Communications in Computer and Information Science   1665

More information about this series at https://link.springer.com/bookseries/7899

Audrius Lopata · Daina Gudonienė ·
Rita Butkienė (Eds.)

Information and Software Technologies

28th International Conference, ICIST 2022
Kaunas, Lithuania, October 13–15, 2022
Proceedings

Springer

Editors
Audrius Lopata 🆔
Kaunas University of Technology
Kaunas, Lithuania

Daina Gudonienė 🆔
Kaunas University of Technology
Kaunas, Lithuania

Rita Butkienė 🆔
Kaunas University of Technology
Kaunas, Lithuania

ISSN 1865-0929   ISSN 1865-0937 (electronic)
Communications in Computer and Information Science
ISBN 978-3-031-16301-2   ISBN 978-3-031-16302-9 (eBook)
https://doi.org/10.1007/978-3-031-16302-9

This Springer imprint is published by the registered company Springer Nature Switzerland AG
The registered company address is: Gewerbestrasse 11, 6330 Cham, Switzerland

Preface

We are pleased to present the proceedings of the 28th International Conference on Information and Software Technologies (ICIST 2022). This yearly conference was held during October 13–15, 2022, in Kaunas, Lithuania. The present volume includes three chapters, which correspond to the three major areas that were covered during the conference, namely, Business Intelligence for Information and Software Systems, Software Engineering, and Information Technology Applications. According to the four special sessions of the conference, the proceedings and the three areas are subdivided into the following sections:

i.   Intelligent Methods for Data Analysis and Computer Aided Software Engineering
ii. Intelligent Systems and Software Engineering Advances
iii. Smart e-Learning Technologies and Applications
iv. Language Technologies

Conference participants not only had the opportunity to present their rigorous research in more specialized settings but also to attend high-quality plenary sessions. This year, as well as the carefully selected papers from researchers and institutions from Europe, Asia, and North America, we also had the pleasure of hearing keynote presentations on topics highly relevant to today's society and the scientific world in general. Filippo Sanfilippo, from the University of Agder, Norway, discussed advancements in robotic technology and snake robots that are already able to imitate a wide array of actions that could enable a variety of possible applications for use in demanding real-life emergency operations as well as industry. Antonio J. R. Neves, from the University of Aveiro, Portugal, delved into the current advances in memory enhancement and moment retrieval from daily digital data.

We would like to express our deepest gratitude to the special session chairs Audrius Lopata (Kaunas University of Technology, Lithuania), Marcin Wozniak (Silesian University of Technology, Poland), Diana Andone (Politehnica University of Timisoara), and Jurgita Kapočiūtė-Dzikienė (Vytautas Magnus University, Lithuania). We acknowledge and appreciate the immense contribution of the session chairs not only in attracting the highest quality papers but also in moderating the sessions and enriching discussions between the conference participants. The entire team working on organizing the conference is proud that despite the uncertainties of the COVID-19 pandemic period, the conference maintained and attracted the interest of numerous scholars across the globe.

Every year ICIST attracts researchers from all over the world, and this year was no exception – we received 66 submissions in total. This indicates that over the years the conference has truly gained international recognition as it still brings together a large number of brilliant experts who showcase the state of the art of the aforementioned fields and come to discuss their newest projects as well as directions for future research. This year, the conference took place in a hybrid way to ensure that participants had the opportunity to participate safely in a remote way. However, this year we also had an increased number of participants preferring to attend the conference and present their papers in person and meet their colleagues from other domestic and foreign institutions.

As we are determined not to stop improving the quality of the conference, only 26 scientific papers were accepted for publication in this volume (a 39% acceptance rate). Each submission was reviewed by at least three reviewers, while borderline papers had an additional evaluation. Reviewing and selection were performed by our highly esteemed Program Committee, who we thank for devoting their precious time to produce thorough reviews and feedback to the authors. It should be duly noted that this year, the Program Committee consisted of 40 reviewers, representing 24 academic institutions and 13 countries.

In addition to the session chairs and Program Committee members, we would like to thank the Local Organizing Committee and the Faculty of Informatics at the Kaunas University of Technology; the conference would not have been a great success without their tremendous support. The proceedings of ICIST 2022 are published as a volume in the Communications in Computer and Information Science series. This would not be possible without the kind assistance that was provided by the Springer team, for which we are extremely grateful. We are very proud of this collaboration and believe that this fruitful partnership will continue for many more years to come.

July 2022

Audrius Lopata
Daina Gudonienė
Rita Butkienė

Organization

The 28th International Conference on Information and Software Technologies (ICIST 2022) was organized by Kaunas University of Technology and was held in Kaunas, Lithuania (October 13–15, 2022).

Conference Chair

Rita Butkienė   Kaunas University of Technology, Lithuania

Local Organizing Committee

Daina Gudonienė (Chair)   Kaunas University of Technology, Lithuania
Rita Butkienė   Kaunas University of Technology, Lithuania
Edgaras Dambrauskas   Kaunas University of Technology, Lithuania
Romas Šleževičius   Kaunas University of Technology, Lithuania
Lina Repšienė   Kaunas University of Technology, Lithuania
Vilma Sukackė   Kaunas University of Technology, Lithuania
Gintarė Lukoševičiūtė   Kaunas University of Technology, Lithuania
Daumantė Varatinskaitė   Kaunas University of Technology, Lithuania

Special Session Chairs

Audrius Lopata   Kaunas University of Technology, Lithuania
Marcin Wozniak   Silesian University of Technology, Poland
Diana Andone   Politehnica University of Timisoara, Romania
Jurgita Kapočiūtė-Dzikienė   Vytautas Magnus University, Lithuania

Program Committee

Audrius Lopata (Chair)   Kaunas University of Technology, Lithuania
Rita Butkienė   Kaunas University of Technology, Lithuania
Daina Gudonienė   Kaunas University of Technology, Lithuania
Aleksandras Targamadzė   Kaunas University of Technology, Lithuania
Andre Schekelmann   Hochschule Niederrhein, Germany
Andrzej Jardzioch   West Pomeranian University of Technology,
                                   Poland
Armantas Ostreika   Kaunas University of Technology, Lithuania
Christophoros Nikou   University of Ioannina, Greece

Contents

Business Intelligence for Information and Software Systems - Special Session on Intelligent Methods for Data Analysis and Computer Aided Software Engineering

Software Engineering - Special Session on Intelligent Systems and Software Engineering Advances

Deep Learning-Based Malware Detection Using PE Headers

Arnas Nakrošis[1,2]([⊠]), Ingrida Lagzdinytė-Budnikė[1],
Agnė Paulauskaitė-Taraseviciene[1], Giedrius Paulikas[1], and Paulius Dapkus[2]

[1] Department of Applied Informatics, Kaunas University of Technology, Studentų St. 50–407,
51368 Kaunas, Lithuania
{arnas.nakrosis,ingrida.lagzdinyte,
agne.paulauskaite-taraseviciene,giedrius.paulikas}@ktu.lt
[2] National Cyber Security Centre Under the Ministry of National Defense, Gediminas Avenue
40, Vilnius, Lithuania
paulius.dapkus@ims.nksc.lt

Abstract. Due to recent advancements in technology, developers of intrusive software are finding more and more sophisticated ways to hide the existence of malicious code in software environments. It becomes difficult to identify viruses in the infected data sent in this way during analysis and detection phase of malware. For this reason, a significant amount of consideration has been devoted to research and development of methodologies and techniques that can identify miscellaneous malware without compromising the execution environment. In order to propose new methods, researchers are investigating not only the structure of malware detection algorithms, but also the properties that can be extracted from files. Extracted features allow malware to be detected even when virus creation tools change.

The authors of this study proposed a data structure consisting of 486 attributes that describe the most important file characteristics. The proposed structure was used to train neural networks to detect viruses. A set of over 400,000 infected and benign files were used to build the data set. Various machine learning algorithms based on unsupervised (k-means, self-organizing maps) and supervised (VGG-16, convolutional neural networks, ResNet) learning were tested. The performed tests were designed to determine the usefulness of the tested algorithms to detect malicious software.

Based on the implemented experimental research, the authors created and proposed a neural network architecture consisting of Dense and Dropout layers with L2 regularization that enables the detection of 8 types of malware with 98% accuracy. The great advantage of the article is the research carried out based on a large number of files. The proposed neural network architecture recognizes malware with at least the same accuracy as solutions offered by other authors and can be practically used to protect workstations against malicious files.

Keywords: Malicious software · Malware · PE header · Machine learning · Deep learning

A. Lopata et al. (Eds.): ICIST 2022, CCIS 1665, pp. 3–18, 2022.
https://doi.org/10.1007/978-3-031-16302-9_1

1   Introduction

As technology advances, developers of malicious software are discovering increasingly sophisticated ways to disguise the way viruses perform their functions and increase the number of existing threats. The amount of malware is growing rapidly both in public and private sectors. These trends have become particularly pronounced with the rise and spread of IoT technologies. During 2021, the number of existing malicious software and cyberattacks increased by approximately 15% [1, 2]. As a result, research is focusing on developing methodologies that can identify a variety of malware without compromising analytical equipment. In order to propose new methods, researchers are studying not only algorithm structure, but also file characteristics that allow to detect contaminated files even if the means for creating viruses have been changed.

A variety of methods have been proposed for the detection of infected files, ranging from static and dynamic algorithms [3] to more sophisticated machine-learning-based solutions [4, 5]. Static algorithms seek to identify malware by analyzing the structure of these files without executing them. This does not endanger the equipment performing the analysis. Meanwhile, dynamic algorithms run the file in a virtual environment and monitor its operation to detect unwanted processes. In the case of static and dynamic algorithms, it is unnecessary to form the data set, which would involve considerable time and human resources. Using these groups of algorithms does not require long training time, which is unavoidable with complex neural network architectures. However, with the development of technology, infected files are becoming more and more structurally clean and use complex encoding procedures, which reduces the efficiency of such algorithms [6, 7]. Algorithms of this type have another significant drawback in having a long and complex procedure of analyzing processes created by the executable file [6, 7]. For these reasons, machine-learning-based algorithms, despite their shortcomings mentioned above, not only remain viable, but have also recently undergone more rapid exploration and successful deployment [5, 8].

An in-depth analysis of research that investigate strategies for detecting malicious files using neural networks shows that they involve the use of different algorithms and neural network architectures, such as random trees, convolutional neural networks, or fully connected neural networks. The choice of method usually depends on data format, the task at hand or the type of analyzed files.

Next, Sect. 2 of this article discusses in detail the research that uses the machine learning paradigm to address the issue of malware detection. At the end of the chapter, problem areas have been identified for which additional attention would be particularly meaningful and necessary; Sect. 3 provides aspects of compiling a dataset using the PE (Portable Executable) header information of a file for virus detection; Sect. 4 discusses the main results of the neural network architectures studied to achieve the highest accuracy in malware detection. Based on these results, the authors developed and proposed a more efficient neural network architecture, which is described in Sect. 5. At the end of the publication, Sect. 6 provides the summary and insights to the conducted research.

2   Analysis of Malware Detection Algorithms and Data Set Structure

2.1   Detection of Malware Using File Images

A popular method for detecting malicious files is to employ convolutional neural networks using strings of data transformed into grayscale images [8, 9]. This strategy takes advantage of the idea that the smallest changes to a file are easily seen graphically and detected by convolutional neural networks. However, using such a strategy requires long series of data that can lead to pictures with high definition. A binary file structure is often used and decomposed into 8-bit vectors that are transformed into grayscale image. The authors of study [10] suggest to use entropy for refining classes that were assigned by CNN in order to improve performance. This strategy allows to identify files infected with viruses, worms, backdoors, or Trojan horses, but requires a large data set for training and testing (21,741 files were used in [10]). It is likely that such data set is not sufficient to investigate network performance in different situations, as most unwanted program code has different characteristics that the neural network will not be familiar with. The authors of study [11], unlike the study discussed earlier, convert the extracted characteristics into a color picture and provide a comparative analysis of the effectiveness of such a strategy with a strategy that uses a grayscale picture. The results of the study showed that better results were obtained using color images, but it should be noted that this study was also performed using comparatively small set of files (14733 infected and 2486 clean samples).

Another option for data set generation is to use PE file headers, which provide extensive information about the file [12, 13]. However, not all PE headers attributes can be directly transformed into image pixels due to small number of possible values. For example, some properties (e.g. has_debug, has_imports, or has_exports) are binary and can only take 0 or 1 values. Therefore, a way for combining properties to obtain more informative images is needed. The compiled picture then is classified using different architectures of convolutional neural networks, such as VGG-16 or ResNet [12, 14].

2.2   Detection of Malware Using a Numeric Data String

Neural network architectures that use numeric data strings can also be used to detect malicious files [15]. The structure of the data series is a deliberate choice by the project developers and depends on the data set available and the accuracy required. Some studies use information obtained from a file signature or hash [16, 17]. In other studies, a subset of file properties is derived from PE headers [8, 9]. The generated data series are presented for classification using various neural networks or other machine learning algorithms, such as random forests, XGBoost [18] or hidden Markov chain [19].

Authors of [20] use the Cascading XGBoost model to detect viruses in infected files. First, the data set is processed using two consecutive XGBoost trees, then the results are processed in a random forest of three trees. In the article, the authors claim to have achieved 99.97% accuracy. A data set of 3,500 files was used to train the neural network, of which 9.6% are infected files.

Unsupervised training can also be used for virus detection [21, 22]. This strategy is effective because no file classification is required before starting the training process. Unsupervised training for malicious file recognition is convenient when a very large data set is available, what allows a more precise definition of class clusters. Unsupervised training algorithms are also used when the scope does not require very high accuracy (e.g. less than 90% is sufficient). Although the training speed of the architecture presented in given articles is high (11.4 ms), it is achieved using a relatively small data set (800 files) with a final accuracy of 62%. This accuracy is significantly lower than that provided by VGG-16, ResNet, or fully connected neural network architectures and in some cases is not acceptable.

2.3   File Characteristics for Identifying Infected Files

Of particular importance for accurate file classification results is the data set format, which provides a large amount of information about the subject under investigation. One of the formats proposed by the authors of study [23] involves information that can be compared to the original file, e.g. the binary structure of the file. The information is analyzed as numeric string or structure, breaking it down into 8-bit numeric combinations and turning it into a grayscale image. However, such method faces certain problems like the shuffling of binary code. This makes it difficult to detect some duplication of properties between different files.

Another problem is the size of the data input (binary code), which can vary depending on the file structure. The authors of [23] study propose a solution to these problems by limiting the size of a binary file and splitting it into an 8-dimensional vector that is processed by a convolutional neural network. However, upon further examination of the proposed architecture, the authors of the study note that it would be very easy for malware developers to avoid such detection system.

Study [24] analyzes the execution of ransomware and determine common processes initiated from the first launch of the program until the virus asks for ransom. This set of processes is further processed using trained transformers. After analyzing the process tree that is created during file execution, three major groups of processes were identified that are created in parallel to the running program and are specific to the type of software requesting a ransom. These groups of processes are associated with the actions of modifying the registry of the Windows operating system and hiding the created files and their extensions [24]. The proposed approach achieves the accuracy of 99.52% in identifying malicious software [24]. Unfortunately, this solution has a major drawback because it requires active processes to detect malware. Such processes are created only when a potentially malicious file is executed. Such situation, without quick response to alerts sent by neural network, can become dangerous and damage the system and its environment.

2.4   Portable Executable Properties for Identifying Infected Files

Information stored in PE header can be used to detect unwanted software packages in PE files. The authors of [25] conducted a study to discover file properties that provide the most relevant information about the infected files. To achieve this goal 3,722 clean and

5,193 infected files were used to train the random forest using a single randomly selected property. During the training of random forest, the table was compiled that showed the accuracy of classification with each property. The best results (92.34%) were obtained using the debug size attribute. Based on the aforementioned research, the authors of that study proposed the data set of 7 attributes – debug size, image version, IatRVA, export size, resource size, virtual size and number of sections. The data set was tested with six different classifiers and average accuracy of about 98% was recorded [25].

[26] present an analysis of the features that are taken from the publicly available data set EMBER [27] and used to identify combinations that provide the best results of detecting viral files. The Ember data set consists of 8 categories of file properties: general file information, header information, imported functions, exported functions, section information, byte histogram, byte-entropy histogram, and string information [27]. In the general case, the Ember dataset consists of 2351 files properties that are distributed over these categories. The authors of study [26] presented the results that were obtained by combining different file properties and evaluating the accuracy, the training time and the size of data string for each corresponding combination. Using these three criteria the best results (83.7% accuracy, 9.12 s training time and 1.562 MB data string size) were achieved by combining generic, header and string properties [26]. The authors also examined the effect of the structure of the proposed data series on classification results by each individual criteria. For example, if classification is evaluated only by accuracy, the best result (92.7%) was achieved by the combination that included all file properties. Results that were close to this accuracy were also obtained using combinations of properties from header, import, file section and byte histogram groups [26].

Summarizing all the studies discussed, it can be seen that the vast majority of them focus on the specifics of a particular malicious software class by offering a neural network architecture or other machine learning methods optimized for this particular case. In cases where the aim is to identify several different types of malware, a relatively small data set is used. Typically, depending on the scope and the number of predicted classes, the selected data set sizes range from 15,000 up to 100 million lines [28, 29]. This suggests that the authors' study of neural network architectures with larger data sets and the ability to identify a wider range of malware is meaningful and fills a gap in broader research currently observed. Based on the discussed file properties analysis, the authors of this article compiled a data set of 420,000 files for further research. This data set is designed to train the neural network to recognize 8 different types of malware.

3 PE Format Data Set and Aspects of Its Composition

PE (Portable Executable) headers were used to train the neural network that would be able to infer whether a file is infected with malware. The PE format is a file system format for Windows OS that includes files with *.dll* or *.exe* extensions. This format allows to extract a large number of file characteristics like file addressing, global variables, constants or program code and also declares the libraries that are used by the file [12, 13].

Based on the PE header analysis performed in [25, 26], it was decided to use characteristics from property groups of header, import, file section and byte histograms. For example, in the case of import group, the use of the most popular libraries in file compilation is considered. Correlation between input and output elements was calculated to determine the relationship that file characteristics have with the fact of infection. The strongest relationship with the output element was found in the attributes of average Shannon entropy, *pe.has_relocations*, and *pe.has_debug*. Details of the PE header characteristics that were selected to identify files infected by viruses are provided in Table 1. In total, the part of PE header that is examined consists of 486 different elements.

Table 1. PE header characteristics that are used for malware detection

File characteristics	Number of elements	Description
PE header flags	11 boolean values	pe.has_configuration, pe.has_debug, pe.has_exceptions, pe.has_exports, pe.has_imports, pe.has_nx, pe.has_relocations, pe.has_resources, pe.has_rich_header, pe.has_signature, pe.has_tls
Normalized elements, representing the first 64 bytes of the PE entry point function	64 elements	
Normalized elements, representing histogram of ASCII symbol repetition	256 elements	
Normalized elements, representing histogram of the usage of selected libraries	150 elements	
Element representing the ratio between PE size on disk and in memory (when file is loaded)	1 element	
The level of file compression	4 elements	-file section contains programming code -file section contains data -average Shannon entropy -average ration between file disk size and memory size

The data set consists of malicious and benign files. The fact that files was infected is detected using the virusTotal API. This tool scans selected files using about 60 different antivirus tools and returns the type of malware each program detected and the number of tools that marked this file as infected. The script that was created to process all collected files arranges files into two main classes: malicious and benign. A file that has been flagged by at least one antivirus program working under virusTotal API is considered infected.

The data set was collected from VirusShare [30], Malware bazaar databases [31]. Our implementation allows to detect different categories of malware, such as: *Viruses; Ransomware; Worms; Trojans; Backdoors; Spyware; Keylogger; Coinminers*. Other types of malicious software, e.g. adware, were not included in the dataset because of the shortage of sample files.

In order to expand the data set with benign files, Windows operating system files, popular software tools and installation files that are commonly used to spread malware were collected. Table 2 provides information on the distribution of benign and infected files in the dataset.

Table 2. Distribution of collected data.

	Malicious files	Benign files
Number of files	198773	220633
Part of the whole dataset (%)	47	53
In total:	419406	

In total, about 420,000 different files were collected for training and testing of neural network, of which 53% were clean and 47% were infected with some kind of malware. Nearly two-thirds (279040 files) of all files in the dataset were executable *.exe* files, and the remaining third (140423 files) were dynamic libraries.

Figure 1 provides information on the malware types and number of files that compose the data set. The largest part of the data set consists of files belonging to the virus class (18.9%), and the smallest – coinminers (9.03%).

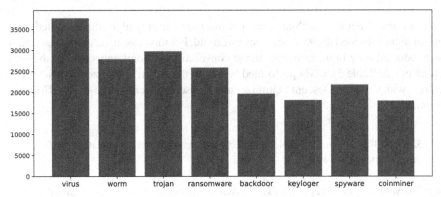

Fig. 1. Malware classes in dataset

LIEF library was used to generate PE headers, it also allows the developed software to read PE format files and extract the selected elements.

4 Analysis of Neural Network Architectures

Various neural network architectures have been trained to determine an effective solution for recognizing infected files from their PE headers. Models such as ResNet, Som, K-means, VGG19, DenseNet, and convolutional neural networks, a total of 25 different neural network architectures and machine learning algorithms, were tested. These architectures were chosen according to their popularity and suitability to security applications [8, 32]. Studies by other researchers have also shown that the selected architectures provide some of the best results in the process of detecting malware [24, 25].

All studied models were constructed using the capabilities of the Ergo-ai framework and Keras library [33]. Ergo-ai framework helped to collect the desired statistical information of the trained neural networks, including metrics as the confusion matrix, the ROC curve and training/testing accuracy and losses. This environment was also used to define the strategy for extracting PE header file attributes that generates the data set in.*csv* format and uses it to train the neural network.

When analyzing neural network architectures, the following parameters were evaluated: classification accuracy, training loss, ROC curve and AUC coefficient. The neural network architectures that were selected during this study were characterized by values that combined the highest accuracy of classification and the lowest training loss. The behavior of the classification model and the ability to distinguish between classification classes were further assessed in terms of the ROC curve [34] and the AUC parameter of the respective model.

The classification results of the examined architectures were analyzed by modifying:

a) number of neural network layers
b) hyperparameters (e.g. learning rate)
c) optimizer
d) loss function.

Of all neural network architectures and machine learning algorithms studied, only some of them exceeded the 95% accuracy threshold. For this reason, further investigation was conducted only in three architectures: convolutional neural networks, ResNet and DenseNet (see Table 3). CNN performed best with the Adam Optimizer, ResNet architecture – with Gradient Descent Optimizer and DenseNet Architecture – with RMSprop Optimizer.

Table 3. CNN, ResNet, and DenseNet architecture parameters and classification results for the detection of 8 types of malware

Neural network	Accuracy	Loss	AUC	Optimizer	Learning rate
CNN	96.1%	0.09	0.982	Adam	0.005
ResNet	96.5%	0.15	0.985	Gradient descent	0.01
DenseNet	96%	0.16	0.99	RMSprop	0.005

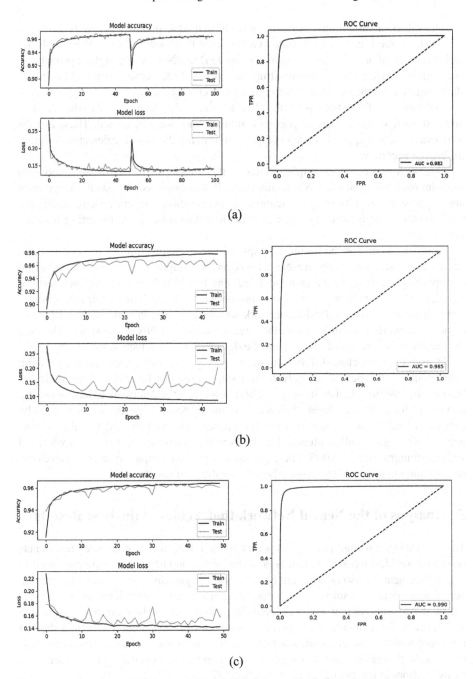

Fig. 2. Statistics of neural networks analyzed during the study: (a) Convolutional neural network loss, accuracy and ROC curve; (b) ResNet loss, accuracy and ROC curve; (c) DenseNet loss, accuracy and ROC curve.

The values of validation accuracy, loss, ROC and AUC parameters and dynamics of these values (see Fig. 2) demonstrate that the given three architectures detect malware with the range of accuracy of 96%–96.5%, while DenseNet has the highest probability to assign the correct class to the resulting data series. ROC curves for all architectures show that none of the mentioned networks assign classes randomly.

In the course of the study, several additional practical aspects related to the architecture and configuration of the respective neural network were identified. These aspects were evaluated and applied at a later stage in optimizing the malware detection solution for greater accuracy.

One such aspect, for example, relates to the transformation of dense layers into convolutional layers in the CNN architecture. It was observed that such change does not improve the results of classification, as convolutional layers require additional transformations of input elements, e.g. extending data series and converting it into a matrix.

Another aspect was the failure to employ ResNet architecture for the tasks of this study with satisfactory results. ResNet is based on layer skipping, which helps to avoid the disappearing gradient and the increase in learning loss [35]. However, this architectural advantage did not work in the context of our research. Figure 2(b) contains the training and validation curves for ResNet network which show that this model has a greater tendency to overfit compared to the other architectures like CNN or DenseNet. That was the reason to exclude this strategy from the design of a new detection toolchain.

DenseNet architecture differs from other already discussed architectures by having layers that use the output not only from a single previous layer, but from all layers before it in order to calculate its output. This allows the neural network to have a smaller number of filters in each layer, thus reducing the number of coefficients that must be optimized [36]. In the course of the study, it was observed that AUC value of this network was significantly influenced by RMSprop optimization function that was used with the training step of 0.005. These parameters were subsequently used to develop a new solution that could demonstrate better classification results.

5   Analysis of the Neural Network that Achieved the Best Results

The best malware recognition results were obtained using a fully connected neural network that was developed by the authors of this article and has its structure presented in Fig. 3. This neural network was built on the best strategies discovered in the research on neural network architectures that was discussed in the previous sections, trying to leverage on the advantages that were observed during practical application of the respective architectures. For example, the experiment with convolutional neural networks showed that more accurate classification is achieved if these networks use dense layers, and better classification results and slowing down of neural network overfitting can be achieved by using dropout layers and L2 regularization [37].

The neural network that achieved best classification results consists of 11 dense layers using the ReLU activation function and 20% of neuron dropout. During the phase of neural network training, the predefined number of randomly selected neurons in dropout layers are ignored. The last dense layer uses the sigmoid activation function. Also, dense

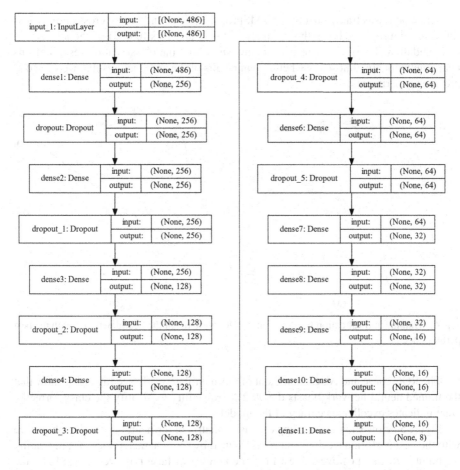

Fig. 3. The proposed structure of the neural network that provided the best classification results

layers use a L2 regularization that replaces the loss function using the expression below (1):

$$Loss = Error(Y, \widehat{Y}) + \lambda \sum_1^n w_i^2 \qquad (1)$$

where:

- Error – the selected loss function
- Y – real labels
- $\widehat{Y}$ – predicted labels
- n – number of neurons
- w – neurons weights
- λ – regularization coefficient, which describes the influence of regularization to the loss function. Excessive values of this coefficient can lead to underfitting of the neural network. This neural network uses the coefficient of 1e−5.

The model was trained using the RMSprop optimizer and binary cross entropy loss function. Figure 4(a) shows the accuracy (97.9%) and loss (0.065) of model training and validation. These characteristics demonstrate that the classification results of this neural network are almost 1,5% better than results of the architectures that were used in previous experiments.

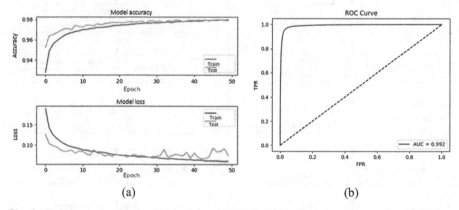

(a)   (b)

Fig. 4. Training and validation results (a) and ROC curve (b) of the neural network with the best performance

The ROC curve and AUC coefficient of this neural network (see Fig. 4(b)) show that the trained neural network boasts the 99.2% probability to identify the class correctly, what indicates excellent accuracy of the model.

Figure 5 below shows the testing confusion matrix of the neural network architecture with the best performance. The matrix is defined by four characteristics: TP, indicating the number of true positive values; FP – the number of false positive values; FN – the number of false negative values and TN – the number of true positive values.

The data of this matrix show that the neural network is more prone to assign a malicious file header to the PE header. As a result, infected files are predicted more accurately (98.81%), but it also leads to higher misclassification of benign files (3.09%). The overall test accuracy of this model is 97.90%. Comparing to other architectures this neural network provided 1.5% better validation accuracy.

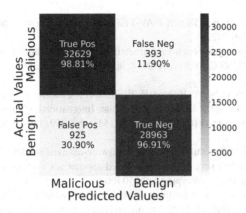

Fig. 5. The best-performing neural network confusion matrix.

6 Conclusion

This study analyzed different neural network architectures and machine learning algorithms for identifying malicious files. The analysis of neural networks was performed using the data set of 400,000 files, while selected properties were extracted from the headers of PE files. The proposed dataset of PE header properties consists of 486 elements.The large number of files allowed to test the examined neural network architectures in a wide range of cases, which was usually lacking in most of the studies of other authors.

As a result of this study, the authors proposed a neural network architecture that uses Dense and Dropout layers and L2 regularization and can improve the performance of other architectures examined. The trained neural network of the proposed architecture allows the detection of 8 types of malware with 97.9% accuracy and can be adapted to protect workstations from malicious files.

The proposed architecture recognizes malware with at least the same accuracy as solutions proposed by other authors that recognize a similar amount of malware types, while using a significantly smaller number of attributes for data analysis (up to 4 times compared to other analyzed studies). For this reason, the implementation and operation of the proposed solution would require less time and physical computer resources (e.g. RAM).

The study can be further expanded by including more malware classes in the dataset (e.g. adware) and by adding a wider range of benign files like samples of new software or dynamic libraries. The results of the authors' research suggest that best performing neural networks may have a relatively simple architecture, therefore it would make sense to explore ever-growing number of neural networks, including models that are composed of a small number of dense layers.

References

1. Malware Statistics & Trends Report | AV-TEST. https://www.av-test.org/en/statistics/mal ware/. Accessed 24 Feb 2022
2. Mahler, T., et al.: Know your enemy: characteristics of cyber-attacks on medical imaging devices. ArXiv180105583 Cs, February 2018. http://arxiv.org/abs/1801.05583. Accessed 24 Feb 2022
3. Samra, A.A.A., Qunoo, H.N., Al-Rubaie, F., El-Talli, H.: A survey of static android malware detection techniques. In: 2019 IEEE 7th Palestinian International Conference on Electrical and Computer Engineering (PICECE), pp. 1–6, March 2019. https://doi.org/10.1109/PIC ECE.2019.8747224
4. Sayadi, H., et al.: Towards accurate run-time hardware-assisted stealthy malware detection: a lightweight, yet effective time series CNN-based approach. Cryptography 5(4), Art. no. 4 (2021). https://doi.org/10.3390/cryptography5040028
5. Patil, S., et al.: Improving the robustness of AI-based malware detection using adversarial machine learning. Algorithms 14(10), Art. no. 10 (2021). https://doi.org/10.3390/a14100297
6. You, I., Yim, K.: Malware obfuscation techniques: a brief survey. In: 2010 International Conference on Broadband, Wireless Computing, Communication and Applications, pp. 297–300, November 2010. https://doi.org/10.1109/BWCCA.2010.85
7. Sung, A.H., Xu, J., Chavez, P., Mukkamala, S.: Static analyzer of vicious executables (SAVE). In: 20th Annual Computer Security Applications Conference, pp. 326–334, December 2004. https://doi.org/10.1109/CSAC.2004.37
8. Awan, M.J., et al.: Image-based malware classification using VGG19 network and spatial convolutional attention. Electronics 10(19), Art. no. 19 (2021). https://doi.org/10.3390/electr onics10192444
9. El-Shafai, W., Almomani, I., AlKhayer, A.: Visualized malware multi-classification framework using fine-tuned CNN-based transfer learning models. Appl. Sci. 11(14), Art. no. 14 (2021). https://doi.org/10.3390/app11146446
10. Xiao, G., Li, J., Chen, Y., Li, K.: MalFCS: an effective malware classification framework with automated feature extraction based on deep convolutional neural networks. J. Parallel Distrib. Comput. 141, 49–58 (2020). https://doi.org/10.1016/j.jpdc.2020.03.012
11. Naeem, H., et al.: Malware detection in industrial internet of things based on hybrid image visualization and deep learning model. Ad Hoc Netw. 105, 102154 (2020). https://doi.org/10.1016/j.adhoc.2020.102154
12. Manavi, F., Hamzeh, A.: A new method for ransomware detection based on PE header using convolutional neural networks. In: 2020 17th International ISC Conference on Information Security and Cryptology (ISCISC), pp. 82–87, September 2020. https://doi.org/10.1109/ISC ISC51277.2020.9261903
13. Rezaei, T., Hamze, A.: An efficient approach for malware detection using PE header specifications. In: 2020 6th International Conference on Web Research (ICWR), pp. 234–239, April 2020. https://doi.org/10.1109/ICWR49608.2020.9122312
14. Chen, Z., Xie, Z., Zhang, W., Xu, X.: ResNet and model fusion for automatic spoofing detection. In: Interspeech 2017, pp. 102–106, August 2017. https://doi.org/10.21437/Inters peech.2017-1085
15. Ha, J., Roh, H.: Experimental evaluation of malware family classification methods from sequential information of TLS-encrypted traffic. Electronics 10(24), Art. no. 24 (2021). https://doi.org/10.3390/electronics10243180
16. Elkhawas, A.I., Abdelbaki, N.: Malware detection using opcode trigram sequence with SVM. In: 2018 26th International Conference on Software, Telecommunications and Computer Networks (SoftCOM), pp. 1–6, September 2018. https://doi.org/10.23919/SOFTCOM.2018.8555738

17. Mohammed, T.M., Nataraj, L., Chikkagoudar, S., Chandrasekaran, S., Manjunath, B.S.: HAPSSA: holistic approach to PDF malware detection using signal and statistical analysis. In: MILCOM 2021 - 2021 IEEE Military Communications Conference (MILCOM), pp. 709–714, November 2021. https://doi.org/10.1109/MILCOM52596.2021.9653097

18. Elnaggar, R., Servadei, L., Mathur, S., Wille, R., Ecker, W., Chakrabarty, K.: Accurate and robust malware detection: running XGBoost on run-time data from performance counters. IEEE Trans. Comput.-Aided Des. Integr. Circ. Syst. 1 (2021). https://doi.org/10.1109/TCAD.2021.3102007

19. Tajoddin, A., Jalili, S.: HM3alD: polymorphic malware detection using program behavior-aware hidden Markov model. Appl. Sci. **8**(7), Art. no. 7 (2018). https://doi.org/10.3390/app8071044

20. Wu, D., Guo, P., Wang, P.: Malware detection based on cascading XGBoost and cost sensitive. In: 2020 International Conference on Computer Communication and Network Security (CCNS), pp. 201–205, August 2020. https://doi.org/10.1109/CCNS50731.2020.00051

21. Feizollah, A., Anuar, N.B., Salleh, R., Amalina, F.: Comparative study of k-means and mini batch k-means clustering algorithms in android malware detection using network traffic analysis. In: 2014 International Symposium on Biometrics and Security Technologies (ISBAST), pp. 193–197, August 2014. https://doi.org/10.1109/ISBAST.2014.7013120

22. Fan, M., et al.: Graph embedding based familial analysis of android malware using unsupervised learning. In: 2019 IEEE/ACM 41st International Conference on Software Engineering (ICSE), pp. 771–782, May 2019. https://doi.org/10.1109/ICSE.2019.00085

23. Demetrio, L., Biggio, B., Lagorio, G., Roli, F., Armando, A.: Explaining vulnerabilities of deep learning to adversarial malware binaries. ArXiv190103583 Cs, January 2019. http://arxiv.org/abs/1901.03583. Accessed 27 Feb 2022

24. Ahmed, M.E., Kim, H., Camtepe, S., Nepal, S.: Peeler: profiling kernel-level events to detect ransomware. In: Bertino, E., Shulman, H., Waidner, M. (eds.) ESORICS 2021. LNCS, vol. 12972, pp. 240–260. Springer, Cham (2021). https://doi.org/10.1007/978-3-030-88418-5_12

25. Al-Kasassbeh, M., Mohammed, S., Alauthman, M., Almomani, A.: Feature selection using a machine learning to classify a malware. In: Gupta, B.B., Perez, G.M., Agrawal, D.P., Gupta, D. (eds.) Handbook of Computer Networks and Cyber Security, pp. 889–904. Springer, Cham (2020). https://doi.org/10.1007/978-3-030-22277-2_36

26. Oyama, Y., Miyashita, T., Kokubo, H.: Identifying useful features for malware detection in the ember dataset. In: 2019 Seventh International Symposium on Computing and Networking Workshops (CANDARW), pp. 360–366, November 2019. https://doi.org/10.1109/CANDARW.2019.00069

27. Anderson, H.S., Roth, P.: EMBER: an open dataset for training static PE malware machine learning models. ArXiv180404637 Cs, April 2018. http://arxiv.org/abs/1804.04637. Accessed 26 Mar 2022

28. Oh, Y., Park, S., Ye, J.C.: Deep learning COVID-19 features on CXR using limited training data sets. IEEE Trans. Med. Imaging **39**(8), 2688–2700 (2020). https://doi.org/10.1109/TMI.2020.2993291

29. Ni, K., et al.: Large-scale deep learning on the YFCC100M dataset. ArXiv150203409 Cs, February 2015. http://arxiv.org/abs/1502.03409. Accessed 01 Apr 2022

30. VirusShare.com. https://virusshare.com/. Accessed 22 Jan 2022

31. MalwareBazaar | Malware sample exchange. https://bazaar.abuse.ch/. Accessed 22 Jan 2022

32. Hemalatha, J., Roseline, S.A., Geetha, S., Kadry, S., Damaševičius, R.: An efficient DenseNet-based deep learning model for malware detection. Entropy **23**(3), Art. no. 3 (2021). https://doi.org/10.3390/e23030344

33. Margaritelli, S.: Evilsocket/ergo (2022). https://github.com/evilsocket/ergo. Accessed 22 Jan 2022

34. Hand, D.J., Till, R.J.: A simple generalisation of the area under the ROC curve for multiple class classification problems. Mach. Learn. **45**(2), 171–186 (2001). https://doi.org/10.1023/A:1010920819831
35. Targ, S., Almeida, D., Lyman, K.: Resnet in Resnet: generalizing residual architectures. ArXiv160308029 Cs Stat, March 2016. http://arxiv.org/abs/1603.08029. Accessed 22 Jan 2022
36. Zhu, Y., Newsam, S.: DenseNet for dense flow. In: 2017 IEEE International Conference on Image Processing (ICIP), pp. 790–794, September 2017. https://doi.org/10.1109/ICIP.2017.8296389
37. van Laarhoven, T.: L2 regularization versus batch and weight normalization. ArXiv170605350 Cs Stat, June 2017. http://arxiv.org/abs/1706.05350. Accessed 22 Jan 202

Survey of Cloud Traffic Anomaly Detection Algorithms

Giedrius Paulikas[1], Donatas Sandonavičius[1], Edgaras Stasiukaitis[1], Gytis Vilutis[1(✉)], and Mindaugas Vaitkunas[2]

[1] Faculty of Informatics, Kaunas University of Technology, Studentu str. 50, 51368 Kaunas, Lithuania
{giedrius.paulikas,donatas.sandonavicius,gytis.vilutis}@ktu.lt,
edgaras.stasiukaitis@ktu.edu
[2] Faculty of Electrical and Electronics Engineering, Kaunas University of Technology, Studentu str. 48, 51367 Kaunas, Lithuania
mindaugas.vaitkunas@ktu.lt

Abstract. Widespread use of cloud computing resources calls for reliable network connections, while anomalies in network traffic impact the availability of cloud resources in a negative way. Anomaly detection tools are essential for identifying and forecasting these network anomalies. In recent years machine learning methods are gaining popularity in implementations of anomaly detection tools. Given the variety of network anomaly types and the availability of diverse machine learning algorithms, developers of anomaly detection software and administrators of cloud infrastructures are presented with a wide range of possible solutions.

This article presents a survey of the most popular machine learning methods that are applicable to detecting anomalies in cloud networks. In order to be able to classify and compare these methods, six major criteria (training approach, training time, preferred areas of application, discovery of unprecedented anomalies, dataset's influence on anomaly prediction and problem of vanishing or exploding gradient) are discerned and discussed in detail, providing their implications on the evaluated methods. Subsequently, the criteria are used to review the features of the main machine learning methods for anomaly detection and to provide insights about using the methods to identify abnormal network behavior.

The last part of the study lists the examined machine learning methods and appropriate tools for anomaly monitoring and detection. The provided lists are then used to draw final conclusions that provide the recommendations for employing the aforementioned algorithms and tools in various cases of anomaly detection.

Keywords: Traffic anomaly · Machine learning algorithms · Network monitoring system

1 Introduction

The recent developments of the Internet of Things (IoT) and proliferation of cloud storage and cloud computing led to a rising demand for computer network resources [1–5].

A. Lopata et al. (Eds.): ICIST 2022, CCIS 1665, pp. 19–32, 2022.
https://doi.org/10.1007/978-3-031-16302-9_2

With an increasing number of devices being connected to the Internet and a big variety of network services, network administration activities, such as device management, traffic monitoring and security assurance, demand a constant development of advanced methods and tools to satisfy their requirements [6–13]. Nowadays improving the reliability of computer network systems is crucial for internet developers and providers. Most problems in computer networks are spotted by detecting traffic anomalies that are caused by them. Detection of anomalies in network behavior requires that a network is continuously monitored for unexpected trends or events [14, 15]. In general, an anomaly is something that is not expected. There are many different causes of anomalies, but is a broad sense they may be classified into three groups:

1. Non-human error – e.g. equipment failure or weather-caused interruptions in radio communication;
2. Human error – e.g. network service outage caused by misconfiguration or accidentally disconnected network cable;
3. Malicious human activity – e.g. cyberattacks that target resources and sensitive data residing within cloud environments, DDoS and other massive attacks.

Among these three, malicious human activity poses the highest threat to network users and generates the biggest financial losses for business. Since the complexity of cyberattacks and malicious events has grown tremendously in recent years, cybersecurity has become one of the hottest topics among researchers who investigate traffic anomalies.

Anomalies themselves can be classified by the area of their origin:

- *Network anomalies* – anomalies where network behavior deviates from what is normal, standard or expected. To detect such anomalies, the owner of the network must have a concept of expected or normal network behavior. Detecting deviations in network behavior demands the continuous monitoring of the network for unexpected trends or events.
- *Application performance anomalies* [16–18]. These are anomalies that can be detected by end-to-end application performance monitoring. Monitoring systems observe application functions and collect data of occurring problems, also tracking the supporting infrastructure and app dependencies. When anomalies are detected, rate limiting is triggered and system administrators are notified about the source and associated data of the issue.
- *Web application security anomalies* [19, 20]. They include any other abnormal or suspicious behavior of web applications that might impact security of the system (e.g. CSS or DDoS attacks).

Anomaly detection is never a simple task. Recently most researchers of traffic anomaly detection systems advocate to detect intruders in local systems by employing various machine learning approaches [21–23]. The efficiency of machine learning techniques depends on application area and data patterns. There are three main groups of machine learning strategies – supervised, semi-supervised and unsupervised – that provide the foundation for anomaly detection algorithms. Supervised machine learning builds a predictive model using a labeled training set with normal and anomalous samples. The most common supervised methods include Bayesian networks, k-nearest neighbors, decision trees, supervised neural networks and SVMs. The advantage of supervised models is that they usually offer a higher rate of detection than unsupervised techniques. This is because these methods are able to return a confidence score of the model's output, incorporate both new data and prior knowledge and encode interdependencies between variables.

Unsupervised methods do not require manual labeling of training data. Instead, they operate based on the presumption that only a small, statistically different percentage of network traffic is malicious and abnormal. These techniques assume the collection of frequent and similar data instances as normal and flag infrequent data groups as malicious. The most popular unsupervised anomaly detection algorithms include Autoencoders, K-means, GMMs, hypothesis tests-based analysis and PCAs.

The term semi-supervised anomaly detection may have different meanings. It may refer to the strategy of creating a model for normal data using a data set that contains both normal and anomalous instances (both unlabeled). This train-as-you-go method is called semi-supervised. A semi-supervised anomaly detection algorithm may also work with a data set that is partially flagged. It builds the classification algorithm on flagged data only and uses that model to predict the status of the remaining data.

In this paper we present a comparative analysis of the latest traffic anomaly detection algorithms and systems. This should help internet providers and network administrators to choose the most suitable means for traffic monitoring and anomaly detection that are relevant to the application scope and the problems they are meant to solve.

2 Criteria for Evaluation of Anomaly Detection Algorithms

All of the articles that discussed the research of anomaly detection methods for cloud environments and that were examined for this study have adopted machine learning algorithms and used them to predict anomalies in real-time. Therefore, our review is based on machine learning algorithms and for comparison uses the criteria that are significant for training models that aim to achieve the preferred accuracy. For this survey, that focuses on methods of anomaly detection in cloud traffic, 6 major criteria for algorithm evaluation were chosen:

- training approach,
- training time,
- preferred areas of application,
- discovery of unprecedented anomalies,
- dataset's influence on anomaly prediction,
- problem of vanishing or exploding gradient.

The listed criteria were selected according to their importance in machine learning methods. Individual criteria points may affect the evaluation of algorithms differently and that mostly depends on the algorithm's training approach that is used for training of the model. As some types of methods are prone to specific tasks, it is essential the selected approach to method's training is effective for the task at hand.

In addition to the strategy of training the machine learning model, training time is also important, especially since various machine learning methods learn parameters of the provided dataset at different rates. This sometimes leads to the high possibility that the model will require multiple iterations of tuning and training with diverse parameters to improve its mediocre prediction accuracy.

The following criterias of preferred areas of application and unprecedented anomaly discovery reflect the strengths and weaknesses of corresponding algorithms and are based on their performance in specific tasks of anomaly detection.

Dataset that is used to train the machine learning method also has a tremendous influence on algorithm's ability to accurately predict anomalies as lots of employed datasets involve noise or highly imbalanced data, which distorts forecasts of the trained model that used that data.

Vanishing and exploding gradient issues only occur in deep learning neural networks, but still it's critical to reduce the risk of this problem since it greatly affects the overall efficiency of the mentioned methods.

All these algorithm comparison criteria will be thoroughly discussed in this section of the article taking into account their relevance to method's capability to accurately predict anomalies in network traffic.

Based on the information of other research and the type of machine learning strategy we grouped anomaly detection algorithms by their *training approach*. Only methods from two well-known machine learning approaches, supervised and unsupervised learning, were selected due to their widespread use for anomaly detection. These methods are regularly adopted for detecting anomalies in cloud environments and each type has their own benefits and drawbacks.

Supervised methods are simpler to train due to the fact that datasets, which are used to train these methods, contain labels that assist machine learning methods in distinguishing if the provided data row should be diagnosed as an anomaly or a normal activity. Supervised methods are also more accurate, owing to having labeled data that aids the prediction. But this kind of learning also has drawbacks. Usually it requires a dataset with rows labeled beforehand. To acquire this kind of dataset, historical data that was gathered from a designated cloud environment must be labeled manually or using traditional anomaly detection methods that use fixed rules or threshold values to determine whether an anomaly occurred or not. However, existing dataset that is specifically constructed for anomaly detection tasks in cloud environments can also be applied. In either case, supervised machine learning methods lack the ability to detect unprecedented anomalies in the provided dataset since they have only two classes of labels for identification of data entries (normal or abnormal). Unsupervised models don't have this limitation and can distinguish diverse outlying data points as anomalies [24].

Contrary to the unsupervised learning models, unsupervised methods do not require labeled data and can be trained based on raw inputs that were collected for the dataset. The dataset is clustered, since there are no labels that can assist in anomaly prediction. In unsupervised methods the substantial amount of clustered data points generally depicts normal usage, while data points that are not assigned to any of the clusters (outliers) can be treated as anomalies. The disadvantages of unsupervised algorithms arise from the fact these methods have to discover the relations in training data and determine the anomalies by themselves just by inspecting for any deviation of available data points. Validation of results often requires human intervention, because the data classification that would help to pinpoint the anomalies is not available [25].

Rating methods by their training time is no less important than employing the appropriate machine learning algorithm. In real-time cloud environments anomaly detection methods must predict possible anomalies of traffic before their occurrence and thus detection methods must be implemented accordingly. Some methods, even though they learn more rapidly, can also achieve far better results. Machine learning methods require time until the satisfactory results are obtained and criteria of training duration is more applicable during this stage when the model's parameters are still tuned and validated. The training duration can also be extremely important when the detection method is retraining on newly gathered data, as time that is needed to acquire an entirely new model might be crucial for identifying unfamiliar new anomalies. That's especially true if the trained method falls into the supervised category as these algorithms and has to be regularly retrained to preserve high rates of anomaly detection.

Different machine learning methods have particular areas of application where they can be used most effectively. The analysis of utilization of these methods for different types of application let us discern four main use cases: intrusion detection, performance monitoring, failure detection and root cause analysis [26].

Intrusion detection methods focus on observing the deviations of traffic from normal usage. Network traffic shifts can be foreseen depending on the type of the attack, e.g.:

- (Distributed) Denial of Service (DoS/DDoS) attacks generate a flood of traffic from a single IP address (DoS) or a range of IP addresses (DDoS).
- Botnets are a crowd of compromised machines, which are coordinated by a single source of influence via remote channel. Botnets are generally difficult to detect, but can be recognized by monitoring unusual activity in network traffic.
- Malware attacks of viruses, worms and rootkits that can be detected by scanning for the presence of their signatures.
- Fraud storms hijack cloud computing resources for fraudulent use.

Performance monitoring observes system performance for occurrences of sudden degradations of performance.

Failure detection is recorded when system services do not satisfy the constraints set by the user of that system.

In cloud computing environments it is usually not sufficient just to identify an anomaly. It's also critical to locate the reason why the anomaly occurred in order to prevent further manifestations. This sort of a problem is called root cause analysis and is most of the time responsible for various types of abnormal emergencies in cloud systems.

Algorithm's capability to accurately predict anomalies is highly susceptible to the collected data. Since machine learning methods are immensely reliant on the dataset they are trained on, datasets that contain lots of noise can dramatically impact the algorithm's ability to accurately predict anomalies. Some methods are affected more than others, but substantial chunks of noise in datasets diminish efficiency of any method. It also should be noted that a few of the analyzed methods perform worse on larger datasets or higher count of parameters, but most of the others use additional data as advantage and achieve greater accuracy [27].

Lastly, machine learning methods that utilize deep neural networks can suffer from a problem called vanishing or exploding gradient. Vanishing or exploding gradient issues commonly occur when certain activation functions, such as sigmoid, have vast differences in variance of inputs and outputs. Besides that, there's a possibility that the initial weights that are assigned to the neural network will become too large and overflow, causing unrepresentable values, which greatly affects the model's ability to determine anomalies. A set of solutions can be applied to reduce vanishing or exploding gradient issues and stabilize neural networks: proper weight initialization, use of non-saturating activation functions, batch normalization and gradient clipping [28].

3 Comparison of Anomaly Detection Algorithms

Methods that are discussed in this section were selected based on their popularity in research and development of anomaly detection tools for cloud environments. Our examination of widely used algorithms relies on existing summaries and explorations of methods that were employed to identify anomalies in diverse cloud environments. The comparison of machine learning algorithm training time and dataset influence was also based on existing summary research, and as a result measurements from the investigated methods of their utilized datasets were observed in Table 1. This section of the article elaborates on criteria that were presented in the previous section, identifying their relation and aspects of applying the criteria to specific methods.

Nearly all methods for anomaly detection that were selected to examine are based on supervised machine learning since supervised algorithms is an established practice for anomaly detection and have the tendency of outperforming unsupervised ones in tasks of classification and categorization. The chosen supervised methods are: Convolutional Neural Network (CNN), Recurrent Neural Network (RNN), Long Short-Term Memory (LSTM), Support Vector Machines (SVM), Decision Tree (DT) and Naive Bayes. These machine learning methods are widely used for anomaly detection because they provide better results, though they require human intervention to appropriately label the data in order to obtain high accuracy of prediction. A couple of methods that are related to unsupervised learning were also included in the survey: Autoencoder and Isolation Forest (iForest). Even if these methods do not attain the same high accuracy as supervised ones, they still provide sufficient efficiency in identifying anomalies [29, 30].

The comparison of algorithms takes into account their training time, i.e. the time that is needed for a method to learn parameters of the dataset. Importance of training duration is especially apparent for supervised methods, because the actual models have a tendency to quickly become obsolete and thus require fast retraining on constantly changing anomalies. For instance, CNNs can be trained more rapidly than RNN and LSTM and are able to achieve excellent prediction accuracy [31]. In addition, CNNs are also faster than SVMs, since SVM training time depends on the size of a dataset and the parameters that were specified during training. While Decision Trees and Naive Bayes train quickly on both small and large datasets. Decision Tree training time depends heavily on dimensionality of the data as time complexity of DT is proportional to the product of data dimensionality and size of the training dataset. In case of unsupervised methods, Autoencoder training time is influenced by the amount of parameters and size of the dataset, whilst Isolation Forests are relatively quick compared to other methods.

When reviewing method application areas, the supervised methods, such as CNN, LSTM and Decision Trees, were found to be frequently applied in intrusion detection and performance monitoring, as these methods attain good accuracies in those fields of application [32]. RNN, Naive Bayes and Autoencoder are commonly employed for intrusion detection in cloud environments. Isolation Forests tend to be applied in performance monitoring, while SVMs act in a wide range of application fields, being used for intrusion detection, performance monitoring and root cause analysis. SVMs perform exceptionally well for classification tasks when the training time is short [33, 34].

As it was already mentioned, supervised algorithms do achieve good prediction accuracy in properly labeled datasets, but in some circumstances unsupervised methods perform better. Unsupervised algorithms of machine learning, like Autoencoder and Isolation Forests, are able to detect unprecedented anomalies, hence increasing their effectiveness in highly variable data. Unsupervised methods are productive in cases where manual labeling of data is more or less impossible due to constant changes of data records. Joining supervised or unsupervised algorithms with other machine learning methods can further improve prediction accuracy. For example, if Autoencoder training and feature extraction is combined with Isolation Forest anomaly detection, it is possible to obtain prediction models that yield high accuracies even on unlabeled datasets. Using Autoencoder can improve the results of Isolation Forest in cases when Isolation Forest alone is not capable of attaining the desired efficiency [35, 36].

Datasets that are employed in machine learning algorithms can have diverse impacts on different methods of machine learning. In supervised methods the impact is essentially based on data labeling, because improperly labeled entries will affect all of supervised methods more or less the same, while large amounts of data noise influence both supervised and unsupervised algorithms. But if these algorithms are compared by their capability of dealing with various sizes of data or training parameters, the results are diversified. Methods like CNN, LSTM, Autoencoder and Isolation Forest attain satisfactory prediction accuracies with large datasets, since these algorithms require lots of data to learn its features. Contrastingly, in case of RNN, SVM and Decision Tree, the method accuracies are highly dependent on the size of dataset or parameter tuning. RNNs suffer from long sequences and long term dependencies that have their performance deteriorated. SVMs perform better on small datasets, because with larger data sizes they have the tendency of becoming extremely complex. Decision Trees are only a valid option if it is possible to reduce the complexity of the tree by pruning without any accuracy loss in the testing dataset. Lastly, Naive Bayes, in contrast with the other methods, operates well enough both on small and large datasets and is able to predict anomalies with high accuracy in either case [37].

Vanishing and exploding gradient problems are only relevant in deep learning neural networks, such as CNN and RNN. Because of the gradient problem, the aforementioned methods fail to recall information during extensive training time. Even though these problems are common in neural networks, they can be resolved by utilizing saturated activation function, gradient clipping or weight regularization [38]. On the other hand, LSTM is a deep neural network, but copes well with the mentioned issues and reduces their impact on accuracy of model predictions by using the unique gradient structure that provides direct access to the activations of forget gate [39]. Other methods for anomaly detection that are considered in this survey do not suffer from gradient issues as their training approach does not involve activation functions in the learning process.

Even though the compared machine learning methods provide high accuracies in discussed scenarios, there are some major challenges that pose problems whilst applying these algorithms in cloud environments. One of the issues is that aforementioned analyzed methods require large quantities of data to be properly trained and thus demand high amounts of cloud computing resources. This is especially prominent in smaller cloud systems, where the resources of the system are quite limited in terms of processing power. Such machine learning methods as Decision Trees and SVMs are quite computationally expensive to train and demand extensive device processing capabilities [40].

Appliance of machine learning algorithms in cloud environments is not solely limited to devices processing power. Frequently, data that will be used to train the model can be difficult to obtain for specific anomaly detection edge cases. In such an instance, it is either required to use an existing dataset that fits the anomaly detection problem or collect the data from a designated cloud environment with which the machine learning model will be applied. The latter alternative might present some issues, specifically, if the utilized machine learning method falls into the supervised category, which does involve additional labor of proper data labeling that is needed to predict possible anomalies.

Generally, a machine learning model that is employed in a cloud environment does not guarantee proper real-time anomaly detections, since there are some major factors that could disturb the model's capability of predicting anomalies. In real-time working cloud applications none of the trained machine learning algorithms can assure that anomalies will be detected as accurately as they were able to predict anomalies on a training dataset. Usually an excellent accuracy on a training dataset does not necessarily indicate great anomaly detection performance in an actual functioning cloud application. Most often trained model's ability to accurately predict anomalies will depend on how close the gathered data of a working system is to the dataset of a trained model [41].

The brief summary of the discussed machine learning algorithms is presented in Table 1. It concludes this section by listing 6 criteria of machine learning methods that were presented in the previous section and relation of these criteria to 8 widely used supervised and unsupervised algorithms for anomaly detection in cloud environments, while showing the advantages and disadvantages of each algorithm.

During this study of machine learning methods, it was discovered that particular algorithms contain a specific edge over other methods if training approach and application areas with different types of datasets are taken into account. It also should be noted that some of the listed neural network algorithms encounter exploding gradient or vanishing gradient issues, while others handle this problem by altering model's structure. Even though the discussed machine learning methods are capable of precise anomaly prediction in cloud environments, there are some algorithms that are more fit for intrusion detection, whilst others are widely applied for device's performance monitoring issue diagnosis. Algorithm's ability to predict anomalies is mainly limited by provided cloud devices computing resources, since many of the reviewed algorithms are computationally expensive.

4   Network Monitoring Systems Able to Recognize Anomalies

There are lots of systems that can monitor network and it's devices: Plixer Scrutinizer [42], Nagios [43, 46], OpenNMS [44], SolarWinds Network Performance Monitor [43, 46], Datadog Network Performance Monitoring [45, 46], ManageEngine OpManager [42, 46], Paessler PRTG Network Monitor [46], Icinga [46], Netflow Analyzer [47], site24x7 [46], Zenoss [48], Zabbix [37, 49], Flowmon ADS [50], WhatsUp Gold [46] and other. Websites that use Netflow Analyzer, site24x7, Zenoss, Zabbix, Flowmon ADS and WhatsUp Gold network monitoring systems declare that they include data analyzers and are able to detect anomalies in the network. Flowmon ADS and WhatsUp Gold use the same Anomaly Detection moule (NBAD) [51] which is created by Flowmon. NBAD [51] currently checks: SSH (Secure SHell) and RDP (Remote Desktop Protocol) attacks, Blacklisted IP addresses, Ports scanning detection, DDoS attacks detection, DNS anomalies, DHCP anomalies and Spammers detection. The systems of anomaly detection that were examined were classified by anomaly type recognition features into 3 main types:

- Application performance: site24x7 has 33 features, Zenoss - 4, Zabbix - 12 and WhatsUp Gold has 8 features;
- Network performance: Netflow Analyzer has 7 features, site24x7 - 9, Flowmon ADS - 13, Zenoss - 4, Zabbix - 9, WhatsUp Gold - 19;
- Web application security: site24x7 has 10 features and Flowmon ADS has 4.

According to features listed above, the best choice for detecting anomalies in application performance and web application security is site24x7. Network anomaly detection is best suited by WhatsUp Gold or Flowmon ADS, since both of them have a comparable amount of network monitoring features and use the same module NBAD for anomaly detection. The best system for web application security anomalies detections is again site24x7.

Table 1. Comparison of machine learning algorithms.

Comparison criteria	Training approach	Training time	Preferred areas of application	Discovery of unprecedented anomalies	Dataset's influence on anomaly prediction	Problem of vanishing or exploding gradient
CNN	Supervised	Rapid training	Performance monitoring and intrusion detection	-	Requires a large dataset for high prediction accuracy	+
RNN	Supervised	Slower than CNN	Intrusion detection	-	Prediction accuracy deteriorates from long sequences and long term dependencies	+
LSTM	Supervised	Slower than CNN	Performance monitoring and intrusion detection	-	Solves RNN drawbacks	-
SVM	Supervised	Slower training with larger datasets, depends on parameters	Intrusion detection, performance monitoring and root cause analysis	-	Training complexity is highly dependent on the dataset, thus better accuracies are achieved on smaller datasets	-
Decision tree	Supervised	Rapid training on large datasets with low dimensionality	Performance monitoring and intrusion detection	-	Requires pruning for optimal accuracy	-
Naive Bayes	Supervised	Rapid training	Intrusion detection	-	Performs well on small and large datasets	-
Autoencoder	Unsupervised	Depends on selected amount of parameters and data size	Intrusion detection	+	Large dataset with minimal noise is needed for attaining best performance	-
Isolation Forest (iForest)	Unsupervised	Rapid training	Performance monitoring	+	Best accuracy is obtained on large datasets	-

5   Conclusion

Based on the conducted survey of algorithms for anomaly detection in cloud traffic, we can assign the analyzed methods to broad types of anomalies that were listed in the introduction. Since all of the researched algorithms are employed for detecting network anomalies, method grouping by anomaly types is feasible. CNNs, LSTMs, SVMs, Decision Trees and Isolation Forests can be assigned to the area of application performance anomalies. Additionally, the same CNNs, LSTMs, SVMs and Decision Trees can also be assigned to the area of web application security anomalies, that group also includes RNNs, Naive Bayes and Autoencoders, because they are capable of achieving high prediction accuracy and recognize various intrusion strategies.

It should be noted that from 8 examined algorithms of machine learning that belong to the supervised section, Naive Bayes seems to be the quickest for model training due to having the lowest time complexity. As the unsupervised section includes only two machine learning methods, Isolation Forests can be given an edge against Autoencoder due to the latter's training time being heavily impacted by the selected parameters and the size of the dataset.

During the analysis of challenges whilst applying machine learning algorithms in cloud environments, it was perceived that such machine learning algorithms as Decision Trees and SVMs are exceptionally expensive in terms of processing power and will pose problems to smaller cloud systems due to them having limited computational resources.

The most popular monitoring systems' that are able to detect anomalies were classified by their supported features related to three main types of anomalies. Following this classification, the best choice to detect anomalies in application performance and web application security is site24x7, while WhatsUp Gold and Flowmon ADS work well detecting network anomalies.

References

1. Kumar, R., Goyal, R.: On cloud security requirements, threats, vulnerabilities and countermeasures: a survey. Comput. Sci. Rev. **33**, 1–48 (2019). https://doi.org/10.1016/j.cosrev.2019. 05.002
2. Dang, L.M., Piran, Md.J., Han, D., Min, K., Moon, H.: A survey on internet of things and cloud computing for healthcare. Electronics **8**(7), art. 768 (2019). https://doi.org/10.3390/ele ctronics8070768
3. Priyanka, E.B., Thangavel, S.: Influence of internet of things (IoT) in association of data mining towards the development smart cities-a review analysis. J. Eng. Sci. Technol. Rev. **13**(4), 1–21 (2020)
4. Pajouha, H.H., Dehghantanhaa, A., Parizib, R.M., Aledharib, M., Karimipour, H.: A survey on internet of things security: requirements, challenges, and solutions. Internet Things **14**, art. 100129 (2021). https://doi.org/10.1016/j.iot.2019.100129
5. Bagchi, S., et al.: New frontiers in IoT: networking, systems, reliability, and security challenges. IEEE Internet Things J. **7**(12), 11330–11346 (2020)
6. Tabrizchi, H., Kuchaki Rafsanjani, M.: A survey on security challenges in cloud computing: issues, threats, and solutions. J. Supercomput. **76**(12), 9493–9532 (2020). https://doi.org/10. 1007/s11227-020-03213-1

7. Du, M.: Application of information communication network security management and control based on big data technology. Int. J. Commun. Syst. **35**(5), art. 4643 (2022). https://doi.org/10.1002/dac.4643
8. Clemm, A., Zhani, M.F., Boutaba, R.: Network management 2030: operations and control of network 2030 services. J. Netw. Syst. Manage. **28**(4), 721–750 (2020). https://doi.org/10.1007/s10922-020-09517-0
9. Arzo, S.T., Naiga, C., Granelli, F., Bassoli, R., Devetsikiotis, M., Fitzek, F.H.P.: A theoretical discussion and survey of network automation for IoT: challenges and opportunity. IEEE Internet Things J. **8**(15), 12021–12045 (2021)
10. Javed, F., Afzal, M.K., Sharif, M., Kim, B.-S.: Internet of things (IoT) operating systems support, networking technologies, applications, and challenges: a comparative review. IEEE Commun. Surv. Tutor. **20**(3), 2062–2100 (2018)
11. Yu, F.R.: From information networking to intelligence networking: motivations, scenarios, and challenges. IEEE Netw. **35**(6), 209–216 (2021)
12. Imran, Ghaffar, Z., Alshahrani, A., Fayaz, M., Alghamdi, A.M., Gwak, J.: A topical review on machine learning, software defined networking, internet of things applications: research limitations and challenges. Electronics **10**(8), art. 880 (2021). https://doi.org/10.3390/electronics10080880
13. Santos, L., Gonçalves, R., Rabada, C., Martins, J.: A flow-based intrusion detection framework for internet of things networks. Cluster Comput. 1–21 (2021). http://hdl.handle.net/10198/23813
14. Hagemann, T., Katsarou, K.: A systematic review on anomaly detection for cloud computing environments. In: 3rd Artificial Intelligence and Cloud Computing Conference (AICCC 2020), pp. 83–96, December 2020. https://doi.org/10.1145/3442536.3442550
15. Fernandes, G., Rodrigues, J.J.P.C., Carvalho, L.F., Al-Muhtadi, J.F., Proença, M.L.: A comprehensive survey on network anomaly detection. Telecommun. Syst. **70**(3), 447–489 (2018). https://doi.org/10.1007/s11235-018-0475-8
16. Jayathilaka, H., Krintz, C., Wolski, R.: Detecting performance anomalies in cloud platform applications. IEEE Trans. Cloud Comput. **8**, 764–777 (2020)
17. Shi, Y., Miao, K.: Detecting anomalies in application performance management system with machine learning algorithms. In: 3rd International Conference on Electronic Information Technology and Computer Engineering (EITCE), pp. 1797–1800 (2020)
18. Baril, X., Coustié, O., Mothe, J., Teste, O.: Application performance anomaly detection with LSTM on temporal irregularities in logs. In: Proceedings of the 29th ACM International Conference on Information & Knowledge Management (CIKM 2020), pp. 1961–1964, October 2020. https://doi.org/10.1145/3340531.3412157
19. Jyothsana, L.P., Anushya, E., Kumari, S.S.: An anomaly-based approach for intrusion detection in web traffic. Int. J. Adv. Res. Basic Eng. Sci. Technol. (IJARBEST) **3**(Special Issue), 360–367 (2017)
20. Tama, B.A., Nkenyereye, L., Islam, S.M.R., Kwak, K.-S.: An enhanced anomaly detection in web traffic using a stack of classifier ensemble. IEEE Access **8**, 24120–24134 (2020)
21. Fotiadou, K., Velivassaki, T.-H., Voulkidis, A., Skias, D., Tsekeridou, S., Zahariadis, T.: Network traffic anomaly detection via deep learning. Information **12**(5), art. 215 (2021)
22. Alshammari, A., Aldribi, A.: Apply machine learning techniques to detect malicious network traffic in cloud computing. J. Big Data **8**(1), 1–24 (2021). https://doi.org/10.1186/s40537-021-00475-1
23. Ergen, T., Kozat, S.S.: Unsupervised anomaly detection with LSTM neural networks. IEEE Trans. Neural Netw. Learn. Syst. **31**(8), 3127–3141 (2020)
24. Pu, G., Wang, L., Shen, J., Dong, F.: A hybrid unsupervised clustering-based anomaly detection method. Tsinghua Sci. Technol. **26**(2), 146–153 (2021). https://doi.org/10.26599/TST.2019.9010051

25. Uddin, S., Khan, A., Hossain, M., et al.: Comparing different supervised machine learning algorithms for disease prediction. BMC Med. Inform. Decis. Mak. **19**, 281 (2019). https://doi.org/10.1186/s12911-019-1004-8

26. Hagemann, T., Katsarou, K.: A systematic review on anomaly detection for cloud computing environments. In: 2020 3rd Artificial Intelligence and Cloud Computing Conference (AICCC 2020), pp. 83–96. Association for Computing Machinery, New York (2020). https://doi.org/10.1145/3442536.3442550

27. Ciriano, I.C., Bender, A., Malliavin, T.E.: Comparing the influence of simulated experimental errors on 12 machine learning algorithms in bioactivity modeling using 12 diverse data sets. J. Chem. Inf. Model. **55**(7), 1413–1425 (2015). https://doi.org/10.1021/acs.jcim.5b00101

28. Ribeiro, A.H., Tiels, K., Aguirre, L.A., Schön, T.: Beyond exploding and vanishing gradients: analysing RNN training using attractors and smoothness, vol. 108, pp. 2370–2380 (2020). https://proceedings.mlr.press/v108/ribeiro20a.html

29. Aouedi, O., Piamrat, K., Bagadthey, D.: A semi-supervised stacked autoencoder approach for network traffic classification. In: 2020 IEEE 28th International Conference on Network Protocols (ICNP), pp. 1–6 (2020). https://doi.org/10.1109/ICNP49622.2020.9259390

30. Alloghani, M., Al-Jumeily, D., Mustafina, J., Hussain, A., Aljaaf, A.J.: A systematic review on supervised and unsupervised machine learning algorithms for data science. In: Berry, M.W., Mohamed, A., Yap, B.W. (eds.) Supervised and Unsupervised Learning for Data Science. USL, pp. 3–21. Springer, Cham (2020). https://doi.org/10.1007/978-3-030-22475-2_1

31. Abdallah, M., Khac, N.A.L., Jahromi, H., Delia Jurcut, A.: A hybrid CNN-LSTM based approach for anomaly detection systems in SDNs. In: The 16th International Conference on Availability, Reliability and Security (ARES 2021), pp. 1–7. Association for Computing Machinery, New York (2021). https://doi.org/10.1145/3465481.3469190. Article 34

32. Habeeb, R.A.A., Nasaruddin, F., Gani, A., Hashem, I.A.T., Ahmed, E., Imran, M.: Real-time big data processing for anomaly detection: a survey (2019). https://doi.org/10.1016/j.ijinfomgt.2018.08.006

33. Haji, S., Ameen, S.: Attack and anomaly detection in IoT networks using machine learning techniques: a review. Asian J. Res. Comput. Sci. **9**, 30–46 (2021). https://doi.org/10.9734/ajrcos/2021/v9i230218

34. Hwang, R.-H., Peng, M.-C., Huang, C.-W., Lin, P.-C., Nguyen, V.-L.: An unsupervised deep learning model for early network traffic anomaly detection. IEEE Access **8**, 30387–30399 (2020). https://doi.org/10.1109/ACCESS.2020.2973023

35. Farzad, A., Gulliver, T.A.: Unsupervised log message anomaly detection (2020). https://doi.org/10.1016/j.icte.2020.06.003

36. Lesouple, J., Baudoin, C., Spigai, M., Tourneret, J.Y.: Generalized isolation forest for anomaly detection (2021). https://doi.org/10.1016/j.patrec.2021.05.022

37. Eltanbouly, S., Bashendy, M., AlNaimi, N., Chkirbene, Z., Erbad, A.: Machine learning techniques for network anomaly detection: a survey. 2020 IEEE International Conference on Informatics, IoT, and Enabling Technologies (ICIoT), pp. 156–162 (2020). https://doi.org/10.1109/ICIoT48696.2020.9089465

38. Roodschild, M., Gotay Sardiñas, J., Will, A.: A new approach for the vanishing gradient problem on sigmoid activation. Progr. Artif. Intell. **9**(4), 351–360 (2020). https://doi.org/10.1007/s13748-020-00218-y

39. Girish, L., Rao, S.K.N.: Anomaly detection in cloud environment using artificial intelligence techniques. Computing (2021). https://doi.org/10.1007/s00607-021-00941-x

40. Alrashdi, I., Alqazzaz, A., Aloufi, E., Alharthi, R., Zohdy, M., Ming, H.: AD-IoT: anomaly detection of IoT cyberattacks in smart city using machine learning. In: 2019 IEEE 9th Annual Computing and Communication Workshop and Conference (CCWC), pp. 0305–0310 (2019). https://doi.org/10.1109/CCWC.2019.8666450

41. Biradar, K., Gupta, A., Mandal, M., Vipparthi, S.: Challenges in time-stamp aware anomaly detection in traffic videos (2019). https://doi.org/10.48550/arXiv.1906.04574

42. Boranbayev, S.N., Kuanyshev, D.D.: Network traffic analysis tools. Eurasian Union Sci. (EUS) **12**(81), 35–38 (2020)

43. Liu, J., Qu, C., Zhou, T.: Design and implementation of cloud computing platform monitoring system based on nagios. In: Huang, C., Chan, Y.-W., Yen, N. (eds.) 2020 International Conference on Data Processing Techniques and Applications for Cyber-Physical Systems. AISC, vol. 1379, pp. 1473–1478. Springer, Singapore (2021). https://doi.org/10.1007/978-981-16-1726-3_191

44. Basu, A., Singh, R., Yu, C., Prasad, A., Banerjee, K.: Designing, developing and deploying an enterprise scale network monitoring system. In: ISEC 2022: 15th Innovations in Software Engineering Conference, Article No. 18, pp. 1–5, February 2022. https://doi.org/10.1145/351 1430.3511446

45. Fournier, G., Afchain, S., Baubeau, S.: Runtime security monitoring with eBPF (2021)

46. Birundha, S., Grace, R.K., Jeyaram, T.: Network monitoring and analysis. In: 2021 7th International Conference on Advanced Computing and Communication Systems (ICACCS), pp. 1400–1403 (2021). https://doi.org/10.1109/ICACCS51430.2021.9441767

47. Krishnamurthy, P., Khorrami, F., Schmidt, S., Wright, K.: Machine learning for NetFlow anomaly detection with human-readable annotations. IEEE Trans. Netw. Serv. Manag. **18**(2), 1885–1898 (2021). https://doi.org/10.1109/TNSM.2021.3075656

48. Ljubojević, M., Bajić, A., Mijić, D.: Centralized monitoring of computer networks using Zenoss open source platform. In: 2018 17th International Symposium INFOTEH-JAHORINA (INFOTEH), pp. 1–5 (2018). https://doi.org/10.1109/INFOTEH.2018.8345528

49. Meman, J.M., Villaverde, J.F., Linsangan, N.B.: Automation of daily monitoring operations of N2N connect Berhad using Zabbix technology. In: ICIEI 2021: 2021 The 6th International Conference on Information and Education Innovations, pp. 140–145, April 2021. https://doi.org/10.1145/3470716.3470739

50. Flowmon ADS. Network anomaly detection system. https://www.flowmon.com/en/products/software-modules/anomaly-detection-system

51. Kortebi, A., Aouini, Z., Juren, M., Pazdera, J.: Home networks traffic monitoring case study: anomaly detection. In: 2016 Global Information Infrastructure and Networking Symposium (GIIS), pp. 1–6 (2016). https://doi.org/10.1109/GIIS.2016.7814852

Real-Time Anomaly Detection for Distributed Systems Logs Using Apache Kafka and H2O.ai

Kęstutis Daugėla[(✉)] and Evaldas Vaičiukynas

Kaunas University of Technology, Faculty of Informatics, Kaunas, Lithuania
kestutis.daugela@ktu.edu

Abstract. System monitoring is crucial to ensure that the system is working correctly. Usually, it encompasses solutions from the simple configuration of static thresholds for hardware/software key performance indicators to employing anomaly detection algorithms on a stream of numerical data. System logs, on the other hand, is another golden source of the system state, but often it is overlooked. Combining system logs with load metrics could potentially increase the accuracy of anomaly detection. We propose a robust pipeline and evaluate several of its variants for solving such a task at scale and in real-time. Experiments with proprietary logs from an enterprise Kafka cluster reveal that preprocessing with an autoencoder prior to applying the isolation forest method can significantly improve the detection performance.

Keywords: Anomaly detection · System logs · Apache Kafka · H2O.ai · Autoencoder · Isolation forest

1 Introduction

Stability and threat detection are essential for any business-critical application, regardless of the sector - healthcare, banks, government, and e-commerce. The malfunction of any critical system can cause financial loss, damage reputation, and decrease the trust of potential or current clients. The big data ecosystem is closely related to distributed systems, and this increases the scope and complexity of monitoring tasks [2,3,8]. Consequently, organizations spend a tremendous amount of resources monitoring such solutions using proprietary or custom tools. Typically, monitoring consists of periodically recording hardware/software metrics and setting up thresholds for alarming. Meanwhile, system logs are often analyzed separately using different techniques. However, this is not the most efficient approach since metrics and logs could benefit from synergistic effects if analyzed simultaneously.

Nowadays, enterprises are widely adopting DevOps and site reliability engineering practices [20]. Using this relatively new approach, injecting as much

A. Lopata et al. (Eds.): ICIST 2022, CCIS 1665, pp. 33–42, 2022.
https://doi.org/10.1007/978-3-031-16302-9_3

automation as possible besides a human-centered approach is an essential direction for progress. Therefore, it is vital to have a robust pipeline for log processing and anomaly detection to deal with high-velocity data streams.

Unlabeled data is one of the biggest challenges in anomaly detection - in most cases, labeling is not possible due to an excessive amount of data [7]. Thus, unsupervised algorithms are used to train the model. Two prominent families of models are often listed for this type of task: traditional models (SVM [24], clustering [18,19], fuzzy rules [5], localization algorithms [4], Isolation Forest [22]), and deep learning approach using autoencoders [25,26,31]. The most similar related work uses these two approaches in sequence (autoencoder compresses features for isolation forest) on OpenStack logs [7], but they did not use hyperparameter tuning, and the architecture of the isolation forest "sandwiched" by two autoencoders seems overcomplicated. As some authors warn, complex anomaly detection schemes are not well suited for real-time processing and big data ecosystem [11]. Even though there are some promising first steps with Apache Kafka / Spark integration [9], many anomaly detection approaches perform well only on toy datasets but are not compelling enough to real-time scenarios or lack accuracy when deployed in production setting [1,33].

We especially lack generic and universal solutions [12], particularly for data streams moving at a high rate of speed. Numerous earlier studies on anomaly detection contain only prototypes or model recommendations and do not result in a finished product for consumers or a universal tool for system preventative maintenance. [7,23,27]. Moreover, the anomaly itself does not indicate the root cause – to create business value, the ultimate solution should help to fix the issue [32], take preventative measures [6,27] or at least understandably indicate the problem [32].

One thing these researchers have in common - they focus only on log data. The importance of data enrichment is widely known for business data, but this method is not widely used for data harvested from network computers. In this article, we will test this hypothesis and merge the log data with system performance metrics. Most of the companies already collect these metrics for monitoring and IT administrative purposes.

2   Methods

2.1   Tool Selection

The first thing to consider is log shipment for high traffic of log data. One of the commonly used software is Logstash. On the other hand, Logstash is limited in terms of scalability. Apache Kafka [17,29], however, is significantly more potent due to its inherent architecture: Kafka is a cluster, while Logstash is a single instance. Moreover, the adoption of streaming architecture guarantees efficient and seamless communication between devices. Regarding performance, Kafka can reach a remarkable 420 000 messages per second steady ingestion rate or 92 MB/s throughput [14]. With a relatively new open source feature named Kafka Connect, it is significantly easier to integrate different sources in Kafka, leaving us with the benefit of processing the data in a near real-time manner. Additionally, the application can remain entirely unaware that its logs are going to Kafka using this approach. This approach is not limited to application logs - using it, it is possible can redirect hardware metrics and enrich log data with it. Linux server monitoring was used for hardware metrics, and all data were transferred to Kafka topic.

While aiming to do all processing in Kafka cluster, there are several options: simple Kafka producer/consumer, Kafka streams application [30], or KSQL [15]. Since the first option can be limited in terms of scalability and the last one lacks flexibility, Kafka Streams is the silver bullet for this job. Apache Kafka is a Java-based solution; thus, the JAVA-based ML framework is a priority. H2O [10] has various algorithms suited for anomaly detection, and it perfectly fits the current ecosystem. All transformations can be done within the Kafka Cluster when using this approach. There are two efficient ways to reuse existing models for Kafka streams applications - MOJO (Maven plain Old Java Object) or POJO (Plain Old Java Object), which can be embedded in Kafka Streams applications. This method perfectly decouples the machine learning model from the whole application. It also enables more convenient version control and model transparency, primarily when several different models are used within the pipeline.

Once scoring is done, there are a couple of options for how to visualize anomalies. For business-critical use cases, notifications could be implemented in the same Kafka Stream application once the anomaly score threshold is reached. However, for analysis purposes, it is way more convenient to retrieve the information from the database. Kafka Connect approach also has sink functionality and supports various sources such as HDFS, Elastic, InfluxDB. For our use case, we have selected InfluxDB, a time-series database, and integrated with various open-source monitoring tools without any effort.

The last step is anomaly evaluation and notification. Due to the nature of unsupervised machine learning, further investigation of anomalies needs to be done by humans. Therefore, interactive dashboards or even a web application are needed for user convenience and would serve as a central place where anomalies can be reviewed. Moreover, to prevent reoccurring false positives and track known anomalies, we suggest implementing the anomaly management approach in the following manner: the user reviews the event and flags the event with a red or green label in a custom-built interface. At this point, technology does not play a considerable role, so it is a matter of preference.

2.2 Framework Overview

The end-to-end pipeline for production was proposed accordingly, considering all selected components (see Fig. 1). First, features are extracted from streaming data and joined in a single data stream. From there, our selected model calculates scores for them, adds anomaly scores, and sinks to the time-series database. Finally, a front-end application represents entries above the baseline threshold, calculates an average anomaly score for each cluster component, and assigns tags depending on the log level and most frequent words.

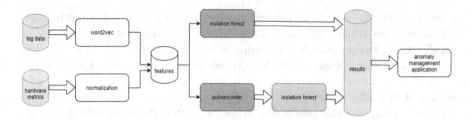

Fig. 1. Details of the proposed pipeline in the platform-independent view. Two approaches are suggested for scoring - pure Isolation Forest and Isolation Forest model enhanced with autoencoder.

System administrators/DevOps can evaluate the anomalies by adding specific event types to the white or black lists depending on the following metrics. Whitelisted events are disregarded in the future, while blacklisted items are constantly tracked until further notice, no matter the anomaly score.

Table 1. Main steps of the proposed anomaly management process. Labelled anomalies can be used for further model training.

Step	Action	People involved
1	Email/phone notification	Support team
2	Evaluate cluster overview	DevOps
3	Evaluate anomalies	Subject matter experts/DevOps
4	Label anomalies	Subject matter experts/DevOps

The low-level production pipeline can be described as follows. Each K-streams application is decoupled depending on the transformation type: source data (logs and hardware metrics), features (word2vec and normalized hardware metrics), and the final stream of scored entries. For example, in the word2vec-autoencoder-isolation forest approach, there is one additional stream for deep learning features (autoencoder output). These features are used for scoring later on.

After the score for each event is calculated (1), it is filtered depending on the suggested threshold and written to the persistent database for further analysis. The final anomaly score is calculated by the isolation forest algorithm [21]:

$$s(x, n) = 2^{-\frac{E(h(x))}{c(n)}} \qquad (1)$$

In this equation, h(x) is the path length of the observation x, c(n) represents the average path length of unsuccessful searches in a Binary Search Tree, and n represents the number of external nodes. Regarding deep learning models, Tanh activation function and MSE stopping metric were selected - according to the research, and this setup provides the best performance for image recognition tasks [16].

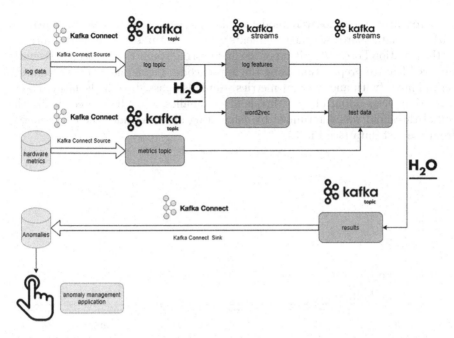

Fig. 2. Details of the proposed pipeline in the platform-specific view. All transformations/scoring are executed within the Kafka cluster. The scoring algorithm is implemented within the Kafka Streams application.

3   Experimental Setup

Kafka was chosen as the source of anomalies because it is the archetypal distributed system. In the trials, we used Apache Kafka service logs in conjunction with and without additional hardware measurements. A financial organization generated the log dataset, which includes one week's worth of usual server behavior. Additionally, anomalies were found within this time frame by administrators and presently used machine learning techniques.

The training was done on log entries which did not contain any anomalies. First of all, a generic word2vec model was created from the training data and additional public log files (OpenStack, HDFS) [13] for corpus enrichment. Vector size of 64 was selected, having a minimum frequency of 100 and a window size of 20. In addition to Kafka's service logs, hardware metrics were added to check our hypothesis regarding data enrichment. Each log line was associated with the corresponding CPU, RAM, network load, and free disk space measure time indicators as well (weekdays, hours, minutes). Metrics were collected each minute and joined depending on the timestamp. The rest of the unseen data was joined with known anomalies which occurred and were used for testing - anomalies consisted only 7.4% of the total test data.

Two feature scenarios were modeled: plain log vectors and log vectors enriched with metadata (hardware measurements). These features were provided directly to the Isolation Forest algorithm in the first scoring scenario. The second scenario involved feature preparation using the autoencoder technique; features from the second layer (with and without metrics) were also passed to the Isolation Forest algorithm. Depending on the threshold, anomalies were discovered, while the initial threshold was determined by calculating an area under the curve metric from the test data (see Fig. 3).

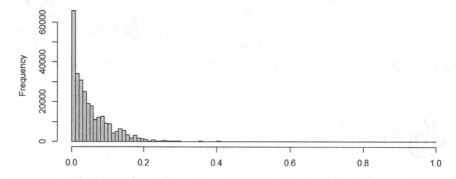

Fig. 3. Histogram for the anomaly score output on the training data. The optimal threshold for the anomaly classification is selected during the validation phase having the test data included.

Optimal hyperparameters were identified using the grid search. Isolation Forest included 256 trees with a maximum depth of 16 and a 20% sample rate. For the sake of the experiment, these parameters were used for all scenarios. Autoencoder had hidden layers of 64, 32, 64, where only the bottleneck of 32 neurons was used for feature engineering. Figure 4 illustrates an example of such a scoring pipeline from the raw input - log event and associated system metrics.

4   Experimental Results

As expected, the Word2Vec - Isolation Forest approach without the use of additional metrics performed the worst amongst other models and slightly outperformed a random guess. On the other hand, additional features significantly improved its performance, with the AUC metric reaching 0.986. Considering the ratio of the anomalies, this could be used as an alternative to the autoencoder approach if the objective is pure performance. Moreover, the extraction of deep features also increased the performance of the Isolation Forest algorithm in our case. While the plain word2vec - Isolation Forest classifier had AUC scores similar to flipping a coin, the rest of the models significantly boosted specificity

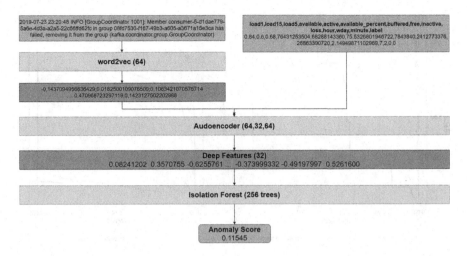

Fig. 4. An example of scoring process using combined encoding of word vectors and metrics.

and sensitivity. The winner was the word2vec - Autoencoder - Isolation Forest model having an AUC score of 0.9985. Autoencoder significantly increased the model's performance using just the plain log vectors - AUC score was surprisingly close to the enhanced features approach. The disparity is more visible in a precision-recall curve, which is recommended over the ROC curve in case of large class imbalance [28]. While the difference in AUC score for all four models is not so different, encoding both word vectors and additional metrics-related features together proved to be superior and had a nearly perfect curve (see Fig. 5).

To prove the model robustness, ten different runs were performed using a random sample of regular server behavior logs, and a central tendency in AUC values was reported (see Table 2). As a result, Autoencoder successfully extracted meaningful features for reconstruction, and all models proved themselves robust even using an additional sampling technique.

Table 2. Model evaluation results after 10 held-out runs.

Method	Dataset	Average **AUC**	Median **AUC**
IsoForest	w2v	0.603	0.585
AE & IsoForest	encoded(w2v)	0.959	0.969
IsoForest	w2v & metrics	0.983	0.983
AE & IsoForest	encoded(w2v) & metrics	0.989	0.995
AE & IsoForest	encoded(w2v & metrics)	**0.995**	**0.998**

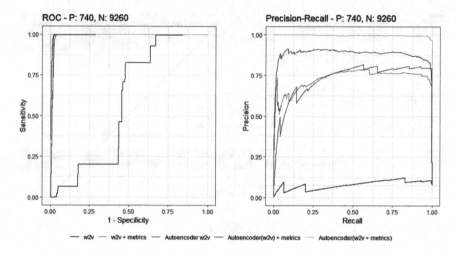

Fig. 5. ROC and Precision-Recall curves: results of the 1st hold-out run.

After the best model was selected, the logic can be extracted as Maven Plain Old Java Object (MOJO) and used in Kafka Streams applications along with a previously trained word2vec model. The algorithm selection will depend on system specification and available resources - Isolation Forest can be used with or without an autoencoder layer, although the incorporation of an autoencoder tends to improve the results with respect to precision and recall. Since the models are decoupled from an application, we suggest implementing a pipeline for retraining an algorithm frequently to get the best and up-to-date results.

5   Discussion and Conclusion

Machine learning-based log anomaly detection approach helps identify anomalies and familiarize with data faster no matter the source system. Furthermore, these models could be used initially to identify suspicious messages and dramatically reduce the scope for searching real anomalies. Word2Vec - Autoencoder - Isolation Forest model with additional metrics proved to be the most robust approach for classifying real-world Kafka logs. All identified anomalies from the anomaly management process can be used for tuning the model later on. Although there were no errors or noticeable disturbances during that time, model insights helped to enhance cluster configuration, to fix minor issues - balance load across the cluster or fix misbehaving applications. The robust data pipeline is vertically and horizontally scalable; therefore, it can ensure near-real-time anomaly detection for any data transmitted via Kafka in production cases. Once the infrastructure is established, it is really easy to onboard any system. Moreover, having all data in Kafka as streams enables fast scoring and data re-usability in real-time use cases for security, auditing, and monitoring purposes. Kafka Connect approach allows to enrich existing data pipelines and divert data streams to persistent storage seamlessly.

References

1. Ahmad, S., Lavin, A., Purdy, S., Agha, Z.: Unsupervised real-time anomaly detection for streaming data. Neurocomputing **262**, 06 (2017)
2. Andreolini, M., Colajanni, M., Pietri, M., Tosi, S.: Adaptive, scalable and reliable monitoring of big data on clouds. J. Parallel Distrib. Comput. **79**, 67–79 (2015). Special Issue on Scalable Systems for Big Data Management and Analytics
3. Chong, F., Chua, T., Lim, E.P., Huberman, B.A.: Detecting flow anomalies in distributed systems. In: 2014 IEEE International Conference on Data Mining. IEEE (2014)
4. Chong, F., Chua, T., Lim, E.P., Huberman, B.A.: Detecting flow anomalies in distributed systems. In: Proceedings of the 2014 IEEE International Conference on Data Mining, ICDM 2014, pp. 100–109, USA. IEEE Computer Society (2014)
5. Decker, L., Leite, D., Giommi, L., Bonacorsi, D.: Real-time anomaly detection in data centers for log-based predictive maintenance using an evolving fuzzy-rule-based approach. In: 2020 IEEE International Conference on Fuzzy Systems (FUZZ-IEEE). IEEE (2020)
6. Dorofeev, A., Kurganov, V., Fillipova, N., Pashkova, T.: Ensuring the integrity of transportation and logistics during the COVID-19 pandemic. Transp. Res. Procedia **50**, 96–105 (2020). XIV International Conference on Organization and Traffic Safety Management in Large Cities (OTS-2020)
7. Farzad, A., Gulliver, T.A.: Unsupervised log message anomaly detection. ICT Express **6**(3), 229–237 (2020)
8. Fu, Q., Lou, J.G., Wang, Y., Li, J.: Execution anomaly detection in distributed systems through unstructured log analysis. In: 2009 Ninth IEEE International Conference on Data Mining. IEEE (2009)
9. Poojitha, G., Sowmyarani, C.: Pipeline for real-time anomaly detection in log data streams using Apache Kafka and Apache Spark. Int. J. Comput. Appl. **182**(24), 8–13 (2018)
10. H2O.ai. H2O: Scalable Machine Learning Platform, 2020. version 3.30.0.6
11. Habeeb, R.A.A., Nasaruddin, F., Gani, A., Hashem, I.A.T., Ahmed, E., Imran, M.: Real-time big data processing for anomaly detection: a survey. Int. J. Inf. Manage. **45**, 289–307 (2019)
12. He, S., Zhu, J., He, P., Lyu, M.R.: Experience report: system log analysis for anomaly detection. In: 2016 IEEE 27th International Symposium on Software Reliability Engineering (ISSRE), pp. 207–218 (2016)
13. He, S., Zhu, J., He, P., Lyu, M.R.: Loghub: a large collection of system log datasets towards automated log analytics. ArXiv, abs/2008.06448, 2020
14. Hesse, G., Matthies, C., Rabl, T., Uflacker, M.: How fast can we insert? a performance study of apache kafka. ArXiv, abs/2003.06452 (2020)
15. Jafarpour, H., Desai, R.: KSQL: streaming SQL engine for Apache Kafka. In: Herschel, M., Galhardas, H., Reinwald, B., Fundulaki, I., Binnig, C., Kaoudi, Z. (eds.) Advances in Database Technology - 22nd International Conference on Extending Database Technology, EDBT 2019, Lisbon, Portugal, 26–29 March 2019, pp. 524–533. OpenProceedings.org (2019)
16. Kochura, Y., Stirenko, S., Alienin, O., Novotarskiy, M., Gordienko, Y.: Performance analysis of open source machine learning frameworks for various parameters in single-threaded and multi-threaded modes. In: Shakhovska, N., Stepashko, V. (eds.) CSIT 2017. AISC, vol. 689, pp. 243–256. Springer, Cham (2018). https://doi.org/10.1007/978-3-319-70581-1_17

17. Kreps, J., Kafka : a distributed messaging system for log processing (2011)
18. Kumarage, H., Khalil, I., Tari, Z., Zomaya, A.: Distributed anomaly detection for industrial wireless sensor networks based on fuzzy data modelling. J. Parallel Distrib. Comput. **73**(6), 790–806 (2013)
19. Kumari, R., Singh, M.K., Jha, R., Singh, N.K.: Anomaly detection in network traffic using k-mean clustering. In: 2016 3rd International Conference on Recent Advances in Information Technology (RAIT), pp. 387–393 (2016)
20. Leite, L., Rocha, C., Kon, F., Milojicic, D., Meirelles, P.: A survey of DevOps concepts and challenges. ACM Comput. Surv. **52**(6), 1–35 (2019)
21. Liu, F.T., Ting, K.M., Zhou, Z.H.: Isolation forest. In: 2008 Eighth IEEE International Conference on Data Mining. IEEE (2008)
22. Liu, F.T., Ting, K.M., Zhou, Z.H.: Isolation-based anomaly detection. ACM Trans. Knowl. Discov. Data **6**(1), 1–39 (2012)
23. Myers, D., Suriadi, S., Radke, K., Foo, E.: Anomaly detection for industrial control systems using process mining. Comput. Secur. **78**, 103–125 (2018)
24. Nguyen, T.-B.-T., Liao, T.-L., Vu, T.-A.: Anomaly detection using one-class SVM for logs of juniper router devices. In: Duong, T.Q., Vo, N.-S., Nguyen, L.K., Vien, Q.-T., Nguyen, V.-D. (eds.) INISCOM 2019. LNICST, vol. 293, pp. 302–312. Springer, Cham (2019). https://doi.org/10.1007/978-3-030-30149-1_24
25. Nixon, C., Sedky, M., Hassan, M. .: Autoencoders: a low cost anomaly detection method for computer network data streams. In: Proceedings of the 2020 4th International Conference on Cloud and Big Data Computing, ICCBDC 2020, pp. 58–62, New York, NY, USA. Association for Computing Machinery (2020)
26. Pang, G., Shen, C., Cao, L., Hengel, A.V.D.: Deep learning for anomaly detection: a review. CoRR, abs/2007.02500 (2020)
27. Rabatel, J., Bringay, S., Poncelet, P.: Anomaly detection in monitoring sensor data for preventive maintenance. Expert Syst. Appl. **38**(6), 7003–7015 (2011)
28. Saito, T., Rehmsmeier, M.: The precision-recall plot is more informative than the ROC plot when evaluating binary classifiers on imbalanced datasets. PLoS ONE **10**(3), e0118432 (2015)
29. Sax, M.J.: Apache Kafka, pp. 1–8. Springer International Publishing, Cham (2018)
30. Sax, M.J., Wang, G., Weidlich, M., Freytag, J.C.: Streams and tables: two sides of the same coin. In: Proceedings of the International Workshop on Real-Time Business Intelligence and Analytics, BIRTE 2018, New York, NY, USA. Association for Computing Machinery (2018)
31. Xu, H., et al.: Unsupervised anomaly detection via variational auto-encoder for seasonal KPIs in web applications. In: Proceedings of the 2018 World Wide Web Conference on World Wide Web, pp. 187–196. International World Wide Web Conferences Steering Committee (2018)
32. Zasadziński, M., Solé, M., Brandon, A., Muntés-Mulero, V., Carrera, D.: Next stop "NoOps": enabling cross-system diagnostics through graph-based composition of logs and metrics. In: 2018 IEEE International Conference on Cluster Computing (CLUSTER), pp. 212–222 (2018)
33. Zhang, X., et al.: Robust log-based anomaly detection on unstable log data. In: Proceedings of the 2019 27th ACM Joint Meeting on European Software Engineering Conference and Symposium on the Foundations of Software Engineering, ESEC/FSE 2019, pp. 807–817, New York, NY, USA. Association for Computing Machinery (2019)

Decomposition of Fuzzy Homogeneous Classes of Objects

Dmytro O. Terletskyi$^{(\boxtimes)}$ and Sergey V. Yershov

V. M. Glushkov Institute of Cybernetics of NAS of Ukraine, Kyiv, Ukraine
{dmytro.terletskyi,ErshovSV}@nas.gov.ua

Abstract. Extraction of new knowledge from earlier obtained and integrated knowledge is one of the main stages of intelligent knowledge analysis. To handle such a task, a knowledge-based system should be able to decompose complex or composite knowledge structures and extract new knowledge items, which were hidden or non-obvious before. Existed approaches to decomposition within object-oriented paradigm provide different variants of partitioning or fragmentation of main knowledge structures, such as objects, classes, and relations among them, however, most of them do not consider semantic structural and functional dependencies among properties and methods of classes that affect on the decomposition process. In this paper, we introduced concepts of fuzzy structural and functional atoms, as well as molecules of fuzzy homogeneous classes of objects, within such a knowledge representation model as fuzzy object-oriented dynamic networks. In addition, we proposed the algorithm for the decomposition of fuzzy homogeneous classes of objects, which implements the idea of universal decomposition exploiter of fuzzy classes of objects, and constructs semantically correct subclasses of a fuzzy homogeneous class of objects by solving appropriate constraint satisfaction problem that defines decomposition conditions. To demonstrate some possible application scenarios, we provided an appropriate example of the decomposition of a fuzzy homogeneous class of objects.

Keywords: Structural atom · Functional atom · Structural molecule · Functional molecule · Decomposition of fuzzy classes

1 Introduction

The analysis of the knowledge base for the extraction of new knowledge is an important task for most modern knowledge-based systems (KBSs), to perform it within a chosen knowledge representation model, a KBS should be able to analyze representation structures, integrated within a knowledge base, and extract implicit or hidden knowledge. Since some knowledge representation structures are complex or composite, therefore they can be decomposed. As the result, we can obtain new knowledge items, which were non-obvious before the decomposition and could not be obtained without it.

© The Author(s), under exclusive license to Springer Nature Switzerland AG 2022
A. Lopata et al. (Eds.): ICIST 2022, CCIS 1665, pp. 43–63, 2022.
https://doi.org/10.1007/978-3-031-16302-9_4

In general, term decomposition can be defined as the splitting of something into smaller constituent parts. Within object-oriented programming (OOP), object-oriented knowledge representation (OOKR), as well as object-oriented databases (OODB), decomposition can be applied to the main representation structures, such as classes, relations, collections of objects, etc. Since a class is one of the main representation structures, decomposition of a class is an important task in all mentioned areas. As it was shown in [35], *decomposition of a class* can be used as an approach to run-time class generation in the OOP and OOKR, which allows the dynamic construction of new classes of objects, that can be useful for knowledge reasoning and integration.

Within the OODB, the term *class decomposition* is also known as *class partitioning* [4–6,19,23–25,29] or *class fragmentation* [6,11–13,30]. According to [11–13,30], there are three main types of database classes fragmentation: *horizontal*, *vertical*, and *hybrid*. Horizontal fragmentation is a decomposition of a class into collections of non-empty subsets of instance objects, called *horizontal fragments*, while vertical fragmentation is a decomposition of a class into collections of non-empty subsets of attributes, called *vertical fragments*. Hybrid fragmentation is a mix of horizontal and vertical approaches to fragmentation, i.e. it is a decomposition of a class into collections of horizontal and vertical fragments.

During the last decades, a variety of schemes and algorithms for horizontal, vertical, and mixed fragmentation/partitioning of objects, classes and relations in OODB were developed [4–6,13,19,20,23–25,29,30]. In addition, some of the proposed schemes and algorithms were generalized for the semi-structured data model and XML [7,8,22,26,27,32], for the data warehouses [3], as well as for the fuzzy querying databases [10]. Since the class decomposition requires analysis of attributes and methods of a class, Ezeife and Barker proposed a taxonomy of class models that classifies decomposition types, types of attributes, and methods of a class [11,12]. According to the proposed taxonomy, there are two kinds of attributes – (simple and complex) and three kinds of methods (simple, contained simple, and complex). The simple attributes are defined as attributes of primitive types, while complex attributes may be determined as objects of other classes. Simple methods are defined as methods, which do not invoke other methods of a class, contained simple methods are determined as simple methods of related classes, while complex methods are methods, which invoke methods of other classes. However, the concepts of a class within OODB and within OOP as well as in OOKR have some differences. The internal structure of a class within the OOP as well as within OOKR is defined as a collection of attributes, which define a structure or internal state of a class. In addition, classes have a behavioral part defined as a collection of methods that provides the external interface allowing access to the class state for reading or modification of particular attributes and their values, when required. Attributes of a class, as well as its methods, can be defined independently from other attributes and methods of the class or based on them. Consequently, attributes and methods of the second kind create internal semantic dependencies within the class. For example, dynamic attributes, which values are computed using particular methods and other attributes, or methods that invoke other methods and (or) use particular attributes during their own invocation. It makes the internal structure of a class more complex and represents its semantic features in more detail.

Usually, within fuzzy object-oriented databases (FOODB) identification and processing dependencies are performed using the concepts of *fuzzy functional object dependency* [31], or *fuzzy attribute dependency* and *fuzzy method dependency* [40,41], which are defined for the fuzzy relation scheme of a database. Such an approach provides an opportunity to formalize the inheritance and aggregation relations, defined among fuzzy classes, objects, as well as classes and objects. That is important and useful for the optimization of the fuzzy database structure and querying over it, however, the approach does not consider internal structural and functional dependencies of attributes and methods within fuzzy classes themselves as well as their instances. Such dependencies define the basis for semantically correct fuzzy class decomposition. In addition, object-oriented databases are used for storage and representation of particular classes, which are models of some essences in certain domains. Automatic saving of classes, represented in terms of a particular object-oriented programming language or knowledge representation model, within the object-oriented database requires performing the corresponding object-relational mapping. As the result, classes will be represented in the database as appropriate tables, where each column defines a corresponding attribute of a class [1]. Therefore all mentioned approaches to class fragmentation/partitioning, which were proposed for OODB, do not consider internal semantic dependencies of classes during the decomposition process. Consequently, these approaches can not be applied to the decomposition of classes within OOP and OOKR. Furthermore, most of the mentioned approaches to class decomposition consider only a crisp model of a class.

Another approach to decomposition, namely decomposition of software systems on subsystems, called *functional decomposition*, was proposed in [14–17]. The main idea of the approach is to consider individual relations among the classes as the atomic design units instead of classes themselves. It means that some functional parts of a system can be dependent or independent from other parts due to some relations, consequently, some parts of the system can or cannot affect some other parts as well. However, when there is a dependency among some parts of the system represented by corresponding relations, such relations represent particular semantic features of certain subsystems, which are important for semantically correct decomposition. Using this idea, to increase the cohesion and decrease coupling of classes via the removal of excessive responsibilities, the method for decomposition of the class responsibilities, based on internal and external relationships of classes, was proposed in [21, 28].

A similar idea for the decomposition of crisp homogeneous classes of objects, based on internal dependencies among properties and methods, was proposed in [35]. Considering all remarks noted above, in this paper, we define concepts of fuzzy structural atoms and molecules as well as fuzzy functional atoms and molecules of fuzzy homogeneous classes of objects within such knowledge representation model as Fuzzy Object-Oriented Dynamic Networks, which was proposed in [33,34] and then extended in [36,37]. Using these concepts, we developed and implemented the algorithm for the decomposition of fuzzy homogeneous classes of objects, which computes a set of all semantically consistent subclasses of the decomposed fuzzy class of objects.

2   Morphology of Fuzzy Classes

As was mentioned above, classes within OOP and OOKR are defined by collections of attributes and methods, which form some internal structural and (or) functional dependencies within a class. Such internal dependencies were analyzed in [35] for such a knowledge representation model as Objects-Oriented Dynamic Networks (OODNs). As a result concepts of structural atoms and molecules, as well as concepts of functional atoms and molecules, were introduced for crisp homogeneous classes of objects. Let us generalize these concepts for fuzzy homogeneous classes of objects, which were proposed in [36,37], as the extension of a fuzzy version of OODNs.

As it was noted in [36,37], a fuzzy homogeneous class of objects can be defined in the following way.

Definition 1. *A fuzzy homogeneous class of objects is a collection*

$$T/M(T) = (P(T)/M(P(T)), F(T)/M(F(T)))/M(T) = ((p_1/\mu(p_1), \ldots,$$
$$p_n/\mu(p_n))/M(P(T)), (f_1/\mu(f_1), \ldots, f_m/\mu(f_m))/M(F(T)))/M(T),$$

where $p_i \in P(T)$ is a crisp or fuzzy property of the class T, $f_j \in F(T)$ is its crisp or fuzzy method, $\mu(p_i) : p_i(A) \to [0,1]$ and $\mu(f_j) : f_j(A) \to [0,1]$ are measures of fuzziness of a property p_i and a method f_j, where A is an object of the class T, and $M(T)$ is a measure of fuzziness of the class T, defined in the following way

$$M(T) = (M(P(T)) + M(F(T)))/2$$
$$= (\mu(p_1) + \cdots + \mu(p_n) + \mu(f_1) + \cdots + \mu(f_m))/(n+m),$$
$$M(P(T)) : P(T) \to (0,1], \ M(F(T)) : F(T) \to (0,1], \ M(T) : T \to (0,1].$$

As we can see, a fuzzy homogeneous class of objects $T/M(T)$ has the specification $P(T)$ and signature $F(T)$, which are collections of fuzzy and (or) crisp properties and methods of the class T respectively. These properties and methods can be defined using some other properties and methods of the class $T/M(T)$ or defined independently from them. Therefore, to classify such properties and methods, as well as dependencies among them, the interpretation of the concept of chemical atoms and molecules was used in [35]. The concept of chemical atoms as the smallest indivisible particles was interpreted as properties and methods defined independently from other properties and methods of the fuzzy class. The concept of chemical molecules as a group of atoms connected with each other in some way was interpreted as a collection determined by a property or a method, and by all properties and methods, used for its definition. Using this interpretation, let us define concepts of the *fuzzy structural atom, fuzzy functional atom, fuzzy structural molecule*, and *fuzzy functional molecule*, based on the correspondent definitions for the crisp homogeneous classes of objects introduced in [35].

Definition 2. *A fuzzy structural atom of a fuzzy homogeneous class of objects $T/M(T)$ is a property $p_i()/\mu(p_i()) \in P(T)$ defined without using any other properties and (or) methods of the fuzzy class $T/M(T)$, where $P(T)$ is its specification.*

Definition 3. *A fuzzy functional atom of a fuzzy homogeneous class of objects $T/M(T)$ is a method $f_i()/\mu(f_i()) \in F(T)$, defined without using any other properties and (or) methods of the fuzzy class $T/M(T)$, where $F(T)$ is its signature.*

Definition 4. *A fuzzy structural molecule of a fuzzy homogeneous class of objects $T/M(T)$ is a collection $SM_i(T) = (p_i/\mu(p_i), x_{j_1}/\mu(x_{j_1}), \ldots, x_{j_n}/\mu(x_{j_n}))$, where $p_i/\mu(p_i)$ is a property defined based on the other fuzzy atoms or smaller fuzzy molecules $x_{j_1}/\mu(x_{j_1}), \ldots, x_{j_n}/\mu(x_{j_n})$, $1 \leqslant j_1 \leqslant \cdots \leqslant j_n \leqslant |P(T) \cup F(T)|$, $1 \leqslant i \leqslant |P(T)|$, and where $P(T)$ is a specification of the fuzzy class $T/M(T)$, while $F(T)$ is its signature.*

Definition 5. *A fuzzy functional molecule of a fuzzy homogeneous class of objects $T/M(T)$ is a collection $FM_i(T) = (f_i/\mu(f_i), x_{j_1}/\mu(x_{j_1}), \ldots, x_{j_n}/\mu(x_{j_n}))$, where f_i is a method defined based on the other fuzzy atoms or smaller fuzzy molecules $x_{j_1}/\mu(x_{j_1}), \ldots, x_{j_n}/\mu(x_{j_n})$, $1 \leqslant j_1 \leqslant \cdots \leqslant j_n \leqslant |P(T) \cup F(T)|$, $1 \leqslant i \leqslant |F(T)|$, and where $P(T)$ is a specification of the fuzzy class $T/M(T)$, while $F(T)$ is its signature.*

Fuzzy structural and functional molecules of a fuzzy homogeneous class of objects define particular *internal semantic connections* among its atoms or other smaller molecules. To model real essences from particular domains, such semantic connections should represent the appropriate internal semantic nature of the modeled entity, otherwise, the corresponding model will be unrealistic and inefficient. Since the decomposition of fuzzy homogeneous classes of objects can be considered as a way to create new fuzzy homogeneous classes of objects, therefore decomposition procedure itself implements the concept of universal exploiters of classes of objects, which was introduced in [33, 34] in the form of the universal union, intersection, difference, and the symmetric difference exploiters of classes of fuzzy objects. Later this idea in the form of the universal intersection, union, and difference exploiters of fuzzy homogeneous classes of objects was extended in [36–39]. Therefore, let us define concepts of internal semantic dependencies and universal decomposition exploiter for fuzzy homogeneous classes of objects, using definitions of fuzzy structural and functional atoms and molecules of a fuzzy homogeneous class of objects.

Definition 6. *Internal semantic dependencies of a fuzzy homogeneous class of objects $T/M(T)$, which defines fuzzy type of objects t, is a set of fuzzy structural and functional atoms and molecules of the class $T/M(T)$, i.e.*

$$ISD(T/M(T)) = \{SA_1, \ldots, SA_n, FA_1, \ldots, FA_m,$$
$$SM_1, \ldots, SM_v, FM_1, \ldots, FM_q\}$$

where SA_{i_1}, $i_1 = \overline{1, n}$ and FA_{j_i}, $j_1 = \overline{1, m}$ are fuzzy structural and functional atoms of the fuzzy class $T/M(T)$, while SM_{i_2}, $i_2 = \overline{1, v}$ and FM_{j_2}, $j_2 = \overline{1, q}$ are its structural and functional molecules respectively.

The set of internal semantic dependencies of the fuzzy homogeneous class of objects $T/M(T)$ can be constructed using the corresponding procedure, which analyzes the specification and signature of the class and detects such dependencies, or via manual detection. The $ISD(T/M(T))$ is a set of constraints that is a basis for the decomposition process, as it guarantees the semantic consistency of each subclass created during the decomposition.

Definition 7. *Decomposition of a fuzzy homogeneous class of objects $T/M(T)$, which defines the fuzzy type of objects t, is a set of its semantically consistent subclasses $D = \{T_1/M(T_1), \ldots, T_n/M(T_n)\}$, i.e. $T_i/M(T_i) \subseteq T/M(T)$, $i = \overline{1, n}$, where each subclass does not contradict any internal semantic dependency of the class $T/M(T)$.*

Since a fuzzy homogeneous class of objects $T/M(T)$, has subclasses of different cardinalities, i.e. with different numbers of properties and methods, not all of its internal semantic dependencies can be applicable to each subclass. However, if the property or method, which defines the corresponding structural or functional molecule of the class $T/M(T)$ belongs to the subclass $T_i/M(T_i) \subseteq T/M(T)$, then all other elements of the molecule also must belong to this subclass, otherwise, such subclass will be semantically inconsistent.

3   Fuzzy Classes Decomposition

As it was noted in [35], the class decomposition procedure should consider all internal semantic dependencies of a homogeneous class of objects, which can be represented as appropriate restrictions for a particular constraint satisfaction problem (CSP). However, in the general case, the corresponding CSP for a full class fragmentation has exponential time complexity, e.g. decomposition of a class, which consists of four properties and four methods, required to find all semantically consistent subclasses among $8^1 + 8^2 + \cdots + 8^7 = 2396744$ possible tuples of the Cartesian product. Therefore, to reduce the time complexity, the internal structure of a homogeneous class of objects was considered as a join-semilattice defined on the power set of the class, where elements of the semilattice are all possible unique combinations of properties and (or) methods of the class. As the result, for the mentioned example, we need to analyze only 255 elements of the corresponding semilattice, which reduces the complexity almost 9399 times.

According to [2,9,18,35], in general, the CSP for the decomposition of a fuzzy homogeneous class of objects $T/M(T)$ can be defined as the following tuple $DFHC = (Y, \Sigma, C)$, where $Y = (y_1, \ldots, y_n)$, $n > 0$, is a fsinite sequence of variables defined on the respective domains $\Sigma = (\Sigma_1, \ldots, \Sigma_n)$, i.e. $y_1 \rightarrow \Sigma_1, \ldots, y_n \rightarrow \Sigma_n$, where $\Sigma_i = \{x_1, \ldots, x_w\}$, $w > 0$, $i = \overline{i, n}$ is a set of all possible values for the variable y_i; C is a set of constraints $C = (c_1, \ldots, c_k)$, $k > 0$, where constraint $c_i = (S_i, R_i)$, $i = \overline{1, k}$, where $S_i \in Y$ is a scope of the constraint, i.e. $S_i = (y_{i_1} \in \Sigma_{i_1}, \ldots, y_{i_n} \in \Sigma_{i_n})$ and $R_i \subseteq \Sigma_{i_1} \times \cdots \times \Sigma_{i_n}$ is a relation defined on the S_i. More precisely, the CSP can be formulated as follows

$$DFHC = (Y, \Sigma, ISD) = ((y_1, \ldots, y_n), (\Sigma_1, \ldots, \Sigma_n),$$
$$(SA_1, \ldots, SA_n, FA_1, \ldots, FA_m, SM_1, \ldots, SM_v, FM_1, \ldots, FM_q)),$$

where Σ_i, $i = \overline{1, n}$ is an i-th antichain of the join-semilattice

$$B(P(T/M(T)), F(T/M(T))) = (p_1(T)/\mu(p_1(T)), \ldots, p_n(T)/\mu(p_n(T)),$$
$$f_1(T)/\mu(f_1(T)), \ldots f_m(T)/\mu(f_m(T)))$$

where $B(P(T/M(T)), F(T/M(T)))$ is a power set of the set of properties and methods of the class $T/M(T)$, while $P(T/M(T))$ and $F(T/M(T))$ is its specification and signature respectively.

Let us extend the approach as well as the algorithm for solving the CSP of decomposition of crisp homogeneous class of objects, which was proposed in [35], for fuzzy homogeneous classes of objects. According to the idea of the universal decomposition exploiter of fuzzy homogeneous classes of objects, a corresponding algorithm for its implementation should analyze the specification and signature of a fuzzy homogeneous class of objects $T/M(T)$ and constructs its semantically consistent subclasses, which satisfy the appropriate constraints in a form of fuzzy structural and functional atoms and molecules of the class $T/M(T)$. To implement the concept of universal decomposition exploiter for fuzzy homogeneous classes of objects, we developed Algorithm 1 based on this idea.

As we can see, Algorithm 1 uses the list of the input parameters, where $T/M(T)$ is a fuzzy homogeneous class of objects, which required to be decomposed; $C = ISD(T/M(T))$ is a collection of structural and functional atoms and molecules, which represent internal dependencies among different properties and methods of the $T/M(T)$ in a form of corresponding constraints; N is the sequence of positive integer numbers, which defines the required cardinalities of subclasses for the class $T/M(T)$ decomposition; M is an interval of real numbers $[a, b] \subseteq [0, 1]$, which determines the required fuzziness of each subclass of the class $T/M(T)$ decomposition; δ is an integer number, which defines the accuracy for computing of the measure of fuzziness for each subclass of the $T/M(T)$. Algorithm 1 performs the decomposition of the fuzzy homogeneous class of objects $T/M(T)$ on the set of subclasses D, which contains fuzzy homogeneous classes of objects $T_1/M(T_1), \ldots, T_k/M(T_k)$, such that $|T_i/M(T_i)| \in N$, $M(T_i) \in M$, and $M(T_i)$ has accuracy δ, $i = \overline{1, k}$. If such subclasses of the class $T/M(T)$ exist, then

---

Algorithm 1. Decomposition of fuzzy homogeneous classes of objects.

Require: $T/M(T)$, C, N, M, δ
Ensure: D

```
 1: D := {};
 2: for n ∈ N do
 3:     Tₖ := {};
 4:     for i = 1, ..., 2ⁿ − 1 do
 5:         if binary(i).count(1) = i then
 6:             for aⱼ ∈ T, j = 1, ..., |T| do
 7:                 if (i & (1 << j)) > 0 then
 8:                     Tₖ.add(aⱼ);
 9:                 μ := compute_fuzziness(Tₖ, δ);
10:                 if μ ∈ M then
11:                     satisfy := true;
12:                     for all c ∈ C do
13:                         if not is_satisfy(Tₖ, c) then
14:                             satisfy := false;
15:                             break;
16:                     if satisfy then
17:                         D.add(Tₖ/μ);
18:             Tₖ := {};
19: return  D.
```

Procedure 1 compute_fuzziness(T, δ)

Input: T, δ
Output: $M(T) \in [0, 1]$

```
 1: sum := 0;
 2: for aᵢ ∈ T, i = 1, ..., |T| do
 3:     sum := sum + μ(aᵢ);
 4: M(T) := round(sum/max(|T|, 1), δ);
 5: return  M(T).
```

Algorithm 1 constructs them as the elements of the set D. To compute the measure of fuzziness for a subclass $T_k/M(T_k)$ of the fuzzy class of objects $T/M(T)$, Algorithm 1 uses Procedure 1, which calculates $M(T_k)$ with accuracy δ according to Definition 1. To solve the corresponding CSP problem for each candidate subclass of the fuzzy class of objects $T/M(T)$, Algorithm 1 uses Procedure 2, which verifies the satisfiability of particular constraint $c \in ISD(T/M(T))$, for a candidate subclass $T_k/M(T_k) \subseteq T/M(T)$. If candidate subclass $T_k/M(T_k)$ satisfies the constraint $c \in ISD(T/M(T))$, then Procedure 2 returns $true$ if $T_k/M(T_k)$ does not satisfy c, it returns $false$, and if c is not relevant for $T_k/M(T_k)$, then it returns $none$.

Algorithm 1 can be used with different configuration parameters, and solve different variations of CSP for the decomposition of fuzzy homogeneous classes of objects. It allows us to solve the CSP for full decomposition of a fuzzy homogeneous class of objects when Algorithm 1 computes all possible semantically

---

Procedure 2 is_satisfy(T_k, c)

Input: T_k, c
Output: satisfy $\in$ {**true**, **false**, **none**}
 1: satisfy := **none**;
 2: **if** $c[0] \in T_k$ **then**
 3:     satisfy := **false**;
 4:     **for** $c[i] \in c, i = 1, \ldots, |c|$ **do**
 5:         **for** $c[i][j] \in c[i], j = 1, \ldots, |c[i]|$ **do**
 6:             **if** $c[i][j] \in T_k$ **then**
 7:                 satisfy := **true**;
 8:             **else**
 9:                 satisfy := **false**;
10:                 **break**;
11:         **if** satisfy **then**
12:             **return** satisfy;
13: **return** satisfy.

---

consistent subclasses of the fuzzy class $T/M(T)$, which satisfy restrictions of subclasses fuzziness. In addition, Algorithm 1 can be used for solving the CSP for partial decomposition of a fuzzy homogeneous class of objects, in this case, it computes all possible semantically consistent subclasses of the fuzzy class $T/M(T)$, which have a defined cardinality and satisfy restrictions for the fuzziness of subclasses. Such application of the algorithm provides an opportunity to reduce the complexity of the decomposition procedure when we definitely know the cardinality of semantically consistent subclasses that we are looking for. In such situations, the algorithm will consider only certain antichains of join-semilattice of a fuzzy homogeneous class $T/M(T)$, which decreases the computation time.

4   Application Example

Universal exploiters of classes of objects can be used for different purposes, in particular for the extraction of implicit or hidden knowledge. For instance, the universal decomposition exploiter, which was proposed in [35], can be used to extract semantic consistent subclasses of a homogeneous class of objects, that are implicit or hidden before the decomposition. In addition, the universal exploiters of union, intersection, and difference of fuzzy homogeneous classes of objects can be used for the efficient integration of fuzzy knowledge, as it was demonstrated in [36–39].

To explain the application of the decomposition exploiter of fuzzy homogeneous classes of objects as well as the developed corresponding algorithm for its implementation, let us consider fuzzy homogeneous classes of objects Pt and Tr, represented in terms of fuzzy object-oriented dynamic networks. Suppose the class Pt defines the concept of a fuzzy point on a plane and has the following structure

$$Pt(p_1 = (x, (v_1 \in V_x, \mathbb{R}))/1,$$
$$p_2 = (y, (v_1 \in V_y, \mathbb{R}))/1,$$
$$f_1 = get\_x(pt, \mathbb{R})/0.92,$$
$$f_2 = get\_y(pt, \mathbb{R})/0.92,$$
$$f_3 = set\_x(pt, (a_x, \mathbb{R}), (b_x, \mathbb{R}), (k_x, \mathbb{R}))/0.95,$$
$$f_4 = set\_y(pt, (a_y, \mathbb{R}), (b_y, \mathbb{R}), (k_y, \mathbb{R}))/0.95,$$
$$)/0.96,$$

where p_1 and p_2 are fuzzy quantitative properties, which mean x and y coordinates of a point, and defined as the fuzzy sets V_x and V_y, determined on the intervals of real numbers $[a_x, b_x]$ and $[a_y, b_y]$, i.e.

$$V_x = \left\{ w_i^-/\mu(w_i^-) + d_x/1 + w_i^+/\mu(w_i^+) \right\},$$
$$V_y = \left\{ q_j^-/\mu(q_j^-) + d_y/1 + q_j^+/\mu(q_j^+) \right\},$$

where $a_x < d_x < b_x$, $a_y < d_y < b_y$, and $d_x = (b_x - a_x)/2$, $d_y = (b_y - a_y)/2$, and k_x, k_y are the increments for the generation of w_i^- and w_i^+, $i = \overline{1, \ldots}$, as well as q_j^- and q_j^+, $j = \overline{1, \ldots}$, where

$$w_i^- = d_x - k_x * i; \quad a_x < d_x - k_x * i < d_x; \quad w_i^+ = d_x + k_x * i;$$
$$d_x < d_x + k_x * i < b_x; \quad q_j^- = d_y - k_y * j; \quad a_y < d_y - k_y * j < d_y;$$
$$q_j^+ = d_y + k_y * j; \quad d_y < d_y + k_y * j < b_y;$$

$$\mu(w_i^-) = \frac{w_i^- - a_x}{d_x - a_x} - \delta_i^-; \quad \delta_i^- = 1 - \mu(w_i^-) - \nu(w_i^-); \quad \nu(w_i^-) = 1 - \mu(w_i^-),$$

$$\mu(w_i^+) = \frac{b_x - w_i^+}{b_x - d_x} - \delta_i^+; \quad \delta_i^+ = 1 - \mu(w_i^+) - \nu(w_i^+); \quad \nu(w_i^+) = 1 - \mu(w_i^+),$$

$$\mu(q_j^-) = \frac{q_j^- - a_y}{d_y - a_y} - \delta_j^-; \quad \delta_j^- = 1 - \mu(q_j^-) - \nu(q_j^-); \quad \nu(q_j^-) = 1 - \mu(q_j^-),$$

$$\mu(q_j^+) = \frac{b_y - q_j^+}{b_y - d_y} - \delta_j^+; \quad \delta_j^+ = 1 - \mu(q_j^+) - \nu(q_j^+); \quad \nu(q_j^+) = 1 - \mu(q_j^+);$$

f_1 and f_2 are fuzzy methods, which compute the defuzzification representation of the fuzzy quantitative properties x and y respectively, and are defined in the following way

$$f_1(pt) = \frac{\sum_{i=1}^{|pt.x.v|} \mu(pt.x.v) \cdot pt.x.v}{\sum_{i=1}^{|pt.x.v|} \mu(pt.x.v)}, \quad f_2(pt) = \frac{\sum_{i=1}^{|pt.y.v|} \mu(pt.y.v) \cdot pt.y.v}{\sum_{i=1}^{|pt.y.v|} \mu(pt.y.v)};$$

f_3 and f_4 are fuzzy methods, which define the fuzzification representation of x and y coordinates for a point on a plane by setting particular intervals of real numbers $[a_x, b_x]$, $[a_y, b_y]$, as well as increments k_x and k_y for the generation of appropriate fuzzy sets V_x and V_y. As we can see according to Definition 1, the fuzzy homogeneous class of objects Pt has a measure of its fuzziness, which is approximately equal to 0.96.

Now let us assume that the class Tr defines the concept of a fuzzy triangle on a plane and has the following structure

$$Tr(p_1 = (vertex_1, (v_1, Pt))/1,$$
$$p_2 = (vertex_2, (v_1, Pt))/1,$$
$$p_3 = (vertex_3, (v_1, Pt))/1,$$
$$p_4 = (is\_a\_triangle, (vf_4(tr), v \in [0,1]))/0.98,$$
$$f_1 = get\_vertex(tr, (n, \mathbb{Z}^+), Pt)/0.96,$$
$$f_2 = set\_vertex(tr, (n, \mathbb{Z}^+), (a_x, \mathbb{R}), (b_x, \mathbb{R}), (k_x, \mathbb{R}^+),$$
$$(a_y, \mathbb{R}), (b_y, \mathbb{R}), (k_y, \mathbb{R}^+))/0.95,$$
$$f_3 = get\_side\_length(tr, (v_a, Pt), (v_b, Pt), \mathbb{R}^+)/0.94,$$
$$f_4 = get\_perimeter(tr, \mathbb{R}^+)/0.91,$$
$$)/0.97,$$

where p_1, p_2, and p_3 are fuzzy quantitative properties, which mean vertices of a triangle, defined as objects of the fuzzy homogeneous class of objects Pt; p_4 is a fuzzy qualitative property, which means satisfiability of the triangle inequality and defined by the following verification function

$$vf_4(tr) : (tr.vertex_1, tr.vertex_2, tr.vertex_3) \rightarrow [0, 1],$$
$$vf_4 = ((s_1 + s_2 > s_3) \wedge (s_1 + s_3 > s_2) \wedge (s_2 + s_3 > s_1)),$$

where, s_1, s_2 and s_3 are defined as follows

$$s_1 = get\_side\_length(tr.get\_vertex(1), tr.get\_vertex(2)),$$
$$s_2 = get\_side\_length(tr.get\_vertex(2), tr.get\_vertex(3)),$$
$$s_3 = get\_side\_length(tr.get\_vertex(3), tr.get\_vertex(1));$$

f_1 is a fuzzy method that computes the defuzzification representation of the fuzzy quantitative property $vertex_n$ and defined in the following way

$$f_1(tr, n) = (tr.vertex_n),$$

f_2 is a fuzzy method, which defines the fuzzification representation of x and y coordinates for a point on a plane and defined in the following way

$$f_2(tr, n, a_x, b_x, k_x, a_y, b_y, k_y)$$
$$= (tr.vertex_n.set\_x(a_x, b_x, k_x), tr.vertex_n.set\_y(a_y, b_y, k_y));$$

f_3 is a fuzzy method that computes the defuzzification representation of the distance between fuzzy vertices $vertex_a$ and $vertex_b$ and is defined as follows
$f_3(tr, v_a, v_b) = \sqrt{d_x + d_y}$, where

$$d_x = (v_a.get\_x() - v_b.get\_x())^2, \quad d_y = (v_a.get\_y() - v_b.get\_y())^2;$$

f_4 is a fuzzy method that computes the perimeter of a fuzzy triangle, and is defined in the following way $f_4(tr) = (a + b + c)$, where

$$a = get\_side\_length(tr.get\_vertex(1), tr.get\_vertex(2)),$$
$$b = get\_side\_length(tr.get\_vertex(2), tr.get\_vertex(3)),$$
$$c = get\_side\_length(tr.get\_vertex(3), tr.get\_vertex(1)).$$

As we can see according to Definition 1, the fuzzy homogeneous class of objects Tr has a measure of its fuzziness, which is approximately equal to 0.97.

Let us consider the internal structural and functional dependencies within the specification and signature of the fuzzy homogeneous class of objects Tr in more detail. As we can see, fuzzy quantitative properties p_1, p_2, and p_3, which determine vertices of a fuzzy triangle, are defined independently from other properties and methods of the fuzzy homogeneous class of objects Tr. Therefore, they form separate fuzzy structural atoms SA_1, SA_2, and SA_3 inside the structure of the class Tr. Fuzzy methods f_1 and f_2 depend on fuzzy quantitative properties p_1, p_2, and p_3 because they use them to get and set coordinates for the vertices of a fuzzy triangle. Consequently, they form corresponding fuzzy functional molecules FM_1 and FM_2 inside the structure of the class Tr. Fuzzy method f_3 depends on fuzzy quantitative properties p_1, p_2, and p_3 because it uses them to compute the length of a fuzzy triangle's sides. Thus, it forms the appropriate functional molecule FM_3 inside the structure of the class Tr. Fuzzy method f_4 depends on fuzzy methods f_3 and f_1 as well ass fuzzy quantitative properties p_1, p_2, and p_3 because it uses them to compute the perimeter of a fuzzy triangle. Hence, it forms the corresponding functional molecule FM_4 inside the structure of the class Tr. And finally, fuzzy qualitative property p_4 also depends on fuzzy methods f_3 and f_1 as well as fuzzy quantitative properties p_1, p_2, and p_3, because it uses them to verify the triangle inequality. Therefore it forms the appropriate structural molecule SM_4 inside the structure of the class Tr.

All noted above structural and functional atoms as well as molecules of the fuzzy homogeneous class of objects Tr can be represented as follows

$$SA_1 = \{p_1/1\},$$
$$SA_2 = \{p_2/1\},$$
$$SA_3 = \{p_3/1\},$$
$$SM_4 = (p_4/0.98, \{p_1/1, p_2/1, p_3/1, f_3/0.94, f_1/0.96\}),$$
$$FM_1 = (f_1/0.96, \{p_1/1\}, \{p_2/1\}, \{p_3/1\}),$$
$$FM_2 = (f_2/0.95, \{p_1/1\}, \{p_2/1\}, \{p_3/1\}),$$
$$FM_3 = (f_3/0.94, \{p_1/1, p_2/1\}, \{p_1/1, p_3/1\}, \{p_2/1, p_3/1\}),$$
$$FM_4 = (f_4/0.91, \{f_3/0.94, f_1/0.96, p_1/1, p_2/1, p_3/1\}).$$

According to the Definition 6, they form the set of all internal semantic dependencies of a fuzzy homogeneous class of objects $Tr/0.97$, i.e.

$$ISD(Tr/M(Tr)) = \{SA_1, SA_2, SA_3, SM_4, FM_1, FM_2, FM_3, FM_4\}.$$

Now let us compute the full decomposition of the fuzzy homogeneous class of objects $Tr/0.97$ using Algorithm 1, with the following parameters $Tr/M(Tr)$, $ISD(Tr/M(Tr))$, $N = [1, 7]$, $M = [0, 1]$, $\delta = 3$. According to the specified parameters, the algorithm should compute all possible semantically consistent subclasses of the fuzzy homogeneous class of objects $Tr/0.97$, which have a cardinality not less than 1 and no bigger than 7, any possible fuzziness, computed with the accuracy of 3. To perform the computational experiment we implemented Algorithm 1 using Python 3.8.5 programming language. As the result of decomposition we obtained the following subclasses of the fuzzy homogeneous class of objects $Tr/0.97$:

$C_1^1(p_1/1)/1;\ C_2^1(p_2/1)/1;\ C_3^1(p_3/1)/1;\ C_1^2(p_1/1, p_2/1)/1;\ C_2^2(p_1/1, p_3/1)/1;$

$C_3^2(p_2/1, p_3/1)/1;\ C_4^2(p_1/1, f_1/0.96)/0.98;\ C_5^2(p_2/1, f_1/0.96)/0.98;$

$C_6^2(p_3/1, f_1/0.96)/0.98;\ C_7^2(p_1/1, f_2/0.95)/0.975;\ C_8^2(p_2/1, f_2/0.95)/0.975;$

$C_9^2(p_3/1, f_2/0.95)/0.975;\ C_1^3(p_1/1, p_2/1, p_3/1)/1;$

$C_2^3(p_1/1, p_2/1, f_1/0.96)/0.987;\ C_3^3(p_1/1, p_3/1, f_1/0.96)/0.987;$

$C_4^3(p_2/1, p_3/1, f_1/0.96)/0.987;\ C_5^3(p_1/1, p_2/1, f_2/0.95)/0.983;$

$C_6^3(p_1/1, p_3/1, f_2/0.95)/0.983;\ C_7^3(p_2/1, p_3/1, f_2/0.95)/0.983;$

$C_8^3(p_1/1, f_1/0.96, f_2/0.95)/0.97;\ C_9^3(p_2/1, f_1/0.96, f_2/0.95)/0.97;$

$C_{10}^3(p_3/1, f_1/0.96, f_2/0.95)/0.97;\ C_{11}^3(p_1/1, p_2/1, f_3/0.94)/0.98;$

$C_{12}^3(p_1/1, p_3/1, f_3/0.94)/0.98;\ C_{13}^3(p_2/1, p_3/1, f_3/0.94)/0.98;$

$C_1^4(p_1/1, p_2/1, p_3/1, f_1/0.96)/0.99;\ C_2^4(p_1/1, p_2/1, p_3/1, f_2/0.95)/0.988;$

$C_3^4(p_1/1, p_2/1, f_1/0.96, f_2/0.95)/0.978;\ C_4^4(p_1/1, p_3/1, f_1/0.96, f_2/0.95)/0.978;$

$C_5^4(p_2/1, p_3/1, f_1/0.96, f_2/0.95)/0.978;\ C_6^4(p_1/1, p_2/1, p_3/1, f_3/0.94)/0.985;$

$C_7^4(p_1/1, p_2/1, f_1/0.96, f_3/0.94)/0.975;\ C_8^4(p_1/1, p_3/1, f_1/0.96, f_3/0.94)/0.975;$

$C_9^4(p_2/1, p_3/1, f_1/0.96, f_3/0.94)/0.975;\ C_{10}^4(p_1/1, p_2/1, f_2/0.95, f_3/0.94)/0.973;$

$C_{11}^4(p_1/1, p_3/1, f_2/0.95, f_3/0.94)/0.973;\ C_{12}^4(p_2/1, p_3/1, f_2/0.95, f_3/0.94)/0.973;$

$C_1^5(p_1/1, p_2/1, p_3/1, f_1/0.96, f_2/0.95)/0.982;$

$C_2^5(p_1/1, p_2/1, p_3/1, f_1/0.96, f_3/0.94)/0.98;$

$C_3^5(p_1/1, p_2/1, p_3/1, f_2/0.95, f_3/0.94)/0.978;$

$C_4^5(p_1/1, p_2/1, f_1/0.96, f_2/0.95, f_3/0.94)/0.97;$

$C_5^5(p_1/1, p_3/1, f_1/0.96, f_2/0.95, f_3/0.94)/0.97;$

$C_6^5(p_2/1, p_3/1, f_1/0.96, f_2/0.95, f_3/0.94)/0.97;$

$C_1^6(p_1/1, p_2/1, p_3/1, p_4/0.98, f_1/0.96, f_3/0.94)/0.98;$

$C_2^6(p_1/1, p_2/1, p_3/1, f_1/0.96, f_2/0.95, f_3/0.94)/0.975;$

$C_3^6(p_1/1, p_2/1, p_3/1, f_1/0.96, f_3/0.94, f_4/0.91)/0.968;$

$C_1^7(p_1/1, p_2/1, p_3/1, p_4/0.98, f_1/0.96, f_2/0.95, f_3/0.94)/0.976;$

$$C_2^7(p_1/1, p_2/1, p_3/1, p_4/0.98, f_1/0.96, f_3/0.94, f_4/0.91)/0.97;$$
$$C_3^7(p_1/1, p_2/1, p_3/1, f_1/0.96, f_2/0.95, f_3/0.94, f_4/0.91)/0.966.$$

As we can see, Algorithm 1 generated 49 semantically consistent subclasses of the fuzzy homogeneous class of objects $Tr/0.97$, among 254 possible ones. A more detailed quantitative comparison of obtained results with all possible subclasses of the fuzzy homogeneous class of objects $Tr/0.97$ is represented in Table 1. The first table row contains cardinality for all possible subclasses of the fuzzy class of objects $Tr/0.97$. The second table row contains a quantity of all formally possible subclasses of certain cardinality, which are structural elements of join-semilattice constructed from the properties and methods of the fuzzy class $Tr/0.97$. The third table row contains a quantity of all semantically consistent subclasses of certain cardinality of the fuzzy class $Tr/0.97$.

Table 1. Quantitative comparison of all possible and semantically consistent subclasses of different cardinality for the class Tr.

Cardinality	1	2	3	4	5	6	7	Total
Possible subclasses	8	28	56	70	56	28	8	254
Consistent subclasses	3	9	13	12	6	3	3	49

For the example of decomposition of the fuzzy class $Tr/0.97$ considered above, we used $Tr/M(Tr)$, $ISD(Tr/M(Tr))$, $N = [1, 7]$, $M = [0, 1]$, $\delta = 3$ as the configuration for Algorithm 1. However, parameter N allows us to choose which subclasses of certain cardinality, that are constituent parts of the decomposition of a fuzzy homogeneous class of objects, must be generated by the algorithm. In addition, we can specify a particular measure of fuzziness for subclasses, which must be generated, as well as the accuracy for their fuzziness computing. Thus, we can configure the decomposition algorithm for different usage scenarios, using these opportunities.

5   Results Interpretation

Now let us analyze subclasses of the fuzzy class $Tr/0.97$ obtained as the result of its decomposition in more detail. Some of them have the appropriate interpretation within the same domain and model valid and common-used essences, while others model essences, which are also valid in the domain but are less used than the first ones. For example, subclasses $C_1^1/1$, $C_2^1/1$, and $C_3^1/1$ have a similar structure, and each of them defines the point on a plane. Subclasses $C_1^2/$, $C_2^2/1$, and $C_3^2/1$ also have a similar structure, and each of them defines two points on a plane. These six subclasses can be used as separate full-fledged concepts, since properties defined by them are objects of the class $Pt/0.96$, which provides procedural abilities to manage points with their use, such as storing or receiving coordinates of points.

Subclasses $C_4^2/0.98$, $C_5^2/0.98$, and $C_6^2/0.98$ also have a similar structure, and each of them defines a point on a plane and provides the ability to get coordinates of the point, i.e.

$$C_4^2(p_1 = (vertex_1, (v_1, Pt))/1,$$
$$f_1 = get\_vertex(tr, (n, \mathbb{Z}^+), Pt)/0.96,$$
$$)/0.98$$

Subclasses $C_2^3/0.987$, $C_3^3/0.987$, and $C_4^3/0.987$ also have a similar structure, and each of them determines two points on a plane and provides the same ability. Similar to them, subclass $C_1^4/0.99$ defines three points on a plane and also provides the same ability. These subclasses also can be used as separate full-fledged concepts, since properties defined by them are objects of the class $Pt/0.96$, which provides the ability to set coordinates of the point.

Subclasses $C_7^2/0.975$, $C_8^2/0.975$, and $C_9^2/0.975$ also have a similar structure, and each of them determines a point on a plane and provides the ability to set coordinates of the point, i.e.

$$C_7^2(p_1 = (vertex_1, (v_1, Pt))/1,$$
$$f_2 = set\_vertex(tr, (n, \mathbb{Z}^+), (a_x, \mathbb{R}), (b_x, \mathbb{R}), (k_x, \mathbb{R}^+),$$
$$(a_y, \mathbb{R}), (b_y, \mathbb{R}), (k_y, \mathbb{R}^+))/0.95,$$
$$)/0.975$$

Subclasses $C_5^3/0.983$, $C_6^3/0.983$, and $C_7^3/0.983$ also have a similar structure, and each of them defines two points on a plane and provides the ability to set coordinates of points. Similar to them, subclass $C_2^4/0.988$ determines three points on a plane and provides the same ability. These subclasses also can be used as separate full-fledged concepts, since properties defined by them are objects of the class $Pt/0.96$, which provides the ability to get coordinates of the point.

Subclasses $C_8^3/0.97$, $C_9^3/0.97$, and $C_{10}^3/0.97$ also have a similar structure, and each of them defines two points on a plane and provides abilities to get and set coordinates of points, i.e.

$$C_8^3(p_1 = (vertex_1, (v_1, Pt))/1,$$
$$f_1 = get\_vertex(tr, (n, \mathbb{Z}^+), Pt)/0.96,$$
$$f_2 = set\_vertex(tr, (n, \mathbb{Z}^+), (a_x, \mathbb{R}), (b_x, \mathbb{R}), (k_x, \mathbb{R}^+),$$
$$(a_y, \mathbb{R}), (b_y, \mathbb{R}), (k_y, \mathbb{R}^+))/0.95,$$
$$)/0.97$$

Subclasses $C_3^4/0.978$, $C_4^4/0.978$, and $C_5^4/0.978$ also have a similar structure, and each of them determines two points on a plane and provides abilities to get and set coordinates of points. Similar to them, subclass $C_1^5/0.982$ defines on a plane and provides the same abilities. These subclasses also can be used as separate full-fledged concepts, because they also provide all minimal required structural and procedural abilities to model some number of points on a plane.

Subclasses $C_{11}^3/0.98$, $C_{12}^3/0.98$, and $C_{13}^3/0.98$ also have a similar structure, and each of them determines two points on a plane and provides the ability to compute the distance between the points, i.e.

$$C_{11}^3(p_1 = (vertex_1, (v_1, Pt))/1,$$
$$p_2 = (vertex_2, (v_1, Pt))/1,$$
$$f_3 = get\_side\_length(tr, (v_a, Pt), (v_b, Pt), \mathbb{R}^+)/0.94,$$
$$)/0.98$$

Similar to them, subclass $C_4^6/0.985$ defines three points on a plane and provides the same abilities. However, these subclasses cannot be used as separate full-fledged concepts because they do not provide abilities to get and set coordinates of points. These subclasses also can be used as separate full-fledged concepts, since properties defined by them are objects of the class $Pt/0.96$, which provides abilities to get and set coordinates of points.

Subclasses $C_7^4/0.975$, $C_8^4/0.975$, and $C_9^4/0.975$ also have a similar structure, and each of them determines two points on a plane and provides abilities to get coordinates of points as well as compute the distance between them, i.e.

$$C_7^4(p_1 = (vertex_1, (v_1, Pt))/1,$$
$$p_2 = (vertex_2, (v_1, Pt))/1,$$
$$f_1 = get\_vertex(tr, (n, \mathbb{Z}^+), Pt)/0.96,$$
$$f_3 = get\_side\_length(tr, (v_a, Pt), (v_b, Pt), \mathbb{R}^+)/0.94,$$
$$)/0.975$$

Similar to them, subclass $C_2^5/0.98$ defines three points on a plane and provides the same abilities. As in the previous case, these subclasses cannot be used as separate full-fledged concepts because they do not provide the ability to set coordinates of points. These subclasses also can be used as separate full-fledged concepts, since properties defined by them are objects of the class $Pt/0.96$, which provides the ability to set coordinates of points.

Subclasses $C_{10}^4/0.973$, $C_{11}^4/0.973$, and $C_{12}^4/0.973$ also have a similar structure, and each of them determines two points on a plane and provides abilities to set coordinates of points as well as compute the distance between them, i.e.

$$C_{10}^4(p_1 = (vertex_1, (v_1, Pt))/1,$$
$$p_2 = (vertex_2, (v_1, Pt))/1,$$
$$f_2 = set\_vertex(tr, (n, \mathbb{Z}^+), (a_x, \mathbb{R}), (b_x, \mathbb{R}), (k_x, \mathbb{R}^+),$$
$$(a_y, \mathbb{R}), (b_y, \mathbb{R}), (k_y, \mathbb{R}^+))/0.95,$$
$$f_3 = get\_side\_length(tr, (v_a, Pt), (v_b, Pt), \mathbb{R}^+)/0.94,$$
$$)/0.973$$

Similar to them, subclass $C_3^5/0.978$ defines three points on a plane and provides the same abilities. These subclasses also can be used as separate full-fledged concepts, since properties defined by them are objects of the class $Pt/0.96$, which provides the ability to get coordinates of points.

Subclasses $C_4^5/0.97$, $C_5^5/0.97$, and $C_6^5/0.97$ also have a similar structure, and each of them determines two points on a plane and provides abilities to get and set coordinates of points as well as compute the distance between them, i.e.

$$C_4^5(p_1 = (vertex_1, (v_1, Pt))/1,$$
$$p_2 = (vertex_2, (v_1, Pt))/1,$$
$$f_1 = get\_vertex(tr, (n, \mathbb{Z}^+), Pt)/0.96,$$
$$f_2 = set\_vertex(tr, (n, \mathbb{Z}^+), (a_x, \mathbb{R}), (b_x, \mathbb{R}), (k_x, \mathbb{R}^+),$$
$$(a_y, \mathbb{R}), (b_y, \mathbb{R}), (k_y, \mathbb{R}^+))/0.95,$$
$$f_3 = get\_side\_length(tr, (v_a, Pt), (v_b, Pt), \mathbb{R}^+)/0.94,$$
$$)/0.97$$

Similar to them, subclass $C_2^6/0.975$ define three points on a plane and provides the same abilities. These subclasses also can be used as separate full-fledged concepts, because they also provide all minimal required structural and procedural abilities to model some number of points on a plane.

Subclass $C_1^6/0.98$ determines a triangle on a plane and provides abilities to get coordinates of the figure vertices, verify if they really create a triangle as well as compute the distance between any two of them, i.e.

$$C_1^6(p_1 = (vertex_1, (v_1, Pt))/1,$$
$$p_2 = (vertex_2, (v_1, Pt))/1,$$
$$p_3 = (vertex_3, (v_1, Pt))/1,$$
$$p_4 = (is\_a\_triangle, (vf_4(tr), v \in [0, 1]))/0.98,$$
$$f_1 = get\_vertex(tr, (n, \mathbb{Z}^+), Pt)/0.96,$$
$$f_3 = get\_side\_length(tr, (v_a, Pt), (v_b, Pt), \mathbb{R}^+)/0.94,$$
$$)/0.98$$

In a similar way, subclass $C_1^7/0.976$ defines a triangle on a plane and provides all the same abilities as subclass $C_1^6/0.98$ and the ability to set coordinates of the figure vertices. Another subclass $C_2^7/0.97$ also determines a triangle on a plane and all the same abilities as subclass $C_1^6/0.98$ and the ability to compute the perimeter of the figure. These subclasses also can be used as separate full-fledged concepts, since properties p_1, p_2, and p_3 defined by them are objects of the class $Pt/0.96$, which provides the ability to set coordinates of points.

Subclass $C_3^6/0.968$ defines a figure on a plane and provides abilities to get coordinates of the figure vertices, compute the distance between any two of them as well as compute the perimeter of the figure, i.e.

$$C_3^6(p_1 = (vertex_1, (v_1, Pt))/1,$$

$$p_2 = (vertex_2, (v_1, Pt))/1,$$
$$p_3 = (vertex_3, (v_1, Pt))/1,$$
$$f_1 = get\_vertex(tr, (n, \mathbb{Z}^+), Pt)/0.96,$$
$$f_3 = get\_side\_length(tr, (v_a, Pt), (v_b, Pt), \mathbb{R}^+)/0.94,$$
$$f_4 = get\_perimeter(tr, \mathbb{R}^+)/0.91,$$
$$)/0.968$$

In a similar way, subclass $C_3^7/0.966$ determines a figure on a plane and provides all the same abilities as subclass $C_3^6/0.968$ and the ability to set coordinates of the figure vertices. These subclasses also can be used as separate full-fledged concepts, since properties p_1, p_2, and p_3 defined by them are objects of the class $Pt/0.96$, which provides the ability to set coordinates of points.

Summarizing all results, we can conclude that all semantically consistent subclasses of the fuzzy homogeneous class of objects $Tr/0.97$, which were extracted by decomposition algorithm, can be used as separate full-fledged concepts since they model real essences from the same domain as the class $Tr/0.97$. It proves that Algorithm 1 can extract implicit or hidden knowledge via decomposition of the fuzzy homogeneous classes of objects.

6   Conclusions

The extraction of hidden or implicit knowledge from earlier obtained knowledge integrated into the knowledge base is an important task for most modern knowledge-based systems. Within object-oriented programming, as well as within object-oriented knowledge representation, this task can be solved by the application of universal exploiters to classes of objects. Therefore in this paper, we defined concepts of fuzzy structural atoms and molecules as well as fuzzy functional atoms and molecules of fuzzy homogeneous classes of objects within such a knowledge representation model as fuzzy object-oriented dynamic networks. Using these notions, we provided the definition of universal decomposition exploiter of fuzzy homogeneous classes of objects and developed the corresponding algorithm for its implementation. The algorithm analyses the internal structure of a fuzzy homogeneous class of objects and computes a set of its semantically consistent subclasses, which satisfy all specified restrictions, by solving the corresponding constraint satisfaction problem. To demonstrate the main idea of the developed algorithm and some of the possible scenarios of its application, we provided an illustrative example of the decomposition of a fuzzy homogeneous class of objects, which defines a concept of a fuzzy triangle. The proposed algorithm can be adapted and integrated for particular object-oriented programming languages as well as for object-oriented knowledge representation models.

Structural and functional atoms and molecules of fuzzy homogeneous and heterogeneous classes of objects can be used to improve universal exploiters of intersection and difference of fuzzy classes of objects, proposed in [34, 36–39]. They can help to verify the semantic consistency of classes of objects generated by such exploiters because not all classes of objects created as the union, intersection, or difference of other classes are semantically consistent ones. In addition, the proposed approach to the decomposition of fuzzy homogeneous classes of objects can be used to develop algorithms for the decomposition of fuzzy heterogeneous classes of objects, as well as complex fuzzy class hierarchies.

Acknowledgments. This research work has been supported by the National Academy of Science of Ukraine (project 0121U111944 Development of Methods and Tools for Construction Domain-Oriented Intelligent Software Systems Based on Object-Oriented Dynamic Networks).

References

1. Ambler, S.W.: Chapter 14 - mapping objects to relational databases. In: Agile Database Techniques: Effective Strategies for the Agile Software Developer, pp. 197–229. Wiley, Indianapolis (2003)
2. Apt, K.R.: Principles of Constraint Programming. Cambridge University Press, New York (2003)
3. Bellatreche, L., Bouchakri, R., Cuzzocrea, A., Maabout, S.: Incremental algorithms for selecting horizontal schemas of data warehouses: the dynamic case. In: Hameurlain, A., Rahayu, W., Taniar, D. (eds.) Globe 2013. LNCS, vol. 8059, pp. 13–25. Springer, Heidelberg (2013). https://doi.org/10.1007/978-3-642-40053-7_2
4. Bellatreche, L., Karlapalem, K., Simonet, A.: Horizontal class partitioning in object-oriented databases. In: Hameurlain, A., Tjoa, A.M. (eds.) DEXA 1997. LNCS, vol. 1308, pp. 58–67. Springer, Heidelberg (1997). https://doi.org/10.1007/BFb0022018
5. Bellatreche, L., Karlapalem, K., Simonet, A.: Algorithms and support for horizontal class partitioning in object-oriented databases. Distrib. Parallel Databases **8**(2), 155–179 (2000). https://doi.org/10.1023/A:1008745624048
6. Bellatreche, L., Simonet, A., Simonet, M.: Vertical fragmentation in distributed object database systems with complex attributes and methods. In: Proceedings of 7th International Conference on and Workshop Database Expert System Application (DEXA 1996), Zurich, Switzerland, pp. 15–21 (1996). https://doi.org/10.1109/DEXA.1996.558266
7. Birahnu, L., Atnafu, S., Getahun, F.: Native XML document fragmentation model. In: Proceedings of 2010 6th International Conference on Signal-Image Technology Internet Based Systems, Kuala Lumpur, Malaysia, pp. 233–240 (2010). https://doi.org/10.1109/SITIS.2010.47
8. Braganholo, V., Mattoso, M.: A survey on XML fragmentation. ACM SIGMOD Rec. **43**(3), 24–35 (2014). https://doi.org/10.1145/2694428.2694434
9. Dechter, R.: Constraint Processing. Morgan Kaufmann Publishers, San Francisco (2003)
10. Drissi, A., Nait-Bahloul, S., Benouaret, K., Benslimane, D.: Horizontal fragmentation for fuzzy querying databases. Distrib. Parallel Databases **37**(3), 441–468 (2018). https://doi.org/10.1007/s10619-018-7250-4
11. Ezeife, C.I., Barker, K.: Horizontal class fragmentation in distributed object based systems. Technical report TR 93-04, University of Manitoba Department of Computer Science, Winnipeg, Manitoba, Canada (1993)

12. Ezeife, C.I., Barker, K.: A comprehensive approach to horizontal class fragmentation in a distributed object based system. Distrib. Parallel Databases **3**(3), 247–272 (1995). https://doi.org/10.1007/BF01418059

13. Ezeife, C.I., Barker, K.: Distributed object based design: vertical fragmentation of classes. Distrib. Parallel Databases **6**(4), 317–350 (1998). https://doi.org/10.1023/A:1008666830313

14. Faitelson, D., Heinrich, R., Tyszberowicz, S.: Supporting software architecture evolution by functional decomposition. In: Proceedings of 5th International Conference on Model-Driven Engineering Software Development (MODELSWARD), Porto, Portugal, pp. 435–442 (2017). https://doi.org/10.5220/0006206204350442

15. Faitelson, D., Heinrich, R., Tyszberowicz, S.: Functional decomposition for software architecture evolution. In: Pires, L.F., Hammoudi, S., Selic, B. (eds.) MODELSWARD 2017. CCIS, vol. 880, pp. 377–400. Springer, Cham (2018). https://doi.org/10.1007/978-3-319-94764-8_16

16. Faitelson, D., Tyszberowicz, S.: Improving design decomposition. In: Li, X., Liu, Z., Yi, W. (eds.) SETTA 2015. LNCS, vol. 9409, pp. 185–200. Springer, Cham (2015). https://doi.org/10.1007/978-3-319-25942-0_12

17. Faitelson, D., Tyszberowicz, S.: Improving design decomposition (extended version). Formal Aspects Comput. **29**(4), 601–627 (2017). https://doi.org/10.1007/s00165-017-0428-0

18. Freuder, E.C., Mackworth, A.K.: Constraint satisfaction: an emerging paradigm. In: Rossi, F., van Beek, P., Walsh, T. (eds.) Handbook of Constraint Programming, chap. 2, pp. 13–27. Elsevier, Amsterdam (2006)

19. Fung, C.W., Karlapalem, K., Li, Q.: Cost-driven vertical class partitioning for methods in object oriented databases. The VLDB J. **12**(3), 187–210 (2003). https://doi.org/10.1007/s00778-002-0084-7

20. Goli, M., Rouhani Rankoohi, S.M.T.: A new vertical fragmentation algorithm based on ant collective behavior in distributed database systems. Knowl. Inf. Syst. **30**(2), 435–455 (2012). https://doi.org/10.1007/s10115-011-0384-6

21. Hamdi, M., Pethe, R., Chetty, A.S., Kim, D.-K.: Threshold-driven class decomposition. In: Proceedings of 2019 IEEE 43rd Annual Computer Software and Applications Conference (COMPSAC), Milwaukee, WI, USA, pp. 884–887 (2019). https://doi.org/10.1109/COMPSAC.2019.00130

22. Hartmann, S., Ma, H., Schewe, K.-D.: Cost-based vertical fragmentation for XML. In: Chang, K.C.-C., Wang, W., Chen, L., Ellis, C.A., Hsu, C.-H., Tsoi, A.C., Wang, H. (eds.) APWeb/WAIM -2007. LNCS, vol. 4537, pp. 12–24. Springer, Heidelberg (2007). https://doi.org/10.1007/978-3-540-72909-9_2

23. Karlapalem, K., Li, Q.: Partitioning schemes for object oriented databases. In: Proceedings of 5th International Workshop Research Issues in Data Engineering-Distributed Object Management (RIDE-DOM 1995), Taipei, Taiwan, pp. 42–49 (1995). https://doi.org/10.1109/RIDE.1995.378746

24. Karlapalem, K., Li, Q.: A framework for class partitioning in object-oriented databases. Distrib. Parallel Databases **8**(3), 333–366 (2000). https://doi.org/10.1023/A:1008769213554

25. Karlapalem, K., Li, Q., Vieweg, S.: Method-induced partitioning schemes for object-oriented databases. In: Proceedings of 16th International Conference on Distributed Computing Systems, Hong Kong, China, pp. 377–384 (1996). https://doi.org/10.1109/ICDCS.1996.507985

26. Kechar, M., Bahloul, S.N.: Hybrid fragmentation of XML data warehouse using K-means algorithm. In: Manolopoulos, Y., Trajcevski, G., Kon-Popovska, M. (eds.) ADBIS 2014. LNCS, vol. 8716, pp. 70–82. Springer, Cham (2014). https://doi.org/10.1007/978-3-319-10933-6_6

27. Kling, P., Özsu, M.T., Daudjee, K.: Scaling XML query processing: distribution, localization and pruning. Distrib. Parallel Databases **29**(5–6), 445–490 (2011). https://doi.org/10.1007/s10619-011-7085-8

28. Lee, J., Kim, D.-K., Kim, S., Park, S.: Decomposing class responsibilities using distance-based method similarity. Front. Comput. Sci. **10**(4), 612–630 (2016). https://doi.org/10.1007/s11704-015-5001-5

29. Lee, S., Lim, H.: Attribute partitioning algorithm in DOODB. In: Proceedings of International Conference on Parallel and Distributed Systems, Seoul, Korea (South), pp. 702–707 (1997). https://doi.org/10.1109/ICPADS.1997.652619

30. Navathe, S.B., Karlapalem, K., Ra, M.: A mixed fragmentation methodology for initial distributed database design. Technical report TR 90-17, CIS Dept, University of Florida, Gainesville, FL, USA (1990)

31. Quang, V.D., Ban, D.V., Ha, H.C.: A method of object identification based on fuzzy object functional dependencies in fuzzy object-oriented databases. In: Proceedings of 4th Fourth International Conference on Knowledge and Systems Engineering (KSE), Danang, Vietnam, pp. 46–53 (2012). https://doi.org/10.1109/KSE.2012.14

32. Schewe, K.D.: Fragmentation of object oriented and semi-structured data. In: Haav, H.M., Kalja, A. (eds.) Databases and Information Systems II, pp. 1–14. Springer, Dordrecht (2002). https://doi.org/10.1007/978-94-015-9978-8_1

33. Terletskyi, D.A., Provotar, A.I.: Fuzzy object-oriented dynamic networks. I. Cybern. Syst. Anal. **51**(1), 34–40 (2015). https://doi.org/10.1007/s10559-015-9694-0

34. Terletskyi, D.A., Provotar, A.I.: Fuzzy object-oriented dynamic networks. II. Cybern. Syst. Anal. **52**(1), 38–45 (2016). https://doi.org/10.1007/s10559-016-9797-2

35. Terletskyi, D.O.: Run-time class generation: algorithm for decomposition of homogeneous classes. In: Lopata, A., Butkienė, R., Gudonienė, D., Sukackė, V. (eds.) ICIST 2020. CCIS, vol. 1283, pp. 243–254. Springer, Cham (2020). https://doi.org/10.1007/978-3-030-59506-7_20

36. Terletskyi, D.O., Provotar, O.I.: Algorithm for intersection of fuzzy homogeneous classes of objects. In: Proceedings of IEEE 2020 15th International Conference on Computer Sciences and Information Technologies (CSIT), Zbarazh, Ukraine, vol. 2, pp. 314–317 (2020). https://doi.org/10.1109/CSIT49958.2020.9321914

37. Terletskyi, D.O., Provotar, O.I.: Intersection of fuzzy homogeneous classes of objects. In: Shakhovska, N., Medykovskyy, M.O. (eds.) CSIT 2020. AISC, vol. 1293, pp. 306–323. Springer, Cham (2020). https://doi.org/10.1007/978-3-030-63270-0_21

38. Terletskyi, D.O., Yershov, S.V.: Difference of fuzzy homogeneous classes of objects. In: Proceedings of 17th International Conference on ICT in Education, Research and Industrial Applications. Integration, Harmonization and Knowledge Transfer, (ICTERI), Kherson, Ukraine, vol. 1, pp. 24–39 (2021)

39. Terletskyi, D., Yershov, S.: Union of fuzzy homogeneous classes of objects. In: Babichev, S., Lytvynenko, V. (eds.) ISDMCI 2021. LNDECT, vol. 77, pp. 665–684. Springer, Cham (2022). https://doi.org/10.1007/978-3-030-82014-5_46

40. Van Thang, D.: Dependence fuzzy objects. In: Proceedings of International Conference on Advanced Technologies for Communications (ATC), Hanoi, Vietnam, pp. 160–166 (2014). https://doi.org/10.1109/ATC.2014.7043376

41. Van Thang, D., Manh, T.Q., Van Han, N.: Fuzzy object dependencies and linguistic quantifier. In: Proceedings on 13th International Joint Conference on Computer Science and Software Engineering (JCSSE), Khon Kaen, Thailand, pp. 1–5 (2016). https://doi.org/10.1109/JCSSE.2016.7748890

Deep Learning in Audio Classification

Yaqin Wang[✉], Jin Wei-Kocsis, John A. Springer, and Eric T. Matson

Purdue University, West Lafayette, IN, USA
{wang4070,kocsis,jaspring,ematson}@purdue.edu

Abstract. Audio processing technology is happening everywhere in our life. We ask our car to make a call for us while driving, or we let Alexa turn off the light for us when we don't want to get out of bed before sleep. In all of these audio-based applications and research, it is AI and ML that makes the computer or the smart phone understand us via our voice [1]. As an important part of artificial intelligence (AI), especially machine learning (ML), which has had great influences in many areas of AI and ML-based research and applications. This paper focuses on deep learning structures and applications for audio classification. We conduct a detailed review of literature in audio-based DL and DRL approaches and applications. We also discuss the limitation and possible future works for audio-based DL approach.

Keywords: Audio classification · Machine learning · Deep learning · Deep reinforcement learning

1 Introduction

Audio processing technology happens everywhere in our life. Siri from Apple, Alexa from Amazon, and Google Home Mini Dot are popular products based on audio processing and AI. In all the audio-based research and applications, it is AI that makes the computer or the smart phone understand us via our voice [1]. The beginning of everything is for the audio-based intelligent system to listen and interact with the environment and to learn and improve their reaction. Such intelligent system can be applied to different applications, such as smart phone application that interact with users with natural language or a computer software that can tell which types of birds are singing in your backyard by listening to the sound. Figure 1 shows the basic processing structure of an audio-based ML system with steps of: audio data pre-processing, windowing, feature selection and extraction, and classification [2]. The initial input of the system can be raw files of the audio data sample. Then the first step is pre-processing, where noise reduction/cancellation or normalization are applied. The next step is to apply window to the pre-processed audio data. The use of sliding window helps to analyze and study the whole length of the audio sample. Different windowing methods can be used according to the characteristics of the audio data. Feature extraction and selection is the next step. The features are the input to feed the ML for training and lastly the classifier makes a prediction.

A. Lopata et al. (Eds.): ICIST 2022, CCIS 1665, pp. 64–77, 2022.
https://doi.org/10.1007/978-3-031-16302-9_5

Fig. 1. ML structure for audio

AI is intelligence presented by machines, like computers, to behave like human. AI techniques includes machine learning, computer vision, natural language processing (NLP), robotics, and more [3]. One way to achieve AI is via ML. ML teaches computer systems learn from experience and improve the performance. Neural Network (NN) is a branch of ML, that processes input data through neurons or nodes in a network, which is how human brain works. Deep Learning (DL) is a branch of NN that the structure must include multiple layers. This paper focuses on deep learning structures and applications for audio classification.

The contribution of this paper is to provide a thorough review of literature in ML types and structures for audio-based detection and classification systems. Section 2 presents research papers in general machine learning process, deep learning and reinforcement learning. Section 3 provides a detailed review of literature in current audio-based DRL algorithms. Section 5 discusses recent deep reinforcement learning (DRL) research in audio-based applications, in the topics of music classification, environmental sound classification, and speech recognition. Section 6 concludes the paper with the limitations and future works for audio-based DRL.

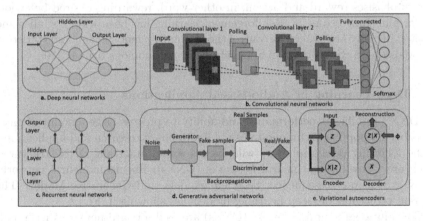

Fig. 2. Graphical illustration of different DL architectures [1]

2   Background of Machine Learning and Deep Learning

2.1   Machine Learning in General

Data needs to be prepare and pre-processed before the phase of training. There are different data preparation methods, including feature engineering, exploratory data analysis (EDA), and data transformation. These can be further divided into subsets. Under feature engineering, there are feature selection, feature extraction methods, feature transformation, and more. Under EDA, there are dimensional reduction, linear methods and more. Under data transformation, there are normalization, integration and more [3,4]. As for the problem of overfitting, many algorithms can be apply, such as adding dropout layer, pruning, and regularization [1,5].

According the assigned task, ML algorithms can be divided into groups, which are supervised learning, unsupervised learning, and reinforcement learning [6]. Supervised learning is defined as a type of machine learning that uses labeled datasets to train models to solve classification or prediction problems [7]. After the input data being fed into the model, the weights are adjusted until the data fits the model properly. Supervised learning are used in many fields of studies and applications, such as your phone can tell what music the radio is playing after listening a few seconds. On the contrary, unsupervised learning is to use unlabeled datasets, usually in analyzing and clustering [8]. Without human intervention, these algorithms can discover patterns and categorize data. Unsupervised learning algorithms can find the differences and similarities hidden in the data, which can be used to solve many real-world problems, such as pattern recognition and anomaly detection. Reinforcement learning (RL) is a type of ML that emphasises reward and action, in other word, rewarding desired behaviors and/or punishing errors [9]. Reinforcement learning has been widely studies and adopted in many areas, such as control theory, multi-agent system, and statistics. It has also been widely used in applications in autonomous driving [10].

2.2   Deep Learning in Audio-Based Applications

For DNN's significant performance and ability to process large amount of data, it has been a popular technique to use in audio-based research and applications. In the following paragraphs, we will discuss some important DNN structures, which are Convolutional neural networks (CNNs), Recurrent neural networks (RNNs), Sequence-to-sequence (Seq2Seq) models, and Generative Models. The different structures of Deep Learning models are showing in Fig. 2.

Convolutional neural networks (CNNs) are feed-forward networks with multiple layers with neurons/nodes. They were specifically designed to process data with grid-like topologies in images [11]. In current and previous works, along with the use of computer vision technique, CNN has produced some of the best results in image processing area, such as image classification, detection, segmentation, and more [12]. Different from DNN, CNN does not require a lot of memory or number of parameters because of two reasons: local receptive fields and their weights sharing. CNNs usually consist of multiple convolutional layers with one ore more dense layers existing afterwards. Fully-convolutional network (FCN) is CNN without the dense layer, which results in even less parameters. Domain adaption can be achieved with extended FCNs, which on the other hand improves the robustness of FCNs [13]. More research have been adopt CNN models for different audio processing applications, including automatic speech recognition (ASR) [14], music genre classification [15], speech enhancement [16], and more. However, with limited receptive fields of CNN, it might be challenging to process raw audio waveform with high sample rates [1]. Dilated convolution layers are intended to deal with this issue. They can also extend the receptive field with zero inserted into their filter coefficients [17].

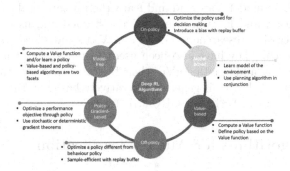

Fig. 3. Different DRL structures [1]

Recurrent neural networks (RNNs) processes differently when it comes to sequential data [18]. The use of recurrent connections between layers enables parameters to be shared recurrently. This unique approach makes them efficient and powerful in understanding and learning temporal data structures from the sequential data input, such as audio and video input [1]. Compare to the traditional Hidden Markov model (HMM) models, RNNs have produced better results in many audio and speech processing applications [19]. Because of these characteristics, two of the most popular RNN structures, Long-Short Term Memory (LSTM) [20] and Gated Recurrent Unit (GRU) network, significantly improved the audio and speech processing applications, and were used to build state-of-the-arts audio-based systems [21]. In the recent years, Time-Frequency LSTMs [22] and Frequency-LSTMs [23] were created based on previous RNN models with information in the frequency domain. To take advantages from both neural networks, Convolutional Recurrent Neural networks (CRNN) was created by integrating CNNs and RNNs with convolutional layers followed by recurrent layers [19]. CRNN has been used in music classification [24], ASR [25], Speech Emotion Recognition (SER) [26], and more.

Sequence-to-sequence (Seq2Seq) models were created to solve problems with sequences of unspecified length [27]. They were used in machine translation first, and later adopted in many different area of research to solve sequence modelling problems. A Seq2Seq model can be divided into two parts: decoder and encoder. Encoder is one RNN generates a vector representation from the input, and the decoder is another RNN generates output by inheriting those learnt features from encoder. The structures of the Seq2Seq model can be unidirectional or bidirectional, single layer or multi-layer [28]. Seq2Seq models has become more popular in speech and audio processing for their capability of converting input to output sequences [1]. Different Seq2Seq models have been created and investigated by research in audio, speech, and language processing topics, including Recurrent Neural Aligner [29], Recurrent Neural Network Transducer [30], Transformer Networks [31], and more.

The three most used types of Generative Models are Generative Adversarial Networks (GANs) [32], autoregressive models [33], and Variational Autoencoders (VAEs) [34]. These models can read and learn the fundamental distributions in the speech dataset, and have been extensively studied and used by the audio and speech processing researchers. GANs and VAEs have been widely used in synthesizing speech. They have also been used to create more training data by generating speech or audio data and/or their features [1]. As for the autoregressive models, future behavior is generated iteratively based on the past behavior by using RNNs, such as LSTM or GRU structures.

3   DRL Algorithms for Audio Classification

RL is a well-studied branch of ML, in which intelligent agents learn to take actions based on error and trial [35]. By combining conventional RL and DL there comes Deep reinforcement learning (DRL). DRL compensated RL in more complicated environment with high computation needs or large state spaces requirements. DRL adopts the structure of DNNs to evaluate model, policy, or value. There are different ways to categorize DRL, such as policy-based vs value-based, model-free vs model-based, or on-policy vs off-policy DRL models. Figure 3 demonstrates the different types of DRL with their main characteristics. In the following paragraphs, we will discuss popular DRL models used in systems based on audio and applications in three sub-categories: model-based DRL, policy gradient-based DRL, adn value-based DRL.

3.1   Model-Based DRL

Model-based DRL algorithms depend on the environment, such as reward functions, along with a planning algorithm. Model-free DRL algorithms usually require a large amount of sample data to achieve acceptable results. Differently, model-based algorithms tend to produce results with improved sample and time efficiency [36]. Simulated policy learning (SimPLe) was proposed by [37]. It is a model-based DRL algorithm for video prediction. Less interactions of agent-environment are needed for SimPle than model-free algorithms. Results show that SimPLe performs better than the state-of-the-art model-free algorithms in the games of Atari. Another model-based DRL algorithm was proposed by [38] called TreeQN. It was designed for a more complicated environment without the presence of the transition model. In TreeQN algorithm, Q-values are estimated by combining model-free and model-based methods.

3.2 Policy Gradient-Based DRL

Policy gradient-based DRL algorithms is another type of DRL that depend on optimizing polices regarding the expected return, such as expected cumulative reward, by gradient descent. This type of DRL utilizes gradient theorems to obtain optimal policy parameters. The estimation of a value function from the current policy are usually required by policy gradient, which can be achieved by utilizing actor-critic architecture. The policy structure is the actor, for it is to select actions, and the estimated value function is the critic, as it criticizes the actions conducted by the actor [49]. [50] demonstrated that even on standard CPU-based computer environment, asynchronous execution of multiple parallel agents can learn efficiently in terms of time and resources. They proposed asynchronous advantage actor-critic (A3C) architecture, which is the asynchronous version of actor-critic. The results showed significant performance in both 2D and 3D games with continuous domains and discrete action spaces.

3.3 Value-Based DRL

[51] built the most well-known value-based DRL algorithms, the Deep Q-network (DQN), that can take and learn from high-dimensional inputs directly. DQN adopts the structure of CNNs to define a policy from estimating a value function $Q(s, a)$. DQN improves the stability of learning by using mainly four techniques: experience replay, target network, clipping rewards, and skipping frames [52]. [53] introduced Double DQN (DDQN) to make up to the possible upward bias caused by DQN with two estimators: one for selecting an action, and one for evaluating an action [1]. [54] indicated that DQN and DDQN performs significantly better if critical experience transitions are emphasized and replay them more frequently.

4   Audio Data Pre-processing and Augmentation

4.1   Data Pre-processing

Audio data needs be pre-processed before feeding into the ML models. In gradient descent based algorithms, feature standardization is commonly used to accelerate the process of convergence [55]. Feature distribution is changed from feature standardization with zero mean and unit variance. Large dynamic range usually appears in environmental sound data. A commonly used solution is logarithmic scaling applied to spectrogram-based features. Pre-processing methods for low-level audio signal include low-pass filtering and speech dereverberation [56] (Table 1).

Table 1. Research papers on DL-based audio application

Research	Application	DL models	Results
[39]	Automatic speech recognition (ASR)	Policy gradient-based RL	Lower Word Error Rate (WER) and better recognition performance than unsupervised methods
[40]	Automatic speech recognition (ASR)	Seq2Seq model	Remarkable improvement in real-world scenario with the combination of a maximum likelihood estimation (MLE) and an RL-based objectives
[41]	Automatic speech recognition (ASR)	DRL	Proposed system achieved lower character error rates of 8.7%
[42]	Speech enhancement	LSTM-based RL	Results showed improvement comparing to methods with no adaptivity in system performance
[43]	Speech enhancement, noise reduction	DRL	Proposed system improved the hearing experience and the user was satisfied with the hearing outcome
[44]	Music generation	LSTM-based DRL	Proposed system can compose polyphonic music based on music theory with better quality
[45]	Music generation	DQN	Results indicated that the proposed model can learn to compose and keep the valuable information of data from supervised training
[46]	Bird sound classification	CNN, NN	The proposed DL approach outperforms the other methods, but the best result from combining all visual, acoustic, and DL learning
[47]	Environmental sound classification	CNN	They achieved state-of-the-art classification results with proposed data augmentation and CNN network
[48]	Music genre classification	CNN	Results indicated that DL-based models had better classification accuracy, and the best result was achieved by the ensemble classifier

In many audio-based applications, such as automatic speech recognition (ASR) and acoustic event detection (AED), background noises sometimes overshadow the foreground sound events. [57] proposed to use per-channel energy normalization (PCEN) to enhance foreground sound events and reduce background noise in environmental audio data. The proposed system adjusted the PCEN parameters with the temporal features of the noise to reduce the noise level, while the foreground sound signal is enhanced. [58] proposed to use two edge detection methods from image processing to enhance the edge-like structures in spectrograms. Those two methods were based on the difference of Sobel filtering and Gaussians (DoG). Meidan filter is used to remove the drift of the mel spectrogram.

Commonly-used pre-processing methods for ASC applications are filtering methods. [3] proposed an ASC system that included a nearest neighbor filter based on repeating pattern extraction technique (REPET) to filter out repetitions appearing intermittently or randomly. The most similar spectrogram frames were replaced by their median. On the other hand, this filter can be used to highlight repetitive sound events in AED, such as horns and sirens. Another commonly used filtering method is harmonic-percussive source separation (HPSS). HPSS splits the spectrogram into horizontal and vertical modules that provides additional features for ASC [59]. All the above pre-processing approaches were relatively new, comparing to the well-established and most-used logarithmic magnitude scaling among the state-of-the-art ASC algorithms [55].

4.2 Data Augmentation

A large amount of training data is essential for deep learning models to learn. In the recent years, the datasets for audio classification are increasing, but still not as much as the image datasets [55], such as ImageNet [60]. The largest audio dataset for now is AudioSet, which includes more than 600 audio classes and almost 2 millions labeled 10s excerpts from YouTube video [61]. But still, there is a need for more publicly available audio datasets. Many research have been trying to compensate this issue with data augmentation techniques. There are mainly two different approaches: to generate new data based on existing ones, and too generate synthetic data from scratch.

The first kind of data augmentation is to generate new training data based on existing one with added signal transformations. Commonly used audio signal transformation methods are pitch shifting, time stretching, and adding noise [47]. [62] proposed to use spectral rolling and mix-up to augment the audio data. The former technique randomly shifts the spectrogram features over the time dimension, and the later one works linearly by combining features from the data and their targets with a given mixing ratio [63] proposed SpecAugment, a simple data augmentation method called SpecAugment. It is used directly on to the feature (log mel spectrogram) of the audio data. The augmentation policy included warping the features, frequency masking, and time masking. [64] used various data augmentation techniques on both time and frequency domain. For the time domain data augmentation, there are mosaicking random segments, time stretching, time interval dropout, and more. And for frequency domain, they used frequency shifting/stretching, piece-wise time, resizing filters, and color filters.

The other kind of data augmentation technique is to generate synthetic data from scratch. The most popular approach for this kind is to use generative adversarial networks (GAN) [32]. An adversarial training strategy was used to train synthesizing models by mimicking the existing audio data. Most data synthesis technique are applied to the audio signal [55].

5   Deep Learning in Audio-Based Applications

This section reviews literature of audio-based DL applications. The literature are usually divided into different categories: sound classification, music generation, automatic speech recognition, spoken dialogue systems, audio enhancement, emotions modelling, and more. In this paper, we will only concentrate on automatic speech recognition, audio enhancement, music generation, and sound classification.

Automatic speech recognition (ASR) is to use algorithms to convert a speech, usually in the form of audio, into text. Contemporary ASR systems have achieved significant results because of the use of DL models, with extensive supervised training and a large numbers of labeled training data. To explore more efficient solutions, RL-based models were also used in ASR, for its capability of learning from action. RL-based ASR systems can generating positive or negative rewards instead of manually preparing these by human [39–41]. [39] proposed a policy gradient-based RL system for ASR. They provided another angle for existing training and modification methods. The proposed system achieved lower word error rate (WER) and better recognition performance than unsupervised methods. The other DL model, sequence-to-sequence models, have demonstrated significant success in ASR. But the issue with Seq2Seq model in ASR was the interference in the real-world speech. [40] proposed a solution for this by using a sequence-to-sequence model trained with a policy gradient algorithm. The proposed system indicated remarkable improvement in real-world scenario with the combination of a maximum likelihood estimation (MLE) and an RL-based objectives, instead of training with the MLE objective alone. There has always been a issue of semi-supervised training with Seq2Seq ASR models. [41] proposed a REINFORCE algorithm for ASR. The algorithm rewarded the ASR to produce more correct sentences for the input data of both paired and unpaired speech. The proposed system achieved lower character error rates of 8.7%.

Audio-based intelligent systems are extremely sensitive to environmental noise, and the system's accuracy decreases when the noise level goes up [65]. Audio enhancement is one of the possible solutions for noise interference. Audio enhancement systems are supposed to filter out the noise and generate an enhanced audio signal. DL-based models have achieved significant performance in speech enhancement, comparing to the traditional methods [42]. [42] proposed a RL-based speech enhancement system to advance the adaptivity. They designed a noise-suppression module in a fashion of a black box, that does not need to understand the algorithm but provides simple feedback from the output. They achieved better performance with LSTM-based agent. [43] proposed a DRL-based approach for hearing aid application. The proposed system can tune the compression from noisy speech according to the individual's preference. Human hearing is non-linear. The system adopted DRL's reward and punishment rule and the DRL model receives preferences from the hearing aid user. Results indicated that the proposed system improved the hearing experience and the user was satisfied with the hearing outcome.

DL-based systems have also been used in generating more data content, such images, music, and text. DL models were first used in music generation because of its ability to learn and compose (generate) any genre of music from existing music database [44, 45]. DRL-based intelligent system can achieve more and provide more ways of learning directly from music theory to compose music with structures that sounds more like real ones [45]. [44] proposed a LSTM-based model that can compose polyphonic music based on music theory with better quality. [45] proposed a system of deep Q-learning structure with a reward function that learns from the probabilistic outputs of an RNN and basic rules of music theory. The results indicated that the proposed model can learn to compose and keep the valuable information of data from supervised training.

Sound classification is another application for DL-based audio system. It can be used in specific tasks, such as bird sound classification [46], environmental sound classification [47], music classification [48] and more. [46] proposed a DL-based bird sound classification system. They utilized CNN for learning generalized features and dimension reduction, with a conventional fully connected layer for classification. The proposed DL approach outperforms the other methods, including acoustic and vision-based system. But they achieved the best result from combining all visual, acoustic, and DL learning. [47] proposed a deep CNN structure for environmental sound classification. Further more, they used data augmentation technique to compensate the lack of publicly available dataset and investigate the performance of different augmentation techniques with proposed deep CNN structure. With the data augmentation and proposed CNN network, they achieved state-of-the-art classification results. [48] evaluated DL-based CNN models and feature engineering based models for music genre classification. CNN structures included VGG-16 CNN with transfer learning, VGG-16 CNN with fine tuning, and fully-connected NN. Feature engineering based models were logistic regression (LR), random forest (RF), support vector machines (SVM), and extreme gradient boosting (XGB). They also built a ensemble classifier with CNN and XGB. Results indicated that DL-based models had better classification accuracy, and the best result was achieved by the ensemble classifier.

6   Conclusion

In this paper, we discussed important architectures of Deep Learning, including CNNs, RNNs, Seq2Seq and more. We also covered some popular DRL algorithms related to audio classification, including model-based DRL, and value-based DRL, and policy gradient-based DRL. To overcome the lack of publicly available audio datasets, different approaches of data augmentation techniques were discussed in Sect. 4. Reviewed literature in Sect. 5 showed the advantages of using DL in audio and speech processing applications. However, most of the systems are not ready to be used in the real-world environment. More work need to be done, such as data collection, system generalization, autonomous learning, knowledge transfer, teaching the systems about commonsense knowledge, and more. Those advanced requirements will need a large number of testing and evaluation in real-world environment, instead of the controlled laboratory environment or simulations. We are still in the right path towards the next milestone.

References

1. Latif, S., Cuayáhuitl, H., Pervez, F., Shamshad, F., Ali, H.S., Cambria, E.: A survey on deep reinforcement learning for audio-based applications. arXiv preprint arXiv:2101.00240 (2021)
2. Sharma, G., Umapathy, K., Krishnan, S.: Trends in audio signal feature extraction methods. Appl. Acoust. **158**, 107020 (2020)
3. Nguyen, G., et al.: Machine learning and deep learning frameworks and libraries for large-scale data mining: a survey. Artif. Intell. Rev. **52**(1), 77–124 (2019)
4. Zhang, S., Zhang, C., Yang, Q.: Data preparation for data mining. Appl. Artif. Intell. **17**(5–6), 375–381 (2003)
5. Ying, X.: An overview of overfitting and its solutions. In: Journal of Physics: Conference Series, vol. 1168, no. 2, p. 022022. IOP Publishing (2019)
6. Bishop, C.M., Nasrabadi, N.M.: Pattern Recognition and Machine Learning, vol. 4, no. 4. Springer, Cham (2006)
7. Caruana, R., Niculescu-Mizil, A.: An empirical comparison of supervised learning algorithms. In: Proceedings of the 23rd International Conference on Machine Learning, pp. 161–168 (2006)
8. Hastie, T., Tibshirani, R., Friedman, J.: Unsupervised learning. In: Hastie, T., Tibshirani, R., Friedman, J. (eds.) The Elements of Statistical Learning. SSS, pp. 485–585. Springer, New York (2009). https://doi.org/10.1007/978-0-387-84858-7_14
9. Wiering, M.A., Van Otterlo, M.: Reinforcement learning. Adapt. Learn. Optim. **12**(3), 729 (2012)
10. Shalev-Shwartz, S., Shammah, S., Shashua, A.: Safe, multi-agent, reinforcement learning for autonomous driving. arXiv preprint arXiv:1610.03295 (2016)
11. Krizhevsky, A., Sutskever, I., Hinton, G.E.: ImageNet classification with deep convolutional neural networks. In: Advances in Neural Information Processing Systems, vol. 25 (2012)
12. Khan, A., Sohail, A., Zahoora, U., Qureshi, A.S.: A survey of the recent architectures of deep convolutional neural networks. Artif. Intell. Rev. **53**(8), 5455–5516 (2020). https://doi.org/10.1007/s10462-020-09825-6
13. Tzeng, E., Hoffman, J., Saenko, K., Darrell, T.: Adversarial discriminative domain adaptation. In: Proceedings of the IEEE Conference on Computer Vision and Pattern Recognition, pp. 7167–7176 (2017)
14. Abdel-Hamid, O., Mohamed, A.-R., Jiang, H., Deng, L., Penn, G., Yu, D.: Convolutional neural networks for speech recognition. IEEE/ACM Trans. Audio Speech Lang. Process. **22**(10), 1533–1545 (2014)

15. Dong, M.: Convolutional neural network achieves human-level accuracy in music genre classification. arXiv preprint arXiv:1802.09697 (2018)
16. Park, S.R., Lee, J.: A fully convolutional neural network for speech enhancement. arXiv preprint arXiv:1609.07132 (2016)
17. Chen, Y., Guo, Q., Liang, X., Wang, J., Qian, Y.: Environmental sound classification with dilated convolutions. Appl. Acoust. **148**, 123–132 (2019)
18. Lipton, Z.C., Berkowitz, J., Elkan, C.: A critical review of recurrent neural networks for sequence learning. arXiv preprint arXiv:1506.00019 (2015)
19. Latif, S., Qadir, J., Qayyum, A., Usama, M., Younis, S.: Speech technology for healthcare: opportunities, challenges, and state of the art. IEEE Rev. Biomed. Eng. **14**, 342–356 (2020)
20. Sherstinsky, A.: Fundamentals of recurrent neural network (RNN) and long short-term memory (LSTM) network. Physica D **404**, 132306 (2020)
21. Cho, K., et al.: Learning phrase representations using RNN encoder-decoder for statistical machine translation. arXiv preprint arXiv:1406.1078 (2014)
22. Sainath, T.N., Li, B.: Modeling time-frequency patterns with LSTM vs. convolutional architectures for LVCSR tasks (2016)
23. Li, J., Mohamed, A., Zweig, G., Gong, Y.: LSTM time and frequency recurrence for automatic speech recognition. In: 2015 IEEE Workshop on Automatic Speech Recognition and Understanding (ASRU), pp. 187–191. IEEE (2015)
24. Ghosal, D., Kolekar, M.H.: Music genre recognition using deep neural networks and transfer learning. In: Interspeech, pp. 2087–2091 (2018)
25. Qian, Y., Bi, M., Tan, T., Yu, K.: Very deep convolutional neural networks for noise robust speech recognition. IEEE/ACM Trans. Audio Speech Lang. Process. **24**(12), 2263–2276 (2016)
26. Sun, T.-W.: End-to-end speech emotion recognition with gender information. IEEE Access **8**, 152 423–152 438 (2020)
27. Sutskever, I., Vinyals, O., Le, Q.V.: Sequence to sequence learning with neural networks. In: Advances in Neural Information Processing Systems, vol. 27 (2014)
28. Schuster, M., Paliwal, K.K.: Bidirectional recurrent neural networks. IEEE Trans. Signal Process. **45**(11), 2673–2681 (1997)
29. Raffel, C., Luong, M.-T., Liu, P.J., Weiss, R.J., Eck, D.: Online and linear-time attention by enforcing monotonic alignments. In: International Conference on Machine Learning, pp. 2837–2846. PMLR (2017)
30. Graves, A.: Sequence transduction with recurrent neural networks. arXiv preprint arXiv:1211.3711 (2012)
31. Pham, N.-Q., Nguyen, T.-S., Niehues, J., Müller, M., Stüker, S., Waibel, A.: Very deep self-attention networks for end-to-end speech recognition. arXiv preprint arXiv:1904.13377 (2019)
32. Goodfellow, I., et al.: Generative adversarial nets. In: Advances in Neural Information Processing Systems, vol. 27 (2014)
33. Shannon, M., Zen, H., Byrne, W.: Autoregressive models for statistical parametric speech synthesis. IEEE Trans. Audio Speech Lang. Process. **21**(3), 587–597 (2012)
34. Kingma, D.P., Welling, M.: Auto-encoding variational bayes. arXiv preprint arXiv:1312.6114 (2013)
35. Sutton, R.S., Barto, A.G., et al.: Introduction to reinforcement learning (1998)
36. François-Lavet, V., Henderson, P., Islam, R., Bellemare, M.G., Pineau, J.: An introduction to deep reinforcement learning. arXiv preprint arXiv:1811.12560 (2018)
37. Kaiser, L., et al.: Model-based reinforcement learning for Atari. arXiv preprint arXiv:1903.00374 (2019)

38. Whiteson, S.: TreeQN and ATeeC: differentiable tree planning for deep reinforce-
    ment learning (2018)
39. Kala, T., Shinozaki, T.: Reinforcement learning of speech recognition system based
    on policy gradient and hypothesis selection. In: 2018 IEEE International Confer-
    ence on Acoustics, Speech and Signal Processing (ICASSP), pp. 5759–5763. IEEE
    (2018)
40. Tjandra, A., Sakti, S., Nakamura, S.: Sequence-to-sequence ASR optimization
    via reinforcement learning. In: 2018 IEEE International Conference on Acoustics,
    Speech and Signal Processing (ICASSP), pp. 5829–5833. IEEE (2018)
41. Chung, H., Jeon, H.-B., Park, J.G.: Semi-supervised training for sequence-to-
    sequence speech recognition using reinforcement learning. In: 2020 International
    Joint Conference on Neural Networks (IJCNN), pp. 1–6. IEEE (2020)
42. Fakoor, R., He, X., Tashev, I., Zarar, S.: Reinforcement learning to adapt
    speech enhancement to instantaneous input signal quality. arXiv preprint
    arXiv:1711.10791 (2017)
43. Alamdari, N., Lobarinas, E., Kehtarnavaz, N.: Personalization of hearing aid com-
    pression by human-in-the-loop deep reinforcement learning. IEEE Access 8, 203
    503–203 515 (2020)
44. Kotecha, N.: Bach2Bach: generating music using a deep reinforcement learning
    approach. arXiv preprint arXiv:1812.01060 (2018)
45. Jaques, N., Gu, S., Turner, R.E., Eck, D.: Generating music by fine-tuning recur-
    rent neural networks with reinforcement learning (2016)
46. Xie, J., Zhu, M.: Handcrafted features and late fusion with deep learning for bird
    sound classification. Eco. Inform. 52, 74–81 (2019)
47. Salamon, J., Bello, J.P.: Deep convolutional neural networks and data augmen-
    tation for environmental sound classification. IEEE Signal Process. Lett. 24(3),
    279–283 (2017)
48. Nam, J., Choi, K., Lee, J., Chou, S.-Y., Yang, Y.-H.: Deep learning for audio-based
    music classification and tagging: teaching computers to distinguish rock from bach.
    IEEE Signal Process. Mag. 36(1), 41–51 (2018)
49. Konda, V., Tsitsiklis, J.: Actor-critic algorithms. In: Advances in Neural Informa-
    tion Processing Systems, vol. 12 (1999)
50. Mnih, V., et al.: Asynchronous methods for deep reinforcement learning. In: Inter-
    national Conference on Machine Learning, pp. 1928–1937. PMLR (2016)
51. Mnih, V., et al.: Human-level control through deep reinforcement learning. Nature
    518(7540), 529–533 (2015)
52. Seno, T.: Welcome to deep reinforcement learning part 1: DQN (2017). https://
    towardsdatascience.com/welcome-to-deep-reinforcement-learning-part-1-dqn-
    c3cab4d41b6b
53. Van Hasselt, H., Guez, A., Silver, D.: Deep reinforcement learning with double
    q-learning. In: Proceedings of the AAAI Conference on Artificial Intelligence, vol.
    30, no. 1 (2016)
54. Schaul, T., Quan, J., Antonoglou, I., Silver, D.: Prioritized experience replay. arXiv
    preprint arXiv:1511.05952 (2015)
55. Abeßer, J.: A review of deep learning based methods for acoustic scene classifica-
    tion. Appl. Sci. 10(6) (2020)
56. Seo, H., Park, J., Park, Y.: Acoustic scene classification using various pre-processed
    features and convolutional neural networks. In: Proceedings of the Detection and
    Classification of Acoustic Scenes and Events Workshop (DCASE), New York, NY,
    USA, pp. 25–26 (2019)

57. Lostanlen, V., et al.: Per-channel energy normalization: why and how. IEEE Signal Process. Lett. **26**(1), 39–43 (2018)
58. Wu, Y., Lee, T.: Enhancing sound texture in CNN-based acoustic scene classification. In: 2019 IEEE International Conference on Acoustics, Speech and Signal Processing (ICASSP), ICASSP 2019, pp. 815–819. IEEE (2019)
59. Mariotti, O., Cord, M., Schwander, O.: Exploring deep vision models for acoustic scene classification. In: Proceedings of the DCASE, pp. 103–107 (2018)
60. Deng, J., Dong, W., Socher, R., Li, L.-J., Li, K., Fei-Fei, L.: ImageNet: a large-scale hierarchical image database. In: IEEE Conference on Computer Vision and Pattern Recognition, pp. 248–255. IEEE (2009)
61. Gemmeke, J.F., et al.: Audio set: an ontology and human-labeled dataset for audio events. In: IEEE International Conference on Acoustics, Speech and Signal Processing (ICASSP), pp. 776–780. IEEE (2017)
62. Koutini, K., Eghbal-zadeh, H., Widmer, G.: Receptive-field-regularized CNN variants for acoustic scene classification. arXiv preprint arXiv:1909.02859 (2019)
63. Park, D.S., et al.: SpecAugment: a simple data augmentation method for automatic speech recognition. arXiv preprint arXiv:1904.08779 (2019)
64. Lasseck, M.: Acoustic bird detection with deep convolutional neural networks. In: Proceedings of the Detection and Classification of Acoustic Scenes and Events 2018 Workshop (DCASE2018), pp. 143–147 (2018)
65. Li, J., Deng, L., Haeb-Umbach, R., Gong, Y.: Robust automatic speech recognition: a bridge to practical applications (2015)

Research of Cryptocurrencies Function of Instant Payments in the Tourism Sector: Risks, Options, and Solutions

Kotryna Laptevaitė, Evaldas Krampas, Saulius Masteika[✉], Kęstutis Driaunys,
Aida Mačerinskienė, and Alfreda Šapkauskienė

Vilnius University, Universiteto str. 3, 01513 Vilnius, Lithuania
saulius.masteika@knf.vu.lt

Abstract. This research aims to provide an overview of the technological solutions of instant payment with cryptocurrencies in the tourism sector. The analysis has been done on various cryptocurrencies and technologies related to them, their transaction processing speed, alternatives on how to optimize it, and what impact it has on cryptocurrency payments adoption to the tourism sector. It was noticed that various places of services in the tourism sector could take a lot of benefits from accepting the cryptocurrency transactions, such as an additional group of clients, eased payment mobility and fast settlement of the received funds, but they are also avoiding accepting the most popular cryptocurrencies due to the volatility of their market, high transactional costs and low transaction confirmation speed, which would cause an issue to manage the customers' queue while comparing to traditional currency payments. This research revealed that there are solutions to avoid the mentioned drawbacks by offering less popular cryptocurrency acceptance or taking the possible risks of accepting 0-confirmation transactions. The prototype of instant payments solution is suggested where cryptocurrency payment adoption in the tourism sector could be reached by accepting 0-confirmation transactions of the most popular cryptocurrencies with an instant exchange to fiat currencies at the merchant side.

Keywords: Bitcoin · Blockchain · Cryptocurrency · Tourism sector · Instant payments

1 Introduction

As service providers want to attract the widest possible range of customers, the customers are looking for the most convenient ways to pay for the service. When talking about the tourism sector we must emphasize the importance of payment managing at the point of service, and define that specific area will be examined, where a service provider and a customer are interacting directly. The research focuses on the tourism sector since crypto point of service payments make more sense when made in different countries, there is no need for currency conversions, and getting to another country is directly

A. Lopata et al. (Eds.): ICIST 2022, CCIS 1665, pp. 78–89, 2022.
https://doi.org/10.1007/978-3-031-16302-9_6

linked to traveling sector. Four main groups of services can be defined: accommodation, spa services, catering, excursions.

The lack of mass adoption of cryptocurrencies thus far may be attributed to several different factors, the main ones being maturation, volatility, technological shortcomings and regulation. However, this is about to change since many governments have already accepted cryptocurrencies as a legal form of payment. In the chart below (see Fig. 1.), Chainalysis presents the crypto adoption index, which is created by adding up all 154 countries' scores - made up of the three components we describe below:

- On-chain cryptocurrency value received, weighted by purchasing power parity (PPP) per capita
- The on-chain retail value transferred, weighted by PPP per capita
- Peer-to-peer (P2P) exchange trade volume, weighted by PPP per capita and the number of internet users.

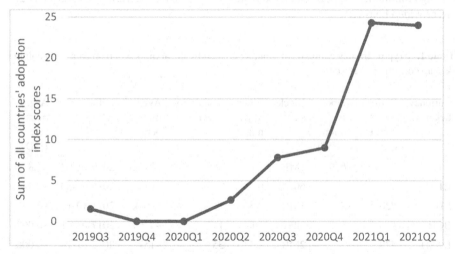

Fig. 1. Chainalysis global crypto adoption index: sum of all countries' index scores by quarter. Source: chainalysis.com

The adoption is increasing heavily due to the obvious advantages of accepting cryptocurrency payments:

- Mobility - foreign customers would not require additional effort, as the cryptographic currency does not need to be changed to local currency.
- Low fees - payment in a cryptographic currency would often cost significantly less than a currency conversion, cash withdrawal, or even a card service fee.
- Fast arrival of funds - when a customer pays with a card, the money is only reserved, and in fact, reaches the service provider much later.
- Additional customer group - a group that seeks to involve their cryptocurrencies as a method of payment.

2 Cryptocurrencies and Instant Payment Options

To decide which currencies should be accepted by point-of-sale (POS) as the most popular ones, we should compare them based on various aspects, such as price, speed of transaction approval, how often they are used and how many users use them, if the popularity of the currency is still increasing/is stable, security, issuer. If we think about cryptocurrencies being a certain form of digital currency or money, then utility tokens might be described as a form of software. It can be used to transfer value and data, but that is generally not the main purpose [1]. Due to that, they will not be included in the analysis. The same would apply for centralized currencies - as the initial purpose of blockchain is to be a decentralized, distributed, and public, digital ledger consisting of records called blocks that are used to record transactions across many computers so that any involved block cannot be altered retroactively, without the alteration of all subsequent blocks [2]. So, let us review several key cryptocurrencies based on the market capitalization and user engagement correlations [3] that already has the trust among cryptocurrency users, the big community support. Gathered results (based on data retrieved in January 2022) are provided below:

Table 1. Cryptocurrency comparison. Source: created by the authors based on data from coinma rketcap.com and ycharts.com

Currency ticker	Rating by market cap	Market cap., billions in USD	Block size	Block time, min	Scalability (tx/s)	Avg. trans. per day	Initial release	Avg. trans. fee, USD
BTC	#1	~669	1MB	10	<7	~215k	2009-01-03	~1,8
ETH	#2	~291	60KB	0,25	15–45	~1106k	2015-07-30	~3,34
LTC	#20	~7	1MB	2,5	56	~104k	2011-10-13	~0.04
BCH	#26	~5	32MB	10	116	~43k	2017-08-01	~0.008
DASH	#79	~1	2MB	2,5	35	~15k	2014-01-18	~0.006

Also, the popularity of the currency can be defined by the number of active wallets (meaning that the wallet has at least one incoming or outgoing transaction per day during the last 6 months). The number of active Bitcoin wallets is currently the same numbers on Ethereum - around 700,000. Litecoin has almost 300k active addresses, BitcoinCash - 100k addresses, and Dash has only over 50,000 active addresses.

The best currency for crypto payments seems to be Dash comparing the data provided in the table. Dash allows users to make fast transactions for a fraction of a cent. However, Dash is widely considered a privacy-enhancing cryptocurrency. For example, the Financial Services Agency (FSA) in Japan forced centralised cryptocurrency exchanges to delist privacy-enhancing crypto such as Monero [4]. Korbit - one of the largest cryptocurrency exchanges in South Korea - delisted the following privacy cryptos: DASH, Monero (XMR), Zcash (ZEC), REP and STEEM. In October 2018, the UK

Financial Conduct Authority proposed the guidelines to "prevent the use of crypto assets for illicit activity" [5]. Governments are seeking to prevent untraceable cryptocurrencies from reaching mainstream adoption, therefore Dash cryptocurrency may not be suitable to be used as an option for daily payments in the tourism sector.

Though Bitcoin, Litecoin and Bitcoin Cash are not fitting the needs of instant payments due to scalability and Ether is currently having fees that would be way higher than acceptable compared to traditional payments or other cryptocurrencies, these currencies cannot be ignored as a payment option, as they are the most popular ones based on market capitalisation, transactions per day and number of active wallets.

2.1 Stablecoins

A stablecoin is a form of cryptocurrency with its value linked to an outside source, such as the American dollar or gold, giving the coin a stable value. This stability is what sets stablecoins apart in the otherwise volatile crypto market. To offer a variety of crypto payment options for a client, acceptance of stablecoins should as well be considered as an instant payment option with a stable value alternative. Based on data found on coinmarketcap.com (values as of January 23rd, 2022), let us review the leading Top 5 stablecoins (USDT, USDC, BUSD, UST and DAI) in the Table 2 below.

Tether (USDT), the largest stablecoin in the crypto market by far in terms of market capitalization, offers the ability to use different blockchains and therefore protocols. We have found that USDT transactions can be processed at a higher speed but with a fraction of typical transaction costs on the Solana Blockchain. Solana works on a unique Proof-of-History mechanism that allows it to process at least 50,000 transactions per second for approximately $0.00001 per transaction. Although Solana's network offers one of the fastest and cheapest transactions, its smart-contract programming language Rust lacks popularity for massive adoption. For this reason, using USDT based on the Ethereum network, particularly the ERC-20 token standard with Solidity program language for smart contracts, would be a better choice considering the current situation. However, the execution of a smart contract costs more than a simple Ether transfer because more data is consumed in the block. Stablecoin transactions in the Ethereum blockchain have recently ranged from $13 to $33 in fees per transaction. Such a high transaction fee becomes unacceptable for daily payments not to mention that there is a high probability of error when transferring a stablecoin in the same name using a different blockchain, resulting in a loss of money. It should also be noted that stable coins are still in a testing phase, with many questions remaining as to their credibility, the adequacy of the guarantee funds (in the case of the USDT), and the stability of the algorithms in the face of larger price changes (in the case of the UST). After considering all the factors and practical solutions, accepting payments with stablecoin is not favorable currently.

2.2 Second Layer Technologies Supporting Nearly Instant Transaction Processing

Despite their growing adoption, cryptocurrencies suffer from poor scalability (as was seen in Table 1). For example, as the Bitcoin network processes 7 transactions per second (TPS), and Ethereum 15–45 TPS, they both pale in comparison to the 1,700 TPS

Table 2. Stablecoins comparison. Source: created by the authors based on data from coinmarke tcap.com

Currency ticker	Blockchains/networks	Market cap., USD	Trade vol. per 24h, USD
USDT	Algorand, Ethereum (ERC-20), EOS, Liquid Network, Omni, TRON (TRC-20), Bitcoin Cash's Standard Ledger Protocol, Solana	~78B	~89B
USDC	Ethereum (ERC-20), Binance Chain (BEP-2), Binance Smart Chain (BEP-20), Avalanche C-chain, Solana, TRON (TRC-20)	~43B	~4,5B
BUSD	Ethereum (ERC-20), Binance Chain (BEP-2), Binance Smart Chain (BEP-20), Avalanche C-chain	~14B	~4,5B
UST	Terra, Binance Smart Chain (BEP-20), Solana	~11B	~354M
DAI	Ehereum (ERC-20) Binance Smart Chain (BEP-20), Avalanche C-chain	~9B	~409M

achieved by the VISA network. Scalability thus remains a major hurdle to the adoption of cryptocurrencies for retail and other large-scale applications. The root of the scalability challenge is the inefficiency of the underlying consensus protocol: every transaction must go through full consensus to be confirmed, which can take anywhere from several minutes to hours [6]. To compete with the popularity of traditional payments merchants might consider sticking to more modern options and applying modern technologies that allow payment transfers to be done instantly, such as Lighting networks or currencies working on protocols that take no time for the transactions to be approved.

DASH: Instant Transactions via InstantSend. Based on the results of the analysis it is the most suitable cryptocurrency for making micro-payments, due to its extremely low transfer cost and fast processing. A key feature of InstantSend technology is the ability to lock a transaction, ensure that it is not illegally reissued, and enable its instant dispatch on the Dash network. An instant transfer is made when a customer initiates an InstantSend transfer - he notifies the network that a certain amount of money will travel from one input to another output address. However, InstantSend can only be used in

Dash wallets that support this feature and considering the previously described privacy issues, scalability limitations merchants might avoid accepting this currency.

Bitcoin Bi-directional Channels. Bi-directional payment channels (Lightning Network) allow payments to be securely routed across multiple peer-to-peer payment channels. This allows the formation of a second layer cryptocurrency network where any peer on the network can pay any other peer even if they do not directly have a channel open between each other [7]. To close the channel, one of the participants commits the latest transaction according to the latest balance sheet, which was signed by both parties and broadcasts it to the Bitcoin network. It will be a single transaction on the Bitcoin network. In this way, the lightning network significantly reduces the load on the main blockchain, as it requires only two transactions on the blockchain: one to open the payment channel and another one to close it. Despite the faster transactions the cost benefits of a lightning network only exist if participants of the channel make more than two transactions, otherwise, it is cheaper to make direct transfers on the main network. Also, the bi-directional channel becomes imbalanced when the transaction rate across it is higher in one direction than the other; the party making more transactions eventually runs out of assets and cannot send further payments without adding more virtual assets to the channel leading to extra transactional costs.

Both promising technologies due to their drawbacks, such as the global distrust in Dash currency and technological solutions for instant reoccurring payments with bidirectional payment channels, as in our case, most of the time transaction is most likely to happen once, are not suitable for POS implementation, so it leaves us with regular BTC, LTC, and BCH currencies to be considered as the ones relevant for testing of cryptocurrency adoption in the tourism sector.

2.3 The Risks of Instant Payments

Confirmation time for cryptocurrency payment becomes more of a problem when the payment is made in a physical location because to pay the bill the customer must wait for his transactions to be confirmed in the chain of blocks.

Bitcoin confirmations are the number of blocks added to the blockchain after a particular transaction has been made and accepted by the rest of the network. Each new block contains information of a previous one, therefore it is considered that – the more confirmations there are – the more likely a transaction will be valid and permanent [8]. The number of required confirmations for a transaction to be accepted by the services provider depends on the provider's security risk tolerance. For example, the world's largest cryptocurrency exchange - Binance - includes BTC deposit as soon as the transaction is added to the first block [9], while Kraken would include BTC to its user's wallet after 4th confirmation. They all protect the providers from these types of double-spending attacks on proof-of-work consensus blockchains:

- The 51% attack (majority attack)
- Race attack and opt-in RBF
- Finney attack.

The 51% Attack (Majority Attack)

There are two ways in which a network's computing power could be taken into control of a bad actor. One of which is collaborating with other network mining pools to centralise 51% of the hashing power. This would require low investment, as the required mining equipment is already in possession of collaborative mining pools. Such an agreement would be practically impossible simply because miners benefit from the network's rewards - they are directly interested in the price of the cryptocurrency increase and blockchain stability. In case of such an attack, the price of the network's native currency would decrease significantly due to loss of trust. The second option is to own the required amount of hashing power by buying equipment and acting as a single bad actor. In this case, the hashing power is equipped by buying equipment, and, in this way, adding more hashing power to the network. Hence, the target hash rate, which we would need to add to the current network's hash rate to control 51% of the total network's hash rate, should be calculated with the following formula:

$$target\ hash\ rate = current\ hash\ rate \frac{target\ rate}{1 - target\ rate} \tag{1}$$

As of 18 February 2022, the hash rate, according to Blockchain.info, on the Bitcoin network was 214,940,499.792 THash/s, therefore, target hash rate = 214,940,499.792 * (0.51/(1 − 0.51)) = 223,713,581.416 THash/s.

At the moment of such attack, the total network's hashing power would be 438,654,081,21 THash/s, while the bad actor's hashing power - 223,713,581.416 THash/s or equal to 51% of the total. This increase of the total network's hashing power from 214,940,499.792 Thash/s to 438,654,081,21 THash/s would be quickly spotted by other miners resulting in detecting an attack not mentioning that it would cost at least 38 billion USD, according to our calculations.

However, even if somebody would get in possession of 51% of the network's hashing power, it would not create a financial sense to attack the network, because of redirecting some transactions in the tourism sector.

Race Attack and Opt-In RBF

A Race attack ensues when two transactions are assembled using the same assets at the same moment with the intent of disbursing the coins twice. A successful Race attack is one where the payment recipient's node receives a spend transaction yet the following block that is minded has a different transaction documenting the spend of the same coins. Thus, the payment recipient's transaction does not get confirmed in the network, and the recipient never receives these coins [10]. For example, the Attacker makes two transactions of which: one sends assets from one of Attacker's wallets to another and the second one pays a bill at a hotel. If the Attacker controls a node, he may reject the second transaction, prioritize the first transaction, and broadcast the first transaction to the rest of the network. Only one transaction can receive confirmations and is verified by miners in the next block.

Another way to make a similar double-spending event is by using opt-in Replace-by-Fee (RBF) - a function embedded in certain Bitcoin wallets (e.g. Electrum). This feature allows rebroadcasting an unconfirmed transaction with a higher fee to get it confirmed faster. RBF allows rebroadcasting of a transaction with a higher fee, effectively trying to double-spend the same assets, so the miners will pick up the new transaction and the old one will get cancelled [11]. The Attacker can use this functionality not to increase the fee of his initial transaction but to cancel it. Luckily, each transaction with opt-in RBF is marked as replaceable (sequence number below MAX-1), therefore the merchant or its crypto payment service provider can set a parameter for RBF compatible transactions to be marked as successful only after first confirmation in a block and mitigate the risk of an unconfirmed transaction becoming changed after purchase at the place is set as paid.

Moreover, to reduce the risk of a Race attack, the merchant should use a trusted third-party provider, i.e., a cryptocurrency exchange. The trusted third-party payment provider has all good practices in-house to protect its nodes from attacks, such as the direct connection from specifics IPs only, constant changes of the main full node operator, double-checking of transaction data by multiple nodes, and similar.

Finney Attack
The Finney attack is a double-spending attack with the following process flow [10]:

1. The attacker mines block normally; in the block, he is trying to find, he creates two transactions - one crediting the merchant (victim) and one crediting his wallet. Both transactions are not yet broadcasted.
2. The attacker keeps the first transaction unsent and proceeds to try mining the second one into a block.
3. When the attacker succeeds (this may take a while), he quickly purchases with the first transaction, once merchants accept the payment and irreversibly provides the service, the attacker broadcasts the pre-mined block with the (second) transaction sending coins to his wallet with that it overrides the unconfirmed transfer to the merchant (first transaction).
4. The first transaction will eventually become invalidated, even if it is replicated through the whole network.

The lower the attacker's hash rate, the lower are the chances he has to carry out this attack. Evaluating that the BTC, LTC and BCH networks are so massive right now, the Finney attack is purely theoretical, and not possible for physical purchases as the buyer has limited time to make a transaction without causing suspicion to the cashier. By making a faulty transaction, the Attack would lose a block reward. Block rewards as of March 2022 are listed below:

- 6.25 units of BTC of Bitcoin network (approx. 225,112 EUR)
- 12.5 units of LTC on Litecoin network (approx. 1,198 EUR)
- 6.25 units of BCH of BitcoinCash network (approx. 1,675 EUR).

For maximum security, it is recommended to wait for a second confirmation if a transaction's value is higher than the block reward of the network. If a payment is considered a high amount - higher than the block reward, which is currently around 1200 EUR for LTC and around 1675 EUR for BCH, then the merchant could ask a client to wait for the second confirmation, which would take additional 5 min in case of LTC and 10 min in case of BCH.

3 Instant Payment Solutions

From what has been discovered during the research, the efficient POS solution should be defined as a system that accepts card payments and most popular cryptocurrencies without the need for a merchant to handle the separate accounting issues, should allow the merchant to choose what currency he would like to receive, and if it is a cryptocurrency - whether to keep it the way it is received or convert it to a chosen fiat-currency making sure the value of the received payment stays as non-volatile.

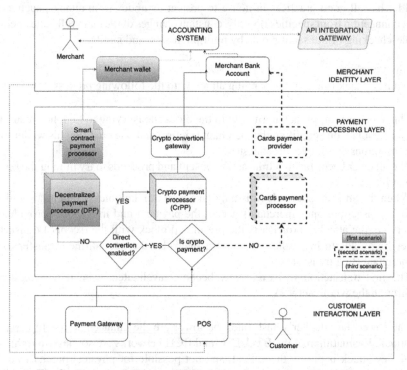

Fig. 2. Concept of all-in-one POS solution. Source: created by authors

In Fig. 2 we propose the main 3 scenarios of how the payment could be processed with the mentioned POS solution:

1. Merchants can accept cryptocurrency payment and keep it as a cryptocurrency (first scenario).
2. Users can stick to a traditional card payment, which would make them acquainted with the fact that a crypto-payment option is also available (second scenario) which might encourage them to use it in future.
3. Merchants can accept cryptocurrency payments and convert the received assets to the fiat currency of their choice (third scenario).

The first scenario describes the part of the procedure where payment is processed and kept in cryptocurrency. A decentralized payment processor would handle the received assets and place them directly into merchant crypto wallets based on the payment currency, where a smart contract payment processor could notify the accounting system based on the received transaction to ease the accounting related information.

The second scenario describes the way payment could be processed if it is initiated and kept in fiat currency. This is the so-called traditional card payment as the majority understands.

The third scenario is most likely to be used to meet both merchants' and customers' needs, which is why we are going to analyze it further. Figure 3 represents required processes of how the crypto payment management inside the payment gateway could be managed in the prototype.

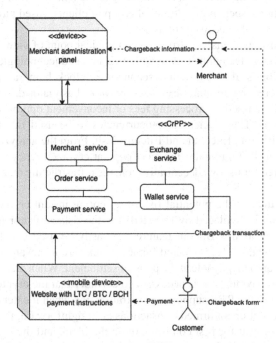

Fig. 3. Concept of crypto payment processor (CrPP), customers' and merchants' interaction. Source: created by authors

In any mobile device/tablet with an internet connection and a browser, a website will be opened which will display the payment instructions, previously defined in a merchant service, for a customer. Received payment will be handled by the payment service, which will inform the order service that the order has been paid. The received amount will be exchanged in exchange service, for fiat currency, and included in the merchant's wallet, which will be managed in wallet service. Merchant, using its computer, via web browser will reach the administration panel and will be able to withdraw the received funds and manage the payments. He will also be able to initiate a chargeback, to customers' wallets based on provided chargeback information (the amount in crypto to be sent will be converted based on received fiat rate in real-time, to match the fiat amount that was paid initially, instead of returning the matching amount in cryptocurrency, as it might have significantly changed trough the time).

4 Conclusions

Research has been done on crypto payments adoption in the tourism sector, providing the technological solutions of instant payment options with cryptocurrencies and specifying differences between currently popular fast payment implementation techniques. As data shows, at least in on-line trading, the adoption rate of cryptocurrencies into day-to-day life is increasing rapidly. Meanwhile, contact payments are still in their infancy. It was noticed that services in the tourism sector could take the benefits from accepting cryptocurrency transactions, such as an additional group of clients, eased payment mobility and faster settlement of the received funds.

A detailed comparative analysis from a technological point of view has shown that some of crypto payment techniques, even with their updated technological approach of increasing transactions scalability, such as second layer blockchain transactions, master nodes approval or creating an inner user's sub-network has major drawbacks, such as low reliability, high transaction processing fees or inconvenient options to operate with one-time transactions. The efficient cryptocurrencies to be used in payments in the tourism sector are Bitcoin, Litecoin and Bitcoin Cash. From the analyzed data sources and indexes, Bitcoin (BTC) remains the most popular cryptocurrency with the highest adoption rate, favored for its high decentralization, the infrastructure created and privacy rating.

An empirical study of the potential risk of accepting instant cryptocurrency payments found that opt-in Replaced-by-Fee (RBF) is the riskiest factor for transactions in the tourism sector, as this Bitcoin feature can easily be used to return an unconfirmed transaction, while 51%, Race and Finney attacks are irrelevant, especially with the reduction in the amount payable at the point of settlement. When creating a prototype for accepting crypto payments, it is necessary to consider that the cryptocurrency payment service identifies the RBF supporting the transaction when it enters the mempool. Preventing the return of unconfirmed transactions is straightforward, the RBF compatible transaction shall wait for first confirmation in the block and then payment can be marked as successful unless the transaction is higher than that specific cryptocurrency block reward - in that case, it is necessary to wait for the second confirmation.

Taking into account the performed research, a POS prototype has been offered, which would enable the acceptance of 0-confirmation transactions of the most popular cryptocurrencies such as BTC, BCH and LTC, with an instant exchange to fiat currencies at the merchant side, which would solve the volatility and transaction speed issues, together with enabling all the benefits described.

Acknowledgement. This project has received funding from European Regional Development Fund (project No 13.1.1-LMT-K-718-05-0006) under grant agreement with the Research Council of Lithuania (LMTLT). Funded as European Union's measure in response to Cov-19 pandemic.

References

1. Häfner, S.: Blockchain platform design (2022)
2. Guo, H., Yu, X.: A survey on blockchain technology and its security. Blockchain: Res. Appl. 100067 (2022). https://doi.org/10.1016/J.BCRA.2022.100067
3. Lahajnar, S., Rožanec, A.: The correlation strength of the most important cryptocurrencies in the bull and bear market. Invest. Manag. Financ. Innova. **17**, 67–81 (2020). https://doi.org/10.21511/IMFI.17(3).2020.06
4. Japan's Financial Regulator Is Pushing Crypto Exchanges To Drop "Altcoins" Favored By Criminals. https://www.forbes.com/sites/adelsteinjake/2018/04/30/japans-financial-regulator-is-pushing-crypto-exchanges-to-drop-altcoins-favored-by-criminals/?sh=65d7798e1b8a. Accessed 27 Feb 2022
5. Cryptoassets Taskforce: final report (2018)
6. Hazari, S.S., Mahmoud, Q.H.: Improving transaction speed and scalability of blockchain systems via parallel proof of work. Future Internet. **12** (2020). https://doi.org/10.3390/FI12080125
7. Antonopoulos, A.M.: Mastering Bitcoin: Programming the Open Blockchain. O'Reilly Media, Inc. (2017)
8. Sunmola, F.T., Burgess, P., Tan, A.: Building blocks for blockchain adoption in digital transformation of sustainable supply chains. Proc. Manuf. **55**, 513–520 (2021). https://doi.org/10.1016/J.PROMFG.2021.10.070
9. Binance Reduces the Number of Confirmations Required for Deposits & Withdrawals on BTC and ETH Networks. https://www.binance.com/en/support/announcement/360030775291. Accessed 11 Feb 2022
10. Karame, G.O., Androulaki, E., Capkun, S.: Two Bitcoins at the price of one? Double-spending attacks on fast payments in bitcoin (2012)
11. Gürcan, Ö., Ranchal Pedrosa, A., Tucci-Piergiovanni, S.: On cancellation of transactions in bitcoin-like blockchains. In: Panetto, H., Debruyne, C., Proper, H.A., Ardagna, C.A., Roman, D., Meersman, R. (eds.) OTM 2018. LNCS, vol. 11229, pp. 516–533. Springer, Cham (2018). https://doi.org/10.1007/978-3-030-02610-3_29

Random Forest Classifier for Correcting Point Cloud Segmentation Based on Metrics of Recursive 2-Means Splits

Karolis Ryselis[✉] [iD]

Kaunas University of Technology, Kaunas, Lithuania
`karolis.ryselis@ktu.edu`

Abstract. Human body segmentation is an intermediate step in many applications. Current state of the art shows the best results of segmentation when deep neural networks are used, however, they require lots of annotated data to learn from. Annotating data for segmentation is a very tedious process since part of the image has to be marked as foreground. This involves much higher amount of manual work by a human than classification where only a correct label must be picked. Geometrical solutions may be used to assist the human, but their mistakes must be corrected manually. The goal of this research is to reduce the total time of segmentation annotation process. This is achieved by a machine learning solution that improves the accuracy of an existing geometric algorithm when applied to human body segmentation. It is trained from 8 introduced metrics acquired after point cloud split based on 2-Means cut. The approach has been trained on two real life datasets that include humans in different positions. Observed results show that accuracy is improved in the most complex scenes at a performance penalty. However, this is a good trade-off in case the original algorithm is unusable due to very low accuracy.

Keywords: Human body segmentation · Random forest · Point cloud

1 Introduction

Depth data processing has seen a lot of active development recently due to its wide applicability. This is a tempting area of research since devices like depth cameras [1] or lidars [2] have low cost and provide acceptable quality of depth images. A large area of the research is segmentation of spatial data [3] provided by depth sensing devices. Depending on an application area, it may be required to extract different objects from the scene. However, current machine learning models that process depth images require a huge amount of data. Xu et al. required over 43k annotated scans [4] to conduct their research. "ShapeNet" dataset consists of 3M models, however, at the time of release only 220k models were annotated [5]. "Kinect" sensor produces 30 depth frames per second, which is 1800 frames per minute of video. These examples show that depth data annotation is a tedious process and is not possible without extra tools that speed

A. Lopata et al. (Eds.): ICIST 2022, CCIS 1665, pp. 90–101, 2022.
https://doi.org/10.1007/978-3-031-16302-9_7

up manual segmentation. However, it is required for high accuracy supervised machine learning models.

One of the most popular off-the-shelf solutions for general segmentation is Point Cloud Library [6]. Euclidean cluster extraction is one of the fastest algorithms presented in the toolkit with algorithmic complexity of $O(n \log n)$. It yields segments of the point cloud by running a radius search on every point in the cloud.

PCL approach can be sped up further by replacing radius search with bounding box search. Let $A = \{a_1, a_2, \ldots, a_n\}$ be a 3D point cloud representing a scene captured using a depth camera. A 3D binary search tree K_A is constructed from point cloud A. Point $a_p \in A$ is selected by human and Euclidean bounding box search is performed. The search can be defined as a function of the search tree, initial point, and bounding box expansion size b:

$$A_S = E(A, a_p, b) \tag{1}$$

A rectangular bounding box around the point a_p is constructed with the point being in the center with dimensions of $2b$ in all directions. A new bounding box is constructed by expanding previous bounding box to make it the smallest bounding box that contains all collected points, expanded by b in all directions. This collect-expand loop is repeated until no new points are added after the expansion. Bounding boxes shift the complexity to $\Theta(n \log n)$ and $\Omega(n)$ because a single bounding box may hold between 1 point and whole point cloud.

This algorithm was implemented by the author of this article previously. It tends to capture multiple objects rather than just the human as a single segment in complex real-life scenes. The accuracy ranges from 24% to 76% with 17 ms processing time per frame [7]. In the context of semi-automatic segmentation this means that a lot of manual corrections are required to remove the extra object. The goal of this research is to improve the accuracy of the worst performing cases of the existing solution in terms of human body with a reasonable performance penalty.

The paper is structured as follows. Section 2 discusses existing solutions for point cloud segmentation. Section 3 describes the suggested algorithm in detail. Section 4 provides the results of accuracy and performance research of the suggested algorithm. Finally, Sect. 5 concludes the article.

2 Related Work

2.1 Depth Data Representations

Depth data is usually provided as depth maps by depth sensors. This is a picture-like 2D matrix where every item represents the depth from the sensor to the object seen in a corresponding pixel. However, this data structure is rarely used to process the depth information. Zhao et al. combine it with RGB data to recognize human activity [8].

A more common data structure is a 3D binary search tree first introduced by Bentley [9]. It is much more applicable because it allows finding neighbor points in $O(\log n)$ time. This is an important property because close points are the basis of algorithms such as segmentation [10–12], clustering [13–15], classification [16–18] and others.

2.2 Point Cloud Segmentation

As mentioned in introduction, PCL solution implements a fast search algorithm - Euclidean search. It was successfully sped up further by Nguyen et al. [19]. The researchers have utilized capabilities of modern GPGPU and achieved significant results. However, memory usage of their solution is high, which makes it difficult to apply for large point clouds.

Point clouds are also processed by extracting bounding boxes for 3D objects. Xu et al. [20] implemented a neural network solution to estimate the bounding boxes. They process both color data and point clouds to achieve better results. However, since this is a machine learning solution, the researchers used publicly available datasets for training. Another solution for a similar problem was suggested by Zhou and Tuzel [21]. They implemented an end-to-end learning neural network architecture that processes depth data to get the bounding boxes. The researchers have also used publicly available datasets for training. A plethora of other neural networks have been proposed to find 3D bounding boxes for different types of objects: a multi-layer perceptron to find bounding boxes from 3D scenes by Yang et al. [22], YOLO3D architecture for bounding box detection in lidar data by Ali et al. [23], point-level supervised network to find bounding boxes in lidar data by He et al. [24], a fully convolutional neural network to find bounding boxes for vehicles in point clouds by Li [25] or a graph neural network for point clouds by Shi and Rajkumar [26]. However, all mentioned methods are based on machine learning and use publicly available datasets for training. Most of them use KITTI dataset [27] which was captured in 2013 and consists of 6 h of traffic scenes. It is still widely used in current research because it takes a lot of time and effort to create a new dataset of that size.

K-Means algorithm first defined by MacQueen [28] is widely used unsupervised machine learning solution to segment point clouds. Saglam et al. achieved over 80% accuracy in building segmentation [29]. Zhou et al. also showed that K-Means algorithm works best for background removal [30]. These results suggest that K-Means could also be used to further segment output of existing segmentation algorithm since part of it may belong to background.

3 Suggested Point Cloud Cut to Improve Segmentation Accuracy

3.1 Problem Statement

While the segmentation algorithm presented with formula 1 is fast, it has no safeguards to prevent including multiple objects in a single segmentation pass. Therefore, A_S should be split into two objects in case this happens. More formally, postprocessing function to optionally remove part of the segmentation result is required:

$$A_T = R(A_S) \tag{2}$$

Here $A_T \subseteq A_S$. This research presents a viable suggestion for function R that improves the accuracy of the standard bounding box search E with a reasonable performance penalty.

3.2 Data Formats and Preprocessing

The point cloud is received from the "Kinect" sensor as a depth map. Segmentation requires preserving object edges, so bilateral filter is applied since it was shown to yield good results [31]. A denoised depth map is acquired. The depth map is then converted to a 3D balanced search tree to enable fast space-local search.

It is assumed that the point cloud is only used for segmentation, therefore, some optimizations are made by modifying the internal state of the search tree. The most important is marking found as removed so that they are not processed repeatedly. This improves performance since the same point will cannot belong to multiple clusters.

3.3 Overview

The whole segmentation process goes as shown in segmentation UML activity diagram in Fig. 1. Activity receives a point cloud, initial point, and bounding box size (same parameters as in formula 1). Actions in purple background are the novelty added by this research and act as function R from formula 2. After the preprocessing step, bounding box-based segmentation is applied as defined by formula 1. This step outputs a cluster that may or may not be correct. Then the system splits the cluster into two using K-Means, computes 8 metrics for these new clusters and runs a random forest classifier to determine if the split was correct. If the split was correct, the split – metrics – predict loop is repeated with an accepted smaller cluster until the split is incorrect. If any part of the original cluster was cut, its points are marked as non-removed and the algorithm outputs its result – a segmented cluster. All software was implemented using Java programming language (OpenJDK 14).

The next subsections present all novelties introduced by this research.

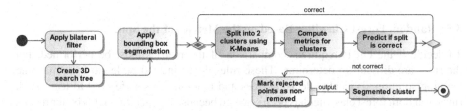

Fig. 1. Generalized segmentation scheme

3.4 2-Means Split and Metrics of the Split

K-Means algorithm is adapted to split the found point cloud into two parts. There are two challenges in this approach – how to split the point cloud and how to decide if the split is good.

One point is provided by a human and is known to belong to the object. To use K-Means clustering, it is required to select other points that would be used as initial points for clustering and then moved. However, it is known that one point is already correct.

This point will act as a fixed centroid that never moves. Since the number of objects that the segmentation will take is unknown, it was chosen to split the point cloud into two clusters repeatedly. The initial point for the second centroid is chosen as the point that is the furthest away from the first centroid. The second centroid is then updated until it converges, but no more than 10 iterations to prevent long runtime. The result of this step is two sub-clusters of points – non-intersecting complete subsets of the base segmentation output.

The next step is determining whether the split improves segmentation output or not. At this point there are 5 pieces of data to analyze:

1. The full cluster of points (input for the split)
2. The sub-cluster that includes the original point
3. The sub-cluster that does not include the original point
4. The original point
5. The computed second centroid.

8 metrics are computed from that data. They consist of six distances – the average distance between all combinations of two centroids and three clusters of points as well as sizes of both sub-clusters.

These metrics were selected due to hypothesis that their value combinations may represent different cluster types. If original segmentation captured a single object, distances between both point clouds and both centroids will be much lower than in case of both clusters representing two distinct objects. If whole background is captured, the false cluster will also be much larger than the true cluster. If two very distinct objects are in the cluster, average distances between sub-clusters and their centroids will be much smaller than the average distance between sub-clusters and the other centroid. These metrics are also relatively fast to compute.

3.5 Random Forest Classifier Based on the Metrics of the Split

To decide if the cut is required, comparison of the metrics must be performed, but the rules are difficult to determine. These rules could instead be learnt by a machine learning solution. Typically, decision trees and random forests are used to learn such rules. Random forest classifier has been selected because it generally yields better results than a single tree. It has been trained to classify the cuts from the described metrics. The training data have been acquired by trying to run segmentation, splitting the point cloud, and checking if its match to ground truth was closer before or after the split. The split is considered correct if it improves the accuracy. The splits are continued until an incorrect split occurs, but no more than 10 splits. Two datasets were used for training. They are self-acquired datasets of depth images of people. The first dataset consists of people in 19 different positions from standing to laying on the ground; the second dataset is people standing still or sitting on a chair. The datasets have been acquired using "Kinect" sensor. They have been labelled semi-automatically with the help of solution without random forest accuracy improvements. The data is short depth-video sequences. 25–30 frames are taken from each video. 22k frames were used for training. 4 random frames are shown in Fig. 2. The first and last frames show examples of the first dataset – one person is seen from the side in a "cobra" position, the other is laying on the ground with his feet up as seen from the back (head is behind the legs). The scene is cluttered with chairs, desks, and objects on the desks. The other frames show examples from the second dataset – two people are standing in a more open space, one of them is facing camera while the other is seen from the side.

Fig. 2. Example frames from the datasets

Table 1. Random forest classification report

	Precision	Recall	F1-score
Incorrect cuts	0.94	0.90	0.92
Correct cuts	0.95	0.97	0.96
Accuracy	**0.95**		

The dataset is split into train (80%) and test (20%) parts video-wise, so that the frames of the same video do not go into both sets since they can be too similar. Classifier has shown 95% accuracy when tested against the test dataset. These results were obtained using 9 tree estimators. It was more accurate classifying the correct cuts, which means there are less false-positive cuts (the cuts that if made would degrade the accuracy). Classification metrics report is shown in Table 1.

One cut may not always remove the whole unwanted part of the cluster. To solve this, the random forest-based cut is performed recursively until the random forest decides that no more cuts are required. Number of cuts is capped at 10. The input for the recursive cut is the correctly cut sub-cluster from the previous cut. This solves the problem of unknown number of sub-clusters that could be found by K-Means by recursively applying 2-Means until it stops making sense to the random forest classifier, effectively increasing the number of "Means" in the K-Means algorithm to a dynamic value which depends on the data.

3.6 Performance Implications

Since the search tree is optimized for a single use, its nodes are marked as removed at the base segmentation step. After the random forest cuts some of the points may be rejected as wrongly added to the cluster. They have to be "returned" to the search tree. This is done by finding each rejected point in the tree and marking it as non-removed. This has algorithmic complexity of $O(m \log n)$, where m is the number of rejected points and n is the number of points in the whole point cloud.

Another extra work to do is computation of the 8 metrics required to make predictions and splitting clusters into two sub-clusters. Split is made 1–10 times per segmentation with algorithmic complexity of $O(m)$, because it involves computing two Euclidean distances for each point and adding it to one of two lists. Computation of cluster sizes is $O(1)$ while other metrics are $O(m)$. This makes the whole extra work for this to have complexity of $O(m)$.

There is also extra time required to make the prediction, however, the prediction time is constant. The prediction is made using "JPMML-Evaluator" library for Java programming language: the model is loaded from a PMML file (during the startup once) and then predictions are made. The model definition takes 6,09 MB of disk space.

4   Experimental Evaluation of Suggested Point Cloud Cut Algorithm

4.1 Performance Results

1000 frames have been randomly selected from the dataset and runtime benchmark was performed using two segmenting algorithms: with and without the cut. The benchmark is run by selecting the first point that does not yet belong to any cluster, performing segmentation starting from that point and repeating the processes until every point belongs to some cluster. Since some parts of the algorithms is common (noise reduction, search tree building etc.), only the segmentation itself is benchmarked. Tree node traversal count is also computed; however, this is always lower without random forest cuts since the points are never returned to the search tree.

Table 2. Algorithm performance comparison

Algorithm	Runtime, ms	Node traversals, M
Bounding box	17.3	2.5
Bounding box + Random Forest cut	54.9	4.4

Performance comparison is shown in Table 2. Random forest cut solution works about 3.2 times slower in this benchmark, however, it also had to make 1.8 times more node traversals, i.e., these traversals would be required anyway if bounding box algorithm was more accurate. Thus, it could be estimated that real performance difference is about 1.80 times. Therefore, extra actions add about 80% of extra work. All benchmarks have been performed using an AMD Ryzen 9 3900X CPU.

4.2 Accuracy Results

The following benchmark has been run for segmentation with and without the cuts: ground truth segmentation mask is read; the middle point is selected, and segmentation is performed starting from this point. Segments are obtained until either at least 90% of ground truth points belong to the segmented clusters or segmentation converges. The clusters are concatenated. This segmentation is repeated with all integer bounding box sizes $b = [1; 10]$ since the best b depends on the data.

Accuracy is measured by computing a cross-set intersection coefficient:

$$a = \frac{n(A \cap G)}{n(A)} \times \frac{n(A \cap G)}{n(G)} \tag{3}$$

Here A is the set of points selected during the segmentation, G – a set of ground truth points. This metric is similar to Dice similarity coefficient [32], however instead of computing the sum of the numerator and denominator, cross-set intersection coefficient computes their products. This metric is stricter because it gives high penalties for mistakes. Moreover, since Dice score computes sums, if one set is completely contained in another that is twice as large as the first one, Dice score will yield a value of 0,67 while cross-set intersection would be stricter with the value of 0,5, which is also more intuitive. This metric is very convenient to estimate the amount of manual work required to correct oversegmentation – value of 0,5 means that half of the output has to be removed.

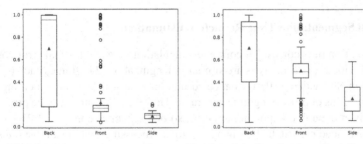

Fig. 3. First dataset accuracy comparison - without random forest cuts on the left, with random forest cuts on the right.

Average values of a have been computed for each frame sequence. The benchmark has been run of the full dataset of 220k depth images. Figure 3 shows the comparison of accuracy impact of recursive random forest decided cuts for the first dataset dissected by position of the camera relatively to the person. The bounding box algorithm works

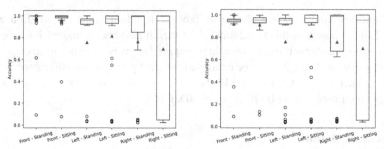

Fig. 4. Second dataset accuracy comparison – without random forest cuts on the left, with random forest cuts on the right.

quite poorly on this dataset because the people are in positions that are more complex, the scene is filled with more objects. The cuts done by the random forest improve the performance by a reasonable margin. Back side on average is processed with similar accuracy, however, the first quartile is much higher. Front and side camera views are processed significantly more accurately. While regular bounding box algorithm fails almost completely with accuracy averages of 21% and 9%, random forest cuts improve this to 50% and 25% respectively. Figure 4 shows a similar comparison for the second dataset. Bounding box approach worked much better on this dataset compared to the first dataset and there are less errors to correct – the clusters are less likely to be constructed in such a way that they hold points that they represent a distinct object. On the other hand, the difference between accuracies reflects the recall values from the classification report – accuracy is the same or lower by 1 percentage point with random forest cuts. In addition to that, since there was a small number of possible improvements to the segmentation by cutting clusters, there is few data with correct segmentation labels. Overall, these results improve accuracy where most needed and does not ruin it where it was already correct, so the algorithm at least partially solves the low-accuracy problem of segmentation.

4.3   Overall Segmentation Time Reduction Estimation

Total segmentation time consists of computer calculation time and manual error correction time. All videos in the datasets are similar in length, about 247 frames each (~220k frames total in 892 videos). Performance results have shown that implementing this solution adds 37 ms of processing time per frame. However, 12 frames can be processed in parallel given enough computational cores, so one sequence consists of 21 batches with 37 ms overhead per batch. This increases total processing time by almost 0,8 s per video sequence – about 11,5 min of added total processing time for full dataset.

Incorrectly labelled frame can be fixed by removing part of the segmentation output manually and this fix can be applied to multiple frames automatically. In static scenes it was estimated to be valid for ~50 frames. This means that segmenter output must be corrected 5 times per video sequence. Manual correction time depends on the size of the cluster to be removed. Clusters of the size of the human take ~5 s to unmark manually, larger clusters take linearly increasing time since larger area must be un-marked. Only two subsets of 210 videos each (front and side views from first dataset) are considered improved. For the subset of front camera data, the cross-section accuracy went from 21% to 50%, so the area to un-mark was reduced from ~4,8x human size to 2x human size saving ~14 s of manual work, which is ~4 h of saved work. Side camera segmentation (9% accuracy) is not worth correcting since full manual segmentation can be done in ~30 s, this would be reduced to ~15 s to correct the smaller error (25% accuracy) of suggested solution instead, so time savings would also be ~4 h. This means that total time savings for manual work is ~8 h which clearly outweighs 11,5 min of added processing time. These results show that segmentation saves a considerable amount of time if suggested algorithm is applied.

5 Discussion and Further Work

5.1 Theoretical and Practical Findings

This paper suggests an extension to bounding-box-based search algorithm to improve its accuracy in complex scenes and reduce the time required to segment the data. The following novelties have been introduced to improve the accuracy:

- Splitting the point cloud into segments using recursive 2-Means algorithm
- Introducing 8 metrics and predicting the correctness of the split based on those metrics
- Accepting or rejecting the split based on the prediction.

The random forest classifier validation accuracy of 95% has shown that the selected metrics carry information required for making the prediction, therefore the hypothesis that the quality of the cut can be evaluated based on these metrics holds true.

Splitting the point cloud segmentation output using the recursive 2-Means algorithm has shown large improvements in accuracy where it was low initially. Cross-set intersection coefficient increasing from sub-0,25 range to much higher values has shown that the original segmentation output contained multiple objects and removing the part of the output increased accuracy (if multiple objects would not have been captured, the accuracy could only decrease when removing parts of segmentation).

2-Means split could be considered the main factor that prevents gaining more accuracy. While metrics and the split acceptance show great accuracy, if the split is sub-optimal and does not increase the accuracy, it cannot be accepted, and accuracy remains low. This was not expected since K-Means usually showed good results in related research.

Despite the issues, the suggested algorithm is worth using because it saves a large amount of time for the human who segments the data if scenes are complex.

5.2 Further Work

The main issue of current solution is the quality of the split and should be investigated more thoroughly. One possibility is to apply a K-Means split with $K > 2$ and cut only a cluster that is furthest from the original point while other clusters would be combined into a single cluster. This would result in more fine-grained control of the splits with the cost of extra calculations required. Large objects would require more splits to be removed, but small objects could be missed by current rough 2-Means split.

Another approach could be applying a K-Means split with a large value of K and then each cluster could be evaluated separately. However, it would require better cut acceptance classifier accuracy to prevent dropping false-positive clusters – if K is 20, 95% accuracy would mean a 64% probability of misclassification of at least one cluster.

References

1. Zhang, Q., Fu, B., Ye, M., Yang, R.: Quality dynamic human body modeling using a single low-cost depth camera. In: Proceedings of the IEEE Conference on Computer Vision and Pattern Recognition, pp. 676–683 (2014)
2. Hu, T., et al.: Development and performance evaluation of a very low-cost UAV-LiDAR system for forestry applications. Remote Sens. **13**, 77 (2020)
3. Chen, L., Lin, Z., Wang, Z., Yang, Y., Cheng, M.: Spatial information guided convolution for real-time RGBD semantic segmentation. IEEE Trans. Image Process. **30**, 2313–2324 (2021)
4. Xu, C., et al.: SqueezeSegV3: spatially-adaptive convolution for efficient point-cloud segmentation. In: Vedaldi, A., Bischof, H., Brox, T., Frahm, J.M. (eds.) Computer Vision – ECCV 2020. Lecture Notes in Computer Science, vol. 12373, pp. 1–19. Springer, Cham (2020). https://doi.org/10.1007/978-3-030-58604-1_1
5. Chang, A., et al.: ShapeNet: an information-rich 3d model repository. arXiv preprint arXiv: 1512.03012 (2015)
6. Rusu, B., Cousins, S.: 3D is here: point cloud library (PCL). In: IEEE International Conference on Robotics and Automation (ICRA) (2011)
7. Ryselis, K., Blažauskas, T., Damaševičius, R., Maskeliūnas, R.: Computer-aided depth video stream masking framework for human body segmentation in depth sensor images. Sensors **22**(9), 3531 (2022)
8. Zhao, Y., Liu, Z., Yang, L., Cheng, H.: Combing RGB and depth map features for human activity recognition. In: Proceedings of the 2012 Asia Pacific Signal and Information Processing Association Annual Summit and Conference, pp. 1–4 (2012)
9. Bentley, J.: Multidimensional binary search trees used for associative searching. Commun. ACM **18**, 509–517 (1975)
10. Xie, Y., Tian, J., Zhu, X.: Linking points with labels in 3D: a review of point cloud semantic segmentation. IEEE Geosci. Remote Sens. Mag. **8**, 35–59 (2020)
11. Te, G., Hu, W., Zheng, A., Guo, Z.: RGCNN: regularized graph CNN for point cloud segmentation. In: Proceedings of the 26th ACM International Conference on Multimedia, pp. 746–754 (2018)
12. Zhang, J., Zhao, X., Chen, Z., Lu, Z.: A review of deep learning-based semantic segmentation for point cloud. IEEE Access **7**, 179118–179133 (2019)
13. Najdataei, H., Nikolakopoulos, Y., Gulisano, V., Papatriantafilou, M.: Continuous and parallel LiDAR point-cloud clustering. In: 2018 IEEE 38th International Conference on Distributed Computing Systems (ICDCS), pp. 671–684 (2018)
14. Zhang, L., Zhu, Z.: Unsupervised feature learning for point cloud understanding by contrasting and clustering using graph convolutional neural networks. In: 2019 International Conference on 3D Vision (3DV), pp. 395–404 (2019)
15. Zhu, W., Zhu, C., Zhang, Y.: Research on deep learning individual tree segmentation method coupling RetinaNet and point cloud clustering. IEEE Access **9**, 126625–126645 (2021)

16. Hackel, T., Savinov, N., Ladicky, L., Wegner, J., Schindler, K., Pollefeys, M.: Semantic3d. net: a new large-scale point cloud classification benchmark. arXiv preprint arXiv:1704.03847 (2017)
17. Uy, M., Pham, Q., Hua, B., Nguyen, T., Yeung, S.: Revisiting point cloud classification: a new benchmark dataset and classification model on real-world data. In: Proceedings of the IEEE/CVF International Conference on Computer Vision, pp. 1588–1597 (2019)
18. Ben-Shabat, Y., Lindenbaum, M., Fischer, A.: 3DmFV: three-dimensional point cloud classification in real-time using convolutional neural networks. IEEE Robot. Autom. Lett. 3, 3145–3152 (2018)
19. Nguyen, A., Cano, A., Edahiro, M., Kato, S.: Fast euclidean cluster extraction using GPUs. J. Robot. Mechatron. 32, 548–560 (2020)
20. Xu, D., Anguelov, D., Jain, A.: Pointfusion: deep sensor fusion for 3d bounding box estimation. In: Proceedings of the IEEE Conference on Computer Vision and Pattern Recognition, pp. 244–253 (2018)
21. Zhou, Y., Tuzel, O.: Voxelnet: End-to-end learning for point cloud based 3D object detection. In: Proceedings of the IEEE Conference on Computer Vision and Pattern Recognition, pp. 4490–4499 (2018)
22. Yang, B., Wang, J., Clark, R., Hu, Q., Wang, S., Markham, A., et al: Learning object bounding boxes for 3D instance segmentation on point clouds. Adv. Neural Inf. Process. Syst. 32 (2019)
23. Ali, W., Abdelkarim, S., Zidan, M., Zahran, M., Sallab, A.E.: YOLO3D: end-to-end real-time 3D oriented object bounding box detection from LiDAR point cloud. In: Leal-Taixé, L., Roth, S. (eds.) ECCV 2018. LNCS, vol. 11131, pp. 716–728. Springer, Cham (2019). https://doi.org/10.1007/978-3-030-11015-4_54
24. He, Ch., Zeng, H., Huang, J., Hua, X., Zhang, L.: Structure aware single-stage 3D object detection from point cloud. In: Proceedings of the IEEE/CVF Conference on Computer Vision and Pattern Recognition, pp. 11873–11882 (2020)
25. Li, B.: 3D fully convolutional network for vehicle detection in point cloud. In: 2017 IEEE/RSJ International Conference on Intelligent Robots and Systems (IROS), pp. 1513–1518 (2017)
26. Shi, W., Rajkumar, R.: Point-GNN: graph neural network for 3D object detection in a point cloud. In: Proceedings of the IEEE/CVF Conference on Computer Vision and Pattern Recognition, pp. 1711–1719 (2020)
27. Geiger, A., Lenz, P., Stiller, C., Urtasun, R.: Vision meets robotics: the KITTI dataset. Int. J. Robot. Res. 32, 1231–1237 (2013)
28. MacQueen, J.: Some methods for classification and analysis of multivariate observations. In: Proceedings of the Fifth Berkeley Symposium on Mathematical Statistics and Probability, pp. 281–297 (1967)
29. Saglam, A., Makineci, H, Baykan, O., Baykan, N.: Clustering-based plane refitting of nonplanar patches for voxel-based 3D point cloud segmentation using K-means clustering. Traitement Signal 37, 1019–1027 (2020)
30. Zhou, J., Fu, X., Zhou, J., Ye, H., Nguyen, H.: Automated segmentation of soybean plants from 3D point cloud using machine learning. Comput. Electron. Agric. 162, 143–153 (2019)
31. Chen, L., Lin, H., Li, Sh.: Depth image enhancement for Kinect using region growing and bilateral filter. In: Proceedings of the 21st International Conference on Pattern Recognition (ICPR2012), pp. 3070–3073 (2012)
32. Chinchor, N., Sundheim, B.: MUC-5 evaluation metrics (1993)

Automated System and Machine Learning Application in Economic Activity Monitoring and Nowcasting

Mantas Lukauskas[1]([✉]), Vaida Pilinkienė[2], Jurgita Bruneckienė[2], Alina Stundžienė[2], and Andrius Grybauskas[2]

[1] Faculty of Mathematics and Natural Sciences, Kaunas University of Technology, Kaunas, Lithuania
`mantas.lukauskas@ktu.lt`
[2] School of Economics and Business, Kaunas University of Technology, Kaunas, Lithuania
`{vaida.pilinkiene,jurgita.bruneckiene,alina.stundziene,`
`andrius.grybauskas}@ktu.lt`

Abstract. The amount of data is growing at an extraordinary rate each year. Nowadays, data is used in various fields. One of these areas is economics, which is significantly linked to data analysis. Policymakers, financial institutions, investors, businesses, and households make economic decisions in real-time. These decisions need to be taken even faster in various economic shocks, such as the financial crisis, COVID-19, or war. For this reason, it is important to have data in as frequent a range as possible, as only such data will reliably assess the economic situation. Therefore, automated systems are required to collect, transform, analyse, visualise, perform other operations, and interpret the results. This paper presents the concept of economic activity, classical and alternative indicators describing the economic activity, and describes the automated economic activity monitoring system. Due to the different economic structures and the different availability of data in different countries, these systems are not universal and can only be adapted to specific countries. The developed automated system uses working intelligence methods to predict the future values of indicators, perform clustering, classification of observations, or other tasks. The application's developed user interface allows users to use different data sources, analyses, visualisations, or results of machine learning methods without any programming knowledge.

Keywords: Economic activity · Nowcasting · Automated systems · Machine learning · Artificial intelligence · Clustering

1 Introduction

Every year, more and more data are collected and used for various purposes. In recent years, it has been observed that the amount of data stored each year is growing faster and faster. Currently, growth is not by a few percent but even by a hundred percent. For example, in 2010, the volume of data/information created, captured, copied, and consumed worldwide was two zettabytes, while in 2025, the projected amount of data is 181 zettabytes. This speed of data collection becomes a real challenge to obtain, process, store, and ultimately interpret. For this reason, automated systems that can collect, transform, analyse, and provide insights are critical to the success of data-driven decision-making. One of the areas where it is imperative to have reliable data and evaluate it properly is economics.

Novelty. Economic assessments are often made using annual data, and at best such assessments are made using monthly data. However, such use of data does not always reflect the exact situation as there are some delays in obtaining and analysing the data. Moreover, they are not considered in sudden changes. An example of this is the recent COVID pandemic or the war in Ukraine. The immediate impact of these events on the economy is significant in the light of these events and the sudden change in the situation. It is also worth noting that each country's economy and freely available data are different, so the assessment for each country may also be different. This makes it difficult to use automated evaluation solutions developed in other countries and requires developing a specific system that allows for the most accurate assessment of economic change. The development of such systems has only recently begun. Therefore, establishing such a system in Lithuania could contribute to a better economic assessment and increase the economy's growth rate. Given the economic differences in each country, it becomes impossible to reuse the systems used by others. Only the OECD currently has a similar partial system, but this system is based only on GDP projections[1]. Our system includes more modules: real estate, goods, and services prices, and satellite data. These data will allow a more accurate assessment of economic activity. Related to this is the unique methodology, adapted to the Lithuanian economic structure and economic entities, which is discussed in the following sections.

For this reason, this work aims to present the idea of monitoring, evaluating, and forecasting automated systems and present the basic principles of data acquisition, transformation, and their use in the developed system. The first part of this work discusses the concept of economic activity factors characterising economic activity. The work also presents an automated system and provides examples of data sources, its use, and its user interface visualization beta version.

2   The Concept of Economic Activity

Policymakers, financial institutions, investors, and households make decisions related to economics in real-time. Based on Eurostat information, economic activity occurs when resources such as capital goods, labour, manufacturing materials, or intermediary products are combined to produce specific goods or services. Therefore, economic activity can be understood as the process with the specific input of some resources and the output of the products, which can be not only goods but also services. Economic activity is a multi-faceted concept, so there is no single specific factor and indicator that characterises this concept. Following the analysis of economic activity, definitions usually combine

---

[1] OECD system: https://www.oecd.org/economy/weekly-tracker-of-gdp-growth.

several interrelated pillars: production, buying, selling, investment, and savings. The set of factors, which stimulate these pillars, and the interaction among these factors, are factors of economic activity. In addition to the economic activity of producing, supplying, or selling goods or services, any activity connected with the production, distribution, or consumption of goods or services is also economic activity. Therefore, economic activities at all levels of the society include any activity involving the exchange of money or goods or services. This understanding justifies why stocks of resources or capital create a flow of goods and services that people partially use to meet their unlimited needs. This process involves the production of goods and services and their distribution among the various members of the community. More broadly, all activities carried out in exchange for money or valuables are economic activities. The understanding of economic activity is usually related to changes in GDP or industrial production [1–4]. Nevertheless, in the COVID-19 environment, the concept of economic activity has been extended to cover a broader range of factors and indicators [5–7]. An example of this is data that was relatively rare or non-existent before the pandemic. For example, Google mobile data or satellite data [5, 8] was previously rare and can be included in assessing economic performance. This can also be assumed to be valid in the current and future war conditions.

It became essential to analyse the data as soon as possible (in real-time or close to real-time if possible) during war or after the onset of the pandemic. Moreover, an analysis is essential because the aim is to assess whether the public decisions taken are useful. For these reasons, the aim is to expand economic activity with high-frequency data such as weekly, daily, or, if possible, hourly [9–11]. No less important is the ability to apply artificial intelligence methods to analyse data, interpret it, and provide more accurate predictions also contribute to this [12] and well as process large amounts of data (big data). Global events, the large amounts of data available, their increasing frequency, and the emergence of new methods and tools for their analysis do not fundamentally change the concept of economic activity, but it is becoming much more dynamic. At the same time, the assessment of economic activity becomes even more informative than conventional analytical methods and data sources. As mentioned earlier, this is crucial for making timely and evidence-based economic decisions.

3 Factors Characterising Economic Activity and Classical and Alternative Indicators

3.1 The New Approach to Economic Activity Analysis

Following Hynes et al. [13] analysing economic activity in a broader systems perspective requires both innovations of economic tools and methodology and the repositioning of the field of economics concerning other critical fields such as the environment, society, and politics at the analytical and theoretical levels and through the integration of policies in practice. Moreover, the performance of traditional forecasting models might be suboptimal in this case, as some reliable econometric relationships in regular times may have broken down during this severe contraction, e.g., because of sudden behavioural changes or nonlinearities [14]. The challenges and requirements of scholars are to broaden the boundaries of economic research and encourage the use of more data. The use of systemic thinking and advanced technologies enables the expansion of economic research and helps in attempts to predict the future and answer the questions of how and why [15]. Next-generation systems analysis models must integrate better real-world dynamics such as social and behavioural heterogeneity [16] and dissect the most salient variables to forecast global economic activity, which should be monitored more closely to predict future shifts in global economic growth, as the latter plays a crucial role as a trigger of domestic economic development in the economy's dependent on external demand [17].

3.2 Factors of Economic Activity and Classical and Alternative Indicators

Existing measurements of economic activity vary significantly within the literature. The most natural approach has been to use the gross domestic product (GDP) and industrial production. However, such traditional measures started to become less popular nowadays (when, in a rapidly changing environment, timely knowledge of information becomes a critical factor in making decisions) as they are published with a significant delay. This makes them less valuable and invalid for addressing economic activities and conditions in real-time. As a result, the concept of economic activity, which is highly correlated with GDP [18] and accurately captures movements in the business cycle [19], has recently received special attention in real-time forecasting. Despite the increasing number of scientific papers [14, 20, 21] confirming the contribution of high-frequency information to providing an accurate nowcast of GDP growth. Studies [22, 23] still refute or require additional research. Mixed results and active discussion among scientists only confirm the relevance of the issue and its novelty.

Different researchers, using both the concept of economic activity and its methodological approach (e.g., Fenz and Stix [14], analysed per demand and supply component of GDP), the availability and availability and reliability of statistics, and considering technological and mathematical computational possibilities, distinguish various factors and indicators characterising economic activity. The most found in the scientific literature is the expression of economic activity through an index to state of the art. However, Burri and Kaufmann [24] proposed a daily fever curve (f-curve) for the health of the Swiss economy based on the publicly available financial market and news data, which provide a warning signal if the economic health takes a turn for the worse.

The most common indicators of economic activity cover the economy along distinct dimensions: private household consumption, production activity, labour market, domestic and international trade, prices, environment (usual pollution), transport, and logistics. However, there is a tendency for researchers to pay relatively less attention to the activity in the service sector compared to other economic activities (most likely due to the availability of data).

It is important to note that individual banks (e.g., the Deutsche Bundesbank (Germany)) are developing and continuously improving their Economic Activity Index (WAI); however, it is not an official forecast instrument.

Exceptionally, more attention among researchers [6, 25–27] receives one group of factors - prices. Following Cavallo [26], online retail markets change retail pricing behaviours, which can have long-lasting effects on inflation dynamics (for example Amazon effect). This distinct group of factors is even equated [6, 25] with economic activity or central in estimating global economic activity [28]. Commodity demand reflects the expectations of firms for future production, which causes it to lead global business conditions. This should prove useful in signalling and forecasting global economic activity [6].

Although there are attempts in the scientific literature to measure the activity of the economy in terms of the prices of individual goods, e.g., price of oil, steel prices, metals prices, copper prices, and iron ore prices [28] but price sets for certain different groups of goods and services are most used. For example, Cavallo et al. [27] used all subsectors of the U.N.'s COICOP classification system for food (and beverages), fuel, and electronics (a total of 267 items). Alquist et al. [25] used 22 commodities that refer to agricultural or food commodities (such as apple, bananas, beef, coffee, potatoes, sugar, Tabaco), five food oils (such as sun/safflower, rapeseed, palm), and 13 industrial commodities (such as aluminium, cement, copper, cotton, wool, rubber). Diaz et al. [6] used prices of energy, beverages, fats and oils, grains, other foods, raw materials, fertilisers, metals and minerals, and precious metals (a total of 47 commodities).

Researchers, faced with the possibility of using indicators for economic activity (for example, cannot keep track of sudden fluctuations [18] or obtaining (for example, do not have access), began to look for alternative or less directly related indicators of economic activity. These indicators are used to justify the reliability of the estimated economic activity indicator or are included directly in the calculation of the indicator itself. Fenz, and Stix [14] used some real-time indicators not directly included in the estimation of the weekly OeNB GDP indicator for plausibility analysis and concluded that these indicators and the OeNB's GDP indicator move almost completely parallel. Eraslan and Götz [20], and Eckert et al. [18] combined unconventional, high-frequency indicators with conventional, low-frequency macro-economic variables. The increasing use of these indicators among researchers indicates that these new indicators will play an important role in economic monitoring in the future. An auspicious data source refers to that card-based payments, as these provide an encompassing view of transactions in the economy [12].

Researchers [14, 18, 20, 28] use a variety of alternative indicators of economic activity, such as daily credit card transactions, energy consumption, traffic volumes, single-voyage ocean shipping freight rates (Kilian's index), mobility behaviour, short-term work, and financial market variables, mobility tracking, the Google mobility index, and internet search hits. The systematization of these indicators allows to divide them into several groups:

- Focus on the physical mobility of people, transport (personal, public, and commercial), smartphones, and other equipment. Mobility data, namely hu-man mobility and use of public transport, was treated by Chen et al. [29] as urban activity, which directly impacts business activity by shifting it from one place to another and economic activity. According to Lourenço and Rua [12] transportation activities are very sensitive to the business cycle. However, their use to track business-cycle fluctuations has been rather limited, although [22] the satisfactory performance of traffic data is already underlined.
- Focus on the frequency of financial transactions.
- Focus on energy consumption or night-time luminosity.
- Focus on the prices of products (usually raw materials), such as oil, metals, etc.

However, the use of alternative indicators also has some drawbacks. For example, following Eckert et al. [18], some indicators may be loosely related to economic activity as measured by statistical offices or cover only particular aspects of economic activity. In addition, the series often fluctuate enormously and are affected by factors unrelated to the business cycle. Furthermore, most of them have only a short history and are subject to irregular patterns of missing observations and publication lags.

The analysis of scientific articles and the perspectives of the discussions allow us to conclude that timely information is critically needed in modern economic conditions, and technological progress allows us to obtain it in real-time. The main challenge for economic recovery is methodological justification and reliability. The main idea of economic activity indicators is to represent reality without much of a delay (almost in "real-time"). However, they should also follow Fenz and Stix [14], not prone to behavioural changes and not biased by fiscal or monetary policy measures or other measures taken to contain the crisis.

Recently, weekly, or even daily indices for tracking real economic activity have been brought forward for various countries [19], such as Germany, the United States, Portugal, Switzerland, Taiwan, and Austria; however, the most significant focus on big open economies or Central or South Europe. There is a lack of attention to a small open economy in Central-Eastern European. After the E.U. accession (in 2004 and 2007), these countries had to transfer from centrally planned to market economies. According to Chen et al. [30], SOEs possess the following features: 1) their business cycle volatility is usually comparable in size to that seen in large wealthy economies, 2) their consumption is less volatile than output, and 3) their interest rates are procyclical (an increase in economic activity is usually associated with an increase in interest rates today and soon). Therefore, it can be argued that small economies need to focus on an open trade for small economies to thrive. Developing an economic activity index following the example of a small open economy country would be an interesting example. It would complement the weekly or even daily indices for tracking real economic activity methodology by integrating small open economy activity specifics.

4 Economic Activity Monitoring System

The handling and processing of large and often complex structured and unstructured data sets have long been a major challenge for macroeconomists. Macroeconomists had encountered the problem of big data analysis when studying phenomena in real-time long before the data began to be used in other areas. For example, in the 1930s, Burns and Mitchell studied business cycles at the NBER, when hundreds of different series were examined. New time series econometric methodologies have allowed the development of real-time forecasting methods and the analysis of economic data. The main idea of Nowcasting is to analyse and interpret the macroeconomic news flow by continuously updating the predictions of key variables, like real GDP growth, for each data release. In 2016, Liberty Street Economics began releasing the New York Fed Staff Nowcast, a weekly estimate of GDP growth using an automated platform for real-time monitoring of economic conditions. 2018 they go one step further by publishing the MATLAB code[2] for the nowcasting model.

Another example is the Now-Casting Economics[3] platform, a London-based consultancy that uses Giannone et al. [31] style methodology to forecast macro indicators. Based on these and other examples, the demand for such systems is considerable. However, the development of such systems has only recently begun. Therefore, establishing such a system in Lithuania could contribute to a better economic assessment and an increase in the economy's growth rate. Given the economic differences in each country, it becomes impossible to reuse the systems used by others. Only the OECD currently has a similar partial system, but this system is based only on GDP projections. Our system includes more used modules: real estate, goods, and services prices, and satellite data. These data will allow a more accurate assessment of economic activity. Related to this is the unique methodology we are developing, adapted to the Lithuanian economic structure and economic entities, which is discussed in the following sections.

4.1 Process of the Economic Activity Monitoring System

To properly extract, transform, store, and analyse large amounts of data, it is critical to have reliable systems capable of doing so. Unfortunately, in Lithuania, such systems do not exist and are usually focused only on one economic factor, or data are obtained at rare intervals; therefore, decision-making is associated with a corresponding delay. For this reason, there is a need for a system capable of extracting, transforming, and analysing data with a minor delay, which is presented in this work. The following is a description of the test system and an abstract description of the data and analytical methods used in this system.

In the first stage, indicators were identified that could describe Lithuania's economic activity and publicly available data sources database was developed and used in further research. Then, depending on the data's availability, structure, and reliability, the sources from which the data could be extracted were selected. The following steps are used in the system being developed during the research:

Stage 1. Data Extraction. Different tools are used to extract the data: Beautiful-Soup, Scrapy, Selenium, and Playwright, which are selected according to the structure of the data sources. It is important to note that all data is retrieved automatically according to a pre-set data acquisition schedule, which is very complicated and often impracticable in the usual way of data collection. Depending on the frequency of data updates, data is retrieved at different intervals. For example, traffic data is received every 15 min, weather data is received hourly, job posting information is received daily, and commodity price information is received weekly. With the data mentioned earlier retrieval tools, data is retrieved based on the structure of the data source and the usability of the source. Some of the data from the sources are extract-ed by visiting various web pages and collecting information from these pages, such as automated page visits. The price of a particular item is taken, and this price is passed on to further system elements. Also, when retrieving

---

[2] https://github.com/FRBNY-TimeSeriesAnalysis/Nowcasting.

[3] https://www.now-casting.com/home.

some data, the data sources have API capabilities when a request is sent from the system we are developing, and the received data is further used in the system and stored.

Prometheus and Grafana monitoring systems have been used in the initial studies to ensure that the data is obtained without problems, but that Prometheus and Grafana monitoring systems are used to ensure uninterrupted data acquisition and to ensure timely system uptime. In this case, Prometheus records errors on the server in the data collection step and in others, and Grafana visualizes this data. These systems are also used to monitor the servers themselves.

Stage 2. Data Transformation. The data extraction step yields pure data from the source, which is not always suitable for further analysis. According to the predefined scheme, each time the data is retrieved, the data is transformed, aggregated, and the derivative values removed. For example, when extracting price data for various goods, it is important to consider precisely how good the goods are and classify them into separate categories. In addition, it is important to remove all non-informative elements from unstructured text data. To ensure data quality, data is always received in the same format. Later, this data is transformed, and during this transformation, various data verification steps are performed: format, values, and others.

Stage 3. Data Storage. All collected and pre-processed data is stored in a database. The models used in the data analysis and visualisation process use the collected and processed data. The use of sensitive data is not foreseen in the initial phase of this system. Most of the data is from freely available sources. The data is stored in a PostgreSQL database that uses a firewall, and the port is open only when connected to the KTU network. Also, as mentioned earlier, a database and complete server monitoring system is used, so the server manager is notified in the event of an emergency. Also, database users are given only specific roles that limit the ability to do any damage to the data. The only sensitive data in this system can be the user logins and passwords that will be encrypted and not accessible to anyone.

Stage 4. Machine Learning Models Training/Retraining/Usage. The data stored in the databases are then used to train machine learning models. The system uses structured and unstructured data, so their analysis is also different. The machine learning model is used for several purposes. The primary task of this module is to perform the forecasting of economic indicators based on available data. Also, for example, having data on the prices of various goods, this module performs clustering of these prices to distinguish the main groups of goods (according to price increases and other factors). Another example of the use of this module is the analysis of textual data, depicting the most used topics in public space and the analysis of sentiments or topics. Depending on the task and the data application, machine learning methods are used in the application:

- Structured data classification. LightGBM, XGBoost, Logistic Regression, Neural Networks, and other classification methods are used to classify structured data.
- Structured data clustering. K-means, MIDE (clustering based on modified inversion density estimation), DBSCAN, and other clustering methods.

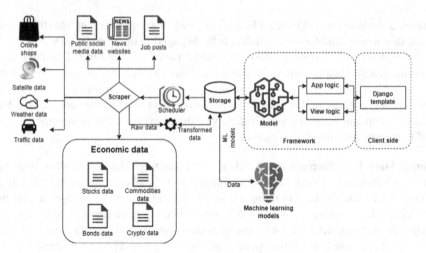

Fig. 1. Scheme of the automatic economic activity monitoring system

- Text data. BERT, DistilGPT2, GPT2, GPTNeo, and other models are used to classify unstructured text data, NER (Named Entity Recognition).
- Time series forecasting. Both one-dimensional and multidimensional forecasting methods are used to forecast time series. Simple linear regression, exponential smoothing, ARIMA methods, as well as recurrent neural network (RNN), long-short term memory neural network (LSTM), support vector machine (SVM), and other machine learning methods are used for prediction.

The resulting models are stored in the database described above. In addition, machine learning tasks are also used to create APIs (Application Programming Interfaces) to which requests for forecasting methods are directed. As a result, models are not retrained according to a pre-determined schedule but as needed so that these models can be retrained depending on the situation. However, due to some of the models' relatively long training time, the models cannot be updated too often. In assessing the accuracy of this machine learning module (the accuracy of the individual models) concerning the purpose of the system, the models must be able to make predictions as quickly as possible. At present, monthly data from the Department of Statistics are used in Lithuania. Therefore, our primary goal is to estimate and forecast economic activity based on higher frequency data. The primary goal is to evaluate the economy once a week while maintaining the same or improving the performance of the Department of Statistics. The exact accuracy of the individual models can only be assessed after complete system preparation and data collection. In this case, data on the Lithuanian economy have been collected for about six months.

Stage 5. User Interface. The obtained results are displayed in the user interface, where the obtained data can be analysed/interpreted without much difficulty and the results of machine learning methods. The following is the beta of the Automated Economic Activity Tracking System. Currently, only authorised users can access the user interface. The dashboard provides information on the latest data updates, the latest and all data in the database, and visualisations of different indicators are used to make economic decisions.

Fig. 2. Example of the beta version automatic economic activity monitoring dashboard user interface

5 Conclusion

The increasing amount of data makes it increasingly difficult to analyse this data each year. Therefore, economics is a particularly important area of data analysis. Furthermore, in the event of various economic shocks, such as the COVID-19 virus or catastrophe, economic data must be evaluated as soon as possible to make appropriate decisions.

At the beginning of this paper, information is provided on economic activity as it is described. Information on factors/indicators describing economic activity is also provided. The monitoring system of economic activity developed during the research is discussed further. The developed automatic economic activity monitoring system provides data collection, processing, storage, machine learning models, and visualisation necessary for effective economic monitoring. The main task of this system is to help economists evaluate economic activity and use artificial intelligence applications in the economy without any programming knowledge. This system allows data to be collected on a pre-arranged schedule and retrieved much more frequently than usual. The data processing process avoids complicated steps of different data cleaning, processing, and aggregation.

Acknowledgements. This project has received funding from European Regional Development Fund (project No 13.1.1-LMT-K-718–05-0012) under a grant agreement with the Research Council of Lithuania (LMTLT). Funded as European Union's measure in response to the Cov-19 pandemic.

References

1. Cooper, I., Priestley, R.: The world business cycle and expected returns. Rev. Finan. **17**, 1029–1064 (2013)
2. Baumeister, C., Hamilton, J.D.: Structural interpretation of vector autoregressions with incomplete identification: revisiting the role of oil supply and demand shocks. Am. Econ. Rev. **109**, 1873–1910 (2019)
3. Kilian, L.: Measuring global real economic activity: do recent critiques hold up to scrutiny? Econ. Lett. **178**, 106–110 (2019)
4. Herrera, A.M., Rangaraju, S.K.: The effect of oil supply shocks on US economic activity: what have we learned? J. Appl. Economet. **35**, 141–159 (2020)
5. Sampi Bravo, J.R.E., Jooste, C.: Nowcasting economic activity in times of COVID-19: an approximation from the Google community mobility report. World Bank policy research working paper (2020)
6. Diaz, E.M., Perez-Quiros, G.: GEA tracker: a daily indicator of global economic activity. J. Int. Money Financ. **115**, 102400 (2021)
7. Angelov, N., Waldenström, D.: The impact of covid-19 on economic activity: evidence from administrative tax registers (2021)
8. Bricongne, J.-C., Meunier, B., Pical, T.: Can satellite data on air pollution predict industrial production? (2021)
9. Orihuel, E., Sapena, J., Navarro-Ortiz, J.: An empirical algorithm for COVID-19 nowcasting and short-term forecast in Spain: a kinematic approach. Appl. Syst. Innov. **4**, 2 (2021)
10. Xin, M., Shalaby, A., Feng, S., Zhao, H.: Impacts of COVID-19 on urban rail transit ridership using the synthetic control method. Transp. Policy **111**, 1–16 (2021)
11. Li, B., Ma, L.: Migration, transportation infrastructure, and the spatial transmission of COVID-19 in China. J. Urban. Econ **15**, 103351 (2020)
12. Lourenço, N., Rua, A.: The daily economic indicator: tracking economic activity daily during the lockdown. Econ. Model. **100**, 105500 (2021)
13. Hynes, W., Lees, M., Müller, J.M.: Systemic thinking for policy making. OECD (2020)
14. Fenz, G., Stix, H.: Monitoring the economy in real time with the weekly OeNB GDP indicator: background, experience and outlook. Monetary Policy Econ. 17–40 (2021)
15. Bruneckiene, J., Jucevicius, R., Zykiene, I., Rapsikevicius, J., Lukauskas, M.: Quantum theory and artificial intelligence in the analysis of the development of socio-economic systems: theoretical insights. In: Developing Countries and Technology Inclusion in the 21st Century Information Society, pp. 22–38. IGI Global (2021)
16. Kirman, A., et al.: Methodologies and tools for integrated systems modelling (2020)
17. Stolbov, M., Shchepeleva, M.: Modeling global real economic activity: evidence from variable selection across quantiles. J. Econ. Asymmetries **25**, e00238 (2022)
18. Eckert, F., Kronenberg, P., Mikosch, H., Neuwirth, S.: Tracking economic activity with alternative high-frequency data. KOF Working Papers 488 (2020)
19. Wegmüller, P., Glocker, C., Guggia, V.: Weekly economic activity: measurement and informational content. Int. J. Forecast. (2021)
20. Eraslan, S., Götz, T.: An unconventional weekly economic activity index for Germany. Econ. Lett. **204**, 109881 (2021)
21. Lewis, D.J., Mertens, K., Stock, J.H., Trivedi, M.: Measuring real activity using a weekly economic index 1. J. Appl. Econ. **37**(4), 667–687 (2021)
22. Fornaro, P., Luomaranta, H.: Nowcasting Finnish real economic activity: a machine learning approach. Empirical Econ. **58**(1), 55–71 (2019). https://doi.org/10.1007/s00181-019-01809-y
23. Banbura, M., Giannone, D., Modugno, M., Reichlin, L.: Nowcasting and the real-time data flow. In: Elliott, G. Timmermann, A. (eds.) Handbook of Economic Forecasting, 2, Elsevier, North Holland (2013)

24. Burri, M., Kaufmann, D.: A daily fever curve for the Swiss economy. Swiss J. Econ. Stat. **156**(1), 1–11 (2020). https://doi.org/10.1186/s41937-020-00051-z
25. Alquist, R., Bhattarai, S., Coibion, O.: Commodity-price comovement and global economic activity. J. Monet. Econ. **112**, 41–56 (2020)
26. Cavallo, A.: More Amazon effects: online competition and pricing behaviors. Nat. Bur. Econ. Res. (2018)
27. Cavallo, A., Diewert, W.E., Feenstra, R.C., Inklaar, R., Timmer, M.P.: Using online prices for measuring real consumption across countries. In: AEA Papers and Proceedings, pp. 483–487 (2018)
28. Kilian, L., Zhou, X.: Modeling fluctuations in the global demand for commodities. J. Int. Money Financ. **88**, 54–78 (2018)
29. Chen, K.-P., Yang, J.-C., Yang, T.-T.: JUE Insight: demand for transportation and spatial pattern of economic activity during the pandemic. J. Urban Econ. **127**, 103426 (2022)
30. Chen, K.-J., Chu, A.C., Lai, C.-C.: Home production and small open economy business cycles. J. Econ. Dyn. Control **95**, 110–135 (2018)
31. Giannone, D., Reichlin, L., Small, D.: Nowcasting: the real-time informational content of macroeconomic data. J. Monet. Econ. **55**, 665–676 (2008)

Business Intelligence for Information and Software Systems - Special Session on Intelligent Methods for Data Analysis and Computer Aided Software Engineering

Artificial Intelligence Solutions Towards to BIM6D: Sustainability and Energy Efficiency

Justas Kardoka[1]([envelope]), Agne Paulauskaite-Taraseviciene[1], and Darius Pupeikis[2]

[1] Faculty of Informatics, Kaunas University of Technology, Studentu 50, Kaunas, Lithuania
{justas.kardoka,agne.paulauskaite-taraseviciene}@ktu.lt
[2] Faculty of Civil Engineering and Architecture, Kaunas University of Technology, Studentu 48, Kaunas, Lithuania
darius.pupeikis@ktu.lt

Abstract. BIM6D is an aspect of building information modeling (BIM) that allows for a detailed analysis of a building's energy performance in order to improve energy and light efficiency, which in turn leads to a more sustainable building utilization. Predictions of a building's energy consumption can have added value in different aspects and for different building actors, be they engineers, architects or the building users themselves. The objective for this study is to explore mathematical and artificial intelligent approaches for predicting thermal energy consumption in buildings and to examine its use for BIM6D. The dataset used in the research includes several years of hourly thermal energy consumption collected in one block of Kaunas city. Experiments have been carried out using different forecasting methods. In terms of prediction accuracy, it is worth highlighting the Extra Trees with $MAE < 3.5$ kWh and Support vector regression (SVR) with $MAE \leq 2.63$ kWh. However, Extra Trees seems to be the best in terms of MAPE (38.65%). Although prediction time is not the most critical parameter, it should be noted, that Extra Trees, SVR and auto-regressive models were found to be the most time-consuming (from 2 to 4 min) to linear models (<1 s) and extreme gradient boosting (~3 s) and that these results may influence the selection of a model for real-life operation.

Keywords: BIM · Forecasting · Energy · Sustainability · Artificial intelligence

1 Introduction

Building information modeling (BIM) is an intelligent software modeling process of creating and managing information for a construction project throughout the entire life cycle of a building or infrastructure [1]. This process uses appropriate technologies to create a coordinated digital description of every aspect of the project. BIM can be viewed as an information platform to generate and distribute relevant data among stakeholders [2]. A comprehensive digital description consists of 3D models and various structured data. BIM, as a methodology, has many dimensions beyond the 3D modeling of a building, including, but not limited to, time (4D), costs (5D) and sustainability (6D) [3]. BIM6D – the aspect of BIM that allows for a detailed analysis of the energy

A. Lopata et al. (Eds.): ICIST 2022, CCIS 1665, pp. 117–135, 2022.
https://doi.org/10.1007/978-3-031-16302-9_9

performance of a building, targeting energy and light efficiency improvements, which in turn leads to a better quality of use and comfort of a sustainable building. Energy consumption forecasts can be useful for engineers, since buildings need to adhere to stricter minimum energy efficiency standards, especially if integrated into the Industry Foundation Classes (IFC)-based BIM models or alongside them. Greenhouse gases emitted by buildings account for approximately 20% of total greenhouse gases emissions [4]. Furthermore, the rate of development of countries is growing steadily, constantly increasing the demand for energy [5]. Energy consumption forecasting for buildings is of great importance for energy efficiency and sustainability research, and accurate energy prediction models have been shown to be of significant importance for building planning and energy optimization [6]. The prediction of thermal energy consumption using machine learning methods is one of the most intensively discussed scientific areas. This is because BEPS - based (Building Energy Performance Simulation), also called White-box methods) methods are not able to accurately estimate the thermal performance of buildings and therefore many boundary conditions are adopted, which negatively affects the final result (usually energy consumption). ML prediction models (called Black-box models) also have shortcomings that need to be investigated:

- The models can only be replicated and applied to buildings of similar type and characteristic;
- There are still many questions from researchers as to which ML approach is the most appropriate for the prediction of time series based thermal energy data;
- How and with which methods to predict thermal energy considering short (up to 48 h) and long (>48 h) time periods.

Analyses and forecasts of energy consumption are therefore crucial for achieving sustainability objectives.

Several studies propose methods for predicting energy consumption based on machine learning algorithms or other artificial intelligence approaches [7–18]. One of the most common models used are linear models. Kim et al. [13] found that a linear regression model and an ANN with the LM-BP algorithm were similarly accurate in terms of CVRMSE (coefficient of variation of the root mean square error) in predicting electricity consumption in campus buildings on non-working days, although the ANN was more stable and accurate on working days. After a series of experiments, it was determined that both, the linear regression, and the ANN model with the LM-BP algorithm met the requirements for the prediction of the long-term and real-time hourly electricity consumption of a building. Linear regression models can be extended to support more than one independent variable [14, 19]. Abdullah and Leong [14] used multiple linear regression for predicting Malaysia's energy consumption using the countries' GDP, population and a tourism feature, achieving a R^2 score of 0.932. Among other methods used to predict the consumption of energy, the radial basis function (RBF) can be utilized [15]. Olanrewaju et al. [15] used RBF networks for calculating the energy consumption of South Africa's industrial sector between the years 1993 and 2000, concluding that the model performed better than a multi-layer perceptron (MLP) model. However, the use of MLP models gives good results for the prediction of energy consumption at different time intervals [16, 17] or even impute missing values [20]. Jang et al. [16] used a MLP model for forecasting the thermal energy consumption of buildings, finding that when used in combination with the Random forest model for feature selection, MLP models can predict with a high accuracy. In the author's study, the model achieved a R^2 score of 0.9877. Khan et al. [17] used a MLP model as part of a hybrid model alongside Catboost and XGBoost as a final step for the prediction of energy consumption of buildings with a mean average percentage error (MAPE) of 2.78% on weekdays and 2.79% for weekends. However deep ANN architectures could be more promising solutions for predicting consumers' demands and energy generations than the shallowed ANN models [21, 22].

Most of these studies seek to identify factors that influence energy demand in buildings, such as socio-demographic and economic [9, 14, 15, 17] appliance and equipment [4], climatic [4, 10, 13, 17, 18] or geographical factors [18].

According to Motalebi et al. [23], BIM-6D, as a digital information model, simulates the buildings' actual energy behavior. Forecasts and simulations can aid engineers and analysts in the task of better understanding a buildings' energy model. By studying a hospital's energy model, Montiel-Santiago et al. [1] found that by modifying a buildings energy model to use more energy efficient solutions, most notably - better utilization of daylight as a renewable energy source, energy savings of up to 47% can be achieved according to performed simulations, turning buildings into more sustainable spaces. Pereira et al. [24] states that integrating BIM with building's energy models could improve the energy efficiency levels in buildings. Bracht et al. [25] proposed a method to link energy consumption predictions directly with a buildings' BIM model, showcasing the possibilities for AI-assisted energy standards labelling for buildings.

2 Methodology

2.1 Data Analysis and Feature Engineering

Thermal energy consumption data for one building in Kaunas, Lithuania was used for this study. The consumed power was measured hourly in kilowatt-hours (kWh), the data encompasses a 2-year period from 2019-02 to 2021-10. The data has been resampled to be exactly hourly. Since the data consists of a single feature, feature engineering was applied to the dataset to generate a wider range of features based on the date-time indexes that could prove useful to the machine learning models. The following Table 1 provides an overview of the engineered features and their description.

Since energy consumption can be influenced by meteorological data, additional meteorological features could prove useful. Alongside the thermal power consumption data, meteorological data was also used and combined with the thermal consumption data into a unified dataset. The meteorological data was obtained from the Iowa Environmental Mesonet (IEM), administered by the Department of Agronomy of Iowa State University [26]. The IEM maintains an automated archive of weather observations from various airports based on their scheduled METAR reports [26]. In this study, meteorological data from the Kaunas Airport was used, as its proximity is closest to the building for which the thermal energy data was collected for. The meteorological data has also been resampled to be hourly and the wind direction feature has been engineered be a set of binary features, each indicating whether if the wind is blowing to a certain direction,

Table 1. Engineered features for the dataset that are based on the date-time index

Name	Description
year	Current year
is_season	Is the current date during the heating season (mid-October to mid-April)
is_evening	Is the current hour in the evening time of day
is_morning	Is the current hour in the morning time of day
is_night	Is the current hour in the night time of day

e.g., to the east. The following Table 2 provides an overview of the features from the meteorological data used.

Table 2. Meteorological features for the data obtained from IEM

Name	Description
temperature_F	Current temperature in degrees Fahrenheit
dew_point_F	Current dew point temperature in degrees Fahrenheit
humidity_%	Current relative humidity percent
wind_speed_kn	Current wind speed in knots
pressure_in	Current pressure in inches
app_temp_F	Current apparent temperature in degrees Fahrenheit
wind_to_north	Whether if the wind is blowing to the north
wind_to_south	Whether if the wind is blowing to the south
wind_to_west	Whether if the wind is blowing to the west

It is reasonable to calculate correlation coefficients r, those provide the strength of the linear relationship between two features. Pearson correlation coefficients values vary between -1 and 1, whereas if $r = 0$, then the variables have no relation; the closer the coefficient is to $+1$ or -1, the stronger the relationship [12, 27]. Sign indicates if the relationship is positive or negative, for example if $r = 1$, then two features have perfect positive relation:

$$r = \frac{\sum (x_i - \underline{x})(y_i - \underline{y})}{\sqrt{\sum (x_i - \underline{x})^2 \sum (y_i - \underline{y})^2}} \tag{1}$$

where value $x_i - x$ variable samples, $y_i - y$ variables sample, $\underline{x}$ - mean of values in x variable, $\underline{y}$ - mean of values in y variable.

The coefficient was calculated for all feature pairs in the dataset (including the meteorological data) excluding non-existing values. The results were visualized with a matrix of all the Pearson's correlation coefficients between features (Fig. 1).

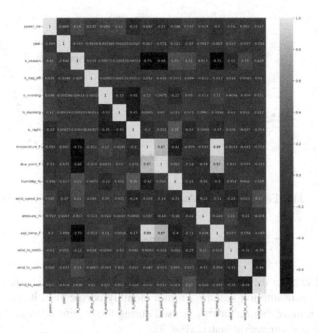

Fig. 1. Pearson's correlation coefficient matrix plot

Analyzing the target feature, it can be observed that on average, less thermal energy is used during the night hours of the day (Fig. 2).

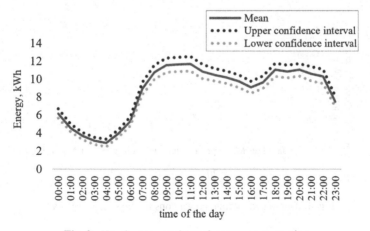

Fig. 2. Hourly average thermal energy consumption

Although there seems to be a visible daily seasonality, the variation in the average energy consumption is not high. It can be observed that although less thermal energy is used during the night hours, it is not significant.

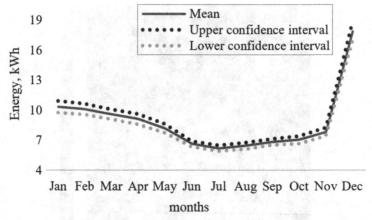

Fig. 3. Monthly average thermal power consumption

This could explain the slight correlation that the binary night feature has with the thermal energy consumption feature. From a monthly perspective, it can be observed that on average, more thermal energy is used during the heating season, though this is not reflected in the correlation matrix (Fig. 3).

Taking a sum of all the thermal energy consumption for every month of the year through the entire length of the data, it can be observed that during most years, thermal energy consumption follows the same pattern of a gradual decrease from the start of the year to August, and from then the thermal energy consumption starts a gradual increase until the end of the year (Fig. 4).

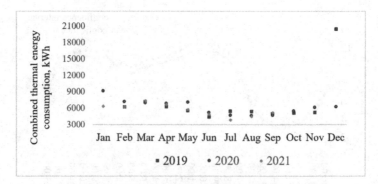

Fig. 4. Combined thermal power consumption for every year

Regarding the seasonality of the data, a seasonal decomposition was performed and based on its results, a daily seasonality can be observed. In later experiments, additional features will be added to the dataset to address the seasonality of the data (Fig. 5).

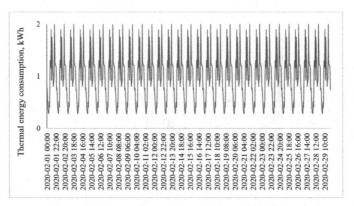

Fig. 5. A seasonal component of a multiplicative seasonal decomposition plot for the thermal power consumption feature

From the same seasonal decomposition plot, the trend component can be observed in Fig. 6. There does not seem to be a significant trend in the time-series. Regarding the target variable's relationship with its lag values, auto-correlation (ACF) and partial auto-correlation (PACF) plots were drawn (Fig. 7).

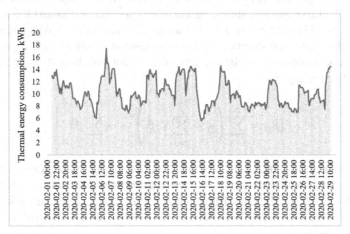

Fig. 6. A trend component of a multiplicative seasonal decomposition plot for the thermal power consumption feature

Drawing conclusions from the plot, the first 2 lag values seem to be the most significant. Judging from the plot, stationarity of the data can be assumed. This assumption was confirmed by performing an augmented Dickey-Fuller test, which can be used for determining the stationarity of a time-series [28]. The test yielded a p-value of $2.544897617122835 \times 10^{-8}$, rejecting the null hypothesis. Since the data is likely to be stationary, no differencing was performed.

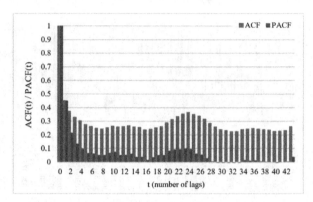

Fig. 7. Autocorrelation and partial autocorrelation for the thermal energy consumption feature

2.2 Machine-Learning Models

11 different machine learning models were used in this study. Among them is Linear regression (LR), Ridge, Lasso, Lars, Lasso-Lars, Elastic net, XGBoost, Extra trees, Support-vector regression (SVR), Multi-layer perceptron (MLP) and SARIMAX. Ridge regression [29], Least absolute shrinkage and selection operator (Lasso) [30], least angle regression (Lars) [31] and Elastic net [32] are broadly used in fields with large datasets [33–37]. Ridge regression differs from linear regression by introducing a penalty that shrinks the coefficients of correlated predictors, but not vanishing them entirely [38]. Ridge is defined in Eq. (2).

$$f(\beta_j) = \sum_{i=1}^{n} \left(y_i - \sum_{j=1}^{p} X_{ij}\beta_j \right)^2 + \lambda \sum_{j=1}^{p} \beta_j^2 \tag{2}$$

where X is a matrix with p variables and n samples, y is the response, whereas β are the regression coefficients and λ is a non-negative tuning parameter, which can be determined with cross validation. Ridge regression introduces a regularization penalty that minimizes the regression coefficients as $\lambda \to \infty$. Since β is squared, coefficients cannot be minimized to 0.

Lasso, defined in Eq. (3), can improve the accuracy of linear regression models [39] and is often used for variable selection [40].

$$f(\beta_j) = \sum_{i=1}^{n} \left(y_i - \sum_{j=1}^{p} X_{ij}\beta_j \right)^2 + \lambda \sum_{j=1}^{p} |\beta_j| \tag{3}$$

Due to the nature of the constraint, Lasso can minimize the size of coefficients to zero.

Lars can be viewed as a more computationally efficient algorithm that analytically selects the step size for the variables forming the model [41], whereas the Lasso-Lars algorithm used is a scikit-learn modification of the Lasso algorithm that implements Lasso using LARS, yielding a piecewise linear function [42].

Elastic net is an algorithm that bridges the gap between the regularization seen in Ridge and in Lasso by providing a combination of L_1 and L_2-norm penalization [37]. Elastic net is defined in Eq. (4).

$$f(\beta_j) = \frac{\sum_{i=1}^{n} \left(y_i - \sum_{j=1}^{p} X_{ij}\beta_j \right)^2}{2n} + \lambda \left(\frac{1-\alpha}{2} \sum_{j=1}^{p} \beta_j^2 + \alpha \sum_{j=1}^{p} |\beta_j| \right) \qquad (4)$$

where α is the mixing parameter between the different penalties seen in Ridge and Lasso.

XGBoost is an open-source, end-to-end tree-boosting system, widely used by data-scientists to achieve state-of-the-art results on many machine learning tasks [43]. XGBoost has the advantage of being faster and more scalable than most other solutions, due to it being heavily optimized for both multi-core, GPU-enabled and low-memory environments [43].

Extremely randomized trees (Extra trees) [44] is a tree-based ensemble method that can be used for regression tasks with large datasets [45]. It was proposed as a more computationally efficient and randomized extension of the random forest algorithm [46].

Support vector regression (SVR) is often used for the prediction of energy consumption [6, 22]. It is a non-linear regression algorithm that utilizes kernels for mapping the original data into a higher dimensional feature space before solving the machine learning problem of convex optimization [10].

Multi-layer perceptron (MLP) is a neural network that uses multiple interconnected layers connected in a feed-forward way, using specialized features for the analysis and prediction of variables that have nonlinear relationships [16].

Seasonal Autoregressive Integrated Moving Average with Exogenous Variables (SARIMAX) is a model that is often used for the prediction of energy consumption [11, 47–49]. SARIMAX differs from a ARIMA model by utilizing a seasonal component and exogenous variables [50]. The parameters for the SARIMAX model were set according to the ACF and PACF plot mentioned above. For a benchmark, two naive models were used. The naïve models predict one value for the entirety of the prediction - the last and average value respectively. The expected result is that the most robust models would outperform these naïve models and perform at least reasonably (20–50%) [51] according to the MAPE error metric.

2.3 Accuracy Evaluation Metrics

The models' results have been evaluated using 5 different metrics. Among them is mean absolute error (MAE), mean absolute percentage error (MAPE) and root-mean-square error (RMSE), defined using Eqs. (5), (6) and (7), respectively.

$$MAE = \frac{\sum\limits_{t=1}^{n} |A_t - F_t|}{n} \tag{5}$$

$$MAPE = \frac{100\%}{n} \sum\limits_{t=1}^{n} \left| \frac{A_t - F_t}{A_t} \right| \tag{6}$$

$$RMSE = \sqrt{\frac{\sum\limits_{t=1}^{n} (A_t - F_t)^2}{n}} \tag{7}$$

where A_t and F_t are the true and prediction values, respectively, and n is the amount of data used in the evaluation.

Additionally, the models were evaluated by the time to fit the model (t_1) and time to predict using the model (t_2) in microseconds. t_1 and t_2 were calculated by finding the difference between the time before after the methods for fitting and predicting using the model, respectively. Though the last 2 metrics are not used to measure the quality of the prediction, they are used to measure the practicality of a method, especially if it would be integrated into a system that it would risk slowing down due to lengthy fitting or prediction time intervals. The coefficient of determination (R^2) was also calculated, but not included due to marginal results, and almost all the methods tested had negative or zero values for R^2.

3   Predictions of Energy Consumption in Buildings

3.1   Overview of the Dataset

A dataset was created from the acquired thermal energy consumption data and the meteorological data mentioned in the previous sections. The time-series dataset was split into 5 train/test samples for further cross-validation. The percentage of the split for train/test samples is 85% for the train data and 15% for the test data. Overall, the test sample consists of around 2 months of hourly data. Cross validation was performed for each model, selecting the best set of hyperparameters.

The dataset was prepared in different variations by modifying its structure or adding additional features. Firstly, a dataset without any modifications was prepared. The second dataset variation had 24 additional lag values for the target feature. 24 lag values were added due to the daily seasonality observed in the seasonal decomposition plot. The next dataset variation did not contain the lowest-scoring features according to the Pearson's correlation coefficient. A dataset variation with added Fourier terms was also prepared. Fourier term features can represent periodic seasonality [52]. A log-transformed dataset variation with 24 added lag values was also prepared. Logarithmic transformation can normalize the distribution of the data. Lastly, a dataset without the added weather attributes, but with the added 24 lag values mentioned earlier was prepared. This last dataset variation consists only of the target feature and the features engineered from the date-time indexes.

3.2 Experimental Results

Predictions were performed on the different variations of the dataset. All the experiments were implemented in Python and run on a computer with a 4-core, 2.2 GHz Intel Xeon CPU and 16 GB of DDR4 RAM. A GPU was not utilized due to not being supported by the scikit-learn Python library (Table 3).

Table 3. Metrics of predictions using an unmodified dataset

Method	*MAE*	*RMSE*	*MAPE, %*	t_1	t_2
Naive (last)	4.38	5.43	49.20	2.77E+00	5.14E+01
Naive (avg)	4.44	5.48	49.33	1.60E+00	2.41E+02
LR	2.71	4.24	49.36	4.73E+04	5.87E+02
Ridge	2.71	4.24	49.31	4.26E+05	7.53E+02
Lasso	2.74	4.22	43.35	5.89E+05	4.80E+02
Lars	2.71	4.24	48.97	2.43E+05	3.89E+02
Lasso-Lars	2.71	4.24	49.36	2.48E+05	3.54E+02
Elastic net	2.71	4.24	48.75	4.97E+05	3.48E+02
XGBoost	2.99	4.46	41.39	3.00E+06	1.01E+04
Extra trees	2.79	**4.19**	**39.11**	1.58E+08	1.97E+05
SVR	**2.52**	4.24	44.95	2.64E+08	2.46E+06
MLP	3.61	4.94	48.55	6.45E+06	4.79E+03
SARIMAX	3.97	5.63	82.46	2.06E+08	3.62E+03

Using an unmodified dataset, it can be observed Extra trees model performs best according to MAPE and RMSE, although the lowest MAE (2.52 kWh) is achieved by the Support-vector regression model (Table 4).

Table 4. Metrics of predictions using a dataset with 24 lag features

Method	*MAE*	*RMSE*	*MAPE, %*	t_1	t_2
Naive (last)	4.38	5.43	49.20	3.78E+00	6.68E+01
Naive (avg)	4.44	5.48	49.33	3.02E+01	2.53E+02
LR	2.71	4.24	49.36	2.29E+04	5.98E+02
Ridge	2.71	4.24	49.31	2.49E+05	8.00E+02
Lasso	2.74	**4.22**	43.35	4.00E+05	4.75E+02
Lars	2.71	4.24	48.97	2.86E+05	3.99E+02

(*continued*)

Table 4. (*continued*)

Method	MAE	RMSE	MAPE, %	t_1	t_2
Lasso-Lars	2.71	4.24	49.36	2.47E+05	3.71E+02
Elastic net	2.71	4.24	48.75	6.53E+05	3.30E+02
XGBoost	2.99	4.46	41.39	3.05E+06	3.53E+04
Extra trees	2.87	4.25	**40.08**	1.35E+08	3.07E+04
SVR	**2.52**	4.24	44.95	2.69E+08	2.53E+06
MLP	3.61	4.94	48.55	6.70E+06	4.87E+03
SARIMAX	3.97	5.63	82.46	2.09E+08	3.65E+03

It can be observed that adding lag values to a dataset does not significantly improve the quality of the predictions, although some minor improvement can be seen regarding the MAPE metric (Table 5).

Table 5. Metrics of predictions using a dataset with 24 lag features and without the least significant features according to the Pearson's correlation coefficient

Method	MAE	RMSE	MAPE, %	t_1	t_2
Naive (last)	4.38	5.43	49.20	3.51E+00	5.74E+01
Naive (avg)	4.44	5.48	49.33	1.96E+01	2.88E+02
LR	2.75	4.29	43.01	2.75E+04	5.34E+02
Ridge	2.75	4.29	43.00	2.45E+05	7.26E+02
Lasso	2.90	4.34	43.16	3.59E+05	3.82E+02
Lars	2.75	4.29	42.97	1.75E+05	3.14E+02
Lasso-Lars	2.75	4.29	42.97	1.62E+05	3.35E+02
Elastic net	2.76	4.29	42.99	4.54E+05	2.91E+02
XGBoost	3.02	4.52	44.26	2.68E+06	9.70E+03
Extra trees	2.89	**4.21**	**40.34**	1.18E+08	1.76E+05
SVR	**2.60**	4.31	44.37	2.17E+08	3.02E+06
MLP	3.32	4.84	49.84	5.33E+06	4.79E+03
SARIMAX	3.97	5.74	62.20	1.63E+08	3.50E+03

Removing some of the least significant features does not offer a significant improvement to the quality of the predictions, although the algorithms do take a shorter time to finish, hence improving the time-based metrics (Table 6).

Fourier terms have not improved the quality of the predictions. The SARIMAX model, which could have benefited from the seasonal features, has made worse predictions from the addition of the Fourier term features (Table 7).

Table 6. Metrics of predictions using a dataset with Fourier terms

Method	MAE	RMSE	MAPE, %	t_1	t_2
Naive (last)	5.45	6.32	51.90	4.05E+00	5.71E+01
Naive (avg)	4.43	5.47	49.30	1.46E+00	2.64E+02
LR	3.20	4.84	279.47	1.05E+04	5.08E+02
Ridge	3.19	4.83	392.96	2.21E+05	6.59E+02
Lasso	2.69	4.32	45.92	3.84E+05	3.62E+02
Lars	2.69	4.33	46.57	1.43E+05	2.86E+02
Lasso-Lars	2.69	4.33	46.57	1.57E+05	2.51E+02
Elastic net	2.74	**4.31**	**43.13**	3.99E+05	2.42E+02
XGBoost	3.20	4.81	82.54	1.76E+06	9.46E+03
Extra trees	3.47	4.62	44.84	1.04E+08	6.15E+04
SVR	**2.63**	4.33	43.86	9.33E+07	2.19E+06
MLP	3.58	4.93	48.60	6.14E+06	1.26E+04
SARIMAX	4.06	5.61	149.86	1.27E+08	4.72E+03

Table 7. Predictions using a log-transformed dataset with 24 lag values

Method	MAE	RMSE	MAPE, %	t_1	t_2
Naive (last)	3.64	5.76	110.45	3.09E+00	5.89E+01
Naive (avg)	4.44	5.48	49.35	1.59E+00	2.49E+02
LR	3.88	5.41	367.74	2.14E+04	6.15E+02
Ridge	3.88	5.41	347.52	3.01E+05	7.90E+02
Lasso	3.64	5.18	845.10	4.89E+05	4.57E+02
Lars	3.86	5.40	504.07	2.63E+05	3.71E+02
Lasso-Lars	3.88	5.41	367.74	2.30E+05	3.82E+02
Elastic net	3.85	5.39	372.78	5.21E+05	3.70E+02
XGBoost	3.02	4.51	42.70	3.08E+06	1.08E+04
Extra trees	2.80	**4.19**	**38.65**	2.13E+08	2.37E+05
SVR	**2.48**	4.34	93.39	2.43E+08	2.47E+06
MLP	3.38	4.86	49.36	5.99E+06	5.37E+03
SARIMAX	5.13	6.59	327.98	1.91E+08	3.62E+03

Logarithmic transformation of data has not improved the quality of the predictions. It can be observed that models like Extra trees performs on a similar level despite the modifications to the dataset (Table 8).

Table 8. Predictions on a dataset with 24 lag values and without the weather features

Method	MAE	RMSE	MAPE, %	t_1	t_2
Naive (last)	4.38	5.43	49.20	3.30E+00	4.81E+01
Naive (avg)	4.44	5.48	49.33	1.61E+00	2.85E+02
LR	2.72	4.24	48.21	1.59E+04	5.10E+02
Ridge	2.72	4.24	48.18	2.62E+05	7.15E+02
Lasso	2.73	**4.22**	44.29	3.36E+05	3.82E+02
Lars	2.72	4.24	48.21	2.06E+05	3.10E+02
Lasso-Lars	2.72	4.24	48.21	1.58E+05	3.52E+02
Elastic net	2.72	4.24	47.49	3.96E+05	3.10E+02
XGBoost	3.21	4.59	42.17	2.83E+06	3.57E+04
Extra trees	3.23	4.51	**39.90**	1.11E+08	1.71E+05
SVR	**2.51**	4.28	48.47	2.29E+08	2.90E+06
MLP	3.78	5.03	48.41	6.63E+06	4.77E+03
SARIMAX	3.95	5.60	80.72	1.47E+08	4.40E+03

The added weather features have little significance to the quality of the predictions. This was previously assumed by the Pearson's correlation coefficient.

Although most of the models performed better than the benchmark Naïve models, the Extra trees model will be further inspected for its consistency regarding the error metrics. Regarding the importance of the features of this model, the mean decrease in impurity (MDI) was plotted alongside the fitted model's attributes (Fig. 8).

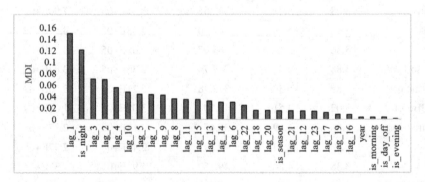

Fig. 8. Feature importance for the fitted Extra trees model's features based on MDI

Regarding the predictions themselves, the Extra trees model can capture the seasonality of the dataset, although its ability to predict more extreme maximum values is lacking (Fig. 9).

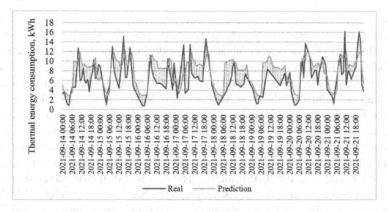

Fig. 9. Weekly prediction using a fitted Extra trees model

The inability of the model to capture the extreme values can be more clearly seen by looking at the prediction for the entire test set (Fig. 10).

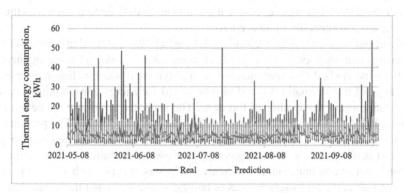

Fig. 10. A prediction for the entire test set using the fitted Extra trees model

4   Conclusion

Energy consumption forecasts can be utilized for better understanding of a building's energy model, and in turn reaching a more sustainable environment. Simulations and forecasts can also aid in constructing a BIM6D model. Although there is no widely agreed upon specification of what information could be included in a BIM6D model, this paper provides a case study for the type of information that could be added to a BIM6D model, which in the case of this study is thermal energy consumption forecasts. Several mathematics and artificial intelligence methods for predicting energy consumption have been analyzed and tested using an hourly thermal energy consumption dataset (one residential building block of Kaunas city in Lithuania) covering a two-year period. In this study 11 different forecasting methods were tested using various dataset modifications.

In terms of prediction accuracy, the different models showed advantages in different experiments, but it is worth highlighting the Extra tree that seems to be the best in terms of MAPE (38.65%). When evaluating the performance of the other models on this metric, XGBoost is the second best performer after Extra Trees, performing 5.66% worse on a dataset without lags or transformations. The Extra trees model seems to perform well with all the variants of the dataset according to MAPE, which is a unique property among the models used in this study. SVR performs noticeably better according to the MAE metric, reaching a maximum MAE of 2.48 kWh on a log-transformed dataset. Regarding the performance of the linear models, it can be observed that most of them perform similarly when compared with each other, although Lasso does seem to perform slightly better according the RMSE metric. The best RMSE metric scores seem to be divided between Lasso and Extra trees, although the best score was achieved by Extra trees on a log-transformed dataset, reaching a RMSE of 4.19. In terms of time, Extra Trees, SVR and SARIMAX are the most time-consuming compared to linear models and XGBoost. It can be concluded that Extra trees generally performs best when trained on the dataset used in the study, although other models like SVR and XGBoost can perform acceptably well. Regarding the pre-processing of the data prior to fitting, it seems that log-transforms and additional lag features can have a positive impact on the quality of the predictions. Our findings suggest that non-linear models perform slower, although their forecasts are generally more accurate.

Further studies should utilize hybrid models, which have potential in robust forecasting of energy consumption based on previous studies. More in-depth feature engineering should also be applied by experimenting with polynomial and non-linear features. A wider range of transformations could also be tested for energy consumption datasets, as they can improve the quality of forecasts. The proposed approach can be used for creating a BIM6D model. This model could be used not only for the 3D representation of a building, but also for displaying energy forecasts. Forecasts performed in our experiments can also be used for evaluating energy expenses in the future and optimizing the buildings' energy consumption. In the future, the aim is to apply such a model to other regions of Lithuania, for different types of buildings, and to predict the missing energy consumption data based on the available data for the nearest districts/zones, the habits of Lithuanian consumers and other factors.

References

1. Montiel-Santiago, F.J., Hermoso-Orzáez, M.J., Terrados-Cepeda, J.: Sustainability and energy efficiency: BIM 6D. Study of the BIM methodology applied to hospital buildings. Value of interior lighting and daylight in energy simulation. Sustain. (Basel Switz.) **12**, 5731 (2020). https://doi.org/10.3390/su12145731
2. Kaewunruen, S., Sresakoolchai, J., Zhou, Z.: Sustainability-based lifecycle management for bridge infrastructure using 6D BIM. Sustain. (Basel Switz.) **12**, 2436 (2020). https://doi.org/10.3390/su12062436
3. Park, J., Cai, H.: WBS-based dynamic multi-dimensional BIM database for total construction as-built documentation. Autom. Constr. **77**, 15–23 (2017). https://doi.org/10.1016/j.autcon.2017.01.021

4. Jang, J., et al.: Development of an improved model to predict building thermal energy consumption by utilizing feature selection. Energies **12**, 4187 (2019). https://doi.org/10.3390/en12214187

5. Chou, J.-S., Tran, D.-S.: Forecasting energy consumption time series using machine learning techniques based on usage patterns of residential householders. Energy **165**, 709–726 (2018). https://doi.org/10.1016/j.energy.2018.09.144

6. Deb, C., Zhang, F., Yang, J., Lee, S.E., Shah, K.W.: A review on time series forecasting techniques for building energy consumption. Renew. Sustain. Energy Rev. **74**, 902–924 (2017). https://doi.org/10.1016/j.rser.2017.02.085

7. Wang, H., Wei, R.: Electricity consumption forecast of energy saving monitoring and management platform based on exponential smoothing model, vol. 194 (2020). https://doi.org/10.1051/e3sconf/202019401006

8. Nazir, S., Aziz, A.A., Hosen, J., Aziz, N.A., Murthy, G.R.: Forecast energy consumption time-series dataset using multistep LSTM models. J. Phys. Conf. Ser. **1933**, 012054 (2021). https://doi.org/10.1088/1742-6596/1933/1/012054

9. Barak, S., Sadegh, S.S.: Forecasting energy consumption using ensemble ARIMA–ANFIS hybrid algorithm. Int. J. Electr. Power Energy Syst. **82**, 92–104 (2016). https://doi.org/10.1016/j.ijepes.2016.03.012

10. Bogner, K., Pappenberger, F., Zappa, M.: Machine learning techniques for predicting the energy consumption/production and its uncertainties driven by meteorological observations and forecasts. Sustain. (Basel Switz.) **11**, 3328 (2019). https://doi.org/10.3390/su11123328

11. Blázquez-García, A., Conde, A., Milo, A., Sánchez, R., Barrio, I.: Short-term office building elevator energy consumption forecast using SARIMA. J. Build. Perform. Simul. **13**, 69–78 (2020). https://doi.org/10.1080/19401493.2019.1698657

12. González-Briones, A., Hernández, G., Corchado, J.M., Omatu, S., Mohamad, M.S.: Machine learning models for electricity consumption forecasting: a review. In: 2019 2nd International Conference on Computer Applications Information Security (ICCAIS), pp. 1–6 (2019)

13. Kim, M.K., Kim, Y.-S., Srebric, J.: Predictions of electricity consumption in a campus building using occupant rates and weather elements with sensitivity analysis: artificial neural network vs. linear regression. Sustain. Cities Soc. **62**, 102385 (2020). https://doi.org/10.1016/j.scs.2020.102385

14. Abdullah, L., Leong, W.H.: The relationship of economic variables and final energy consumption: multiple linear regression evidence. In: MATEC Web of Conferences, vol. 189, p. 10025 (2018). https://doi.org/10.1051/matecconf/201818910025

15. Oludolapo, O.A., Adisa, J.A., Pule, K.A.: Comparing performance of MLP and RBF neural network models for predicting South Africa's energy consumption. J. Energy South. Afr. **23**, 40–46 (2017). https://doi.org/10.17159/2413-3051/2012/v23i3a3171

16. Jang, J., Baek, J., Leigh, S.-B.: Prediction of optimum heating timing based on artificial neural network by utilizing BEMS data. J. Build. Eng. **22**, 66–74 (2019). https://doi.org/10.1016/j.jobe.2018.11.012

17. Khan, P.W., Kim, Y., Byun, Y.-C., Lee, S.-J.: Influencing factors evaluation of machine learning-based energy consumption prediction. Energies **14**, 7167 (2021). https://doi.org/10.3390/en14217167

18. Chen, H.-Y., Lee, C.-H.: Electricity consumption prediction for buildings using multiple adaptive network-based fuzzy inference system models and gray relational analysis. Energy Rep. **5**, 1509–1524 (2019). https://doi.org/10.1016/j.egyr.2019.10.009

19. Babatunde, A.A., Abbasoglu, S.: Predictive analysis of photovoltaic plants specific yield with the implementation of multiple linear regression tool. Environ. Prog. Sustain. Energy **38**, 13098 (2019). https://doi.org/10.1002/ep.13098

20. Jung, S., Moon, J., Park, S., Rho, S., Baik, S.W., Hwang, E.: Bagging ensemble of multilayer perceptrons for missing electricity consumption data imputation. Sensors (Basel Switz.) **20**, 1772 (2020). https://doi.org/10.3390/s20061772

21. Hamedmoghadam, H., Joorabloo, N., Jalili, M.: Australia's long-term electricity demand forecasting using deep neural networks (2018)

22. Aslam, S., Herodotou, H., Mohsin, S.M., Javaid, N., Ashraf, N., Aslam, S.: A survey on deep learning methods for power load and renewable energy forecasting in smart microgrids. Renew. Sustain. Energy Rev. **144**, 110992 (2021). https://doi.org/10.1016/j.rser.2021.110992

23. Motalebi, M., Rashidi, A., Nasiri, M.M.: Optimization and BIM-based lifecycle assessment integration for energy efficiency retrofit of buildings. J. Build. Eng. **49**, 104022 (2022). https://doi.org/10.1016/j.jobe.2022.104022

24. Pereira, V., Santos, J., Leite, F., Escorcio, P.: Using BIM to improve building energy efficiency – a scientometric and systematic review. Energy Build. **250**, 111292 (2021). https://doi.org/10.1016/j.enbuild.2021.111292

25. Bracht, M.K., Melo, A.P., Lamberts, R.: A metamodel for building information modeling-building energy modeling integration in early design stage. Autom. Constr. **121**, 103422 (2021). https://doi.org/10.1016/j.autcon.2020.103422

26. Iowa State University: Iowa Environmental Mesonet Global METAR Archive. https://mesonet.agron.iastate.edu/request/download.phtml

27. Liu, Y., Wang, W., Ghadimi, N.: Electricity load forecasting by an improved forecast engine for building level consumers. Energy **139**, 18–30 (2017). https://doi.org/10.1016/j.energy.2017.07.150

28. Mehedintu, A., Sterpu, M., Soava, G.: Estimation and forecasts for the share of renewable energy consumption in final energy consumption by 2020 in the European Union. Sustainability **10**, 1515 (2018). https://doi.org/10.3390/su10051515

29. Hoerl, A.E., Kennard, R.W.: Ridge regression: applications to nonorthogonal problems. Technometrics **12**, 69–82 (1970). https://doi.org/10.2307/1267352

30. Tibshirani, R.: Regression shrinkage and selection via the lasso. J. R. Stat. Soc. Ser. B (Methodol.) **58**, 267–288 (1996)

31. Efron, B., Hastie, T., Johnstone, I., Tibshirani, R.: Least angle regression. Ann. Stat. **32**, 407–451 (2004). https://doi.org/10.1214/009053604000000067

32. Zou, H., Hastie, T.: Regularization and variable selection via the elastic net. J. R. Stat. Soc. Ser. B (Stat. Methodol.) **67**, 301–320 (2005)

33. Fraley, C., Hesterberg, T.: Least angle regression and LASSO for large datasets. Stat. Anal. Data Min. ASA Data Sci. J. **1**, 251–259 (2009). https://doi.org/10.1002/sam.10021

34. Bottmer, L., Croux, C., Wilms, I.: Sparse regression for large data sets with outliers. Eur. J. Oper. Res. **297**, 782–794 (2022). https://doi.org/10.1016/j.ejor.2021.05.049

35. Yu, Q., Miche, Y., Eirola, E., van Heeswijk, M., Séverin, E., Lendasse, A.: Regularized extreme learning machine for regression with missing data. Neurocomputing **102**, 45–51 (2013). https://doi.org/10.1016/j.neucom.2012.02.040

36. Yu, X., Liong, S.-Y.: Forecasting of hydrologic time series with ridge regression in feature space. J. Hydrol. **332**, 290–302 (2007). https://doi.org/10.1016/j.jhydrol.2006.07.003

37. Hans, C.: Elastic net regression modeling with the orthant normal prior. J. Am. Stat. Assoc. **106**, 1383–1393 (2011). https://doi.org/10.1198/jasa.2011.tm09241

38. Ogutu, J.O., Schulz-Streeck, T., Piepho, H.-P.: Genomic selection using regularized linear regression models: ridge regression, lasso, elastic net and their extensions. BMC Proc. **6**, S10 (2012). https://doi.org/10.1186/1753-6561-6-S2-S10

39. The best model of LASSO with the LARS. Library of Science. https://bibliotekanauki.pl/articles/1076395

40. Iturbide, E., Cerda, J., Graff, M.: A comparison between LARS and LASSO for initialising the time-series forecasting auto-regressive equations. Procedia Technol. **7**, 282–288 (2013). https://doi.org/10.1016/j.protcy.2013.04.035
41. Khan, J.A., Van Aelst, S., Zamar, R.H.: Robust linear model selection based on least angle regression. J. Am. Stat. Assoc. **102**, 1289–1299 (2007). https://doi.org/10.1198/016214507 000000950
42. LARS Lasso documentation. https://scikit-learn.org/stable/modules/linear_model.html#lars-lasso
43. Chen, T., Guestrin, C.: XGBoost: a scalable tree boosting system. In: Proceedings of the 22nd ACM SIGKDD International Conference on Knowledge Discovery and Data Mining, pp. 785–794 (2016). https://doi.org/10.1145/2939672.2939785
44. Geurts, P., Ernst, D., Wehenkel, L.: Extremely randomized trees. Mach. Learn. **63**, 3–42 (2006). https://doi.org/10.1007/s10994-006-6226-1
45. Alawadi, S., Mera, D., Fernández-Delgado, M., Alkhabbas, F., Olsson, C.M., Davidsson, P.: A comparison of machine learning algorithms for forecasting indoor temperature in smart buildings. Energy Syst. **13**, 689–705 (2020). https://doi.org/10.1007/s12667-020-00376-x
46. John, V., Liu, Z., Guo, C., Mita, S., Kidono, K.: Real-time lane estimation using deep features and extra trees regression. In: Bräunl, T., McCane, B., Rivera, M., Yu, X. (eds.) PSIVT 2015. LNCS, vol. 9431, pp. 721–733. Springer, Cham (2016). https://doi.org/10.1007/978-3-319-29451-3_57
47. Eskandarnia, E., AlHammad, M.: Predication of future energy consumption using SARIMAX, pp. 657–662 (2021). https://doi.org/10.1049/icp.2021.0853
48. Zhou, Y.: Regional energy consumption prediction based on SARIMAX-LSTM model. Acad. J. Comput. Inf. Sci. **4** (2021). https://doi.org/10.25236/AJCIS.2021.040307
49. Elamin, N., Fukushige, M.: Modeling and forecasting hourly electricity demand by SARIMAX with interactions. Energy **165**, 257–268 (2018). https://doi.org/10.1016/j.energy.2018.09.157
50. Fathi, M.M., Awadallah, A.G., Abdelbaki, A.M., Haggag, M.: A new Budyko framework extension using time series SARIMAX model. J. Hydrol. **570**, 827–838 (2019). https://doi.org/10.1016/j.jhydrol.2019.01.037
51. Lewis, C.D.: Industrial and Business Forecasting Methods: A Practical Guide to Exponential Smoothing and Curve Fitting. Butterworth-Heinemann, Oxford (1982)
52. Rausch, T., Albrecht, T., Baier, D.: Beyond the beaten paths of forecasting call center arrivals: on the use of dynamic harmonic regression with predictor variables (2021). https://doi.org/10.15495/EPub_UBT_00006037

The Only Link You'll Ever Need: How Social Media Reference Landing Pages Speed Up Profile Matching

Sergej Denisov[✉] and Frederik S. Bäumer

Bielefeld University of Applied Sciences, Bielefeld, Germany
{sergej.denisov,frederik.baeumer}@fh-bielefeld.de

Abstract. The Web is characterized by user interaction on Online Social Networks, the exchange of content on a large scale, and the presentation of one's own life on several digital channels using different media. Users strive to reach as many people as possible with their content while also distributing traffic across the various networks. To simplify this, there are Social Media Reference Landing Pages where users can bring together their numerous social media profiles. Our research project investigates the threat to users posed by the shared content, such as blackmailing or doxing. An important step is finding and merging different user profiles, primarily based on hints, similar user names, or links. In this paper, we show how Reference Landing Pages make it easier to create comprehensive Digital Twins, which we can use to compute and make tangible the risk of thoughtless sharing of information to users.

Keywords: Online Social Networks · Profile matching · Anonymity

1 Introduction

The Web is all about participating and creating, sharing, and interacting. Users can share information more efficiently than ever before, discuss topics, present themselves on the Web and link up with contacts. Online Social Networks (OSNs) have already been essential user platforms for years, providing the necessary foundations, setting new trends, and increasingly blurring the digital and real worlds. However, OSNs offer different functions, set different priorities, and appeal to different user groups. Therefore, users are motivated to provide several OSNs with content and maintain several user profiles. According to DataReportal [10], the average number of social media accounts per Internet user worldwide amounts to 7.5 in 2022. This allows users to present themselves in different ways on different profiles and, in addition to thematic focuses, to disclose private information exclusively or to explicitly conceal it. This quickly creates the illusion of keeping profiles separate from one another and, for example, protecting one's privacy and anonymity as needed.

However, the opposite can also be found: Users who want to have traffic on all social media profiles push the interlinking between the profiles and even boost

A. Lopata et al. (Eds.): ICIST 2022, CCIS 1665, pp. 136–147, 2022.
https://doi.org/10.1007/978-3-031-16302-9_10

it utilizing external services [7]. Using so-called Social Media Reference Landing Pages (SMRLP), various links can be combined on one page so that only one central link needs to be shared in order to gain access to all of a user's profiles [7]. What seems practical is questionable from the point of view of anonymity and privacy, but also for reasons of data protection (GDPR[1]). A very prominent service, with over 23 million users worldwide, is Linktree [17].

Since there are many different OSNs, it is challenging to select the relevant platforms, find matching profiles, and weigh the information on these networks. Bringing different profile links centrally via SMRLPs makes it easy to obtain extensive data from a user in terms of data acquisition. Without these central pages, finding and validating user profiles is costly and time-consuming, e.g., by means of hints in the profiles. By linking users in multiple OSNs, very comprehensive profiles of users can be created so that on the one hand, their entire profile and behavior and, on the other hand, their preferences, activities, and friend network can be reconstructed. In the area of cybercrime, such as cyber-bullying or the propagation of fake news, the digital footprint can be used to track and target such users and create digital twins (DTs) [8]. In this paper, we explore the value of SMRLPs for data acquisition tasks and highlight the threats that can arise from these link collections.

All of these considerations are taking place as part of the ADRIAN[2] research project, which is dedicated to exploring and developing Machine-Learning-based methods for detecting potential threats to individuals based on online datasets [8]. For this purpose, we discuss related work in Sect. 2. After that, we describe the research concept in Sect. 3.1 before giving an overview of the collected data and presenting our analysis in Sect. 3.2. Finally, we discuss our findings in Sect. 4 and draw our conclusions in Sect. 5.

2 Related Work

In this section, we discuss the notion of DTs (cf. Sect. 2.1) in the context of cyber threats and present related works on user profile matching (cf. Sect. 2.2).

2.1 Digital Twins in the Context of Cyber Threats

The term DT is ambiguous and is used in a variety of areas in research and practice. It can be found in mechanical engineering, medicine, and computer science [3]. Developments in the field of artificial intelligence have given the term a wider usage. More generally, "DTs can be defined as (physical and/or virtual) machines or computer-based models that are simulating, emulating, mirroring, or 'twinning' the life of a physical entity, which may be an object, a process, a human, or a human-related feature" [3].

In the ADRIAN research project, we understand the term to mean the digital representation of a real person instantiated by information available on the

---

[1] See https://frame-for-business.de/?page_id=14485 (2022-03-14).

[2] Authority-Dependent Risk Identification and Analysis in online Networks.

Web [8]. In this context, the DT can never reflect the entire complexity of a real person, but reproduces features that, alone or in combination with other characteristics, can pose a threat to the real person. In this way, the DT makes it possible to model the vulnerability of a person and make it measurable. The modeling of DTs is based on established and freely available standards of the semantic web, such as Schema.org and FOAF (Friend of a Friend). This makes it possible to easily connect and extend DTs. At the same time, the sheer number of possible sources of information, the quality of the data, and a multitude of contradictory data make modeling challenging. However, studies show that a large amount of relevant information is knowingly and, to a large extent, unknowingly revealed by users themselves [4,5]. It is precisely this fact, that knowingly and unknowingly shared information on the Web can be merged and thus pose a threat to users, that the ADRIAN research project aims to highlight [8].

2.2 Matching User Profiles Across Social Media

The approaches presented so far for profile matching across social media are mainly based on public user profile information and observable user behavior.

OSN users disclose a range of personal information on their profiles that can be used to uniquely identify specific individuals. These attributes are usually openly accessible and can be retrieved via corresponding APIs of the platform [1]. Traditional string matching methods are used to match this data. These mainly include three approaches: (i) phonetic encoding, (ii) pattern matching, and (iii) token-based comparisons [23]. Most of the studies focus on the names of a user. Thus, only user and display names in different social media were compared to match the profiles of a user [16]. It was shown that the accuracy drops drastically when there is only a slight difference in the display names on the different OSNs [2]. Another approach is based on the observation that most users have certain patterns in generating their display names. Therefore, the degree of similarity between both names is calculated [24]. In other works, additional features are considered besides the usernames.

Thus, not only the analysis of the language and writing style used in the posts provide a starting point for recognition, but user's behavior and movements can also be derived from the content information, such as the timing of posts or profile/status updates, places visited, etc. [11] For profile matching, Xing et al. [25] developed a two-level information entropy-based scoring method to weight each attribute. Furthermore, an intelligent system has been proposed to analyze three different aspects by measuring the similarity of Twitter profiles [21]. First, time-series information is used to analyze the consistency and habits of users; second, each user's followers and follower accounts are extracted to build a network; and third, the content provided by users is analyzed. The Features were extracted by using TF-IDF and DistilBERT. TF-IDF calculates the vectors based on the frequency of appearance of the words. DistilBERT is a pre-trained language model, which is the encoding part of the transformer architecture. Finally, the cosine similarity is calculated based on the features. In addition, Halimi et al. [12] calculated the similarities between location, gender, activities, interests, and also profile photos. Uploaded profile pictures can also be used for profile matching with the help of face recognition algorithms [22]. Graph-based approaches look at the underlying graph structure of social media. In addition, they analyze a user's network and merge it using similarity measures. Therefore, the friend relationships of a user in different OSNs are analyzed and profile matching is performed by using user features as well as profile pictures and friend relationships [9,14,15,19].

While Kasbekar et al. [14] used the graph structure of OSNs for friend relationship detection as well as features such as username and profile image, Müngen et al. [19] addressed the network alignment and similarity problem with both user profile features and their relationships with other users. Bennacer et al. [6] take advantage of the fact that some users have already linked their profiles on the social media platforms they use. In their approach, both network topology and personal information (attributes) disclosed on profiles are used for matching. Based on the existing cross-links, initial profile pairs can be identified. Then, equally weighted profile attributes (first name, last name, username) are compared to match profiles across platforms with high precision (94 %). Based on matches found, the algorithm iteratively tries to identify and uncover more profile pairs by using newly found matches to locate more new matches.

3   Backtracking of Digital Traces

Individual pieces of information found on the Web make it possible to create DTs. The question is where to start searching for information. This question has to be answered on the one hand by the expected information quality and on the other hand by the digital tracks, which in turn lead to new data sources. In the following, we discuss the procedure of compiling DTs (cf. Sect. 3.1) and show which starting points are suitable for information search, based on a conducted data collection (cf. Sect. 3.2).

3.1   Towards Digital Twin Compilation

As mentioned earlier, an average OSN user has multiple accounts on different platforms. A threat to users arises when information from different platforms is combined and, in aggregate, provides a more comprehensive picture of the real person than the scattered individual pieces of information, which was never intended to be so by the users of the platforms. Accounts must be created or populated with different usernames, content, and images for the different OSNs to avoid the aggregation of information. However, users interlink profiles to get more followers or likes in reality. For this reason, an uncomplicated merging of the profiles is possible. Our approach for cross-platform profile linking consists of four phases: (1) Twitter Data Processing, (2) Linktree Data Processing, (3) Linked OSNs Analysis, and (4) Profile Matching (cf. Fig. 1).

The first phase is dedicated to collecting the data from Twitter. It is a pre-destined entry point because, on the one hand, it is possible to collect a large

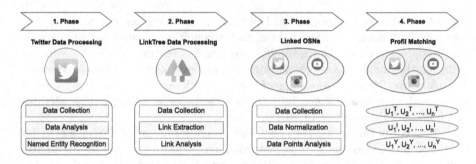

Fig. 1. ADRIAN's profile matching pipeline.

amount of data; on the other hand, the data can be filtered directly. For the filtering, we focus on tweets that contain a link to the Linktree platform. After a detailed data analysis, personal names must be detected. The second phase is to crawl all the linked Linktree pages. Once acquired, the goal is to extract all links within the Linktree pages and analyze them. The frequencies of the linked OSNs and the overlaps between them are fundamental here. The third phase involves collecting data from the extracted links of Linktree pages. Data normalization, e.g., location, date, and geodata, must be performed next. At this point, data points within the profiles in the OSNs need to be analyzed, and relevant data points need to be selected appropriately for profile matching. Finally, this forms the basis for verifying that it is the same individual. In the fourth phase, the various aspects of the profiles are checked for similarity. The goal is to merge the profiles into one cross-platform profile if the metrics for measuring similarity reach predefined values and it is accordingly the same user on two or more platforms.

Due to a large number of OSNs and profiles, it is impossible to search in all OSNs. So the alternative to our approach would be first to collect the data from one OSN and then follow the links to additional OSNs. This would require significantly more time and resources. The decision to use Linktree pages as a starting point is the possibility of quickly creating a dataset of cross-platform profiles. Therefore, when collecting information for DT compilation using this pipeline, the following two questions arise: how to identify as many cross-platform profiles as possible and how to validate the linkage between these profiles in the OSNs? The above-mentioned pipeline was created to answer these questions.

In this paper, we focus on YouTube, Twitter, and Instagram. In the ADRIAN research project, the goal is to add more social media and social sports platforms as well as business networks [8]. Sports platforms provide high-quality location information about shared running routes, while business networks put detailed biographical data online in a semi-structured form.

3.2   Dataset and Link Analysis

Our goal is to investigate how users engage in different OSNs and what links exist so that profiles can be linked together. For this reason, we have collected data from Twitter that includes a Linktree link for almost two months (2022-01-01–2022-02-23). An analysis of the links revealed that a tweet can contain up to ten links. A detailed breakdown of how many links the tweets include is shown in Table 1. After removing all duplicate URLs, we first analyzed the occurrence of the linked domains within the Twitter dataset. To create a cross-platform profile, we build a dataset from the links contained on the Linktree page. For this, we extracted all the links from the Linktree page by using BeautifulSoup[3]. A breakdown of the top 10 linked domains for the Twitter and Linktree datasets is shown in Table 2. First, we can see that accounts linking to the Linktree page are often connected to other online social networks such as Instagram, YouTube, and Facebook. These are our primary data sources for building cross-platform profiles with Twitter. For Linktree, 102,621 of the 109,735 could be resolved, and the remaining URLs were unreachable. Secondly, we can observe that Instagram, YouTube, and Facebook are among the top 4 linked to on Linktree pages. LinkedIn did not appear in the top 10, and it has 8,467 links. Other OSNs that are also of interest to us are Flickr (217 links) and Strava (26 links), which are significantly underrepresented.

Table 1. Statistics and link analysis for the Twitter dataset

Statistics	#	Link analysis	#
Tweets	4,105,016	Author links	1,582,272
Total users	1,013,209	Tweets with 1 link	2,298,522
Tweets per user (min)	1	Tweets with 2 links	1,076,128
Tweets per user (mean)	3.57	Tweets with 3 links	243,468
Tweets per user (max)	4.77	Tweets with 4 links	79,051
Links per tweet (min)	0	Tweets with 5 links	29,686
Links per tweet (mean)	1.19	Tweets with 6 links	7,015
Links per tweet (max)	11	Tweets with 7 links	2,083
Links per user (min)	1	Tweets with 8 links	784
Links per user (mean)	6	Tweets with 9 links	234
Links per user (max)	51,575	Tweets with 10 links	36

The first task is to perform an overlap analysis for the different OSNs. For this purpose, we select the OSNs relevant to our research project. The overlaps of these are displayed in Table 3. It can be noticed that when it comes to two social media platforms, Twitter and Instagram overlap the most with 52,265, and YouTube and Facebook overlap the least with 17,033. We also see that all four major social media platforms overlap in 13,768 cases. If we add the business

---

[3] See https://pypi.org/project/beautifulsoup4/ (2022-03-14).

Table 2. Top 10 links for domains extracted from Twitter and Linktree

Twitter	# of links	Linktree	# of links
Twitter	410,761	Twitter	74,334
Linktr	109,735	Instagram	73,152
Instagram	24,268	YouTube	46,352
Carrd	13,139	Facebook	36,601
YouTube	17,107	TikTok	24,515
OnlyFans	8,521	Apple	20,940
Twitch	5,805	Spotify	20,094
Bit	5,435	Google	18,945
Facebook	5,211	Bit	15,025
OpenSea	4,963	Amazon	14,156

network LinkedIn, only 2,735 overlaps remain. In our research project, we want to realize cross-platform profiling and threat detection for individuals, so it is essential to first identify factors that indicate that the account belongs to an individual. In general, on online social networks, a distinction must be made between accounts of organizations and individuals.

In this step, we focus only on the Twitter data for now. We have applied the following heuristics to ensure that a profile belongs to an individual: (I) Separation of persons and organizations by using Named Entity Recognition[4], (II) Name-parsing[5] to split first and last names and (III) comparison with a name-dataset[6] to determine if it is a valid first and last name.

Table 3. Profile intersections among OSNs

Online social networks	Intersections
Twitter ∩ Instagram	52,265
Twitter ∩ YouTube	27,953
Twitter ∩ Facebook	25,283
Instagram ∩ YouTube	27,822
Instagram ∩ Facebook	26,651
YouTube ∩ Facebook	17,033
Twitter ∩ Instagram ∩ YouTube	24,118
Twitter ∩ Instagram ∩ YouTube ∩ Facebook	13,768
Twitter ∩ Instagram ∩ YouTube ∩ Facebook ∩ LinkedIn	2,735

---

[4] See https://huggingface.co/flair/ner-english (2022-03-14).
[5] See https://github.com/derek73/python-nameparser (2022-03-14).
[6] See https://github.com/philipperemy/name-dataset (2022-03-14).

For the platform individual data acquisition, we select our data still following criteria: (1) we remove duplicates based on the author name and description, (2) we select English as language, and (3) we select profiles that intersect between Twitter, YouTube, and Instagram. Data collection using APIs for Twitter and YouTube is very convenient compared to a hand-crafted crawler for Instagram, where we can only access a limited amount of data. Therefore, for the initial profile comparison, we randomly select a sample of 500 Linktree pages that contain links to Twitter, YouTube, and Instagram profiles. The collected profiles provide the foundation for the second task, profile similarity analysis. First, we examine which data points within the profiles across the three OSNs are suitable for profile matching. Then, we assign the diverse data points within the profiles to the different types of information (cf. Table 4).

Table 4. Types of information and examples for data points

Type of information	Data points
User identity	User id, name, username
User information	Description, created (timestamp), private, verified
Content information	Post id, created (timestamp), caption, text, language, source, like/view count, hashtags, keywords
Image or video links	User image, content image/Video
External links	Profile URL, Post URL
Geo information	Location, coordinates, bounding box
User metrics	Followers, following, content count, view count

The seven types of information indicate under which aspects the profiles are similar and form the basis for the similarity analysis of profiles and the initialization of DTs. Also, different methods and approaches are generally needed to perform similarity analysis of the different information types. A semantic text similarity approach is applied to compute the similarity for the user identity and user information data points. We calculate the degree of similarity between profile names and descriptions based on the *all-mpnet-base-v2*[7] model and cosine similarity. The results are presented in the following two histograms.

After calculating the similarity, the results were checked manually. In Fig. 2 the distribution of the similarity scores for the names within the Twitter, YouTube, and Instagram data is shown. As for the interpretation of the results, a cosine similarity score between 0.75 and 1 reveals mainly perfect matches. If the score goes towards 0.75 then the names in most cases have some other words such as "*official*", "*podcast*" and "*nft*" included. For a score between 0.5 and 0.75, also a large number of matches can be found. These matches often lack the first or last name or contain additional information or emojis. For scores below 0.50,

---

[7] See https://huggingface.co/sentence-transformers/all-mpnet-base-v2 (2022-03-14).

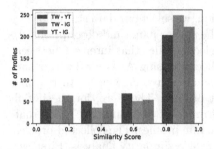
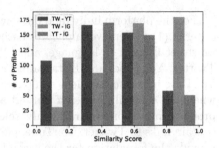

Fig. 2. STS for names

Fig. 3. STS descriptions

almost no more matches are found here. In total, the distribution for different OSNs is almost even, with the highest value achieved between Twitter and Instagram names. In Fig. 3 the distribution of the similarity scores for descriptions is shown. Our analysis conducts that significantly worse similarity scores are achieved for descriptions. While for names 80.01 % have a similarity value above 0.5, it is only 53.80 % for descriptions. Also, the distribution between different platforms is very uneven. Here the similarity of the descriptions on Twitter and Instagram stand out with high similarity scores.

4   Discussion

As described earlier, users of OSNs may face threats due to the large amount of information shared on different OSNs. It is irrelevant when and where the information was shared if attackers can find and link multiple profiles and validate the information. In the ADRIAN research project, we address how to make this threat visible. Naively, users assume that information in one place cannot be

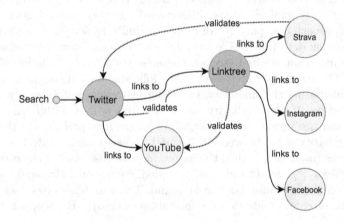

Fig. 4. Matching and validation of OSN user profiles

found and merged by attackers in another place or do not have a clear overview of what is happening with their data [18,20]. Often, the assumption stems from attackers' inability to monitor all websites and OSN profiles.

In this paper, we primarily followed a technical question: whether the value of SMRLPs such as Linktree is given and can speed up the acquisition of matching user profiles. However, we also want to focus on the danger for users at this point. Offering numerous OSN links centrally not only simplifies acquisition immensely but also enables validation on a first level (cf. Fig. 4). In principle, it is even possible to validate or deny the actual entry point (Twitter) if it is also stored on Linktree. Figure 4 also shows how the different OSNs can validate each other and thus place more confidence in the connections between the OSNs. The more often a profile appears through the link structure analysis, the more reliable the affiliation appears. Nevertheless, further validation of the profiles is necessary: In the Linktree data analysis, non-related profiles are linked, or Linktree profiles of groups that merge links. This shows that Linktree as a product is more broadly positioned and, for example, enables money transfer and donations and the landing page function. The different application scenarios lead to different usage and, thus, landing pages with links from multiple users. Since we have to achieve very high quality in merging the profiles, a validation of the information has to be done on a detailed level. Nevertheless, SMRLPs like Linktree are a considerable help to identify entry pages and profile candidates and monitor user activities (e.g., OSN registrations). That said, for our ADRIAN research project, Linktree's advertising slogan therefore primarily reflects the truth: "*The Only Link You'll Ever Need*".

5   Conclusion

We have collected Twitter data containing links to Linktree pages for our work. We analyzed how many links are included in Linktree pages, which OSNs are linked, and how frequently. We were able to extract 109,735 Linktree pages for a period of almost two months. As a result, we found that a large number of Linktree links exist on Twitter, and all major social media sites are linked from the Linktree pages. For this reason, Linktree is a valuable data source for the future initialization of DTs. For further work, we also need to analyze and add other available landing pages, like BrideURL or ManyLink [13].

Furthermore, one of our goals is to improve the distinction between accounts of organizations and individuals. Detecting individuals using NER and the name dataset worked well, but a large amount of data was filtered out. We want to improve our existing approach to be more granular and identify and use more relevant data points in future work. That said, we have already discovered relevant data points on Facebook that can provide us with information on whether a user is an organization or an individual. This could lead us to a machine learning approach to train models to distinguish profiles.

After collecting data from different OSNs, profile matching is essential. This work used an approach with the current best transformer model for Semantic

Text Similarity (STS) and computed the cosine similarity for the names and descriptions. As a result, we demonstrated the similarity of the names in different OSNs. However, this is only the first step in the ADRIAN research project. In the future, all available data points for analysis will be investigated, and methods for this purpose will need to be identified and analyzed. Of particular importance is the content posted by users. The analysis of images (e.g., face or location recognition) and geospatial information (e.g., walking routes) presents new challenges due to the heterogeneous nature of the data. In addition, it is essential to analyze content and user behavior over time. The challenge here is that the persistence of the data we collect is severely limited: Content on the web is highly volatile and changes quickly. In addition, we do not want to store the data longer than it exists in the real world.

Finally, it appears that the use of SMRLPs poses an invisible threat to users by facilitating the merging of profiles and the creation of extensive data collections and instantiation of DTs. We are taking this finding into account in our further work and will also take this into account in our educational work.

Acknowledgements. This research is funded by dtec.bw – Digitalization and Technology Research Center of the Bundeswehr.

References

1. Agarwal, A., Toshniwal, D.: SmPFT: social media based profile fusion technique for data enrichment. Comput. Netw. **158**, 123–131 (2019)
2. Ahmad, W., Ali, R.: User identification across multiple online social networks using cross link attribute and network relationship. J. Interdiscip. Math. **23** (2020). https://doi.org/10.1080/09720502.2020.1721713
3. Barricelli, B.R., Casiraghi, E., Fogli, D.: A survey on digital twin: definitions, characteristics, applications, and design implications. IEEE Access **7**, 167653–167671 (2019). https://doi.org/10.1109/ACCESS.2019.2953499
4. Bäumer, F.S., Grote, N., Kersting, J., Geierhos, M.: Privacy matters: detecting nocuous patient data exposure in online physician reviews. In: Damaševičius, R., Mikašytė, V. (eds.) ICIST 2017. CCIS, vol. 756, pp. 77–89. Springer, Cham (2017). https://doi.org/10.1007/978-3-319-67642-5_7
5. Bäumer, F.S., Kersting, J., Orlikowski, M., Geierhos, M.: Towards a multi-stage approach to detect privacy breaches in physician reviews. In: SEMANTICS Posters & Demos (2018)
6. Bennacer, N., Nana Jipmo, C., Penta, A., Quercini, G.: Matching user profiles across social networks. In: Jarke, M., et al. (eds.) CAiSE 2014. LNCS, vol. 8484, pp. 424–438. Springer, Cham (2014). https://doi.org/10.1007/978-3-319-07881-6_29
7. Bettendorf, S.: Hilfreiche Programme. In: Instagram-Journalismus für die Praxis, pp. 97–101. Springer, Wiesbaden (2020). https://doi.org/10.1007/978-3-658-31484-2_14
8. Bäumer, F.S., Denisov, S., Su Lee, Y., Geierhos, M.: Towards authority-dependent risk identification and analysis in online networks. In: Halimi, A., Ayday, E. (eds.) Proceedings of the IST-190 Research Symposium (RSY) on AI, ML and BD for Hybrid Military Operations (AI4HMO), October 2021

9. Cai, C., Li, L., Chen, W., Zeng, D.D.: Capturing deep dynamic information for mapping users across social networks. In: 2019 IEEE International Conference on Intelligence and Security Informatics, ISI 2019, May 2019. https://doi.org/10.1109/ISI.2019.8823341

10. Data Portal, January 2022. https://datareportal.com/reports/digital-2022-global-overview-report

11. Goga, O., Lei, H., Parthasarathi, S.H.K., Friedland, G., Sommer, R., Teixeira, R.: Exploiting innocuous activity for correlating users across sites. In: Proceedings of the 22nd International Conference on World Wide Web, pp. 447–458 (2013)

12. Halimi, A., Ayday, E.: Efficient quantification of profile matching risk in social networks using belief propagation. In: Chen, L., Li, N., Liang, K., Schneider, S. (eds.) ESORICS 2020. LNCS, vol. 12308, pp. 110–130. Springer, Cham (2020). https://doi.org/10.1007/978-3-030-58951-6_6

13. Kammakomati, M., Battula, S.V.: MergeURL: an effective URL merging and shortening service (2020)

14. Kasbekar, P., Potika, K., Pollett, C.: Find me if you can: aligning users in different social networks. In: Proceedings of the 2020 IEEE 6th International Conference on Big Data Computing Service and Applications, BigDataService 2020, August 2020, pp. 46–53. https://doi.org/10.1109/BigDataService49289.2020.00015

15. Li, Y., Ji, W., Gao, X., Deng, Y., Dong, W., Li, D.: Matching user accounts with spatio-temporal awareness across social networks. Inf. Sci. **570**, 1–15 (2021)

16. Li, Y., Peng, Y., Zhang, Z., Yin, H., Xu, Q.: Matching user accounts across social networks based on username and display name. World Wide Web **22**(3), 1075–1097 (2018). https://doi.org/10.1007/s11280-018-0571-4

17. Linktree: Linktr.ee: About (2022). https://linktr.ee/s/about/

18. Metzger, M.J.: Effects of site, vendor, and consumer characteristics on web site trust and disclosure. Commun. Res. **33**(3), 155–179 (2006). https://doi.org/10.1177/0093650206287076

19. Müngen, A., Gündoğan, E., Kaya, M.: Identifying multiple social network accounts belonging to the same users. Soc. Netw. Anal. Min. **11**, 29 (2021)

20. Sheehan, K.B., Hoy, M.G.: Dimensions of privacy concern among online consumers. J. Public Policy Mark. **19**(1), 62–73 (2000). http://www.jstor.org/stable/30000488

21. Shoeibi, N., Shoeibi, N., Chamoso, P., AlizadehSani, Z., Corchado, J.: Similarity approximation of twitter profiles (2021)

22. Sokhin, T., Butakov, N., Nasonov, D.: User profiles matching for different social networks based on faces identification. Hybrid Artif. Intell. Syst. 551–562 (2019). https://doi.org/10.1007/978-3-030-29859-3_47. http://dx.doi.org/10.1007/978-3-030-29859-3_47

23. Soltani, R., Abhari, A.: Identity matching in social media platforms. In: 2013 International Symposium on Performance Evaluation of Computer and Telecommunication Systems (SPECTS), pp. 64–70 (2013)

24. Xing, L., Deng, K., Wu, H., Xie, P., Gao, J.: Behavioral habits-based user identification across social networks. Symmetry **11**, 1134 (2019). https://doi.org/10.3390/sym11091134

25. Xing, L., Deng, K., Wu, H., Xie, P., Zhang, M., Wu, Q.: Exploiting two-level information entropy across social networks for user identification. Wirel. Commun. Mob. Comput. **2021**, 1–15 (2021). https://doi.org/10.1155/2021/1082391

Enhancing End-to-End Communication Security in IoT Devices Through Application Layer Protocol

Rimsha Zahid[1]([✉]), Muhammad Waseem Anwar[2], Farooque Azam[1], Anam Amjad[1], and Danish Mukhtar[1]

[1] Department of Computer and Software Engineering, CEME, NUST, Rawalpindi, Pakistan
{rzahid.cse20ceme,dmukhtar.cse20ceme}@student.nust.edu.pk,
{farooq,anam.amjad}@ceme.nust.edu.pk
[2] School of Innovation, Design, and Engineering, Malardalen University, Västerås, Sweden
muhammad.waseem.anwar@mdu.se

Abstract. The Internet of Things (IoT) has combined the hardware components with software elements by providing users with remote control and management facilities. From safety-critical systems to security devices and industrial appliances, every appliance makes use of IoTs. Whereas security issues such as SQL injections, Denial of Service/Distributed Denial of Service (DOS/DDOS) attacks, the forged transmission of messages, or man in the middle (MITM) are major security threats among smart devices. Any purging of data causes privacy issues while the subsequent assessments made using modified information are also erroneous. This security hole needs comprehensive non-cryptographic data-security techniques and frameworks which would help developers in creating secure systems on heterogeneous devices. Algorithms like blowfish and Data Encryption Standard (DES) do not have the uniquity which AES does, making them more vulnerable to attack this research paper focuses on the communication security issues in IoT systems. We have proposed an End-to-End Encryption using AES in IoT (EAES-IoT). Validation of the proposed algorithm has been done in a case study of the Smart Voice Pathology Monitoring System (SVPMS) by sending the encoded data to the application layer through Application Programming Interface (API). We compared results to ensure the authenticity of the data and they were found promising. Data access is provided only to authorized individuals by providing a shared key for decryption of the alphanumeric string of data shared between devices. The proposed algorithm will provide future directions to meet security challenges in the IoT.

Keywords: Internet of Things · Security · Data privacy · Application layer protocol · Encryption in IoT · AES

1 Introduction

The Internet of Things is termed as a network of real-world objects (known as "things" in the world of IoT) which have embedded sensors and embedded systems connecting

A. Lopata et al. (Eds.): ICIST 2022, CCIS 1665, pp. 148–159, 2022.
https://doi.org/10.1007/978-3-031-16302-9_11

and transmitting the data. Machine learning procedures, commodity sensors, real-time analytics and reporting, and ubiquitous computing have evolved things. Smart is the word that usually accompanies the appliances or system which integrates things and could be controlled using devices. These days' huge numbers of gadgets are associated with the internet, and we can undoubtedly get to use them on daily basis. One of the prime drivers of IoT is remote communication and organization. In a world where things are getting automated and devices are communicating directly as humans do, however, we are facing security challenges.

Due to the security concern of IoT devices, we are close to the misuse of IoT-related products and services. The Internet of Things or IoT is paving the way for analytical change by disrupting businesses, governments, and consumers. Meanwhile, IoT is gradually becoming a priority, with companies such as Google, Cisco, IBM, Intel, and others leading the transformation. It puts a big question on whether industry 4.0 would be able to protect all of these security-related threats or not?

The ways of our living, working, and traveling would soon change with the IoT revolution. Soon we would be in control of every aspect of life by connecting to any device from connected houses and self-driving cars, from smart toasters to smart buildings. IoT explosion, on one hand, is creating opportunities for both manufacturers and consumers, while on other hand it has led to significant security concerns by threatening safety. For the efficient working of IoT objects, there is a need to secure hardware, software, and connectivity without which the connected devices are likely to be hacked. Once the connected objects are hacked, the user's digital data is at risk. It can easily be stolen by the hacker by usurping the object's functionality.

On the other hand, SQL injections, denial of service attacks, and forged transmission of messages are some of the exemplary events recorded due to poor handling of messages transmitted over the internet. These issues need comprehensive systems security; non-cryptographic data-security techniques and frameworks which would help developers in creating secure systems on heterogeneous devices. More research is needed on cryptographic security services as they are capable of operating on resource-constrained devices. Security of messages sent and received by IoT devices, communication confidentiality, reliability, and data integrity should also be addressed for secure communication. A feature where one-to-one communication of devices is possible was much needed where no third person could see what kind of data is being transmitted.

To deal with the security challenges faced by communicating IoT devices at the application layer, we have proposed a solution that involves end-to-end encryption using cloud-based libraries for addressing the security issues. The proposed solution is validated on a case study of smart voice pathology to ensure that the data is sent in encrypted form before it flows over the network. This framework is objected to guarantee secure communication at the application layer between IoT devices.

Later portions of this paper are organized as Sect. 2 provides a synopsis of related research works which have been done in the same domain and the problem statement which we have derived after carrying out an analysis of literature. Section 3 illustrates the proposed methodology for dealing with the security challenges faces by IoT devices while communicating. Section 4 covers proof of concept for the proposed methodology whereas discussion and limitations are discussed in Sect. 5. For the conclusion and future work, details are provided in Sect. 6.

2   Literature Review

In this section, we have reviewed background data that was available on online databases for carrying out the research study on a topic under consideration. We have analyzed the previously identified security loopholes in IoT communication, the significance of availability and integrity of data, the proposed solutions, and what were the future endeavors presented by researchers.

Authors in [1] have stated that establishing a secure route is a key challenge in IoTs. It is because messages sent over a network are vulnerable to malign data injection attacks. In such attacks, a device is injected into the IoT system which sniffs all wireless traffic. It could be worst-case when forged messages are passed or make the system unavailable to the intended users. For dealing with data transmission, security algorithms used with IoTs grant a protected route for data communication between nodes.

H. Sufyan et al. [2] proposed Secure Multichip Routing [SMR] which embeds multilayer parameters into the routing algorithms. This is done to ensure that the communication in an IoT system is suitable when there are data privacy concerns. The details of permissible connected devices are saved so that the least information is stored when communication channels are populated. This routing protocol has security implications concerning authentication to safeguard the verification threats.

IPv6 is preferred to be used in low-power Wireless Networks. Whereas network layer in IoT makes use of Datagram Transport Layer Security (DTLS) while Transmission Control Protocol (TCP) is used by conventional networks. Constrained Application Protocol (COAP) is used at the application layer most often however conventional networks make use of Hypertext Transport Protocol (HTTP) [3].

In [4], Sicari et al. investigated the security concerns of the IoT arena including secrecy, reliability, and validation. Devices connected through the internet, in an IoT system, have a trustworthy relationship that encourages them to communicate. However, the concerns of implementing reliance negotiations for dealing with access control and data stream were not addressed. These were crucial for the security of the data being communicated in heterogeneous environments. Policies addressing security threats and dealing with adaptable infrastructure and scalability must be deployed.

In the main application areas, WAN is an efficient protocol for protecting sensitive pieces of data. Thus, a peer-to-peer security protocol is proposed by H. Zhang and T. Zhang in [5] to meet this requirement. Open-source platforms in IoT rely on secure communication as it requires fewer handshakes once a connection is made while dynamic adjustments for security ensure that the demands of IoTs are fulfilled. Message encapsulation and encapsulation is the responsibility of message handles which also oversee the routing of the message to other components in the network. Security while making configuration is done at the message configuration level as the security manager gives operations access to meet the secure communication goals of IoTs [6].

L. Costa et al. [7] proposed protocols that are used in the application layer, while working with CoAP and HTTP. The proxy suggested in this paper maintains the nature of messages, allowing seamless communication between devices. It is an independent entity that works by intercepting Swarm communication. Afterward, it maps CoAP and HTTP to extend the network rather than working on all components one by one.

Table 1. Comparison of encryption algorithms

Ref.	Encryption algorithm	Input size	Encryption time	Decryption time	Throughput
[18]	AES	100 B	63 ms	2	NA
[22]	DES	90 Kb	38.15 s	NA	10.13 MBps
[21]	3DES	1 MB	114.8 ms	49.9 ms	NA
[19]	Blowfish	NA	4.2 ms	4.9 ms	2619 MBps
[19]	Twofish	NA	3.1 ms	4.1 ms	3548 Mbps
[18]	RSA	100 B	45 ms	141	NA
[20]	Salsa20	1 mb	1.35 s	1.36 s	NA

In [8], authors have proposed encryption using the AES algorithm to ensure the confidentiality and integrity of data that information sharing between two parties is done through a trusted communication channel. IoTs are encapsulated in RESTful Application Programming Interfaces (APIs), using these services application complexity can be reduced and software reusability could be enhanced. These endeavors helped to devise principles and conventions for IoT which are dependent on the compositional Web components, called IoTs [9].

IoTs have been introduced in the healthcare sector, but many countries still have outdated healthcare facilities, this can easily be changed with the usage of modern technology will assist various operations, such as sharing reports with relevant stakeholders of the system. Maintaining patient records and medicine delivery would go a long way in changing the healthcare industry [10].

Large numbers of the advantages are offered by IoT applications in medical care. Well-programmed transmission of information is fundamental for streamlining the data. Smart devices empower patient-driven capacities, diagnosing their health issues and conveying updated data [11]. Sensors attached to patients will improve the procedures for estimating and observing patients' vitals like temperature, cholesterol, glucose, and pulse, just to name a few. The uses of IoT and IoE are extended with the introduction of IoNT. Healthcare applications are an essential objective of IoNT.

In IoT, message transmission from device to device is done through Pushing or Polling [12]. Compared to the surveying convention, the Push convention is the proper message correspondence convention for IoT gadgets since it is incorporated into a low transfer speed organization. The MQTT, XMPP and CoAP conventions have been executed through these push message administrations. MQTT has been used as it was expected to run on low-power machines as a lightweight convention [13]. A comparison of encryption algorithms at application layer protocol is presented in Table 1.

MQTT was intended to send information precisely under long organization postponement and low data transmission conditions. MQTT trades a scope of control bundles. There are fourteen control parcels and each of them contains three sections. In MQTT, the distributor distributes messages and clients buy into subjects which are viewed as a distribute/buy in the model [12]. With the help of IoT devices, bringing real-world objects to the virtual realm is made possible. This has been made possible by various tagging technologies such as 2D, NFC, and RFID barcodes which have made it possible to identify and reference physical objects on the internet [14]. However, there are numerous inadequacies in IoT gadgets as IoT lies on existing Wireless Sensor Networks (WSNs). In this way, IoT acquires structurally a similar secrecy and security issues as WSN [15]. Different attacks on IoT frameworks demonstrate that there is a requirement for broad security plans. Numerous shortcomings have been recorded in smart devices, related to the framework being deployed and navigating down to their security issues, integrity concerns, and availability problems [16, 17].

IoT has become the future of automation it is not only the manufacturing industry, but academia has also drawn its focus on research studies related to this technology. The objective of this research study is to analyze the security issues of data communicated in an IoT-based system. Since the availability of data is also a major concern, any security breaches or attacks might lead to the misinterpretation of novel information. Therefore, we will be working to improve the security of such systems and look for future endeavors in the same domain.

3   Methodology

This section illustrates the proposed methodology for securing the data being communicated on the application layer in an IoT-based system. We have proposed a solution to ensure that data being sent and received from any devices for controlling the devices based on decision-making algorithms is reliable and available on time (see Fig. 1).

3.1   Encryption Using AES in IoT (EAES-IoT)

API-based end-to-end encryption is used to resolve security issues related to the communication of packets over application layer protocol. This is achieved by the AES. The algorithm devised for coping with the security challenges faced by IoT devices makes use of AES and API to send requests and receive responses in encrypted form. By calling API before communicating the data over the network, it will be converted into encoded data which is then transmitted. The receiving devices are also provided with an API call which would decrypt the data using a shared key. The concept of using a shared key for encoding and decoding the data makes this algorithm a safe choice as unauthorized users can't get access to crucial information and it stays unaffected.

Firstly, the data is divided into separate blocks as AES computations are made on bytes. For example, if you are using 128-bits techniques then a four-by-four column would be created which is then multiplied to 8 for converting bytes into bits. The block creation depends upon the technique which is being chosen for AES-based encryption as the number of bits are differ as per the procedure being selected and followed. Rijndael's key schedule is used for key expansion which is a crucial step of this encryption algorithm. Afterward, the round keys are added using an XOR cipher, known to be an additive encryption process.

In the process, called substitute bytes, each byte is substituted with the next one. It makes use of the old techniques where letters are swapped. In the next round, AES shifts rows in a manner that the second rows are shifted one place to the left, the third moves two places left, fourth shifts three places, and so on. Once row shifting is completed, columns are mixed in the next step and then another round key is added again following Rijnhael's key schedule.

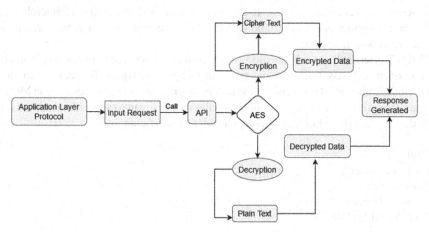

Fig. 1. Proposed approach for ensuring end-to-end encryption in IoT devices

Bytes are again substituted and following this process, row shifting is started. After column mixing, another round key is added. This round repetition depends upon the encryption keys followed. When 128-bit key encryption is used, there are 9 rounds in total whereas, for 192-bit, these rounds count to 11. If you are using a 256-bit key then in that case, there are 13 rounds in total.

Once the data is encoded after following the number of rounds against the respective key encryption process, they travel over the application layer through any selected protocol. For the scope of this research, we have used HTTPS and MQTT however others are also being worked upon as the proposed approach provides a generic security solution for IoT devices. The ciphers at receiving end follow the inverse of steps that were being used for encryption. Once the rounds are completed, the data gets decrypted and could be used for further processing while its integrity was maintained when it traveled over the transmission channels.

4   Proof of Concept

End-to-end encryption using APIs is proposed in this research work which utilizes AES-based algorithms. We have worked on making a secure packet transmission on the application layer as it is the last in the OSI model which is most often used for communication over the internet. It is utilized by the client-end programming side so that users can send and receive data by providing useful information after making an analysis and disseminating the information to the intended customer. HTTP, HTTPS, Simple Mail Transfer Protocol (SMTP), Domain Name System (DNS), File Transfer Protocol (FTP), and Post Office Protocol (POP) are the ones that reside on the application layer.

4.1 Selected Protocols

HTTPS makes use of encoded data transmission using Transport Layer Security (TLS) and Secure Sockets Layer (SSL). It ensures bidirectional encryption of interchanges between a customer and worker and secures the correspondences against listening in and data tampering attacks.

MQTT is termed as a publish/subscribe, lightweight message transmission protocol. It is an open and easy-to-implement protocol that is used where the network has low bandwidth. Embedded devices with limited memory resources and processors run MQTT for data transmission. You cannot publish or subscribe to any message without connecting both devices to a shared broker. Message in MQTT must contain:

- Payload
- Message Identifier
- Fixed Header
- Variable Header
- MQTT and UTF-8

4.2 Use Case

We have used Node-Red for validating the proposed solution to meet communication-related security challenges of packets between HTTP and MQTT. Node-Red is built on Node.js thus it takes advantage of its non-blocking, event-driven models. It is used for creating dynamic flows of IoTs and wiring together the hardware devices, online services, and APIs. Command Prompt executes in the background keeping a track of flows and errors for easy debugging.

1) Smart Voice Pathology Monitoring System (SVPMS)

Our case study is based on voice pathology [23, 24]. Voice pitch and frequency is everyone's unique feature. However, the natural phenomena of generating the voice are sometimes disturbed when individuals continuously speak for longer periods or habitual to communicate in a louder voice. Musicians, teachers, and sometimes the kids who shout very often face some distortion in their voice, called voice pathology. Other than poor vocal practices, smoking, dehydration, and laryngeal infection can also deteriorate voice quality causing fatigue and strain on vocal cords.

We will be creating an SVPMS which would be monitoring the patient's health attributes to identify their current condition. This automated system would be handled through an IoT-based system. SVPMS tracks patients' health with sensors and sends encrypted packets over the application layer to notify paramedics about the health condition of the patient. The process involves gathering the data, processing it, and finally analyzing it to evaluate a finalized decree so that patient gets on-time medical assistance. In case any patient doesn't need any help from medical staff, then transmission of false data could also be prohibited so that forged sensor values are not communicated to relevant paramedics, and the patients who need medical surveillance could be attended.

4.3 Implementation

For validating the proposed approach, we have devised a system as illustrated in Fig. 2. Moreover, we have carried out a case study to ensure that data integrity is maintained when it's communicated over a network. As the encoded string is transferred over network lines that could not be altered without a shared key the inclusion of third-party is least to zero.

Node-red is the tool that we have used for simulating SVPMS. We simulated the workflow in the node-red dashboard and analyzed how packets are sent over different protocols. We have evaluated the performance of encrypted data packets over HTTP and MQTT using their size and transmission time. Before sending packets over the network, they are encrypted using C# to ensure their safety.

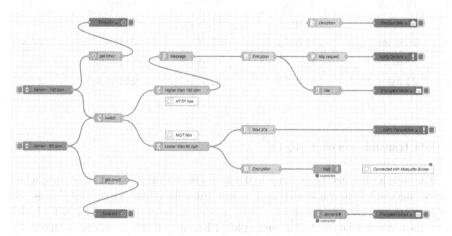

Fig. 2. SVPMS implementation in Node-Red

Sensors will be attached to individuals to monitor their heartbeat based on which, it would be analyzed whether their voice is pathological or normal. In the above diagram, two input nodes are used to inject different readings into the flow. Heartbeat less than 60 and greater than 100 is dangerous so both limitations are passed to the simulated network. Get time methods are used at the point where sensors inject data. A switch is attached to the sensors which evaluate the data depending upon the threshold values and forward the messages to the relevant branch. At this stage, the flows are separated.

4.4 Results

In this part, we have illustrated the working of our proposed system in Node-Red and carried out an analysis of results obtained from communicating data over HTTP and MQTT. Packet sizes are calculated before and after encryption whereas the size of the encoded packet is also checked. Moreover, we have calculated the time difference of packet when it is sent by sensor, passes through the encryption process, and finally reaches at receiver end by using API and time nodes in Node-Red.

1) Data Transmission over HTTPS

Flow using HTTPS has another switch attached to it that cross-checks incoming sensor values. A function is used to convert the data into useful information so that receiving devices can present it to users in a readable format. The next node in the flow is used for calling API for encryption. The average time for data flow over HTTPS is 2.74 as details are shown in Table 2.

Table 2. Data transmission over HTTPS

Sr#	Packet size before encryption	Packet size after encryption	Size difference	Packet size after decryption	Time
1	18 Bytes	64 Bytes	46 Bytes	18 Bytes	2.9 s
2	24 Bytes	88 Bytes	64 Bytes	24 Bytes	2.6 s
3	26 Bytes	88 Bytes	62 Bytes	24 Bytes	2.6 s
4	13 Bytes	44 Bytes	31 Bytes	13 Bytes	3.1 s
5	22 Bytes	62 Bytes	40 Bytes	22 Bytes	2.5 s

2) Data Transmission over MQTT

The switch transfers the message to the flow where another switch is attached which decides the value to be transferred next. Afterward, the payload is transmitted to an API for generating an encrypted response. This encoded message flows over MQTT which is later attached to a debug node. To connect MQTT-in and MQTT-out nodes, we have used the Mosquitto broker to specify the shared port. This works as a point of connection to connect nodes wirelessly and publish data to be received by another node. Throw-catch blocks are used to track errors. 0.93 s is the average recorded time for data flow using MQTT. Details of this encryption process at MQTT are shown in Table 3.

5 Discussion and Limitation

Technologies evolve with time, so the protocols and procedures used to secure messages on WAN need to be enhanced to provide reliability and security. Thus, we have worked on encrypted data transfer in IoT with two protocols i.e., MQTT and HTTPS.

Table 3. Data transmission over MQTT

Sr#	Packet size before encryption	Packet size after encryption	Size difference	Packet size after decryption	Time
1	9 Bytes	44 Bytes	35 Bytes	9 Bytes	0.57 s
2	24 Bytes	88 Bytes	64 Bytes	24 Bytes	1.2 s
3	15 Bytes	44 Bytes	29 Bytes	15 Bytes	1.1 s
4	23 Bytes	64 Bytes	41 Bytes	23 Bytes	0.82 s
5	13 Bytes	44 Bytes	31 Bytes	44 Bytes	0.96 s

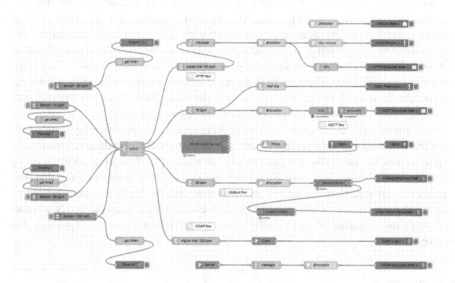

Fig. 3. Implementation of EAES-IoT with four application layer protocols

The results were encouraging and would be enhanced in the future for other protocols which lie at the application layer. We have also tested the proposed algorithm with four protocols and promising throughput was observed (see Fig. 3).

The case study is mapped on Node-Red where messages are injected into the flow. Messages are forwarded based on payload value. Encoding messages before they stream over the network has been achieved by calling API which has unique keys for encryption and decryption to ensure security. It is deployed on azure servers to ensure that both flow and encryption data do not reside on the same machine. EAES-IoT has the facility of changing keys in case of a security threat. AES is one of the efficient algorithms in terms of memory and computation. Lengthy key sizes make it robust against malicious attacks.

When the key size is the strength of the proposed methodology, at the same time, it adds to the limitations as well. The more the size, the more time it takes to travel and in the worst case, it'd affect the performance. It should be worked upon so that a consolidated output could be retrieved without affecting any functional or non-functional characteristics of the system. Moreover, servers should be kept awake so that API calling is possible whenever needed. Resource management is also a matter to be investigated as we have limited resources when working with IoT systems to ensure quality and performance attributes are satisfied.

6 Conclusion and Future Work

IoT possesses a security challenge so building an IoT with fundamental firewalls and dependable enough for coping with future attacks is crucial so that it remains reliable for high and low-level devices connected across a network to share messages. To give a comprehensive elucidation, this paper proposed a security-enhancing algorithm that provides end-to-end encryption through API to ensure that messages are communicated in the encoded form before then travel over the network. EAES-IoT is recommended to be configured to an IoT system as AES used in the proposed solution follows a combination of data shifting and shuffling while keeping on adding extra bytes in a row to keep itself safe from vulnerabilities. The system is designed in such a way that unauthorized users cannot pass the multi-layer firewalls to hamper the encryption algorithm whereas data communication to the network uses API to ensure augmented safety.

For carrying out future work, we are working on other application layer protocols and a few proposals include making an analysis of these protocols and investigating the outputs to pick the most efficient one. Moreover, working with a private Virtual Proxy Network (VPN) is also suggested for adding an extra security layer to ensure that data is safe from any unauthorized access and malicious attacks. It can also be extended by creating an extra security layer using hashes (blockchain techniques) to verify whether there were any incidents of data purging or not so that relevant countermeasures could be taken.

References

1. Chze, P.L.R., Leong, K.S.: A secure multi-hop routing for IoT communication. In Proceedings of IEEE World Forum of Internet of Things (WF-IoT), USA, pp. 428–432 (2014)
2. Hameed, S., Idrees, K.F., Hameed, B.: Understanding security requirements and challenges in Internet of Things (IoT): a review. J. Comput. Netw. Commun. 11, 1–14 (2019)
3. U-Blox Homepage. https://www.u-blox.com/en/blog/IP-versus-soap-iot-communications. Accessed 18 July 2021
4. Sicari, S., Rizzardi, A., Miorandi, D., Cappiello, C., Coen-Porisini, A.: A secure and quality-aware prototypical architecture for the Internet of Things. Inf. Syst. 58, 43–55 (2016)
5. Zhang, H., Zhang, T.: Short paper: 'A peer to peer security protocol for the internet of things': secure communication for the sensible things platform. In 18th International Conference on Intelligence in Next Generation Networks, France, pp. 154–156. IEEE (2015)
6. Kajwadkar, S., Jain, VK.: A novel algorithm for DoS and DDoS attack detection in Internet of Things. In 2018 Conference on Information and Communication Technology (CICT), India, pp. 1–4. IEEE (2018)
7. Esquiagola, J., Costa, L., Calcina, P., Zuffo, M.: Enabling CoAP into the swarm: a transparent interception CoAP-HTTP proxy for the Internet of Things. In: 2017 Global Internet of Things Summit (GIoTS), Switzerland, pp. 1–6. IEEE (2017)

8. Babitha, M.P., Babu, K.R.R.: Secure cloud storage using AES encryption. In: 2016 International Conference on Automatic Control and Dynamic Optimization Techniques (ICACDOT), India, pp. 859–864. IEEE (2016)
9. Colitti, W., Steenhaut, K., Caro, N.D.: Integrating wireless senso: networks with the web. In: Extending the Internet to Low Power and Lossy Networks (2011)
10. Mano, Y., et al.: Exploiting IoT technologies for enhancing Health Smart Homes through patient identification and emotion recognition. Comput. Commun. **89**(90), 178–190 (2016)
11. Miraz, M., Ali, M., Excell, P., Picking, R.: Internet of nano-things, things and everything: future growth trends. Future Internet **10**(8), 68 (2018)
12. Soni, D., Makwana, A.: A survey on MQTT: a protocol of Internet of Things (IoT). In: International Conference on Telecommunication, Power Analysis and Computing Techniques (2017)
13. Hwang, H.C., Park, J., Shon, J.G.: Design and implementation of a reliable message transmission system based on MQTT protocol in IoT. Wirel. Pers. Commun. **91**(4), 1765–1777 (2016)
14. Razzak, F.: Spamming the Internet of Things: a possibility and its probable solution. Procedia Comput. Sci. **10**, 658–665 (2012)
15. Alansari, Z., et al.: Internet of Things: infrastructure, architecture, security and privacy. In: 2018 International Conference on Computing, Electronics and Communications Engineering (iCCECE), UK, pp. 150–155. IEEE (2018)
16. Sundareswaran, V., Mahesh, K., Rajesh, M., Salmon, S.: Survey on smart agriculture using IoT. Int. J. Innov. Res. Eng. Manage. (IJIREM) **5**(2), 62–66 (2018)
17. Tadejko, P.: Application of Internet of Things in logistics-current challenges. Econ. Manag. **7**(4), 54–64 (2015)
18. Hussain, I., Negi, M.C., Pandey, N.: Proposing an encryption/decryption scheme for IoT communications using binary-bit sequence and multistage encryption. In: 2018 7th International Conference on Reliability, Infocom Technologies and Optimization (Trends and Future Directions) (ICRITO), India, pp. 709–713. IEEE (2018)
19. Jhosh, A.: Comparison of encryption algorithms: AES, Blowfish and Twofish for security of wireless networks. Int. Res. J. Eng. Technol. **7**(6), 4656–4658 (2020)
20. Panda, M., Nag, A.: Plain text encryption using AES, DES and SALSA20 by Java based bouncy castle API on Windows and Linux. In: 2015 Second International Conference on Advances in Computing and Communication Engineering, India, pp. 541–548. IEEE (2015)
21. Dibas, H., Sabri, K.E.: A comprehensive performance empirical study of the symmetric algorithms: AES, 3DES, Blowfish and Twofish. In: 2021 International Conference on Information Technology, Jordan, pp. 344–349. IEEE (2021)
22. Rihan, S.D., Khalid, A., Osman, S.E.: A performance comparison of encryption algorithms AES and DES. Int. J. Eng. Res. Technol. **4**(12), 151–154 (2015)
23. Muhammad, G., Rahman, S.K.M.M., Alelaiwi, A., Alamri, A.: Smart health solution integrating IoT and cloud: a case study of voice pathology monitoring. IEEE Commun. Mag. **55**(1), 69–73 (2017)
24. Github Homepage. https://github.com/RimshaZahid/IOTEncryption

Rationale, Design and Validity of Immersive Virtual Reality Exercises in Cognitive Rehabilitation

Jovita Janavičiūtė[2(✉)], Andrius Paulauskas[1], Liuda Šinkariova[2], Tomas Blažauskas[1], Eligijus Kiudys[1], Airidas Janonis[1], and Martynas Girdžiūna[1]

[1] Kaunas University of Technology, Kaunas, Lithuania
[2] Vytautas Magnus University, Kaunas, Lithuania
`jovita.janaviciute@vdu.lt`

Abstract. The application of virtual reality solutions for rehabilitation is hard, because stroke patients usually suffer motor, gait, and visual field impairments. This article discusses important aspects that should be addressed when developing programs of a similar nature. The system for stroke patients' cognitive rehabilitation is introduced. The development process of the system is described in detail. The results were validated using the Content Validity Index (CVI). The validation results revealed that the tasks created are suitable for stroke patients' cognitive rehabilitation.

Keywords: Virtual reality · Post-stroke rehabilitation

1 Introduction

Cognitive function impairments usually affect 20–80% of stroke survivals [1]. Although stroke is commonly classified as a disease of the elderly, the epidemiology of morbidity has changed in recent decades. Due to the significantly younger age of stroke survivals [2], people lose their jobs, or they are not able to do the same work tasks as before the stroke, which increases the economic burden of stroke. Despite the fact that cognitive functions are crucial to everyday activities, job tasks, most of all services of stroke rehabilitation target motor, but not cognitive impairments [3]. Cognitive impairments can be difficult to notice, but not detected cognitive impairments lead to difficulties in everyday activities, worsen quality of life, cause long-term disability, worsen rehabilitation outcomes [4, 5]. Furthermore, the decline in working memory was associated with poor functional outcomes in young (<50) stroke survivals [6]. Due to the wide prevalence of cognitive impairments, younger age of stroke survivals and increased economic burden, more effective and involving methods of cognitive rehabilitation are crucial.

Convenient rehabilitation methods are not attractive, engaging, and optimizing neuroplasticity processes in stroke patients. Traditional rehabilitation methods are based on various tasks which take cognitive effort but those are not necessarily based on everyday activities or important tasks for patients. Most recently the focus has been on more

A. Lopata et al. (Eds.): ICIST 2022, CCIS 1665, pp. 160–170, 2022.
https://doi.org/10.1007/978-3-031-16302-9_12

innovative computerized methods for cognitive function improvement in rehabilitation settings. The most promising virtual reality (VR) methods [7]. These methods help to improve impaired functions, motivation, and most important is that these methods optimize the neuroplasticity processes in the brain [8]. Immersive VR distinguishes high ecological validity because of the technical features which ensure a high level of immersion, true-to-life tasks, and user's interaction with the virtual environment [9].

In recent years, immersive VR technologies are used as an intervention tool in neurorehabilitation settings, and researchers have spotted beneficial effects of it. It is found that 6 immersive VR sessions have improved stroke patients' spatial orientation and reduced symptoms of spatial neglect [10]. Other researchers' findings suggest that immersive VR increases motivation during gait rehabilitation [11]. Furthermore, there is clear benefit of immersive VR in balance training [12]. Furthermore, the results of this research suggest that these methods are suitable for older patients, because of no significant complications or adverse effects. Moreover, resent research revealed that immersive VR is a useful and effective way to improve upper limb functions, as well as increase adherence rates [13]. Innovative technologies usually are used for motor, but not for cognitive rehabilitation [14], so it is important to fill this gap and develop an immersive VR program for cognitive rehabilitation.

The main goal of this article is to present the development process of the immersive VR program for stroke patients' cognitive rehabilitation and analyze its content validity.

2   Methods

The program was developed according to four stages [15]: 1) initial development stage; 2) program construction; 3) program testing; 4) final development stage. Each stage of the development of immersive VR tasks for cognitive rehabilitation is presented.

Stage 1. Initial development stage. At this stage, the main goal is to provide task content that is appropriate for the immersive VR program which will be suitable for cognitive rehabilitation in stroke patients. To achieve the goal, a literature review, about cognitive rehabilitation and important efficacy factors in stroke patients, was made. Immersive VR provides the ability to create a high level of task fidelity conditions that would allow patients to perform everyday tasks in a safe manner. Task fidelity is an important leading factor that provides improved function transfer to daily tasks [16]. Furthermore, the literature revealed that the program efficiency of cognitive function improvement is related to the level of presence [9] and flow [17] senses.

Most computerized rehabilitation programs are developed according to the principles of flow theory. Immersive VR methods are distinguished by the fact that the sense of flow is increased due to the technical capabilities. Flow theory describes a person's involvement in an activity that maintains the balance between the challenges and the available skills. This balance describes the fact that the challenges posed in a task are sufficient to be successfully overcome with optimal effort. If the challenges are too great, stress and anxiety arise, and if they are too small, participants will be bored [18]. One of the key features of immersive VR is the ability to vary the level of complexity of the tasks according to each person's capabilities [17]. This aspect, together with the well-designed interactivity and technique of the task, provides all the necessary conditions to evoke a sense of flow. To ensure the sense of flow, tasks in this study were created according to the following aspects [19]:

- Clear goals. The goal can be long-term or short-term, but it is important for the consumer to know what he or she needs to do.
- Feedback. The user receives multimodal feedback on each action taken, so they know if the action was performed correctly or incorrectly.
- Challenges meet skills.
- Focus.
- Ability to control the task or its aspects.
- Loss of self-awareness.
- Altered sense of time. The user loses sense of time, or the user feels that time is running faster.
- Activities are rewarding and stimulating.

Consequently, immersive VR tasks for stroke patients' cognitive rehabilitation should be simple, easy to use, replicate everyday activities which are challenging, and have clear goals. Cognitive rehabilitation will be more effective if the sense of presence is achieved during the tasks, so during the activities, it should be easy to control the aspects of tasks. Furthermore, tasks should maintain the user's attention, and other external stimuli, that may interfere with the concentration of attention, should be limited. During the task, it is important to reward correct action with positive feedback, so the user can learn and be involved. Immersive VR tasks for stroke patients' cognitive rehabilitation were created according to all mentioned principles.

Stage 2. Program construction. At this stage, the main goal is to conceptualize the content of the task according to the literature review, and technical program development. During this stage, the interdisciplinary team worked together to build the program.

Figure 1 shows the main use cases of the created system. The software requires two people for operation. One person should control the flow of the tasks (control tasks use case). Normally it is a physician. The second person (patient) is the one that performs tasks.

There are two tasks to be performed within a virtual reality application: sequence recall: cooking (perform sequence recall task) and object recall: remembering the products (perform object recall task).

Sequence Recall: Cooking. Participant is asked to remember the sequence of the cooking ingredients lighting and put them in the bowl in a particular order (see Fig. 2). The task environment is the ordinary kitchen. Each time participant should remember a different variation of the sequence. If the research participant successfully completes the task twice with a sequence of X products, one additional product is added. The participant always sees more products than he or she needs to remember. When the recall of the sequence is done correctly, an image of the dish appears as a reward. Also, a participant gets multimodal feedback which informs if the task is done correctly or not. When the task is completed correctly points are awarded.

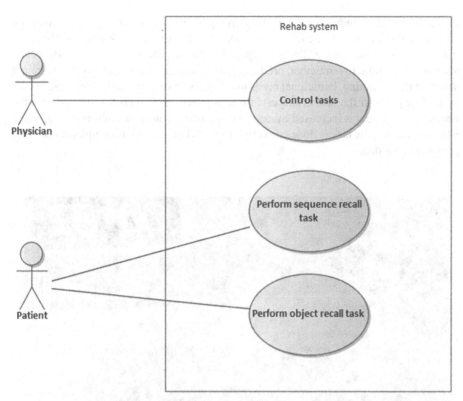

Fig. 1. Presented rehabilitation system context.

Fig. 2. The sequence recall task illustration.

Object Recall: Remember the Products. Participant is to remember products that are shown for a limited time (see Fig. 3). This task is like an everyday task when the shopping list needs to be remembered. The participant is asked to remember shown products and after the given time to remember, products appear together with products that were not shown at the beginning. Participant needs to select and take the products that were shown in the first place. If the task is successfully completed twice with X products, then the number of products is increased by one. Also, a participant gets multimodal feedback which informs if the task is done correctly or not. When the task is completed correctly points are awarded.

Fig. 3. The object recall task illustration.

Figure 4 shows the major components of the system. At the moment the application is dedicated to Windows machines, although later it can be compiled onto different platforms, including mobile ones (like Oculus Quest or similar). The patient wears virtual reality glasses and uses one controller to grab and put items. The physician uses the Bluetooth keyboard to select the tasks. The keyboard is connected to virtual reality glasses and interacts with the same application that is used by the patient.

Stage 3. Program testing. At this stage, the main goal is to test and evaluate the technical features of the tasks and their suitability for a stroke patient's cognitive rehabilitation. This stage was organized into two sub-stages: 1) program testing among the development team; 2) program testing among the experts. After every program testing among the team corrections were made. Most of the corrections during the first sub-stage were technical.

To evaluate tasks' content validity and suitability for stroke patients, the second sub-stage was made. This stage involved experts who work with stroke patients in a rehabilitation center. Experts were asked to perform the created immersive VR tasks, and after that they were asked to fill out the questionnaire. The procedure and instructions

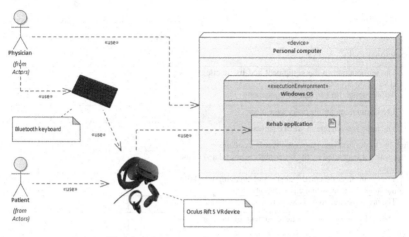

Fig. 4. The proposed system deployment.

were standardized and 16 experts participated: 1 neurologist, 3 physical medicine and rehabilitation physicians, 3 health psychologists, 4 occupational therapists, 3 physiotherapists, and 2 Doctors in Psychology. Experts were asked to perform created immersive VR tasks and evaluate their suitability for stroke patients' cognitive rehabilitation in three sections: 1) procedure suitability; 2) suitability of the first task; 3) suitability of the second task. Experts were asked to fill out a questionnaire (see Fig. 5). The questionnaire was conducted according to the example of judges' evaluation used in the study by Cordoso et al. (2017) [15]. The 12-item questionnaire was created and contained 3 subscales: procedure evaluation (4 items), the first task evaluation (4 items), and the second task evaluation (4 items). Each item was evaluated using a 4-points Likert scale (1 – strongly disagree; 2 – disagree; 3 – agree; 4 – strongly agree). Also, to identify recommended changes or suggestions, open-ended questions were used.

Stage 4. Final development stage. The main goal is to make final corrections and the program finalization. A Content Validity Index (CVI) was calculated to evaluate the program's suitability for stroke patients' cognitive rehabilitation. CVI shows the agreement between experts on suitability and content validity of the tasks [20]. Open-ended questions were analyzed to determine the key areas for the final program improvement.

3   Results

Results will be presented for the last stage of program development.

3.1   Content Validity

To evaluate content validity CVI was calculated for the separate item, for the sub-scale, and for the total questionnaire.

The level of agreement (CVI) of the experts on the suitability of the procedure shows that the procedure is suitable (see Table 1). Also, everyone evaluated that they

No.	Question	Strongly Disagree	Disagree	Agree	Strongly Agree
Procedure suitability					
1.	The introduction to the equipment and its functions was clear.				
2.	Allow enough time to test the equipment.				
3.	The instructions for the tasks were clear.				
4.	The tasks are suitable for stroke patients.				
Suitability of the first task (*Sequence recall: cooking*)					
5.	I was not distracted by the other objects not related to the task.				
6.	The environment seemed realistic and engaging (i.e. I did not think I was in virtual environment).				
7.	The task is related to daily activities.				
8.	The task focuses on the development of memory and attention.				
Suitability of the second task (*Object recall: remember the products*)					
9.	I was not distracted by the other objects not related to the task.				
10.	The environment seemed realistic and engaging (i.e. I did not think I was in virtual environment).				
11.	The task is related to daily activities.				
12.	The task focuses on the development of memory and attention.				
Open-ended questions					
13.	What was the most difficult in the tasks?				
14.	What aspects, if any, could be improved?				

Fig. 5. Questionnaire used for suitability and content validity of tasks in testing among the experts.

had enough time to test the equipment. Almost everyone felt that the instructions for the tasks were clear, except one expert who wanted more detailed instructions. All the experts evaluated that the tasks are suitable for stroke patients. The average CVI of the procedure suitability sub-scale shows that the procedure meets a satisfactory level, and thus the procedure of the immersive VR tasks has achieved a satisfactory level of content validity.

The level of agreement (CVI) of the experts on the suitability of the first task (see Table 2) and the second task shows that the tasks are suitable. The level of agreement on the separate question shows that both tasks are related to daily activities and focus on improving memory and attention. Almost all the experts evaluated that they were not distracted, and the virtual environment seemed realistic and engaging. That shows good immersion of the tasks. The average CVIs of both tasks' suitability show that the tasks

Table 1. Content validity of the procedure

Heading level	E1	E2	E3	E4	E5	E6	E7	E8	E9	E10	E11	E12	E13	E14	E15	E16	CVI
I was not distracted by the other objects not related to the task	1	1	1	1	1	1	1	1	1	1	1	1	1	1	1	1	1
The environment seemed realistic and engaging (i.e., I did not think I was in a virtual environment)	1	1	1	1	1	1	1	1	1	1	1	1	1	1	1	1	1
The task is related to daily activities	1	1	1	1	1	1	1	1	1	1	1	1	1	0	1	1	0.94
The task focuses on the development of memory and attention	1	1	1	1	1	1	1	1	1	1	1	1	1	1	1	1	1
S-CVI/ave																	0.98

Note. E – Expert, S-CVI/ave – the average of CVI scores across all items in the sub-scale, 1 – expert evaluated the item as suitable (on a 4-points Likert scale marked 3 or 4), 0 – expert evaluated the item as unsuitable (on a 4-points Likert scale marked 1 or 2).

meet a satisfactory level, and thus the tasks of the immersive VR tasks have achieved a satisfactory level of content validity (Table 3).

Table 2. Content validity of the first task (Sequence recall: cooking)

Question	E1	E2	E3	E4	E5	E6	E7	E8	E9	E10	E11	E12	E13	E14	E15	E16	CVI
I was not distracted by the other objects not related to the task	1	1	1	1	1	1	1	1	1	1	1	1	0	1	1	1	0.94
The environment seemed realistic and engaging (i.e., I did not think I was in a virtual environment)	1	1	1	1	1	1	1	1	1	1	1	0	1	1	1	1	0.94

(*continued*)

Table 2. (*continued*)

Question	E1	E2	E3	E4	E5	E6	E7	E8	E9	E10	E11	E12	E13	E14	E15	E16	CVI
The task is related to daily activities	1	1	1	1	1	1	1	1	1	1	1	1	1	1	1	1	1
The task focuses on the development of memory and attention	1	1	1	1	1	1	1	1	1	1	1	1	1	1	1	1	1
S-CVI/ave																	0.97

Table 3. Content validity of the second task (Object recall: remember the products).

Question	E1	E2	E3	E4	E5	E6	E7	E8	E9	E10	E11	E12	E13	E14	E15	E16	CVI
I was not distracted by the other objects not related to the task	1	1	1	1	1	1	1	1	1	1	1	1	1	1	1	1	1
The environment seemed realistic and engaging (i.e., I did not think I was in a virtual environment)	1	1	1	1	1	1	1	1	1	1	1	0	1	1	1	1	0.94
The task is related to daily activities	1	1	1	1	1	1	1	1	1	1	1	1	1	1	1	1	1
The task focuses on the development of memory and attention	1	1	1	1	1	1	1	1	1	1	1	1	1	1	1	1	1
S-CVI/ave																	0.98

3.2 Open-Ended Questions Analysis

During the analysis of the open-ended questions the experts' answers were divided into two groups: 1) related to the instructions; 2) related to the technical characteristics of the tasks. Even though the level of agreement between experts shows satisfactory content validity and that the tasks are suitable for stroke patients' cognitive rehabilitation, some suggestions arise.

Adjustments and Changes Related to the Instructions. Three experts considered that stroke patients must have enough time to try out the controller without a head-mounted display because it could be a new experience for stroke patients, and it should be clear how to use the technology. Two experts pointed out that the products in the tasks should be more stable or participants should be notified that products may fall. Due to fall risk prevention, one expert considered that participants who have motor impairments should sit in front of the table.

Adjustments and Changes Related to the Technical Characteristics of the Tasks. Three experts noted that a wide field of vision is necessary to complete the task, therefore it could be difficult for stroke patients to see all products. Moreover, five experts considered that the view could be more detailed and clearer, and two experts noted that the environment could be more realistic. Seven experts announced that the products should be less far away, and participants should reach them without any effort.

4   Conclusions

The purpose of this article was to present the development process of the immersive VR program for stroke patients' cognitive rehabilitation and analyze its content validity. The application of virtual reality solutions for rehabilitation is hard, because stroke patients usually suffer motor, gait, and visual field impairments. The implementation and initial testing revealed important aspects that should be addressed when developing programs of a similar nature. As the results show, it is important to organize objects closely; objects should be in the concentrated visual field, easily identified, and clear. The validation results, acquired using the content validity index, revealed that the created tasks are suitable for stroke patients' cognitive rehabilitation. To sum up, the design of the development process of the immersive VR program for stroke patient's cognitive rehabilitation is suitable.

This study presents some limitations as well. The sample in this study was convenient; the experts work in the same institution which limits the generalizability of our results. Furthermore, patients were not involved in the study; this study do not reveal the usability of the program from patient's point of view. Future research should consider these limitations, and analyze the system usability of the patients' point of view.

References

1. Sun, J.H., Tan, L., Yu, J.T.: Post-stroke cognitive impairment: epidemiology, mechanisms and management. Ann. Transl. Med. **2**(8) (2014)
2. Benjamin, E.J., et al.: Heart disease and stroke statistics—2019 update: a report from the American Heart Association. Circulation **139**(10), e56–e528 (2019)
3. Langhorne, P., Bernhardt, J., Kwakkel, G.: Stroke rehabilitation. Lancet **377**(9778), 1693–1702 (2011)
4. McDowd, J.M., Filion, D.L., Pohl, P.S., Richards, L.G., Stiers, W.: Attentional abilities and functional outcomes following stroke. J. Gerontol. B Psychol. Sci. Soc. Sci. **58**(1), P45–P53 (2003)

5. Jehkonen, M., Laihosalo, M., Kettunen, J.: Anosognosia after stroke: assessment, occurrence, subtypes and impact on functional outcome reviewed. Acta Neurol. Scand. **114**(5), 293–306 (2006)
6. Synhaeve, N.E., et al.: Cognitive performance and poor long-term functional outcome after young stroke. Neurology **85**(9), 776–782 (2015)
7. Coupar, F., Langhorne, P., Rowe, P.J., Weir, C.: Effectiveness of interventions for upper limb recovery after stroke: a systematic review. In: XVIII European Stroke Conference (2009)
8. Kleim, J.A., Jones, T.A.: Principles of experience-dependent neural plasticity: implications for rehabilitation after brain damage (2008)
9. Tieri, G., Morone, G., Paolucci, S., Iosa, M.: Virtual reality in cognitive and motor rehabilitation: facts, fiction and fallacies. Expert Rev. Med. Devices **15**(2), 107–117 (2018)
10. Huygelier, H., et al.: An immersive virtual reality game to train spatial attention orientation after stroke: a feasibility study. Appl. Neuropsychol.: Adult 1–21 (2020)
11. Kern, F., Winter, C., Gall, D., Käthner, I., Pauli, P., Latoschik, M.E.: Immersive virtual reality and gamification within procedurally generated environments to increase motivation during gait rehabilitation. In: 2019 IEEE Conference on Virtual Reality and 3D User Interfaces (VR), pp. 500–509 (2019)
12. Rebêlo, F.L., de Souza Silva, L.F., Doná, F., Barreto, A.S., Quintans, J.D.S.S.: Immersive virtual reality is effective in the rehabilitation of older adults with balance disorders: a randomized clinical trial. Exp. Gerontol. **149**, 111308 (2021)
13. Elor, A., Teodorescu, M., Kurniawan, S.: Project star catcher: a novel immersive virtual reality experience for upper limb rehabilitation. ACM Trans. Accessible Comput. (TACCESS) **11**(4), 1–25 (2018)
14. Domínguez-Téllez, P., Moral-Muñoz, J.A., Salazar, A., Casado-Fernández, E., Lucena-Antón, D.: Game-based virtual reality interventions to improve upper limb motor function and quality of life after stroke: systematic review and meta-analysis. Games Health J. **9**(1), 1–10 (2020)
15. Cardoso, C.D.O., Dias, N.M., Seabra, A.G., Fonseca, R.P.: Program of neuropsychological stimulation of cognition in students: emphasis on executive functions-development and evidence of content validity. Dementia Neuropsychologia **11**, 88–99 (2017)
16. Saposnik, G., et al.: Effectiveness of Virtual Reality Exercises in STroke Rehabilitation (EVREST): rationale, design, and protocol of a pilot randomized clinical trial assessing the Wii gaming system. Int. J. Stroke **5**(1), 47–51 (2010)
17. De Luca, R., et al.: Effects of virtual reality-based training with BTs-Nirvana on functional recovery in stroke patients: preliminary considerations. Int. J. Neurosci. **128**(9), 791–796 (2018)
18. Csikszentmihalyi, M., Csikszentmihalyi, I.S. (eds.): Optimal Experience: Psychological Studies of Flow in Consciousness. Cambridge University Press, Cambridge (1992)
19. Jones, M.G.: Creating electronic learning environments: games, flow, and the user interface. In: Selected Research and Development Presentations at the National Convention of the Association for Educational Communications and Technology (AECT) Sponsored by the Research and Theory Division (1998)
20. Yusoff, M.S.B.: ABC of content validation and content validity index calculation. Resource **11**(2), 49–54 (2019)

IoT Applications Powered by Piezoelectric Vibration Energy Harvesting Device

Chandana Ravikumar[✉]

Kaunas University of Technology, 44249 Kaunas, Lithuania
chandana.ravikumar@ktu.edu
http://linkedin.com/in/chandana-ravikumar-a5302b110

Abstract. Regarding IoT applications, the efficiency has immensely upgraded, though the product features remain the same, the progress in extremely low power sensing and computing has boosted the efficiency and thereby the power consumption of IoT devices have drastically dropped. With this change happening for the first time in history, it is actually feasible to tap into this appreciable energy available in our surroundings to power such electronic devices. The tapped energy from environment not only enables self-reliant electronics but also gives a chance for addition of newer features in IoT applications. This paper is devoted to the development of a multilayer PVDF based piezoelectric vibration energy harvesting device for powering wireless sensor networks and low power electronic devices. The purpose of the device is to be the power supply to endless applications of information technology.

The designed energy harvester successfully generates an average power of $9.2\,\mu\mathrm{W/g/mm^3}$ with a resonant frequency of 43 Hz, generating at least 15 V rms voltage and 495 μW power for acceleration 1 g. The commercial piezo sensors generate power of only $10\,\mathrm{nW/g/mm^3}$. This work reveals the challenges and limitations involved in constructing a realistic piezoelectric energy harvesting system and how to overcome them with the proposed harvester design. The method of fabrication and design of the proposed energy harvester are also discussed. Comparison of the harvester results with other author works is presented. Future recommendations, suitable application areas and market size information is also provided.

Keywords: Self-reliant electronics · Powering IoT applications · Energy harvesting · Piezo sensor · Frequency response · Power efficiency

1 Introduction

One key component of the IoT are wireless sensors that measure a wide variety of data. For many wireless applications where sensors are used in moving components, embedded systems, or human body, a battery is required to power the sensor. A grid of wireless sensor networks needs wireless sensor nodes. Every sensor node is a combination of sensor, processing electronics, wireless communications, and power supply. It is not effective to have multiple nodes of batteries for a wireless network system to function properly and would therefore lead to a performance compromise.

The problem is that currently, 99% of sensors installed are powered by batteries that can provide them with the energy they need on average only for three years. This means that within a span of three years, a person must come to each sensor and replace the battery so that it can continue to operate. However, access to these sensors is mostly difficult or even dangerous, and the cost of that replacement is expensive. It is estimated that on average, for replacement of a single-sensor battery it costs around 200 euros [1, 2]. In most cases we will have to give up one the project idea because the money involved in maintaining and owning the system far outweighs the cost of installation. Either the battery replacement problem must be solved or the idea itself is abandoned. The solution for this problem will be game changer for many electronic companies.

Disposing of batteries is also a big concern for environment. Use of batteries have some limitations due to the limited lifetime and need for replacement. Their disposal poses an environmental hazard since batteries contain chemicals which are harmful to environment and human [3]. Traditionally, power has always been brought to the device, either through a cable or a battery. There are technical issues with the practical deployment of such sensors, mainly because of the difficulty in the installation of the sensors itself and the cost of power cables which supply power and transfers the signal to remote locations.

We must change the paradigm. Now power supply has to be done differently using the energy already available at the device's location, entering the field of energy harvesting. Extracting energy from moving objects that often experience stress, such as shoes or parts in a factory, could be a way to power small devices to conserve electricity. Attempts have been made to integrate piezoelectric components into backpacks and shoes with a demonstrated power output enough to power small devices such as phones [4, 5]. Piezoelectric polymers have been considered for applications in therapeutics [6], as they are more flexible than some alternatives, and are able to produce ultrasonic waves for ultrasound imaging [7], tissue surgery [8], and potential cancer treatment [9], all while being incorporated into small thin devices or into the body. Alternatively, piezoelectric materials could be used for more precise and accurate robotic surgery assistants by incorporating piezoelectric elements into sensors that could relay pressure information to a computer [10]. For the transformation of kinetic energy to electrical energy, piezoelectric elements are often the defining feature of such innovations. Piezoelectric materials have drastically transformed many aspects of science and technology since their discovery.

More often than not these materials are crystals like quartz or ceramics or polymers like PVDF (polyvinylidene fluoride) or biological tissues such as silk, bone [11–13] and also microbes and specific viruses or even cane sugar [14–16] which has interlocking electrical domain which gives them a neutral charge. Whenever these materials are compressed or deformed their symmetry is broken releasing electrical charge which can then be syphoned. Piezoelectric polymers, currently the fastest growing class of piezoelectric materials, offer several benefits over ceramic and crystal piezoelectric materials. Piezoelectric polymers have strong inherent molecular dipoles due to aligned alternating electronegative and electropositive groups, with fluorine often serving as the electroneg-ative group. When the polymer is exposed to pressure, the change in dipole density gen-erates an electric field. Most conventionally available piezoelectric polymers are poly (vinylidenes) such as PVDF or PVDC. These materials usually have lower piezoelectric coefficients than ceramics but offer advantages such as flexibility and low mechanical impedance [17, 18].The shapes of piezoelectric elements also play a role in materials selection, and piezoelectric polymers are being developed so quickly in part due to their malleability and low density. Polymers are also more impact resistant than ceramics, and have low dielectric constants, which makes them very voltage sensitive. The variety of synthesis methods for polymeric piezoelectric material has made these materials much cheaper, and methods for combining several polymers or nanopatterning polymers have made them the material of choice for extensive applications [19].

This study proposes a piezoelectric energy harvester that works on the principle of piezoelectric effect and is made from available raw polymer PVDF material. Polyvinyli-dene difluoride is a non-reactive semi crystalline fluoropolymer produced by the poly-merization of vinylidene difluoride [20]. The emergence of the new 3D printing manu-facturing technique to make β phase -PVDF material more resistance to high and low temperatures will unfold new application areas in the field of energy harvester tech-nology [21]. One of the most significant properties is the piezoelectric coefficient, as a higher electrical output for a given pressure, or vice versa, is favorable for many appli-cations. The β phase -PVDF has high piezoelectric d_{31} coefficient of 25 pC/N and hence becomes a suitable material to be incorporated in the proposed energy harvester.

The reminder of this paper is structured as follows. Section 2 shows the problems involved in building piezoelectric energy harvesting systems. Section 3 presents the experiment methodology, block diagram of the proposed energy harvesting system, fabrication process of harvester and experiment setup. Results are given in Sect. 4. Discussion of results and possible application areas are presented in Sect. 5. Section 6 concludes and outlines future lines of work.

2   Challenges in Building a Piezoelectric Energy Harvesting System

The frequencies in the natural environment must be in tune to match its oscillating energy harvesting characteristics and that also requires the design of the converter for different uses and functions in energy conversion environment. To deal with the energy range of frequencies, it would be much better if such transducers could be adapted. Sensor and transducer energy conversion is necessary for the conditioning electronics to supply electrical power in a form that is acceptable to the system electronics.

Although energy is always around us in one form or the other, energy harvesting is probably still one of the oldest ideas alive today. It lacks large-scale commercial application mainly because of some critical issues as discussed below.

- **Low energy output**
    The energy obtained by tapping into the wasted natural vibration present in our surroundings is obviously trivial, mostly the power generated is in μWat range. There-fore, mobile phones or laptops are unlikely to be powered by energy harvesting. But

when it comes to IoT applications, there is a big possibility since product efficiency is high, power requirement for computing and sensing is minimum. This scenario opens an interesting opportunity to actually use the small energy that surrounds us to power devices. With this development the first challenge of using low level energy is resolved by the reduction of power consumption.

- **Low voltage output**

  The output voltage derived from energy harvesting is usually between 40 mV to 100 mV. Most electronic devices operate from 3.6 V or more hence this level of voltage will not be suitable. In recent research, there is now a way to upgrade this low level voltage to a higher voltage using the benefit of MPPT (Artificial Intelligence Powered Maximum Energy Point Tracking) with over 92% efficiency [22].

- **Large number of external components**

  A large number of external components causes a high form factor The footprint on the printing circuit becomes too large and hence renders unsuitable for the application, as it cannot integrate into a very small watch or tracking device [23]. Therefore, less external components can be recommended.

- **High form factor on PCB**

  The most challenging part of the electronics involved in an energy harvesting system is the charge lost between the internal and external capacitance of the main circuit of the system. This wasted charge reduces the amount of electrical energy output and indirectly the efficiency of the standard circuit is compromised. The only way to reduce this conversion loss is by ensuring accurate impedance matching (e.g. Using MPPT). This puts pressure on the PCB designer to achieve energy neutrality and raises concerns about the size of the PCB layout(defined by form factor) which is supposed to be within a couple of mm^2 area [24].

3   Methodology

3.1   Block Diagram of Proposed Energy Harvesting System and Supercapacitors

A self-powered piezoelectric vibration energy harvesting system generally consists of various parts mainly a vibration source, a piezoelectric energy transducer, an electrical interface circuit that converts the generated alternating current into direct current, and a storage unit. The electrical interface circuit is nothing but a rectifier circuit. In our design, four Schottky diodes SMD case number SOT23-6-1 were used to form a complete rectifier bridge, a 1nF capacitor was used as C_L, shown in Fig. 1. With the use of Schottky diodes the voltage drop is between 0 V to 0.6 V unlike the case in conventional silicon diodes where ethe voltage drop is 1.2 V. In this way our design helps to optimize the power output performance of the harvester circuit. After passing through the load capacitance (C_L) and load resistance (R_L) the rectified voltage is accumulated in a storage device. Our device uses a supercapacitor to accumulate and store energy for intermittent use.

A supercapacitor is a amalgamation of a battery and a capacitor. It is best of both worlds because it has the energy storage characteristics of a battery with the discharge characteristic of a capacitor. The supercapacitor is a promising replacement of traditional batteries becoming a key to enabling IoT applications with its added benefits of high-speed charging, improved safety, and reliability.

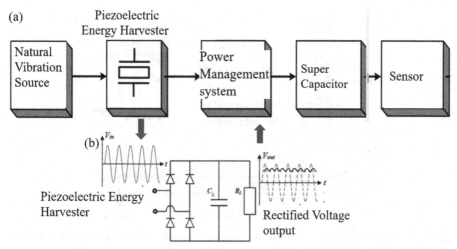

Fig. 1. (a) Block diagram of IoT sensor powered by a Vibration Energy Harvester (b) Harvester rectifier circuit

3.2   Principle of Operation and Fabrication of Energy Harvester

The harvester design focuses on overcoming the difficulties and limitations in proper technological application of harvester device in real life scenario. The design of electronic circuit for a real practical energy harvesting device is very critical in the technical point of view as far as energy conversion is concerned.

It is a grass root level concept and is majorly focused to develop a piezoelectric cantilever beam energy harvester from available raw materials like steel base core, polarized PVDF sheet etc. The proposed energy harvester is made of not just with one but three substances -polymer based PVDF material, thin metal plate and tipmass made of structural steel and a strong bonding adhesive made of epoxy resin. The harvester prototype is made of two layers of metal coated PVDF sheet of 30 μm thickness, stuck back-to-back on a passive base made of 100 μm thick steel, attached by conductive electrodes along with a tipmass weighing 25 g as seen in the Fig. 2(b) This PVDF material is purchased from Jinzhou kexin electronic material Co. ltd, having a d_{31} piezoelectric constant of 25 pC/N. The material parameters of piezoelectric material in energy harvester are shown in Table 1.

By varying the tipmass and the gap between the tipmass and the tipmass end is known to alter the resonant frequency and the voltage generated by the cantilever beam, for more relevant information refer to the previous published work in reference [25]. With enough simulation and experimental investigation of the harvester done in the previous work, a proper optimized bimorph piezoelectric cantilever design is constructed that proves to have a higher overall efficiency and a wider frequency spectrum as compared to other such products in the market. Comparison is shown in Table 2.

The Fig. 2(b) shows the principle of operation of the energy harvesting device. Due the tipmass weight attached to the end of PVDF layers, when the device vibrates, there is simultaneous expansion and compression of the top and bottom PVDF layers. The principle of operation of the product is based on the direct piezo effect -electrical

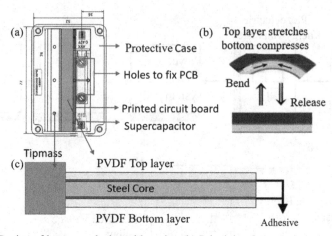

Fig. 2. (a) Design of harvester device with casing (b) Principle of direct piezoelectric effect (c) Constituent structure of Harvester device

Table 1. Parameters of piezoelectric material in energy harvester

PVDF	Units	Harvester
Operating temperature	°C	−40~80
Thickness	μm	30
Relative permittivity	$\varepsilon/\varepsilon_0$	9.5
Density	kg/m^3	1780
d_{31} Piezoelectric constant	pC/N	25
Yield strength	N/m^2	45~55
Young's modulus	MPa/psi	2500

technology that performs the conversion of kinetic energy generated by vibration into electricity. When the device is stretched and the upper PVDF layer receives tensile stress while the PVDF film below receives compressive stress. When the device is stretched, the curvature of the PVDF film changes and an electric charge is formed at the two electrodes of the PVDF film due to the changing stress on the PVDF film. With simultaneous repeating of stretching and relaxation movements the PVDF film will produce a voltage output. Figure 2(a) shows the design of whole harvester device enclosed in a casing along with the electronics and supercapacitor to store the generated energy.

3.3 Experiment Setup

Vibration power generators produce huge power if the frequency of the generator is same as frequency of ambient generator as these generators are in resonant system. The natural source vibration condition for the harvester is complicated. The source of vibration in the natural environment could be a combination of multiple vibrations like the hammering motion or a drilling motion or even stone cutting motion. To simulate such a vibration, one may use a simple sinusoidal vibration, or a complex random vibration, or even a sine vibration superimposed on random vibration.

The flow chart of experiment setup and the photo of the setup is shown in Fig. 3(a) and Fig. 3(b) respectively. The signal generator provides a particular frequency signal, once the signal is amplified the signal is used to energize the exciter to vibrate. This excitation is measured by a digital accelerometer. The acceleration values are seen on the computer screen. The prototype is fixed on the exciter. The output peak-to peak value is measured by an oscilloscope and rms value by a multimeter. The digital accelerometer is mounted on the exciter diaphragm to show the vibration acceleration supplied to the prototype.

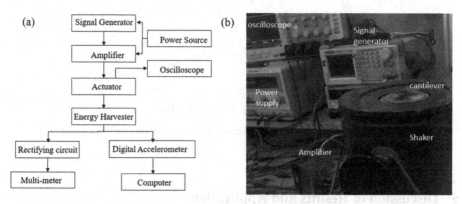

Fig. 3. (a) Flowchart of Experiment setup (b) Photo of Experiment setup in Laboratory

4 Result

The only purpose of a vibration energy harvester is to produce more and more output voltage from the available source of vibration. For validation of the harvester model, we manufactured real prototypes of the harvester design and tested the performance of the prepared harvesters. The output voltage generated by the harvester for various supply frequencies is observed, in order words the frequency response for the harvester is measured. At resonance frequency of 43 Hz the rms voltage generated is 10 V, 21 V and 25 V for acceleration levels 0.2 g, 1 g and 3 g respectively when the applied load impedance is 890 KΩ. The results are plotted in Fig. 4.

Hence after testing of the harvester prototypes made in the laboratory, it is seen that harvesters successfully generate power up to 500 μW per g (g referred to acceleration due to gravity on earth 9.8 m/s^2) which is just about sufficient to self-power any small electronic system. The area of piezoelectrical material in the prototype is 54 mm^3 hence the calculated power density is 9.2 μW/g/mm^3.

The rms voltage generated by the harvester is more than 5 times of that of commercially available piezo films. Also, power density is one thousand times more than power density of piezo films. This improved result is attributed to many reasons mainly bimorph PVDF layers of high piezoelectric coefficient, steel plate support allowing higher amplitude of cantilever deflection and bigger length to width ratio width of the cantilever. Along with the added high power generation capacity the harvester is more reliable because of its strong base and optimized structure.

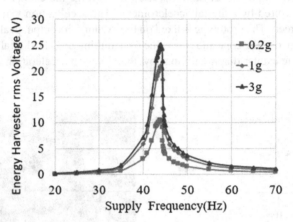

Fig. 4. Frequency response of Energy Harvester at acceleration levels 0.2 g, 1 g, 3 g.

5   Discussion of Results and Applications

For the purpose of comparison, results of energy harvester are tabulated along with other published works in Table 2. The proposed harvester is one of the best among the PVDF based energy harvesters within the similar volume reported so far.

The significance of this technology is that it does not require any wires and it can literally be placed into any product or machine-like grass movers or wood cutting machines that require electricity to operate and that show kind of vibration to turn the machine into a self-sufficient regenerative machine. Piezoelectricity does not emit any pollution similar to wind and solar energy. It only needs to be placed in or underneath the structures we already have in place today making it a preferrable solution to our crowded urban cities. Possibility within the next few years many mechanical aspects of the city like streetlamps, trolleys, subways perhaps even buildings themselves may be completely powered by the implementation of piezoelectric energy harvesters which will be able to gather the kinetic energy of cars riding on top of asphalt embedded with piezo harvesters. There is possibility that if the vehicle is electric in nature, it may even be able to derive its energy directly from the road itself, removing almost entirely the need for backup gasoline.

The main segment of industrial application will be wireless sensor manufacturers and IoT solution integrators. Its uses can also expand to Automotive, Logistics and Smart City area. In other words, harvesters will be used in monitoring the operation of various equipment, machine tools, following logistics processes, calculating passing cars and

Table 2. Comparison of proposed harvester with other published works

Sl no	f_{res}(Hz)	PVDF volume	$P_{max}(\mu W)$	$P_{Density}\left(\frac{\mu W/mm^3}{g}\right)$	Ref
1	33	70	0.9	0.035	[26]
2	30	70	4.5	0.116	[27]
3	17	82	16	0.15	[28]
4	30.8	54.88	8.59	0.220	[29]
5	55	52.5	4.3	0.38	[30]
6	103.8	97.41	10.6	1.94	[31]
7	34.4	130	112.8	7.22	[32]
8	43	54	495	9.26	Our proposal

yet endless solutions, and all that is needed for the harvester operation is the wasted vibration available in our surroundings.

The idea is to implant our proposed energy harvesters in outdoor power products like chainsaws, trimmers, garden tractors, mowers, tools for construction and stone industries which have abundant mechanical vibration that can be converted to electricity. The energy extracted can be used to power the sensors like the temperature sensors or location trackers or any other IoT device application. Another application of the harvester is to be assembled in after-asphalt and sidewalks in order to effectively generate electric power for electronic sensors targeted towards effective measurement of parameters relating to road conditions, traffic usage and patterns, vehicle speed, mass, tire condition and axle quality etc. This study identifies the need to automatically self-power electronics and sensors for real-time sensing and energy efficient data transfer in autonomous vehicles. With this energy system, a potential clean and reliable energy source is developed to scavenge energy from traffic-induced vibrations.

Fig. 5. (a) Zoomed photo of Harvester prototype in working condition (b) Photo of Harvester prototype mounted on a Stone cutting machine during installation.

In the picture given in Fig. 5(a), the proposed harvester prototype is fixed on a stone cutting machine. Since the harvester device has fixed geometry, it should be mounted as close as possible to the driving surface to harvest maximum energy from running machinery. The weight of tipmass and movement of tipmass in resonant configurations helps to convert wide or narrow-band vibration to piezoelectric generated electricity.

6 Conclusion

Regenerative technology appears to have the potential to break through the energy-efficiency roadblock and gives rise to the evolution of self-powered electronics. The ongoing research in this domain using the state-of-the-art laboratory equipment has played a key role to improve overall generated electricity significantly which contributes to reduce cost, encourage zero-carbon emission and sustainable energy generation through creation of alternative energy source using environmental mechanical vibrations. This in turn benefits the global growth of individuals by creating affordable and clean energy thus, developing innovative ideas on eco-friendly products and diversifying renewable energy sources.

The proposed energy harvester device within a volume of $53.76\,mm^3$ shows an output power of $495\,\mu W$ which is comparable to that of the best-performing PVDF-based energy harvesters within the similar volume reported so far. The frequency response of the proposed harvester is discussed and is compared with commercially available piezo sensors. The calculated power density of the harvester is $9.2\,\mu W/g/mm^3$. Whereas the power density of commercial piezo sensors is calculated to be $10\,nW/g/mm^3$. The rms voltage generated by the harvester is more than 5 times of that of piezo sensor at resonant frequency. Hence harvester power density is nearly one thousand times more than that of commercial piezo sensors.

Thus, based on our findings, it is proven that PVDF material can be used as a tool for piezoelectric conversion. Yet, there is still space for improvement in capacity of energy generated. Nevertheless, with sufficient research funding and in-depth study of piezoelectric material harvesters, the power generated can be significantly increased so in years to come it will be just as efficient as the solar technologies are now, thus it will become one more significant source of renewable energy.

References

1. Schmitz, J.A., Sherman, J.M., Hansen, S., Murray, S.J., Balkir, S., Hoffman, M.W.: A low-power, single-chip electronic skin interface for prosthetic applications. IEEE Trans. Biomed. Circuits Syst. 13(6), 1186–1200 (2019). https://doi.org/10.1109/TBCAS.2019.2948006
2. Kaustubh, P., Vaish, N.: Highly efficient PVDF film energy harvester for self charging vehicle system. In: Proceedings of the 9th Conference on Industrial and Commercial Use of Energy, ICUE 2012, pp. 179–183 (2012)
3. Rasheed, A., Iranmanesh, E., Andrenko, A.S., Wang, K.: Sensor integrated RFID tags driven by energy scavenger for sustainable wearable electronics applications. In: 2016 IEEE International Conference on RFID Technology and Applications, RFID-TA 2016, pp. 81–86 (2016). https://doi.org/10.1109/RFID-TA.2016.7750757
4. Snehalika, Bhasker, M.U.: Piezoelectric energy harvesting from shoes of soldier. In: 1st IEEE International Conference on Power Electronics, Intelligent Control and Energy Systems, ICPEICES 2016, pp. 1–5 (2017). https://doi.org/10.1109/ICPEICES.2016.7853116

5. Wang, Z.L., Chen, J., Lin, L.: Progress in triboelectric nanogenerators as a new energy technology and self-powered sensors. Energy Environ. Sci **8**, 2250 (2015). https://doi.org/10.1039/c5ee01532d

6. Keim, R.G.: The future is now. J. Clin. Orthod. **51**(1), 9–10 (2017)

7. Zhang, X., Sessler, G.M., Xue, Y., Ma, X.: Audio and ultrasonic responses of laminated fluoroethylenepropylene and porous polytetrafluoroethylene films with different charge distributions. J. Phys. D. Appl. Phys. **49**(20) (2016). https://doi.org/10.1088/0022-3727/49/20/205502

8. Varga, M., et al.: Direct piezoelectric responses of soft composite fiber mats. Appl. Phys. Lett. **102**(15), 1–5 (2013). https://doi.org/10.1063/1.4802593

9. Finot, E., Passian, A., Thundat, T.: Measurement of mechanical properties of cantilever shaped materials. Sensors **8**(5) (2008). https://doi.org/10.3390/s8053497

10. Aparna, Karanth, P.N., Kulkarni, S.M.: Modeling of cantilever type piezoelectric polymer actuator. In: 2018 3rd International Conference on Control and Robotics Engineering, ICCRE 2018, no. 1, pp. 274–279 (2018). https://doi.org/10.1109/ICCRE.2018.8376479

11. Afroze, S., Binti Haji Bakar, A.N., Reza, M.S., Salam, M.A., Azad, A.K.: Polyvinylidene fluoride (PVDF) piezoelectric energy harvesting from rotary retracting mechanism: imitating forearm motion. In: IET Conference Publications, vol. 2018, no. CP750, pp. 2–5 (2018). https://doi.org/10.1049/cp.2018.1591

12. Liu, H., Zhong, J., Lee, C., Lee, S.W., Lin, L.: A comprehensive review on piezoelectric energy harvesting technology: materials, mechanisms, and applications. Appl. Phys. Rev. **5**(4) (2018). https://doi.org/10.1063/1.5074184

13. Kaczmarek, H., Królikowski, B., Klimiec, E., Kowalonek, J.: New piezoelectric composites based on isotactic polypropylene filled with silicate. J. Mater. Sci.: Mater. Electron. **28**(9), 6435–6447 (2017). https://doi.org/10.1007/s10854-016-6329-9

14. McCall, W.R., Kim, K., Heath, C., La Pierre, G., Sirbuly, D.J.: Piezoelectric nanoparticle-polymer composite foams. ACS Appl. Mater. Interfaces **6**(22), 19504–19509 (2014). https://doi.org/10.1021/am506415y

15. Programme of the 23rd International Conference-School 'Advanced Materials and Technologies 2021' of Traces of Molecules, pp. 23–27 (2021)

16. Ghosh, S.K., Mandal, D.: Efficient natural piezoelectric nanogenerator: electricity generation from fish swim bladder. Nano Energy **28**, 356–365 (2016). https://doi.org/10.1016/j.nanoen.2016.08.030

17. Zhao, Y., Zhang, Y., Xu, J., Zhang, M., Yu, P., Zhao, Q.: Frequency domain analysis of mechanical properties and failure modes of PVDF at high strain rate. Constr. Build. Mater. **235**, 117506 (2020). https://doi.org/10.1016/j.conbuildmat.2019.117506

18. Eddiai, A., Meddad, M., Farhan, R., Mazroui, M., Rguiti, M., Guyomar, D.: Using PVDF piezoelectric polymers to maximize power harvested by mechanical structure. Superlattices Microstruct. **127**, 20–26 (2019). https://doi.org/10.1016/J.SPMI.2018.03.044

19. Król-Morkisz, K., Pielichowska, K.: Thermal decomposition of polymer nanocomposites with functionalized nanoparticles. Polym. Compos. Funct. Nanoparticles Synth. Prop. Appl. 405–435 (2018). https://doi.org/10.1016/B978-0-12-814064-2.00013-5

20. Ray, S., Cooney, R.P.: Thermal degradation of polymer and polymer composites. In: Handbook of Environmental Degradation of Materials, 3rd edn., pp. 185–206 (2018). https://doi.org/10.1016/B978-0-323-52472-8.00009-5

21. Tarbuttona, J., Leb, T., Helfrichb, G., Kirkpatrickb, M.: Phase transformation and shock sensor response of additively manufactured piezoelectric PVDF. Procedia Manuf. **10**, 982–989 (2017). https://doi.org/10.1016/J.PROMFG.2017.07.089

22. Savanth, A., Weddell, A.S., Myers, J., Flynn, D., Member, S., Al-hashimi, B.M.: Direct operation for energy harvesting systems. **64**(9), 2370–2379 (2017)

23. Home - Nowi. https://www.nowi-energy.com/. Accessed 22 Mar 2022
24. Kim, W.K.: Design and Analysis of Switching Circuits for Energy Harvesting in Piezostrutures (2012)
25. Cepenas, M., et al.: Research of parameters of plastic piezoelectric harvester for practical model implementation. In: Proceedings of the 13th International Conference on ELEKTRO 2020, vol. 2020-May (2020). https://doi.org/10.1109/ELEKTRO49696.2020.9130273
26. Rammohan, S., Chiplunkar, S., Ramya, C.M., Kumar, S.J., Jain, A.: Multi-layer piezoelectric energy harvesters for improved power generation, no. Fig 1, pp. 1–6 (2014)
27. Rammohan, S., Ramya, C., Jayanth Kumar, S., Anjana, J., Rudra, P.: Low frequency vibration energy harvesting using arrays of PVDF piezoelectric bimorphs. J. Inst. smart Struct. Syst. 3(1), 18–27 (2014)
28. Jiang, Y., Shiono, S., Hamada, H., Fujita, T., Higuchi, K., Maenaka, K.: Low-frequency energy harvesting using a laminated PVDF cantilever with a magnetic mass. Maenaka Human-Sensing Fusion Project, Japan Science and Technology Agency, Himeji, Japan, no. November (2009)
29. Sriramdas, R., Chiplunkar, S., Cuduvally, R.M., Pratap, R.: Performance enhancement of piezoelectric energy harvesters using multilayer and multistep beam configurations. IEEE Sens. J. 15(6), 3338–3348 (2015). https://doi.org/10.1109/JSEN.2014.2387882
30. Takise, H., Takahashi, T., Suzuki, M., Aoyagi, S.: Fabrication of piezoelectric vibration energy harvester using coatable PolyVinylidene DiFluoride and its characterisation. Micro Nano Lett. 12(8), 569–574 (2017). https://doi.org/10.1049/mnl.2017.0128
31. Cao, Z., Zhang, J., Kuwano, H.: Vibration energy harvesting characterization of 1 cm^2 poly(vinylidene fluoride) generators in vacuum. Jpn. J. Appl. Phys. 50(9), PART 3, 13–17 (2011). https://doi.org/10.1143/JJAP.50.09ND15
32. Song, J., Zhao, G., Li, B., Wang, J.: Design optimization of PVDF-based piezoelectric energy harvesters. Heliyon 3(9), e00377 (2017). https://doi.org/10.1016/J.HELIYON.2017.E00377

Holistic Approach for Representation of Interaction Scenarios in Semantically Integrated Conceptual Modelling

Remigijus Gustas[✉] and Prima Gustiene

Department of Information Systems, Karlstad University, Karlstad, Sweden
{Remigijus.Gustas,Prima.Gustiene}@kau.se

Abstract. One of the problems with conventional conceptual modelling methods is that they do not take into account certain important semantic interdependency types between the static and dynamic aspects. Integrity of dimensions is crucial for successful reasoning and solving problems that occur in conceptual modelling. Typically, conceptual modelling methods project various aspects of information systems using different graphical representations. Therefore, to reach semantic integration of various architectural aspects is very difficult. This paper presents semantically integrated conceptual modelling method. This method enables stability and flexibility of the diagrams that are very important for managing constant changes of organizational and technical requirements. It shows how alternative actions introduced into different scenarios. This is also important for controlling semantic integrity and for maintaining holistic representations of different aspects. Holistic modelling approach enables reasoning about system architecture across organizational and technical system boundaries. On a simple hotel reservation system scenario, it is demonstrated how different actions can be decomposed into more primitive underlying interaction loops. Integrated conceptual modelling method is important for evaluation of expressive power of conceptual modelling languages.

Keywords: Conceptual modeling · Semantic integration · Interaction dependency · Basic interactions · Alternative interactions

1 Introduction

Information systems (IS) architectures are complex engineering products that can be defined on various levels of abstractions and represented using different dimensions. Integration of these dimensions is critical, because they represent the same system. The traditional conceptual modelling methods do not provide an effective support in distinguishing crosscutting concerns, which span across various types of diagrams. It does not matter, whether system developers use structured analysis and design methods, object-oriented or component based methods. The modelling techniques used are poor in separation of concerns and this is one of the reasons why the conceptual modelling

© The Author(s), under exclusive license to Springer Nature Switzerland AG 2022
A. Lopata et al. (Eds.): ICIST 2022, CCIS 1665, pp. 183–196, 2022.
https://doi.org/10.1007/978-3-031-16302-9_14

of systems is rather primitive. Managing complexity of IS specifications in system engineering is a problem that can be certainly linked to various limitations of traditional IS modelling and design methods. When the requirements implied by one concern are modified, it is necessary to identify all related aspects and components, which can be affected by introduced changes. Especially, modifying requirements, which are specified in different diagrams, becomes quite problematic. Having a poor understanding of concerns, makes it difficult to introduce new changes or extensions in IS specifications.

The declarative nature of value flows oriented design [15, 17] enables system developers to analyze underlying business events, which are quite comprehensible for business experts, enterprise architects, and users. Value exchanges and related coordinating events can be used as the guidance for system designers to move smoothly from system analysis to design, without having no demand to represent a complete solution. Interaction-based thinking is fruitful in the area of enterprise engineering. However, there is a paradigmatic mismatch between the traditional object-oriented modelling methods and interaction-based system analysis approaches. The paradigmatic differences is the obstacle in finding a solution for the alignment of business process design with Information Technology (IT) operations. The principles, of how the blending of traditional system analysis and enterprise engineering methods, are unclear. The goal of this paper is to introduce SICM method [11]. The biggest advantage of this modelling method is that it provides a new way of enterprise modelling and integration. SICM method challenges the existing integration problems among interactive, behavioural and static aspects of IS.

DEMO approach [3] benefits with the focus on modelling of organizational interactions. This approach provides with the concise model of enterprise construction and operation. To analyse interactions it is very important in redesigning and reengineering organizations [12]. The advantage of modelling organizational interactions is that interactions remain relatively stable over time. It helps stakeholders to understand the essential business model before and after new changes take place. However, the significant efforts are necessary to align new changes of interactions with the corresponding modifications of static and dynamic aspects of IS specifications. A limited human mind is capable to focus on a particular concern at a time in isolation, without paying too much attention to other concerns. One particular concern usually comprises both static and dynamic aspects. Conventional system analysis and design methods separate various dimensions of enterprise architecture [16]. Therefore, these methods used have the problem of bridging static and dynamic aspects of different concerns. The lack of semantic integration principles for graphical representations of different aspects of enterprise system [9, 10] is a problem in conceptual modelling. Nearly all object-oriented modelling methods deal with the collections of models. Modelling of data flows between subsystems using Unified Modelling Language (UML) is rather awkward [14]. It is not clear how coordination flows, which are necessary for the initiation of value flows, can be explicitly defined using traditional IS analysis and design methods. To reach integrity among interactive, behavioral and structural aspects is not an easy task, because typically the constructs of different modelling traditions do not deal with the integration principles and fail in providing a holistic approach. In this situation, system designers are forced to use semantically inconsistent or incomplete graphical representations.

Semantically Integrated Conceptual Modelling (SICM) method [11] can be used for defining graphical representations of e-business scenarios. Usually different aspects of scenario specifications such as interactive, behavioral and structural aspects, are described using a narrative text. SICM modelling method provides with a possibility to replace a narrative text by the integrated representation of business process and data. The expressive power of the developed conceptual modelling method is sufficient for the composition of both software and business process scenarios. The new design principles of semantically integrated conceptual modelling method should provide significant competitive advantages for organisations, because they help to separate crosscutting concerns. Separation of crosscutting concerns by decomposing conceptual representations of scenarios into simple interaction loops provides with a flexible way to represent new changes in order to meet evolving needs of stakeholders in the area of IS. The modelling language could be roughly classified as a mixture between DEMO [3] and OPM [4]. As such, and in particular with respect to some additional concepts like overlays and underlying loops, it could be used as a technique for separation of concerns. Relative simplicity of SICM method and clear link with basic traditional techniques like use-cases, is an effective way of modelling e-business scenarios.

2 Main Concepts of Semantically Integrated Conceptual Modelling

Bunge [1] ontological principles are important to understand the core conceptual modelling constructs of the SICM method. Bunge [1] states that world is composed of things. Things can be seen as subsystems, which can be viewed as interacting actors. When two subsystems interact, they cause changes to certain things. Changes to things are defined via properties. Any subsystem can be viewed as an active object, but not every object can play a role of subsystem. According to Bunge [1], just interacting things (which cause objects to change) can be viewed as active subsystems. It is necessary to analyze interactions between subsystems in order to justify why a subsystem is useful. Interaction dependencies between two concepts indicate that these concepts should be interpreted as actors. An actor represents a collection of subsystems, which are characterized by the same set of rights, responsibilities or commitments.

The focus of conceptual modelling is to represent certain aspects of human perceptions about things. Ontology distinguishes between concrete things and conceptual things [6]. Concrete things can be defined as objects or systems. Every autonomous subsystem can be viewed as a system on its own. If an object represents a set, it can only be a concept. Whether an object is an individual or a set is relatively not important. The individual in one context may become a set in another context. Any system can be interpreted as an object, but not every object is a system. Two interacting subsystems can be viewed as an entirely new system. The interpretations of concepts in the SICM method are represented in Fig. 1.

Actors in SICM are active concepts, which are characterized by interaction dependencies. Organizational actors can be represented as humans or as organizational subsystems, which are composed of humans. Technical actors are represented as artefacts of a physical world, they are interpreted as software or hardware components. A concept can be passive and active at the same time. There is no clearly defined criterion

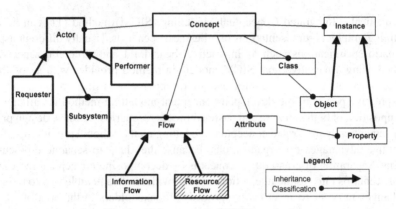

Fig. 1. Main concepts of SICM method

for distinguishing between these two types of modeling artifacts in conceptual modeling languages. Usually passive concepts are represented by classes or entities, which are characterized by attributes, relationships and state changes. In SICM method interactions between active concepts may affect instances of passive concepts. The effects of interactions are expressed by creation and termination actions. The effects of these actions describe structural changes in various classes of objects [10]. An actor is a special instance of the concept characterized by a unit of functionality, which is exposed to the environment. It depends upon the responsibilities of an individual actor, what type of value or coordination flow an actor is supposed to send or to receive. In DEMO [3], initiators and executers are viewed as active elements, which are represented by actors. Such actors are entitled as service requesters and service providers [9]. In the SICM method, we define these actors correspondingly as requesters and performers. Any value flow requires the initiation of some coordinating interactions, which are necessary for the provision of value flows. The DEMO approach [3] distinguishes between two kinds of actions: production acts and coordination acts. Coordination acts are normally initiated by requesters and they are necessary to make commitment regarding the corresponding production act. This act is supposed to bring a value flow to requester. Production acts are normally activated by performers and they should always be associated with some value flows.

3 Interaction-Based Way of Modelling

It is very important to have the way of modelling, which enables to explicitly represent interaction flows, that are crucial for the identification of discontinuity and other undesirable characteristics in IS specifications. By identifying essential workflows, which can be presented as a set of purposeful interactions among organizational and technical component, it is possible to conceptualize different business process scenarios. Technical components can be enterprise subsystems such as machines, software and hardware. Organizational components can be humans, organizations and their divisions. These components are called actors, can be represented by the roles they play. Interaction dependencies among actors are important to identify business actions. Interaction dependencies help to explore various situations in which enterprise system components can be useful. In this section, we are going to demonstrate how interaction flows can be composed into workflow loops [2]. A workflow loop is considered as a basic element of scenario, which describes interplay between two different actors that could be seen as requester and performer. A workflow loop here is viewed as a response to a request that provides some value to service requester [8].

An instance of an actor is an autonomous subsystem. Its existence and relevance can be motivated by a set of interaction dependencies with other actors that keep this subsystem viable. Interaction dependency R(A▪▪▪▪▶B)between two concepts indicates that A is an agent. It performs action R on one or more instances, which are represented by recipient B. The graphical notations of two types of interaction dependencies between actors are presented in Fig. 2.

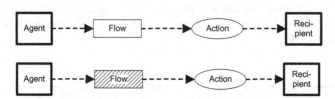

Fig. 2. Two main dependencies of the interaction model

The notation for actors are denoted by square rectangles and actions are represented by ellipses. Solid rectangles are used to represent resource flows and light rectangles are used to indicate information flows. Interaction dependencies (▪▪▪▪▶)are represented by broken arrows. They correspond to moving things that could be information or resource flows. Actors may view all moving flows either as coordination flows [3] or value flows [15] such as materials, financial resources, etc. The interaction dependencies can be represented as expressions in the following way:

Action (Agent ▪▪▪▪▶ Flow ▪▪▪▪▶ Recipient),
Action (Agent ▪▪▪▪▶ <u>Flow</u> ▪▪▪▪▶ Recipient).

Here 'Flow' denotes an information flow and <u>Flow</u> denotes a resource flow. It should be noted that the expression Action (Agent ▪▪▪▪▶ Recipient)may denote either a decision flow or that the flow is undecided yet.

Business process scenarios can be seen and analyzed as the compositions of service interaction loops. Taking into account the nature of service concept, which is based on interaction between different actors to capture value [13], is the way of thinking that can be applied in business process analysis. Interaction loops are very useful in analyzing the discontinuity of value creation process, which capture service value in an exchange between two or more actors. Business process as a service can be defined by interaction flow into opposite direction between service requester and service performer. Both requests and responses can be viewed as elementary interactions and such understanding of requests and responses is consistent with the ontological foundation of service process [5]. Services cannot be transferable, because they are events, not objects. Service providers are actors who receive service requests transforming them into service responses, which are delivered to service requesters.

Service responses cannot be delivered without providing service requests. A response can be viewed in a number of ways. It can be represented by a promise to deliver a desirable result to service requester or it can be viewed as a production action. Two interaction dependencies are coupled into two opposite directions by the following expression:

If Request (Requester ⋯▶ Provider)then
Response (Provider ⋯▶ Requester).

Legal sequences of actions represent possible event flows for actors to communicate with each other. Interaction loops can be delegated to various organizational and technical actors. For instance, two interaction loops among participants, which represent system component such as Customer, Room Guest, Hotel Reservation System and Hotel are represented in Fig. 3.

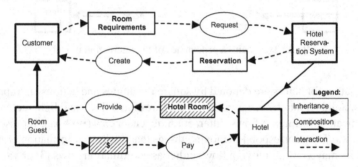

Fig. 3. Two interaction loops in a Hotel System

The diagram represents four interaction possibilities, available to four actors. Actors can be related by inheritance, composition and classification dependencies [8]. These dependencies are used to reason about various ways in which interaction loops can be composed, merged or overlaid on the top of each other. The actions that are available to the actors can be also viewed as their rights and responsibilities. A customer has a right to request a room by informing a Hotel Reservation System about Room Requirements. If the requested type of room is available, then a Hotel Reservation System has responsibility to Create reservation. By taking advantage of the available actions, the actors may enter into commitments regarding their obligations. For instance, the effect of successfully executed Create Reservation action is the new commitment from the Hotel to provide a room. Interaction dependencies can be inherited by the more specific actors and they are propagated to the compositional wholes according to the special inference rules [12]. Most conventional IS analysis and design methods do not provide enough reasoning power regarding commitments and obligations.

4 Semantically Integrated Conceptual Modelling

The dynamic and static aspects of interactions can be analyzed in terms of creation and termination of communication actions. The changes can be expressed according to specified transition links. The reclassification of object is defined in terms of communication action that terminates an object in one class and creates a new object in another class. The graphical representation of a reclassification construct can be viewed in Fig. 4(a). This construct is specified according to by the following expression:

Action (Pre-condition Class ──▶ Post-condition Class).

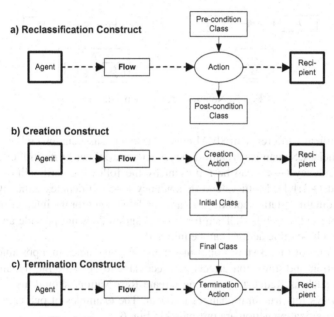

Fig. 4. Representation of three types of constructs

Two kinds of changes happen during any reclassification event. A creation action is denoted by the outgoing transition arrow to an initial class. Graphical notation of the creation (──▶)construct is represented in Fig. 4(b), which can be also denoted by the following expression:

Action (⊥──▶Initial class)Here ⊥ is an empty class. It is used for representation of a new object creation.

A termination action is represented by the transition dependency directed from a final class. The graphical notation of the termination construct is represented in Fig. 4(c). It corresponds to the following expression:

Action (Final Class ──▶⊥).

A communication action manipulates the properties of one object, otherwise, this action is not purposeful. The changes of object properties may trigger transition from one class to another. Changes of objects can be clearly presented by declaration of static features. Dynamic properties are represented as actions. Static features are represented by the attributes of classes. Both single-valued and multi-valued attribute dependencies denote static properties [8]. Graphical notation of various cases of static dependencies is represented in Fig. 5.

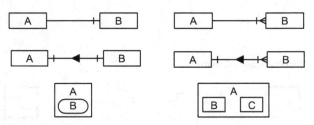

Fig. 5. Notation of static dependencies

One significant difference in SICM method is that the association ends of static relations are nameless. Semantics of static dependencies are defined by multiplicities. Single-valued dependency (─>) can be represent by the following cardinalities: (0,1;1,1), (0,*;1,1) and (1,1;1,1). Multi-valued dependency (─>>) denotes either (0,1;1,*) or (1,1;1,*) cardinality. Static dependencies are not defined yet for the interaction diagram, which is represented in Fig. 3. Therefore, this diagram does not provide any semantic details in which possible actions can be initiated.

The diagram of Fig. 3 shows only interactive dependencies in a possible scenario. Both interaction and transition effects are necessary to describe the dynamic aspect. The actions such as Request Room and Create Reservation, should also specify the acceptable ways for structural changes to occur. The examples of one creation action and one reclassification action are presented in Fig. 6.

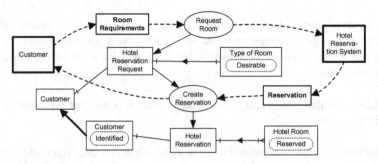

Fig. 6. Examples of creation and reclassification actions

A simple interaction loop between requester and performer can be viewed as the basic construct of any communication process [2]. In carrying out the work, a performer may in turn initiate further interactions. In this way, a network of the loosely coupled actors with various roles comes into interplay to fulfill the original service request. If some actors are unclear or missing, then they may cause breakdowns of business scenarios.

5   Basic Interaction Loops

Interaction dependencies among actors are important for the identification of business or technical actions. By following interaction dependencies, it is possible to explore various ways in which enterprise system components can be used. Components are important for representation of enterprise system architecture, which may describe internet of things. Components are represented by the roles these actors play. In this section, we are going to demonstrate how interaction flows can be composed into workflow loops [2]. A workflow loop is considered as a basic element of scenario, which describes interplay between various actors that are be seen as requesters and performers. In its most general form, a workflow loop is viewed as a response to a request that provides some value to requester [8]. Various kind of components are represented in Fig. 7. These different representations of components may replace actors in different business scenario representations on the lower level of abstraction.

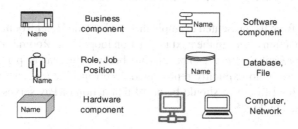

Fig. 7. Different representations of actors

The main idea behind a conversation for action schema can be explained as turn-taking [18]. The purpose of it was motivated by creating computer-based software for conducting conversations. Any business scenario can be characterized by the same four types of events: a) Request, b) Promise, c) State and d) Accept. Requester initiates a request action and then is waiting for a particular promise or a service provision action from Performer. Request, promise and acceptance are typical coordination actions [3], which are triggered by the corresponding types of basic events. We will show how creation and termination constructs of the SICM method can be used to define the new facts of the basic transaction pattern [13]:

1)   If Request (Requester ⋯▶ Performer)
         then Promise (Performer ⋯▶ Requester),
         Request (⊥ ──▶ Request),Promise (Request ──▶ Promise).

It should be noted that the first Request (verb) in the expression Request ($\perp$ ───▶ Request),denotes the action and the second Request (noun) denotes the initial class. These two concepts represent two completely different things.

2) If State (Performer ····▶ Requester)
   then Accept (Requester ····▶ Performer).
   State (Promise ───▶ Result),Accept (Result ───▶ Payment),
   Payment ──> Result.

New facts occur from four basic events, which are instantiated by such classes of objects as Request, Promise, Stated Result and Accepted Result. Created or terminated objects and their features can be interpreted as classes, which represent requests, promises and statements about delivered or accepted results. For instance, the Create Reservation action can be interpreted as a promise to Provide Hotel Room. For example, the sequence two different interaction loops can be defined as follows:

If Request Room (Customer ····▶ Hotel Reservation System)
then Create Reservation (Hotel Reservation System ····▶ Customer).
If Provide Hotel Room (Hotel ····▶ Room Guest)
then Pay (Room Guest ····▶ Hotel).
Hotel Reservation System ─▶─Hotel,
Room Guest ══▶Customer.
Here: ─▶─is composition link and ══▶is an inheritance link.

It is obvious from the presented example that the Provide Hotel Room action can be viewed as a production event. In the next interaction loop, Hotel Room is exchanged for money. Some represented actions can be missing, because they can be performed tacitly. For example, there is no explicitly represented acceptance action for the production action Provide Hotel Room. It should be noted that action of Pay serves this purpose. This is represented by Fig. 8.

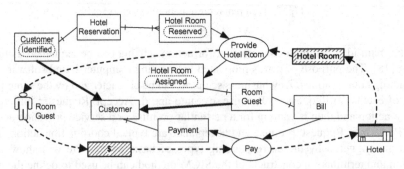

Fig. 8. Example of two production actions in a resource exchange

This diagram defines the case when Requester and Performer agrees on each other's communication actions. For a communication action to be successfully performed the following two conditions are applied:

1) A requester initiates the interaction flow by triggering a communication action,
2) A performer agrees to accept the resulting interaction flow, which is generated by communication action.

Analysis of goals and problems [7] may help to understand why different actors may react or not act at all. There are many alternative actions, which may take place if one of two presented conditions are violated. Alternative actions can be introduced to handle possible breakdowns in the basic interaction pattern. These alternatives can be represented by various transitions in the conversation for action schema [18]. They are necessary for the actors involved to deal with unexpected situations.

6 Alternative Interactions

Alternative actions are necessary to handle breakdowns in the basic pattern of a transaction. Actors, representing autonomous subsystems, may have different goals. If coordination and production actions are initiated, then they generate noteworthy events, which can be defined by creation, termination or reclassification effects in various classes of objects. This extended schema is known as the standard pattern of transaction [3]:

1) If Request (Requester ···· ▶ Performer)
    then Reject (Performer ···· ▶ Requester),
    Request ($\perp$ ── ▶ Request),Reject (Request ── ▶ Rejection).
    Rejection ──> Request.
2) If Perform (Performer ···· ▶ Requester)
    then Decline (Requester ···· ▶ Performer),
    Perform (Promise ── ▶ Result),
    Decline (Result ── ▶ Declination),
    Result ──> Promise, Declination ──> Result.
    In practice, it is also common that either requester or performer is willing to completely revoke some events. For example, the requester may withdraw his own request. There are four cancellation patterns, which may lead to partial or complete rollback of a transaction. Every cancellation action can be performed, if the corresponding fact exists. For instance, the Withdraw Request action can be triggered, if a request was created by the Request action:
3) Withdraw Request (Requester ···· ▶ Performer),
    Withdraw Request (Request ── ▶ $\perp$).
    For instance, Withdraw Reservation Request action can be added for the termination of a Hotel Reservation Request. The requester may agree or disagree to accept the consequences of the Withdraw Promise action. It should terminate the Promise and to preserve the Request:
4) Withdraw Promise (Performer ···· ▶ Requester),
    Withdraw Promise (Promise ── ▶ Request).
    Another cancellation event can be represented by the option Cancel Result. It should be initiated by Performer to avoid a Decline action by the requester. The requester typically allows canceling result, because after this action the Promise is still not terminated:

5) Cancel Result (Performer ····▶Requester),
    Cancel Result (Result ──▶Promise),Result ──> Promise.
        Yet another cancellation event may take place when the whole transaction was
    completed, but the requester discovers some problem and he regrets his acceptance:
6) Cancel Acceptance (Requester ····▶ Performer),
    Cancel Acceptance (Payment ──▶Cancellation of Payment),
    Cancellation of Payment ──> Result.

    All listed alternative actions can be typically introduced into different scenarios to
take care of various breakdowns in business processes. We use the following example
of business scenario, which is represented in Fig. 9. In this example, it is possible to see
the class of Hotel Reservation Request. It corresponds to the Request in the previous
alternative interactions. Hotel Reservation would match the promise, which is created
by the Hotel Reservation System.

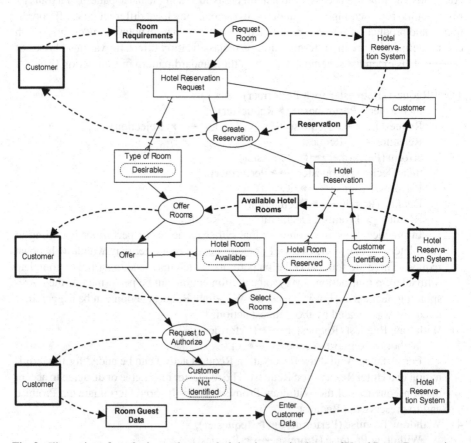

Fig. 9. Illustration of overlaying and two underlying interaction loops of Hotel Room Reservation

    The first interaction loop of Hotel Room Reservation scenario can be completed,
if one or more desirable types of rooms are offered (second interaction loop). If there

are no available rooms in this hotel, then the overlaying action would fail. For the first interaction loop to be executed correctly, two second underlying interactions must be completed as well. According to the second underlying loop, the create reservation action would fail if the Request to Authorize is not satisfied. The underlying interaction scenario represents Customer's response to the Hotel Reservation System's request. If the customer expects to receive a Reservation flow from the Hotel Reservation System, it is necessary for him to Select Rooms. The request and reply in the underlying loop is specified as follows:

If Offer Rooms (Hotel Reservation System ····▶ Customer),
then Select Rooms (Customer ····▶ Hotel Reservation System).

The actions of the first underlying loop are synchronized with the primary interaction loop. The Create Reservation is a reclassification action, which is composed of the Select Rooms and Offer Rooms actions on the lower granularity level. The Select Room action can be performed several times for each Hotel Room [Available]. Hotel Reservation is a composed object. When it is created, such parts as Hotel Room [Reserved] and Customer [Identified] must be created as well. The third interaction loop is necessary for provision of necessary data about the Customer [Identified]. Creation of Customer [Identified] object requires the Request to Authorize action and Enter Customer Data action in the third loop to be triggered.

7   Concluding Remarks

The goal of this paper was to present a holistic SICM method, which can be used in conceptual modelling in order to reach semantic integration of static and dynamic aspects of business scenario. Conventional conceptual modeling methods analyze business processes and data in isolation. In this situation, it is difficult to achieve semantic integration when several concerns are combined together. It was shown how business scenarios can be conceptualized by identifying the essential business actions, which are expressed as a set of interactions. We have demonstrated the main principles of holistic approach to conceptual modelling, which allows designers to construct scenarios in a more comprehensible way. This way of modeling is built on interaction loops, which can be either gradually replaced on demand, or enhanced on the lower levels of decomposition. Modeling based on interactions facilitates the control of business process continuity and semantic integrity in order to overcome discontinuities in IS specifications.

It was demonstrated how interaction dependencies can be augmented with the traditional semantic relations in the area of system analysis and design. Possible breakdowns in the basic pattern of a transaction can be avoided by designing the alternative interaction loops. Alternatives help designers to meet evolving needs of stakeholders. It was demonstrated how the basic and alternative interactions can be used for reasoning on conceptual representations of scenarios. If the alternative scenarios are not designed into the system, it increases working overload and gives rise to customer complaints. SICM method, provides a holistic way of modelling, which is critical in detecting breakdowns and discontinuities in IS specifications. Breakdowns in scenarios, which define software processes, can be viewed as hidden requirement defects.

References

1. Bunge, M.A.: Treatise on Basic Philosophy, vol. 4, Ontology II: A World of Systems. Reidel Publishing Company, Dordrecht (1979)
2. Denning, P.J., Medina-Mora, R.: Completing the loops. Interfaces **25**, 42–57 (1995)
3. Dietz, J.L.G.: Enterprise Ontology: Theory and Methodology. Springer, Heidelberg (2006)
4. Dori, D.: Object-Process Methodology: A Holistic System Paradigm. Springer, Heidelberg (2002)
5. Ferrario, R., Guarino, N.: Towards an ontological foundation for services science. In: Domingue, J., Fensel, D., Traverso, P. (eds.) FIS 2008. LNCS, vol. 5468, pp. 152–169. Springer, Heidelberg (2009). https://doi.org/10.1007/978-3-642-00985-3_13
6. Evermann, J., Wand, Y.: Ontology based object-oriented domain modeling: representing behavior. J. Database Manag. **20**(1), 48–77 (2009)
7. Horkoff, J., Yu, E.: Interactive analysis of agent-goal models in enterprise modeling. Int. J. Inf. Syst. Model. Des. **1**(4), 1–23 (2010). https://doi.org/10.4018/jismd.2010100101
8. Gustas, R.: A look behind conceptual modeling constructs in information system analysis and design. Int. J. Inf. Syst. Model. Des. **1**(1), 79–108 (2010). https://doi.org/10.4018/jismd.2010092304
9. Gustas, R.: Modeling approach for integration and evolution of information system conceptualizations. Int. J. Inf. Syst. Model. Des. **2**(1), 45–73 (2011)
10. Gustas, R., Gustiene, P.: Conceptual modelling method for separation of concerns and integration of structure and behavior. Int. J. Inf. Syst. Model. Des. **3**(1), 48–77 (2012)
11. Gustas, R., Gustiené, P.: Principles of semantically integrated conceptual modelling method. In: Shishkov, B. (ed.) BMSD 2016. LNBIP, vol. 275, pp. 1–26. Springer, Cham (2017). https://doi.org/10.1007/978-3-319-57222-2_1
12. Gustas, R., Gustiené, P.: A semantically integrated conceptual modelling method for business process reengineering. In: Zimmermann, A., Schmidt, R., Jain, L.C. (eds.) Architecting the Digital Transformation. ISRL, vol. 188, pp. 163–177. Springer, Cham (2021). https://doi.org/10.1007/978-3-030-49640-1_9
13. Gustas, R., Gustiené, P.: Semantically integrated conceptual modelling method and modelling patterns. In: Systems and Software Development, Modelling and Analysis: New Perspectives and Methodologies, pp. 1–33. IGI Global (2014)
14. OMG: Unified Modeling Language Superstructure, version 2.2. www.omg.org. Accessed 19 Jan 2018
15. Gordijn, J., Akkermans, H., van Vliet, H.: Business modelling is not process modelling. In: Liddle, S.W., Mayr, H.C., Thalheim, B. (eds.) ER 2000. LNCS, vol. 1921, pp. 40–51. Springer, Heidelberg (2000). https://doi.org/10.1007/3-540-45394-6_5
16. Zachman, J.A.: A framework for information systems architecture. IBM Syst. J. **26**(3), 276–292 (1987). https://doi.org/10.1147/sj.263.0276
17. Wieringa, R., Gordijn, J.: Value-oriented design of service coordination processes: correctness and trust. In: Proceedings of the the 20th ACM Symposium on Applied Computing, pp. 1320–1327. ACM Press (2005)
18. Winograd, T., Flores, R.: Understanding Computers and Cognition: A New Foundation for Design, Ablex Norwood (1986)

A Model-Driven Framework for Design and Analysis of Vehicle Suspension Systems

Muhammad Waseem Anwar[1]([✉]) [iD], Muhammad Taaha Bin Shuaib[2] [iD],
Farooque Azam[2] [iD], and Aon Safdar[2] [iD]

[1] School of Innovation, Design and Engineering, Malardalen University, Vasteras, Sweden
muhammad.waseem.anwar@mdu.se
[2] Department of Computer and Software Engineering, College of Electrical and Mechanical
Engineering, National University of Sciences and Technology (NUST), Islamabad, Pakistan
mtshuaib.cse20ceme@student.nust.edu.pk, farooq@ceme.nust.edu.pk,
aon.safdar20@ce.ceme.edu.pk

Abstract. The design and implementation of vehicle suspension systems is complex and time-consuming process that usually leads to production delays. Although different Model Driven Engineering (MDE) technologies like EAST-ADL/AUTOSAR are frequently applied to expedite vehicle development process, a framework particularly dealing with design and analysis of vehicle suspension is hard to find in literature. This rises the need of a framework that not only supports the analysis of suspension system at higher abstraction level but also complements the existing standards like EAST-ADL. In this article, a **M**odel driven framework for **V**ehicle **S**uspension **S**ystem (**MVSS**) is proposed. Particularly, a meta-model containing major vehicle suspension aspects is introduced. Subsequently, a modeling editor is developed using Eclipse Sirius platform. This allows the modeling of both simple as well as complex vehicle suspension systems with simplicity. Moreover, Object Constraint Language (OCL) is utilized to perform early system analysis in modeling phase. Furthermore, the target MATLAB-Simulink models are generated from source models, using model-to-text transformations, to perform advanced system analysis. The application of proposed framework is demonstrated through real life Audi A6L Hydraulic active suspension use case. The initial results indicate that proposed framework is highly effective for the design and analysis of vehicle suspension systems. In addition to this, the analysis results could be propagated to EAST-ADL toolchains to support full vehicle development workflow.

Keywords: Model Driven Engineering (MDE) · Vehicle suspension system · Meta-modeling · OCL · EAST-ADL

1 Introduction

The advancements in automotive industries allow vendors to introduce luxury vehicles with premier comfort level. The vehicle component responsible to provide comfort level during ride is known as suspension system. Technically, the system of a vehicle which allows motion between the chassis and wheels, relative to each other, of the vehicle is known as suspension system. Particularly, it is a connection between a vehicle's body and wheels. Components like spring and shock absorber combine to form up the suspension, while tires and air in the tires can be counted too. Shock absorbers or dampers are used to release the kinetic energy by converting it into heat or other forms of energy. Avesta Goodarzi [1] explains that suspension system serves the purpose of both the car's handling and stability, which contributes to a smooth and comfortable ride. Generally, suspension systems are categorized into three main types i.e. passive suspension [2], semi-active suspension [3] and active suspension [4].

In the context of current advancements in vehicle manufacturing, the suspension system is highly important. Therefore, researchers and practitioners continuously proposing different approaches (e.g. [5, 6]) for the improvements of vehicle suspension systems. However, such approaches mostly deal at lower abstraction level with high implementation complexities. Furthermore, system analysis is usually performed after complete implementation of system design that delays the overall analysis process. Due to such issues, industries are suffering from low productivity and higher time-to-market issues. On the other hand, Model Driven Engineering (MDE) is a renowned system development approach [7] where system design is developed at higher abstraction level with simplicity. Furthermore, it provides early system analysis features through transformation process.

Although industries are adopting different MDE approaches like EAST-ADL/AUTOSAR[1] for vehicle manufacturing, a MDE framework particularly dealing with vehicle suspension system is hard to find in literature and industrial projects. As suspension system is highly important in modern vehicles, it is a need of a day to develop a MDE framework that not only supports the analysis of suspension system at higher abstraction level but also complements the existing standards like EAST-ADL. To achieve this, a **M**odel driven framework for **V**ehicle **S**uspension **S**ystem (**MVSS**) is proposed in this article. Firstly, a meta-model for vehicle suspension system is proposed where all major vehicle suspension concepts are introduced. Secondly, a modeling tool is developed by utilizing Eclipse Sirius Platform[2]. The tool allows the effective modeling of suspension systems with simplicity. Moreover, OCL constraints are incorporated in the tool to perform system analysis in modeling phase. Furthermore, the model-to-text transformations are applied to generate MATLAB-Simulink models from source models to realize advanced system analysis capabilities. Finally, the application of MVSS is demonstrated through Audi A6L Hydraulic Active Suspension use case. The results indicate that proposed framework is highly effective for the design and analysis of suspension systems. In addition to this, the analysis results could be propagated to EAST-ADL development flow through Requirements/Verification-Validation (V&V) package.

This article is organized as: Literature review is provided in Sect. 2. The MVSS is proposed in Sect. 3 where meta-model is given in Sect. 3.1 and Tool support is described in Sect. 3.2. The application of MVSS through use case is given in Sect. 4. The discussion and limitations are given in Sect. 5. Finally, article is concluded in Sect. 6.

---

[1] https://www.east-adl.info/Specification.html.

[2] https://www.eclipse.org/sirius/.

2 Literature Review

Vehicle suspension systems are usually categorized into three main classes i.e. passive suspension [2], semi-active suspension [3] and active suspension [4]. There are several advantages of active suspension systems over passive systems [13]. Therefore, active vehicle suspension is an attractive research area for researcher and practitioner of the domain [5]. Kuan-Yu Pan et al. [14] propose a novel approach to improve the stability of active vehicle suspension system by utilizing the pneumatic muscle actuators through haar wavelet series. The significant improvements are observed in ride comfort during experiments. Xi Wang et al. [6] applied machine learning approach to improvement of active vehicle suspension system. Authors utilize deep reinforcement learning technique to train the active suspension system and subsequently, achieve more ride stability. In another study, Jing Na et al. [9] propose a cost-effective vehicle suspension approach where non-linear parameters are managed without applying approximator functions for real time adaption.

Model Driven Engineering (MDE) is a renowned system development paradigm with early system design and analysis features [8]. To get the benefit from MDE in vehicle manufacturing industry, EAST-ADL was introduced [10]. It provides several modeling entities at different level of abstractions and supports full vehicle development activities. Although different aspects of EAST-ADL have been frequently researched in state-of-the-art [11, 12], its application particularly on vehicle suspension system is hard to find in literature to the best of our knowledge. On the other hand, the approaches like [6, 9, 14] perform certain improvements in active vehicle suspension, however, these operate on lower abstraction level with several complexity. Furthermore, these approaches work in-isolation and their integration with full vehicle development workflow (like EAST-ADL) is problematic. Therefore, it is a need of a day to develop a MDE framework that not only supports the analysis of suspension system at higher abstraction level but also complements the existing standards like EAST-ADL. To achieve this, MVSS is proposed in this article.

3 MVSS – Model-Driven Framework for Vehicle Suspension System

In this section, MVSS is proposed for the modeling and analysis of vehicle suspension systems. Particularly, meta-model is proposed in Sect. 3.1. The details regarding tool support are provided in Sect. 3.2.

3.1 Proposed Meta-model

The proposed meta-model, as shown in Fig. 1, allows the modeling of different active suspension systems i.e. air suspension, hydraulic suspension, electro-magnetic suspension and electro-pneumatic suspension. Several concepts essential for the modeling of suspension system are included in the meta-model. It can be seen from Fig. 1 that Suspension is a main container that contains chassis where all other concepts like spring, damper etc. are contained for modeling purposes. For the modeling of complex active suspension systems, several relevant concepts are included like chassis (weight of the body of the car), spring, damper, tyre, actuators, accelerometer, height sensor, motor driver, controller (with PID), reservoir, compressor, air-springs, electromagnets, and amplifiers. Furthermore, each concept has attributes to achieve desired modeling objectives e.g., Spring has spring-constant, and damper has damping-coefficient attributes, actuator maximum speed and maximum weight attributes and so forth. All concepts are systematically connected with each other through different relationships and cardinalities to achieve the full modeling environment. For example, chassis links the bump hence the accelerometer relates to the chassis to read the acceleration. Furthermore, the accelerometer relates to the controller (with implementation of PID) to feed the value of acceleration to the controller. To conclude, the comprehensive modeling of vehicle suspension systems can be achieved through the proposed meta-model. This can be evident through the modeling of use case in Sect. 4.

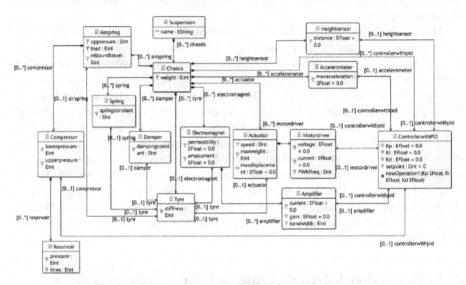

Fig. 1. Proposed meta-model for vehicle suspension system

3.1.1 Early Analysis Through OCL

To provide system analysis at modeling level, Object Constraint Language (OCL) has been utilized. Particularly, several OCL constraints have been included at meta-model level to ensure the correctness of suspension system in early modeling stage. Here we utilize the concept of invariant (always true during model instance) to specify different meta level constraints. Few sample constraints are given in Table 1 for demonstration purposes. For example, first constraint in Table 1 deals with the value of the 'maxdisplacement' which an actuator can counter. The maximum allowed value of 'maxdisplacement' is less than 0.3 (approx. 1 feet). The error will be displayed during modeling phase whenever value of 'maxdisplacement' equals or exceeds 0.3 threshold. Similarly, second constraint in Table 1 ensures that the number of springs should always be less than or equal to the number of tyres. Note that OCL constraints in Table 1 are specified for demonstration purposes only and more complex constraints could be written through proposed framework as per requirements.

Table 1. OCL meta-model level constraints for analysis

Description	OCL syntax
Maximum displacement that an actuator may counter should be less than 0.3m (1ft approx.)	`Context Actuator` **`invariant inv1:`** **`self`**`.maxdisplacement < 0.3;`
Number of springs should be less or equal to the number of tyres in the system	`Context Spring` **`invariant inv2:`** `Spring->size() <= Tyre->size();`
Number of dampers should be less or equal to the number of tyres in the system	`Context Damper` **`invariant inv3:`** `Damper->size() <= Tyre->size();`
Number of actuators should be less or equal to the number of tyres in the system	`Context Actuator` **`invariant inv4:`** `Actuator->size() <= Tyre->size();`
Number of motor-drivers should be equal to the number of actuators in the system	`Context Motordriver` **`invariant inv5:`** `Motordriver->size() = Actuator->size();`
If there are Airsprings included in the model then Compressors must also be included into the model	`Context Compressor` **`invariant inv6:`** `Chassis->count(Airspring)>0` **`implies`** `Chassis->count(Compressor)>0;`
If there are Actuators included in the model then Motordrivers must also be included into the model	`Context Actuator` **`invariant inv7:`** `Chassis->count(Actuator)>0` **`implies`** `Chassis->count(Motordriver)>0;`

3.2 Tool Support

Based on the proposed meta-model in Sect. 3.1, a full graphical modeling tool is developed using Sirius Platform features as shown in Fig. 2. Particularly, it contains graphical notations for all concepts as defined in the proposed meta-model. The palette on the right side of the Fig. 2 contains all the components required to create a graphical depiction of the model. These components can be dragged and dropped in the workspace for effectively modeling of suspension system. For example, a chassis, a tyre and an association between them is modeled by utilizing drag and drop functionality as shown in Fig. 2. Similarly, other options like resizing, properties view etc. are also available for seamless modeling of suspension systems. The modeling of complete use case is available in Sect. 4.

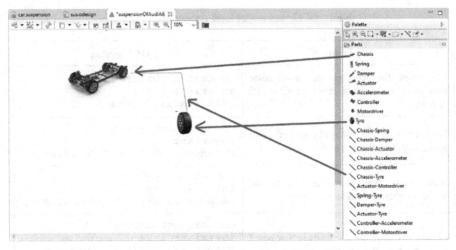

Fig. 2. Modeling editor with workspace (on the left) and palette (on the right)

3.2.1   Model Transformation for MATLAB Code

The OCL constraints allow to perform initial analysis at modeling stage. However, correctness of suspension system cannot be established without performing detailed analysis. For this, we have performed model-to-text transformations using Acceleo tool in order to generate MATLAB code from models. Subsequently, the generated code can be simulated in Simulink for detailed analysis. We have developed several transformation rules and implemented through different Acceleo templates. A sample Acceleo template is shown in Fig. 3.

4   Proof-of-Concept

The application of proposed framework is demonstrated through "**A6L Limousine (C8) | 2019–2020**" use case. Particularly, the design of hydraulic active suspension is modeled (Sect. 4.1) where different calculations (using weight of car i.e. 2000 kg) and formulas (e.g. Newton's law of motion for force on each tyre etc.) have been performed. Furthermore, the system analysis is done in Sect. 4.2.

```
📄 generate.mtl ⊠   📄 ActiveSuspension.m    📄 Suspension.xmi
    [comment encoding = UTF-8 /]
    [module generate('http://www.example.org/suspension')]

⊖ [template public generate(a : Suspension)]
    [comment @main /]
        [file (a.name.replaceAll('\\.','/').concat('.m'), false, 'Cp1252')]
    clear all
    clc
    kt = [a.chassis.tyre.stiffness/]; \\Tyre Stiffness
    mt = [a.chassis.tyre.mass/]; \\Tyre Mass
    k = [a.chassis.spring.springconstant/]; \\Spring Constant
    c = [a.chassis.damper.dampingconstant/]; \\Damping Constant
    ChassisWeight = [a.chassis.weight/]; \\Total chassis weight
    Mc = ChassisWeight/4; \\Weight of chassis on each tyre
    kp = [a.chassis.controllerwithpid.Kp/]; \\Value of kp
    ki = [a.chassis.controllerwithpid.Ki/]; \\ Value of ki
    kd = [a.chassis.controllerwithpid.Kd/]; \\ Value of kd
        [/file]
    [/template]
```

Fig. 3. Sample acceleo template for MATLAB code

4.1 Modeling

The modeling editor contains palette (Fig. 2) where different components are available for the modeling of suspension system. The model of an Audi A6L limousine suspension system has been developed using the palette components as shown in Fig. 4. Particularly, Audi A6L has 4 tyres and subsequently all the tyres have each individual working component. Each tyre has its own components containing accelerometer, controller-with-PID, motor driver, actuator, damper and spring. The system is supposed to work in a way that the accelerometer reads the value of the acceleration with which the chassis is initially experiencing after going over a bump. This acceleration is fed to the controller which then calculate the amount of force required to counter this bump with the help of PID. This value of force is fed to the actuator with which it moves and helps countering the bump. Hence, each tyre has its own set of components in order to work independently as shown in Fig. 4. It is important to mention that it is not necessary for a vehicle to have all the tyres working independently, therefore, appropriate changes can be made in model as per requirements by using available options. Here, this use case is focused on the development of hydraulic active suspension; hence, this model has been created containing all the components which are required in the hydraulic active suspension. Similarly, other active suspension systems can be modeled as available in the proposed meta-model. The only requirement is to include the required features in modeling tool accordingly.

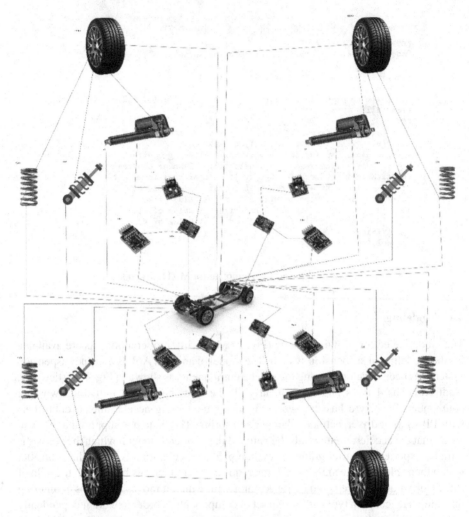

Fig. 4. Design Model of Audi A6L Limousine Suspension System in MVSS

4.2 Analysis

Once modeling of Audi A6L suspension system is successfully accomplished through modeling editor as given in Sect. 4.1, the initial analysis of system model is performed through OCL constraints. The analysis is performed through different OCL meta-model level constraints as given in Sect. 3.1.1. Here, analysis results for one OCL Constraint (i.e. actuator displacement – first constraint in Table 1) is shown in Fig. 5. The given OCL constraints ensure that the maximum displacement catered by an actuator can only be less than 0.3 m (1 ft). This constraint has been violated (Fig. 5) as maximum displacement value is 0.4m. The error message specifies the violated constraint including exact information about pertaining component i.e., Actuator 0. Similarly, in case of multiple constraints violation, the relevant constraints will be shown in pop-up window.

To summarize, the proposed framework allows the analysis at modeling phase through OCL constraints.

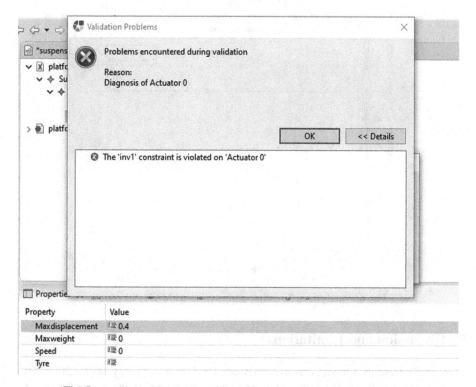

Fig. 5. Analysis of Audi A6L Suspension System through OCL Constraint

After the successful initial analysis of system at modeling level through OCL constraints, the detailed analysis can be performed in MATLAB-Simulink by utilizing the model-to-text transformations. Here, we generate the MATLAB code from Audi suspension system model and subsequently, performed the detailed analysis through simulation in Simulink as shown in Fig. 6.

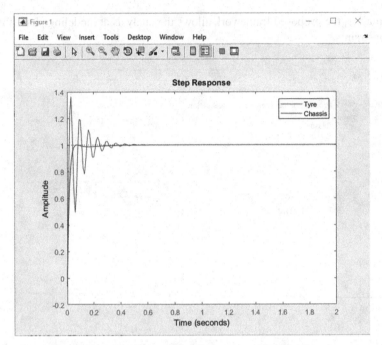

Fig. 6. Analysis in Simulink using generated MATLAB code

5   Discussion and Limitations

This article presents a model driven framework for design and analysis of vehicle suspension systems. This is the first model driven framework particularly meant for vehicle suspension system. The proposed framework complements the existing standards like EAST-ADL in full vehicle development workflow. Particularly, the modeling and analysis of vehicle suspense systems can be accomplished through proposed framework. Subsequently, the analysis results can be propagated to EAST-ADL to support complete vehicle development flow. To achieve this, one option is to associate the suspension system requirements through EAST-ADL requirement package. Subsequently, the analysis results of proposed framework can be linked with EAST-ADL verification-validation sub-package. This way the satisfiability of suspension system requirements with respect to analysis results could be established in EAST-ADL workflow. Another option is that the generated MATLAB code through proposed framework could be linked with EAST-ADL through Behavior package using Simulink parameter for function-behavior. The more complex but flexible integration option is to implement EAXML transformations in the proposed framework and subsequently, directly integrate the MVSS models into existing EAST-ADL tool chains like EATOP. To summarize, the proposed framework can be utilized for the design and analysis of vehicle suspension system individually. Furthermore, it could be integrated in existing EAST-ADL vehicle development workflow at different level of abstractions.

In vehicle suspension system, temporal design and verification characteristics are highly important. Currently, the proposed framework does not provide the temporal features for system design. Essentially, an effective modeling and analysis of complex suspension systems is hard to achieve without temporal characteristics. This is the major limitation of proposed framework, and we are working on it. Particularly, we are incorporating few timing concepts from EAST ADL/AUTOSAR meta-model into proposed meta-model. As a result, temporal design and verification characteristics will be available in the proposed framework in next version.

The proposed framework allows the analysis features through OCL constraints at modeling level. However, such OCL based analysis is only helpful while dealing with large and complex suspension systems. For advanced analysis features, we have implemented model-to-text transformations to generate MATLAB code from source models. Currently, these transformations are implemented for demonstration purposes with limited rules and only applicable to few small use cases. We are working on the design and implementation of more generic transformation rules that could be applicable to several use cases broadly.

6 Conclusion and Future Work

This article presents a Model driven framework for Vehicle Suspension System (**MVSS**). Particularly, a meta-model for vehicle suspension system is proposed. Moreover, Object Constraint Language (OCL) constraints are incorporated at meta-model level to provide system analysis features in modeling phase. Furthermore, a complete modeling tool is developed by utilizing Eclipse Sirius platform. In addition to this, model-to-text transformations are implemented to generate MATLAB code from models for detailed analysis in Simulink. Consequently, MVSS allows the seamless modeling and analysis of both simple as well as complex vehicle suspension systems. The applicability of MVSS is established through Audi A6L Hydraulic Active Suspension use case. The experimental results show that MVSS provides solid platform for the design and analysis of vehicle suspension systems.

In future, we intend to explore and achieve the seamless integration of MVSS in exiting EAST-ADL tool chains at different level of abstractions. Furthermore, more generic model-to-text transformations will be implemented to be applied on broader use cases.

Acknowledgement. This work was partially supported by the Knowledge Foundation through MoDev project.

References

1. Goodarzi, A., Khajepour, A.: Vehicle Suspension System Technology and Design. Springer, Heidelberg (2017)
2. Eligar, S.S., Banakar, R.M.: A survey on passive, active and semiactive automotive suspension systems and analyzing tradeoffs in design of suspension systems. In: 2018 International Conference on Recent Innovations in Electrical, Electronics & Communication Engineering (ICRIEECE), pp. 2908–2913 (2018)

3. Wu, J., Zhou, H., Liu, Z., Gu, M.: Ride comfort optimization via speed planning and preview semi-active suspension control for autonomous vehicles on uneven roads. IEEE Trans. Veh. Technol. **69**(8), 8343–8355 (2020)
4. Zhang, H., Zheng, X., Li, H., Wang, Z., Yan, H.: Active suspension system control with decentralized event-triggered scheme. IEEE Trans. Ind. Electron. **67**(12), 10798–10808 (2020). https://doi.org/10.1109/TIE.2019.2958306
5. Xue, X.D., et al.: Study of art of automotive active suspensions. In: International Conference on Power Electronics Systems and Applications, Hong Kong, China, pp. 1–7 (2011)
6. Wang, X., Zhuang, W., Yin, G.: Learning-based vibration control of vehicle active suspension. In: 18th International Conference on Industrial Informatics (INDIN), pp. 94–99 (2020)
7. Anwar, M.W., Rashid, M., Azam, F., Kashif, M., Butt, W.H.: A model-driven framework for design and verification of embedded systems through SystemVerilog. Des. Autom. Embed. Syst. **23**(3–4), 179–223 (2019). https://doi.org/10.1007/s10617-019-09229-y
8. Anwar, M.W., Rashid, M., Azam, F., Naeem, A., Kashif, M., Butt, W.H.: A unified model-based framework for the simplified execution of static and dynamic assertion-based verification. IEEE Access **8**, 104407–104431 (2020)
9. Na, J., Huang, Y., Pei, Q., Wu, X., Gao, G., Li, G.: Active suspension control of full-car systems without function approximation. IEEE/ASME Trans. Mechatron. **25**(2), 779–791 (2020). https://doi.org/10.1109/TMECH.2019.2962602
10. Blom, H., Chen, D.-J., Kaijser, H., Papadopoulos, Y.: EAST-ADL: an architecture description language for automotive software-intensive systems in the light of recent use and research. Int. J. Syst. Dyn. Appl. **5**(3), 1–20 (2016). https://doi.org/10.4018/IJSDA.2016070101
11. Bucaioni, A., et al.: MoVES: a model-driven methodology for vehicular embedded systems. IEEE Access **6**, 6424–6445 (2018). https://doi.org/10.1109/ACCESS.2018.2789400
12. Mubeen, S., Nolte, T., Sjödin, M., Lundbäck, J., Lundbäck, K.-L.: Supporting timing analysis of vehicular embedded systems through the refinement of timing constraints. Softw. Syst. Model. **18**(1), 39–69 (2017). https://doi.org/10.1007/s10270-017-0579-8
13. Soudani, M.S., Aouiche, A., Chafaa, K., Aouiche, E., Taleb, M., Fares, Z.: Comparison between a passive and active suspension vehicle using PID and fuzzy controllers with two entries applied on quarter vehicle model. In: 2019 1st International Conference on Sustainable Renewable Energy Systems and Applications (ICSRESA), pp. 1–6 (2019)
14. Pan, K.-Y., Hsu, L.-T., Lee, L.-W., Chiang, H.-H., Li, I.-H., Wang: Development and control of active vehicle suspension systems using pneumatic muscle actuator. In: 2017 International Conference on Real-Time Computing and Robotics (RCAR), pp. 617–622 (2017)

Financial Process Mining Characteristics

Audrius Lopata[1], Rimantas Butleris[1], Saulius Gudas[1], Kristina Rudžionienė[1],
Liutauras Žioba[1], Ilona Veitaitė[1(✉)], Darius Dilijonas[2], Evaldas Grišius[2],
and Maarten Zwitserloot[3]

[1] Faculty of Informatics, Kaunas University of Technology, Studentų g. 50, 51368 Kaunas,
Lithuania
{Audrius.Lopata,Rimantas.Butleris,Saulius.Gudas,
Vytautas.Rudzionis,Liutauras.Zioba,Ilona.Veitaite}@ktu.lt
[2] Intellerts, UAB, Studentų g. 3A-9, 50232 Kaunas, Lithuania
{d.dilijonas,e.grisius}@intellerts.com
[3] Intellerts B.V, Europalaan 400-7, 3526 KS Utrecht, The Netherlands
m.zwitserloot@intellerts.com

Abstract. The purpose of this paper is to present continuous results of the research in financial data analysis. Many organizations face challenges by processing a colossal quantity of financial data for evaluation of the current state of the organization, for analysis of future strategies and other purposes. One of the possible ways to analyse financial data is to use process mining techniques. This paper proceeds with analysis and usage of financial data cubes dimensions using General Ledger information of particular organizations in the Netherlands. The research project is funded by European Regional Development Fund according to the 2014–2020 Operational Programme for the European Union Funds' Investments under measure No. 01.2.1-LVPA-T-848 "Smart FDI". Project no.: 01.2.1-LVPA-T-848–02-0004; Period of project implementation: 2020–06-01–2022–05-31.

Keywords: Process mining · Data preparation · Finance analytics · Process discovery

1 Introduction

Financial data analysis helps to evaluate organization's performance and identify probable trends, but it is a very challenging process. The main source of data are organization's financial statements, balance sheets, annual reports, general ledger, etc. According gathered data the analyst can use diverse types of analysis, what rely on main financial analysis goals and depends on data quality [1, 4, 12, 14, 17].

Process mining as a bridge between process-centric approaches and more data-centric approaches like data mining and machine learning. It is difficult to distinguish between process mining and Business Process Intelligence (BPI). BPI could be defined as Business Intelligence (BI) with particular attention to processes. However, this is exactly what process mining is about. Process mining is particularly concentrated on

A. Lopata et al. (Eds.): ICIST 2022, CCIS 1665, pp. 209–220, 2022.
https://doi.org/10.1007/978-3-031-16302-9_16

analysis of historical data of process implementation in the form of event logs [1, 2, 3, 18, 19]. There are many process mining tools, technologies and applications which can provide fact-based support process enrichments and solutions. [1–3, 13, 14]. Despite that during the short period of time process mining has developed very quickly, it is quite fresh to the financial and accounting literature [4–6, 7, 9–12].

Business process mining is a quite new and increasing research field, which concentrates on analysis of business processes by approaching different data mining methods on event data [2, 5, 8, 10, 11, 16]. Plenty of latest discoveries in process mining research make it possible to discover, analyse, and improve business processes according to event data [1, 11, 12, 14].

The process cube is a multidimensional space used to specify process models and event logs. [1, 3, 13]. The idea of process cubes explains that events and process models are organized using different dimensions. The process cube is very like the data cube – online analytical processing (OLAP). An OLAP Cube is a data structure that allows fast analysis of data according to the multiple dimensions that define a business problem [1, 2, 13, 15, 16, 19].

Research is continued according to early presented meta-model [15], where financial data about companies from the Netherlands are analysed. The type of financial data is general ledger, which consists of separate files such as general ledger account opening balance, journal, journal entry, ledger account, vat code and general ledger trail descriptions. Research process starts with data quality evaluation. Then the process of data preparation begins. Data must be transformed to a more convenient structure for further analysis, in this case process mining process. Prepared data is analysed by using process mining algorithms and filling the data cube dimensions by certain data set fields. After process mining phase data is also processed by machine learning tools and techniques for outlier detection. There are prepared reports of each phase, reports on statistics and all these results are presented to the user – financial analyst. The main focus of research described in this paper is to present data dimensions with their members, data preparation process and presentation on how data dimensions may be covered with certain financial data [15].

2   Basic Concepts of Financial Data Space

Description of key concepts used to systematize financial data:

- Financial data are data records on all activities and entities of the enterprise (accounts payable, accounts receivable, customers, creditors, suppliers and etc.) are located in the Finance Data Space.
- Financial accounting object (FO) – any name of the file field (data record field), i.e. the column name of the excel table), except for time attributes.
- Finance Data Space consists of a set of Dimensions with meaningful names. Dimensions correspond to some type of Financial Object. There can be several dimensions of FO, it depends on the experts who provide the FO classification.
- Dimension – a type of FO (cluster) that corresponds to an aspect of financial accounting or performance management practices. Each dimension corresponds to one axis of the Finance Data Space.

- Dimensions consist of dimension members that specify the hierarchical structure of the FO, i. identifies a more detailed classification of the FO type (Fig. 1).

Dimension members are assigned attributes (identifiers) that correspond to the data record fields (quantities, values, or codes).

Different dimensions can form combinations of Members if they have at least one common attribute (identifier).

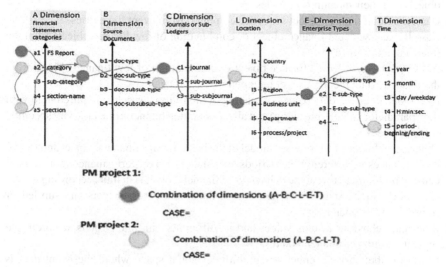

Fig. 1. Dimensions can form combinations specifying a process mining project

A financial data analysis system, with a user-friendly interface created using financial data space and process mining techniques, provides new capabilities. Such a system combines the traditional Data mining technique and the Financial Process Mining technique adapted to the specifics of financial data.

2.1 Financial Process Mining Aspects

The specification of Financial Process Mining tasks (projects) quite often has fundamental differences from traditional Process Mining. The Process Mining technology is aimed to discovery of process model from process related data records named Eventlog.

Financial processes refer to the methods and procedures completed by the Office of Finance. They include but aren't limited to: Accounting, Budgeting, Planning and other categorized under varied titles depending on the finance policies and procedures.

Since each finance department function has a list of finance business processes involved, drawing up process maps can bring a clear understanding of the tasks and people involved.

Finance Process definition in terms of process mining technology: Finance process is fixed as a set of finance data records in the company's database and can be discovered, visualized and linked to static indicators using Process Mining (PM) technology.

2.2 Basic Concepts of Finance Process Mining

Basic concepts of finance process mining necessary for current research are explained below:

- Financial (accounting) object (FO): any name of the file field (data record field), i.e. the column name of the excel table), except for time attributes.
- Source data: A subset of financial data records, each record being a set of financial objects and their meanings or codes.
- Case: a unique finance object sequence compiled from event log entries
- Case ID: any selected finance object or combination of few finance objects from the financial data record
- Activity ID: any selected finance object or combination of few finance objects from the financial data record, except included to Case ID.
- Event: one financial data record consisting of the following fields: required field with time parameter value (timestamp) and all others called financial objects (with specified value or code)
- Outcome of finance PM: process model of the behavior of a financial object and its and its differences in different time periods, and statistics (key performance indicators).
- Current problem: to reveal the behaviour of financial objects in time, according to data clusters (financial statement types, source document types, ledgers and sub ledger (journals, other documents.)).
- Relevant: behaviour of data values and its differences in time periods, according to separate groups of financial data.).
- Process Cube: Process cubes are multidimensional space where the event data is presented and organized using different dimensions. Each cell in the process cube corresponds to a set of events which can be used as an input by any process mining technique. This notion is related to the well-known OLAP (Online Analytical Processing) data cubes, adapting the OLAP paradigm to event data through multidimensional process mining.

3 Specification of a Financial Process Mining Project

The conceptual schema of Financial Process Mining (PM) project specification (with example) is depicted in Fig. 2. The principle schema of Financial Process mining based on the Process Cube is presented in Fig. 3.

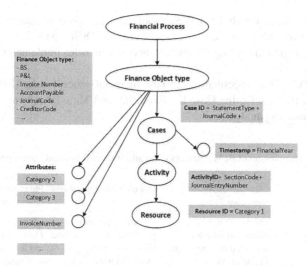

Fig. 2. Financial Process Mining (PM) project specification (example)

Each cell in the Process Cube corresponds to a some eventlog (sublog) containing events (financial data records) and is associated with process models (derived by PM or given as input, i.e. a predefined models).

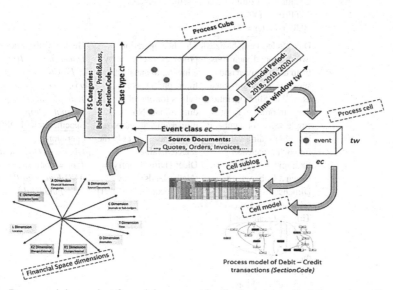

Fig. 3. Process mining project financial process cube dimensions: vertical dimension – Case type; horizontal dimension – event class, diagonal dimension – time stamp

Next we consider the classical OLAP operations (Table 1) in the context of our Process Cubes.

In terms of data set, the ROLL UP operation forms a subset of financial accounting data (a subset of records) that meets user requirements. Drill Up (Roll Up) operation is the based on the expert knowledge – financial accounting rules implemented in the code of operation.

Next, the PM task is specified in the new financial process cube (FPC) of higher level of granularity by selecting Case ID, Event ID, and Time ID relevant for the audit or financial accounting analysis.

Table 1. The classical OLAP, process cube and financial process cube operations

Operation	Classical OLAP operations	Process Cube Operations	Financial Process Cube Operations
Slice	The Slice OLAP operations take one specific dimension from a cube given and represent a new sub-cube. It can create a new sub-cube by choosing one or more dimensions Example: Slice (dimension = Location) for (dimension = TIME = (Year = 2020, Quarter = Q1))	The slice operation produces a new sub-cube view by allowing the analyst to filter (pick) specific values for attributes within one of the dimensions, while removing that dimension from the visible part of the cube. Slice: {Dim Country = (Netherlands)}	Given a Cube where *Dimensions = {(Case ID = FS Categories), Time = Financial Year), (Event ID = JournalType)}* Specification of SLICE operation: *SLICE on {FS Category (Case type = (FS Category AND Section)}*
Dice	Dice (Select) emphasizes two or more dimensions from a cube given and suggests a new sub-cube, as well as Slice operation does. In order to locate a single value for a cube, it includes adding values for each dimension Example: Given a Cube where Dimensions = {(Location = Cities), Time = Quaternar-ies), (Products types = Items)} then Dice for (Location = "Venice" or "Florence") and (Time = Seasons = ("Winter" or "Spring") and (Product type = (Item = "components" or "clothining")	The dice operation produces a subcube by allowing the analyst to filter (pick) specific values for one of the dimensions. No dimensions are removed in this case, but only the selected values Dice: {Dim Country = (Netherlands); gran(Location) = City)}	Given a Cube where *Dimensions = {(Case ID = FS Categories = (a1, a5), Time = Financial Year, (Event ID = JournalType)}* Specification of DICE operation: *DICE on {Document Type = (doc-subtype3) AND Financial Period = (t3 – Financial Year)}*

(continued)

Table 1. (*continued*)

Operation	Classical OLAP operations	Process Cube Operations	Financial Process Cube Operations
Drill Down (Roll Down)	OLAP Drill-down is an operation opposite to Drill-up. It is carried out either by descending a concept hierarchy for a dimension or by adding a new dimension. It lets a user deploy highly detailed data from a less detailed cube. Example: Given a Cube where Dimensions = {(Location = Cities), (Time = Seasons), (Products = Product types)} then Drill Down on Dimension = {(Time) from Seasons to Month)}	The roll up and drill down operations do not remove any dimensions or filter any values, but only change the level of granularity of a specific dimension [p826] Drill down (Roll Down) operation is intended to show the same data with more detail (granularity)	Given a Cube, where Dimensions = {(Case ID = FS Categories = ((*Debit-Credit), Category3, Category2, Category1, Statement Type*), Time = Financial Year, (Event ID = Source documents)} Specification of DRILL DOWN (ROLL DOWN) operation: *DRIL DOWN on {FS Category (from Case type = (Debit – Credit) to Case type = Section)}* Results are sub-cube: Dimensions = {(Case ID = FS Categories = (*Section code, Debit-Credit), Category3, Category2, Category1, Statement Type*), Time = Financial Year, (Event ID = Source documents)}
Drill Up (Roll Up)	Summarize data: Climbing up hierarchy or by dimension reduction in order to receive measures at a less detailed granularity Example: Given a Cube where Dimensions = {(Location = Cities), Time = Seasons), (Products = Product types)} then Drill Up on Dimension = (Location = Country)	The roll up and drill down operations do not remove any dimensions or filter any values, but only change the level of granularity of a specific dimension [p826] Roll Up (Drill Up) operation is intended to show the same data with less detail (granularity)	Given a Cube, where Dimensions = {(Case ID = FS Categories = (*Section code, Debit-Credit), Category3, Category2, Category1, Statement Type*), Time = Financial Year, (Event ID = Source documents)} Specification of ROLL UP (DRILL UP) operation: *ROLL UP on {FS Category (from Case type = Section to Case type = (Debit – Credit))}* Results are sub-cube

4   Financial Process Mining Project Specification

Financial Process Mining Project specification is presented and described in steps below.

Step 1. Mapping of Finance Data Space dimensions to the Process Cube dimensions
There is need to select the Financial Data Space dimension (or multiple dimensions) and their members [15] that correspond to the Financial Process Cube dimensions (Case type dimension in Fig. 1 and 3): vertical, horizontal and diagonal dimensions. Financial Process Cube dimensions may be associated with the different Financial Data Space dimensions in the different way.
Financial Process Cube dimensions in the example (Fig. 34) are associated with the Financial Data Space dimensions as follows:

- Case type dimension is associated with the Financial Statement Category (dimension A) and etc.
- Event class dimension is associated with the Document Type (dimension B),
- Time window dimension is associated with the Financial Period (dimension T).

Step 2. Specification and visualization of the required Finance Process Cube
The Financial Process Mining tool composes the Financial Process Cube according to the user specification and displays (visualizes) PC dimensions and their members.
It is possible to say, user requirements are as follows:

- Case type dimension is associated with the Financial Statement Category (dimension A) members a1 – FS Category and a5 – Section,
- Event class dimension is associated with the Document Type (dimension B) members, b3 – Doc-subtype3,
- Time window dimension is associated with the Financial Period (dimension T), t3 – FinancialYear.

The Process Cube dimensions and members according to the user requirements specification are as follows (Fig. 4):
PC = { Case type (a1, a5); (Event class (b3); (Times window (t1)}.
Step 3. Specification of Process Mining project
The next step is to specify the parameters of the PM project according to the objectives of the analysis performed. We select Case ID, Activity ID, and Timestamp ID from existing cube dimensions and their members.
The example of PM project specification is as follows (Fig. 4):

- Dimension FS Category: Case ID: a1 – Category, a5 – Section Code;
- Dimension Document types: Activity ID: b3 – Doc-subtype3 (Invoice);
- Dimension TimeWindow: Timestamp: t3 – Financial Year.

Initial Event log relevant to PM project specification is depicted in Fig. 5 (example, screenshot of Disco tool).
The execution process of a Financial Process Mining project is described by multidimensional process cube operations: SLICE, DICE, ROLL UP and others as defined in Table 1.
Step 4. Specification of project EventLog

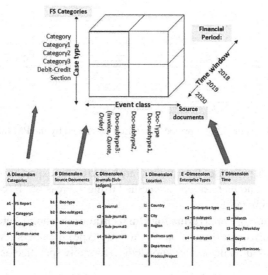

Fig. 4. The financial process cube required by the user includes dimensions A = case type, B = source document and T = time window

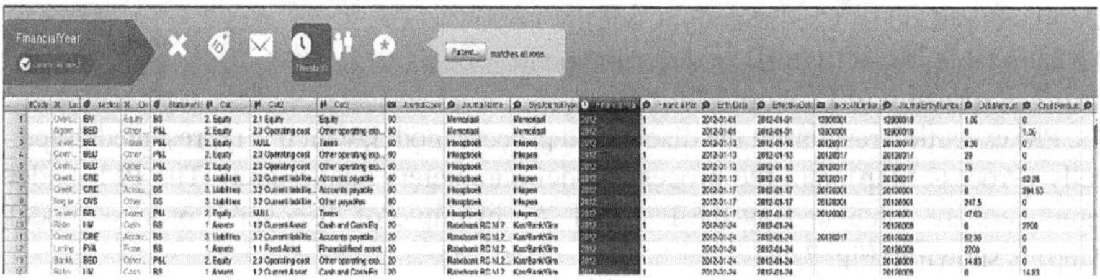

Fig. 5. Initial event log example (Disco tool)

In this step, according to the project specification, the PM tool creates a project EventLog (Fig. 5) from the existing data set (i.e. Initial Event), on the basis of which the PM process will be started:

- CaseID = (CaseID1 = StatementType AND CaseID2 = SectionCode),
- ActivityID = InvoiceNumber (i.e. doc-subtype3),
- Timestamp = FinancialYear.

Figure 6 shows an example of a project EventLog generated by the PM tool Disco.

Step 5. Specification of constraints for Vertical dimension (Case type)

Case type (CaseID1 and CaseID2,..) can be associated with financial process rules (constraints) defined through data record attributes and their values.

These rules of the financial process make it possible to distinguish between permissible and non-permissible transactions, i.e. allows you to detect inadequate records.

	A	B	C	D	E	F	G	H	I	J	K	L	M	N	O	P	Q	R	S	T	U
1	Case ID	Activity	Resource	Complete	Variant	Variant index	LodgerAcc	Cat1	Cat2	Cat3	JournalCode	JournalNo	SysJournal	Financial	EntryDate	EffectiveDate	JournalEnt	DebitAmo	CreditAmc	DebtorCoc	CreditorCodc
2	BS-EIV	13900001	2. Equity-2.	00:00.0	Variant 1	1	750	2. Equity	2.1 Equity	Equity	90	Memorias	Memorias	1	2012-01-01	2012-01-01	12900019	1.05	0		
3	BS-EIV	15900010	2. Equity-2.	00:00.0	Variant 1	1	750	2. Equity	2.1 Equity	Equity	90	Memorias	Memorias	3	2015-03-05	2015-03-05	15900010	40000	0		
4	BS-EIV	15900011	2. Equity-2.	00:00.0	Variant 1	1	750	2. Equity	2.1 Equity	Equity	90	Memorias	Memorias	3	2015-03-05	2015-03-05	15900011	40000	0		
5	BS-EIV	16900002	2. Equity-2.	00:00.0	Variant 1	1	750	2. Equity	2.1 Equity	Equity	90	Memorias	Memorias	12	2015-12-31	2015-12-31	15900024	4.11	0		
6	BS-EIV	16900003	2. Equity-2.	00:00.0	Variant 1	1	750	2. Equity	2.1 Equity	Equity	90	Memorias	Memorias	4	2016-09-12	2016-09-12	16900001	62500	0		
7	BS-EIV	16900024	2. Equity-2.	00:00.0	Variant 1	1	750	2. Equity	2.1 Equity	Equity	90	Memorias	Memorias	12	2016-12-31	2016-12-31	16900024	1.19	0		
8	BS-EIV	17900013	2. Equity-2.	00:00.0	Variant 1	1	750	2. Equity	2.1 Equity	Equity	90	Memorias	Memorias	1	2017-01-17	2017-01-17	17900013	45000	0		
9	BS-EIV	17900014	2. Equity-2.	00:00.0	Variant 1	1	750	2. Equity	2.1 Equity	Equity	90	Memorias	Memorias	12	2017-12-31	2017-12-31	17900014	1.34	0		
10	BS-EIV	18900004	2. Equity-2.	00:00.0	Variant 1	1	750	2. Equity	2.1 Equity	Equity	90	Memorias	Memorias	12	2018-12-31	2018-12-31	18900004	1.39	0		
11	BS-EIV	18900005	2. Equity-2.	00:00.0	Variant 1	1	750	2. Equity	2.1 Equity	Equity	90	Memorias	Memorias	12	2018-12-31	2018-12-31	18900004	60000	0		
12	BS-EIV	19900005	2. Equity-2.	00:00.0	Variant 1	1	750	2. Equity	2.1 Equity	Equity	90	Memorias	Memorias	12	2019-12-31	2019-12-31	19900005	50000	0		
13	P&L-BED	13900001	2. Equity-2.	00:00.0	Variant 2	2	5550	2. Equity	2.3 Operat	Other ope	90	Memorias	Memorias	1	2012-01-01	2012-01-01	12900019	0	1.05		
14	P&L-BED	20120017	2. Equity-2.	00:00.0	Variant 2	2	5552	2. Equity	2.3 Operat	Other ope	60	Inkoopbos	Inkopen	1	2012-01-13	2012-01-13	20120017	29	0		2
15	P&L-BED	20120017	2. Equity-2.	00:00.0	Variant 2	2	5552	2. Equity	2.3 Operat	Other ope	60	Inkoopbos	Inkopen	1	2012-01-13	2012-01-13	20120017	15	0		2
16	P&L-BED	20120003	2. Equity-2.	02:00.0	Variant 2	2	5560	2. Equity	2.3 Operat	Other ope	20	Rabobank	Kas/Bank/	1	2012-01-24	2012-01-24	20120009	14.83	0		
17	P&L-BED	20120003	2. Equity-2.	00:00.0	Variant 2	2	5552	2. Equity	2.3 Operat	Other ope	60	Inkoopbos	Inkopen	2	2012-02-01	2012-02-01	20120003	122.31	0		6
18	P&L-BED	20120016	2. Equity-2.	00:00.0	Variant 2	2	5552	2. Equity	2.3 Operat	Other ope	60	Inkoopbos	Inkopen	2	2012-02-10	2012-02-10	20120016	15	0		2

Fig. 6. An example of a project EventLog generated by the PM tool Disco

The rules of financial processes (constraints) are based on the expert knowledge presented in natural language and then formally specified using expression IF (conditions) THEN (Action) and decision tables.

Step 6. Specification of constraints for Horizontal dimension (Activity type)
Constraints for Horizontal dimension (= Activity type) members (ActivityID = doc-subtype3,….) is based on the expert knowledge (formally specified as decision table or otherwise.
The list of doc-subtype3 possible values:
doc-subtype3 = (Invoice, Quote, Order, …).
Example of the Decision table for ActivityID = doc-subtype3 when Transaction type = (DebitSectionCode – CreditSectionCode):
Decision table for ActivityID = doc-subtype3.

Step 7. Execution of Process Mining
The PM execution results are the discovered process model, which is represented graphically (Process Map), and the process model parameters (static data). The PM model parameters are calculated by the PM tool. An example of discovered process model (Map) is shown in Fig. 7.

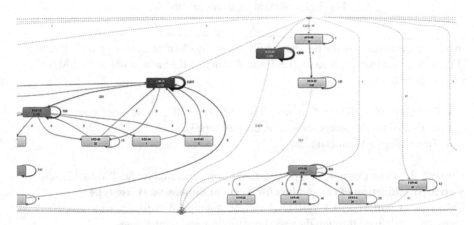

Fig. 7. An example of discovered process model

5 Conclusion

Process mining aims to discover, monitor and improve real processes by extracting knowledge from event logs readily available in today's information systems. Process mining gathers data from these event logs taken from a business's systems or a data warehouse. The minimum data requirements needed to map a process are the activity name, a unique case ID, and a timestamp for each case.

First part defines basic concepts of financial data space and explains the main differences between financial process mining tasks from traditional process mining.

Second part presents the specification of a financial process mining project, where financial process mining based on a process cube is presented. There is clearly explained continual research focusing on the comparison of classical OLAP, process cube and financial process cube operations.

Third part defines financial process mining project specification depicted by steps, starting from the mapping of finance data space dimensions to the process cube dimensions, continuing with the specification of the required finance process cube, of a process mining project, of project EventLog, of constraints for vertical dimension and horizontal dimension and finishing with the execution of process mining processes by presenting discovered process map.

Acknowledgments. This paper presents the primary results of the research project "Enterprise Financial Performance Data Analysis Tools Platform (AIFA)". The research project is funded by European Regional Development Fund according to the 2014–2020 Operational Programme for the European Union Funds' Investments under measure No. 01.2.1-LVPA-T-848 "Smart FDI". Project no.: 01.2.1-LVPA-T-848–02-0004; Period of project implementation: 2020–06-01 – 2022–05-31.

References

1. van der Aalst, W.M.P.: Process Mining: Discovery, Conformance and Enhancement of Business Processes. Springer, Berlin, Heidelberg (2011). https://doi.org/10.1007/978-3-642-193 45-3
2. Aalst, W.M.P.: Process cubes: slicing, dicing, rolling up and drilling down event data for process mining. In: Song, M., Wynn, M.T., Liu, J. (eds.) AP-BPM 2013. LNBIP, vol. 159, pp. 1–22. Springer, Cham (2013). https://doi.org/10.1007/978-3-319-02922-1_1
3. Aalst, W.V., Kees, M.V., Werf, J.M.V., Verdonk, M.: Finance process mining auditing 2.0: using process mining to support tomorrow's auditor. Computer **43**(3), (2010) http://www.pad sweb.rwth-aachen.de/wvdaalst/publications/p593.pdf
4. Adriansyah, A., Buijs, J.C.A.M.: Mining process performance from event logs. In: La Rosa, M., Soffer, P. (eds.) Business Process Management Workshops, pp. 217–218. Springer, Berlin, Heidelberg (2013). https://doi.org/10.1007/978-3-642-36285-9_23
5. Abdulrahman, A.: Audit focused process mining: the evolution of process mining and internal control. PhD Thesis (2019). https://rucore.libraries.rutgers.edu/rutgers-lib/60514/PDF/1/play/
6. Das, K., Schneider, J.: Detecting anomalous records in categorical datasets. In: Proceedings of the 13th ACM SIGKDD international conference on Knowledge Discovery and Data Mining August 2007 pp.220–229 https://doi.org/10.1145/1281192.1281219

7. Earley, C.E.: Data analytics in auditing: opportunities and challenges. Bus. Horiz. **58**, 493–500 (2015)
8. Debreceny, R.S., Gray, G.L.: Data mining journal entries for fraud detection: an exploratory study. Int. J. Acc. Inf. Syst. **11**(3), 157–181 (2010)
9. Amani, F.A., Fadlalla, A.M.: Data mining applications in accounting: A review of the literature and organizing framework. Int. J. Acc. Inf. Syst. **24**, 32–58 (2017)
10. Frederik, G., Guido, G.: Business process modeling: an accounting information systems perspective. Int. J. Acc. Inf. Syst. **15**(3), 185–192 (2014). https://doi.org/10.1016/j.accinf.2014.08.001
11. Gehrke, N., Mueller-Wickop, N.: Basic principles of financial process mining a journey through financial data in accounting information systems. Association for Information Systems AIS Electronic Library (AISeL) (2010)
12. Gepp, A., Linnenluecke, M.K., O'Neill, T.J., Smith, T.: Big data techniques in auditing research and practice: current trends and future opportunities. J. Acc. Lit. **40,** 102–115 (2018)
13. Gosselin, M.: An empirical study of performance measurement in manufacturing firms. Int. J. Product. Perform. Manag. **54**(5/6), 419–437 (2005). https://doi.org/10.1108/17410400510604566
14. vom Brocke, J., Rosemann, M. (eds.): Handbook on Business Process Management 2. Springer, Berlin, Heidelberg (2010). https://doi.org/10.1007/978-3-642-01982-1
15. Lopata, A., et al.: Financial data preprocessing Issues. In: Lopata, A., Gudonienė, D., Butkienė, R. (eds.) ICIST 2021. CCIS, vol. 1486, pp. 60–71. Springer, Cham (2021). https://doi.org/10.1007/978-3-030-88304-1_5
16. Mamaliga, T.: Realizing a process cube allowing for the comparison of event data. Master Thesis. Eindhoven University of Technology (2013)
17. Mieke, J., Alles, M., and Vasarhelyi, M.: The case for process mining in auditing: sources of value added and areas of application. Int. J. Acc. Inf. Syst. **14**(1), 1–20 (2013). https://doi.org/10.1016/j.accinf.2012.06.015.
18. OLAP Council, OLAP: On-Line Analytical Processing. http://www.olapcouncil.org/research/glossaryly.htm Accessed 21 Feb 2022
19. Werner, M., Gehrke, N., and Nuttgens, M.: Business process mining and reconstruction for financial audits. In: 45th Hawaii International Conference on System Sciences, pp. 5350–5359 (2012). https://doi.org/10.1109/HICSS.2012.141
20. Werner, M.: Financial process mining - accounting data structure dependent control flow inference. Int. J. Acc. Inf. Syst. **25**, 57–80 (2017). https://doi.org/10.1016/j.accinf.2017.03.004

Intelligent Method for Forming the Consumer Basket

Khrystyna Lipianina-Honcharenko[1] , Carsten Wolff[2] , Zoriana Chyzhovska[1] ,
Anatoliy Sachenko[1] , Taras Lendiuk[1(✉)] , and Sergii Grodskyi[1]

[1] West Ukrainian National University, Lvivska Str., 11, Ternopil 46000, Ukraine
{as,tl}@wunu.edu.ua
[2] Fachhochschule Dortmund, Otto-Hahn-Str. 23, Dortmund, Germany
carsten.wolff@fh-dortmund.de

Abstract. Authors developed an intelligent method of forming a consumer basket based on data from supermarket chains, which allows modifying the set of goods in the consumer basket and defining a living wage. The consumer basket is forming on a base of k-means clustering approach. The algorithmic structure of the proposed method is described. Experimental research is carried out using the Customer Personality Analysis dataset from the Kaggle platform. After data normalization and clustering, the clusters relative to the amount (USD) of purchased goods for 2 years were analyzed. As a result, the cluster (consumer basket) was selected which includes 27% of middle-aged customers of various ages and counts such goods as fish, meat, sweets, wine and equipment. The novelty of the paper is the automated and intelligent forming the set of goods in the consumer basket, which may promote survival during humanitarian and economic disasters, especially in times of economic crisis (war, pandemic).

Keywords: Consumer basket · Clustering · k-means · Dataset

1 Introduction

Nowadays, the method of defining the consumer basket is an extremely important issue, because based on the consumer basket is formed a living wage, according to which pensions, social benefits and payments are calculated. For example, in Ukraine, the Cabinet of Ministers of Ukraine is directly involved in the formation of the consumer basket. Based on the data of the consumer basket and the consumer budget, such indicators as the minimum wage and the minimum pension are calculated.

The value of the consumer basket depends on the level of retail prices for goods and tariffs for paid services (for example, utility bills). This practice is common throughout the civilized world. For each type of needs, the calculation includes the purchase of relatively cheap goods, usually at government fixed prices. If, for example, in the market this product or service is sold at lower prices, the lowest level is taken as a basis.

The concept of the consumer basket exists in many countries around the world. Its price and national characteristics vary from country to country. For example, the

American consumer basket includes 350 products and services, the French – 507, the Englishman – 350, the German – 475. The Ukrainian consumer basket has recently been expanded to 297 items.

People's purchasing power can change dramatically with respect to crises such as war and pandemics. Therefore, the assessment of the consumer basket and its variable must be rapid, in order to prevent humanitarian catastrophes and increasing poverty.

Hence, a development of an intelligent method for forming a consumer basket based on data from supermarket networks – a subject of this paper, is relevant.

The novelty of the paper is the automated and intelligent formation of a set of goods in the consumer basket, which may promote survival during humanitarian and economic disasters, especially in times of economic crisis (war, pandemic).

Based on the proposed method the analysis of clusters, relative to the amount (USD) of purchased goods for 2 years is made, and the cluster (consumer basket) was defined. It includes the 27% of middle-aged customers of various ages and counts such goods as fish, meat, sweets, wine and equipment.

The paper is distributed as follows. Section 2 describes the analysis of related work. Section 3 presents an intelligent method of the consumer basket forming. Section 4 considers the case study and Sect. 5 contains a discussion. Section 6 summarizes the outcomes of the study.

2 Related Work

The paper [1] identified tools for a consumer basket forming in different areas and levels, including national laws, government policies and local government initiatives, and analyzed them with the various forms of short supply chains available in France that are key components of the local food system such as direct marketing, producer shops, urban agriculture and catering. In [5] the evolution of fluctuations between consumer price index classes is investigated, and a weighted Granger Causal Network (WGCN) for each G7 country is constructed. In [6] the consumer price index in the United Kingdom as a complex network is modelled and clustering and optimization techniques are applied to study the evolution of the network over time. The paper [7] analyzes the similarity of consumer patterns in 10 Asian countries, using three well-known system-wide demand models, namely Rotterdam, CBS and AIDS. None of the papers above consider the intelligent methods for classifying customers.

In paper [9], an intuitive fuzzy clustering algorithm was applied to supermarket customer data according to the amount spent on some product groups. The analysis of the general consumer basket is not carried out in this paper.

The paper [2] attempted to predict a segment of the mid-Atlantic wine market – based on purchasing behavior, attitudes and socio-demographic characteristics. Cluster analysis is used to segment the mid-Atlantic wine market. The paper [3] analyzed the market basket using an a priori algorithm to find consumer models in the goods purchase by transaction data. In [4] a study of the integration of disparate data sources from the grocery store based on methods of market basket analysis is proposed. The paper [8] examines and implements a recommendation mechanism on a well-known Portuguese e-commerce platform specializing in clothing and sportswear to increase customer engagement by providing a personalized experience with different types of recommendations on the platform. The paper [10] attempted to fill a gap in the study by using big data analytics to analyze approximately 44,000 point-of-sale transaction records for 26,000 Taiwanese retailer customers to understand how the consumer's personality traits are related to country of origin (COO), traits (brand identity) of beer brands, as well as to predict the Customer Lifetime Value (CLV). In those papers above, the possibility of determining the consumer basket is not considered, they deals with the segmentation of customers by individual products only.

The paper [11] proposed the modifications of the CDFCM algorithm due to certain shortcomings identified in it, which resulted in the formation of a modified dynamic fuzzy c-algorithm means (MDFCM). In this paper, the detailed analysis of cluster analysis approaches is absent.

The paper [12] evaluates the effectiveness of different data clustering approaches for finding profitable consumer segments in the UK hospitality industry. The papers [13, 28] are based on the RFM (Review, Frequency and Monetary) model and uses the principles of data set segmentation using the K-Means algorithm.

The sales results obtained in this way are compared with various parameters, such as recent sales, sales frequency and sales amount. In the paper [14, 15] a forecasting model is presented, it is based on the behavior of each customer using data analysis methods. The proposed model uses a supermarket database and an additional database from Amazon, which contains information about customer purchases. In paper [16, 27], customer segmentation was performed by clustering K-means in uncontrolled machine learning. Target customers are classified using clustering based on demographic information (e.g., gender, age, income, etc.), geographic information, psychography, and behavioral data. A drawback is, that customer segmentation is done from the marketing side only.

Paper [22] discusses the possibilities of how big data affects retailers, including the five main dimensions of data – customer, product, time, (geospatial) location and channel. In order to study the use of smart technologies in terms of marketing and retail, this paper provides the approach to disciplines that are driven by continuous improvement of technology [23]. Its focus is aimed on smart technologies for consumer behavior through a more integrated and modern perspective that combines marketing and retail with other disciplines such as psychology, media research and sociology. The authors carried out the analysis of possible technologies that can be used to determine the consumer basket in real time, but the implementation is absent.

The paper [21] focuses on intelligent consumers who voluntarily participate in value creation activities to conceptualize joint Smart Experience Creation (SEC) and intelligent service systems.

The above-mentioned papers mostly analyze the customer in terms of supermarket marketing. There are no papers where the customer is evaluated as a consumer, the consumer basket is defined, and the living wage is found.

Therefore, the purpose of this paper is to fill the existing gap and develop the intelligent method of a consumer basket forming.

3 Proposed Method

The proposed method is illustrated schematically (Fig. 1) and represented by the following steps:

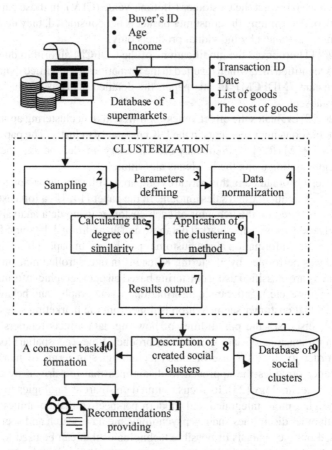

Fig. 1. Algorithmic structure of intelligent method for forming the consumer basket.

Step 1. Collection of data from supermarkets (Block 1), namely information about the customer (Customer ID, Age, Revenue) and customer's purchases (Transaction ID, Date, List of goods, Product price). When collecting data, it is possible to expand the database of pharmacies, food and non-food products.
Step 2. Data clustering.

Step 2.1. Selection of objects for clustering (Block 2).
Step 2.2. Defining the set of variables (Block 3), which will be evaluated objects in the sample.

Step 2.3. Normalization (Block 4) of variable values.

Step 2.4. Calculating the values of similarity degree between objects (Block 5).

Step 2.5. Application of clustering method (Block 6) for creating the groups of similar objects (clusters).

Step 2.6. Presentation of results analysis (Block 7).

Step 3. Description of obtained clusters, namely the definition of the social cluster (Block 8), and the transfer of existing social clusters in a separate database (Block 9) for automatization of processing and clusters formation.

Step 4. Forming the consumer basket (Block 10) and providing recommendations (Block 11).

4   Experimental Results

The Python language was selected to implement the proposed method of forming the consumer basket. Customer Personality Analysis data from the Kaggle platform was used as input [18]. This dataset presents the analysis of customer's personality as the US dollars amount spent over 2 years (Table 1).

Table 1. Dataset structure.

Parameter	count	mean	min	max
Income	2240.0	52247.25	1730.0	666666.0
Kidhome	2240.0	0.44	0.0	2.0
Teenhome	2240.0	0.51	0.0	2.0
Recency	2240.0	49.11	0.0	99.0
Wines	2240.0	303.94	0.0	1493.0
Fruits	2240.0	26.30	0.0	199.0
Meat	2240.0	166.95	0.0	1725.0
Fish	2240.0	37.52	0.0	259.0
Age	2240.0	52.19	25.0	68.0
Total_Spend	2240.0	602.25	5.0	2525.0

Normalization must be run before clustering. We are also interested in knowing the costs per month, so we divide all the cos t values by 24 months. This will get the values ready to form a consumer basket.

Several methods of clustering [9, 11, 13, 15–17, 19] were analyzed and method of k-means clustering was selected [15, 19] as a common and simplest one.

To define the number of clusters, the Elbow method is used [20]. This method is calculated as the square sum of distances of the points from the center of the cluster according to each value of k – a number of clusters. Then a graph is plotted per each value of k (Fig. 2). The point of the elbow on the graph, where the difference between the results begins to decrease, is defined as the most appropriate value of k. For our example, the optimal number of clusters is three (see Fig. 2).

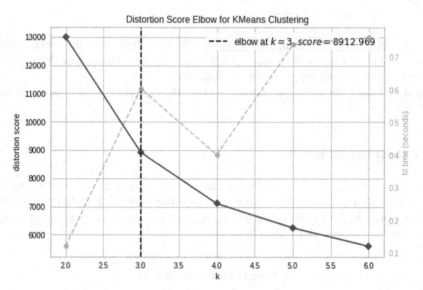

Fig. 2. Selection of clusters number by the Elbow method.

Next, let's consider the visualization of the obtained three clusters. As can be seen (Fig. 3a) the cluster number zero counts the most customers. The interpretation of the obtained clusters (Fig. 3b) is made in accordance with the characteristics of income and total costs:

- Cluster 2: high costs – average income;
- Cluster 1: high costs – high income;
- Cluster 0: low costs – low income.

If we consider clusters as social, then it is important that Cluster 2 and Cluster 0 are taken into account first. So, let's focus on the of the consumer basket formation, using these two clusters. Namely, to form a consumer basket based on Cluster 2 for an economically stable situation, and the consumer basket based on Cluster 0 for crises.

When considering the customers age category of (Fig. 4), it is seen that the distribution of clusters is uniform. Therefore, the authors believe that age does not affect purchasing power.

Next, let us consider in more detail the clusters relation to the amount (USD) of purchased goods (Fig. 5) for 2 years. Boxplot charts show the best the point of determining the average number of purchased goods in the cluster. As it is seen from Fig. 5 the Cluster 1 spends just a little money on fish, meat, sweets, wine, and the Cluster 2 shows larger amounts spent on these products. If we consider technological products,

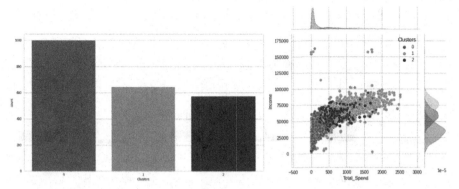

Fig. 3. Visualization of clusters: (a) number of customers in clusters; (b) distribution of customer income and expenses.

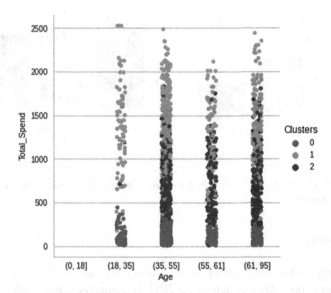

Fig. 4. Clusters visualization: age distribution.

then all customers spend approximately the same costs (Fig. 5e). Hence, in terms of goods sales, the authors believe that Cluster 2 has the optimal values for the consumer basket formation.

Therefore, let us describe Cluster 2 in more details, and use it as the base of recommendations for the consumer basket formation. The consumer basket (Cluster 2) includes 27% of middle-income customers with the different age and counts following goods purchased for the month: fish in the amount of 25 USD; meat in the amount of 100 USD; sweets in the amount of 20 USD; wine in the amount of 400 USD; equipment in the amount of 50 USD.

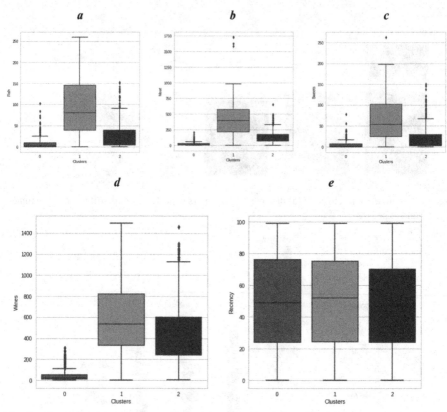

Fig. 5. Clusters visualization by distributing the purchased goods: (a) fish; (b) meat; (c) sweets; (d) wine; (e) equipment.

5 Discussion

To test the proposed method, authors have used training dataset Customer Personality Analysis, which was created in September 2021. In comparison with analogues [9, 11, 16] the developed method allows to form the set of goods in the consumer basket and define the living wage. The last includes 27% of middle-aged customers of various ages, and can count such goods (purchased for the month) as fish in the amount of 25 USD; meat in the amount of 100 USD; sweets in the amount of 20 USD; wine in the amount of 400 USD; equipment in the amount of 50 USD.

Authors realize that the proposed method allows working in real time, therefore changes of market situation will influence on result correspondingly. Authors believe that a full data collection from online supermarkets can give results that are more accurate. This can provide the monitoring of people's purchasing power in real time. Therefore, the authors are going to investigate the method of predicting the changes in the consumer basket formation in the future research.

6   Conclusions

The proposed intelligent method of forming the consumer basket is based on data from supermarket networks enabling to change quickly the set of goods in the consumer basket and define the living wage.

As the input, the Customer Personality Analysis from the Kaggle platform was used presenting the analysis of the customer's personality. To implement a posed task, the method of clustering k-means was selected. The analysis of clusters, relative to the amount (USD) of purchased goods for 2 years, was made, and the cluster (consumer basket) was defined. It includes the 27% of middle-aged customers of various ages and counts such goods as fish, meat, sweets, wine and equipment.

The proposed method allows working in real time, therefore changes of market situation will influence on result correspondingly.

Unlike analogues, the developed method allows to form the set of goods in the consumer basket and define the living wage, which may promote survival during humanitarian and economic disasters, especially in times of economic crisis (war, pandemic).

In the future research, we plan to investigate the method of predicting the changes in the consumer basket formation. In addition, the cross-cluster analysis will be performed with different approaches [24–26] to determine the best one.

References

1. Kapała, A.M.: Legal instruments to support short food supply chains and local food systems in France. Laws **11**(2), 21 (2022). https://doi.org/10.3390/laws11020021
2. Govindasamy, R.: Cluster analysis of wine market segmentation – a consumer based study in the mid-Atlantic USA. Econ. Aff. **63**(1), 151–157 (2018)
3. Qisman, M., Rosadi, R., Abdullah, A.S.: Market basket analysis using apriori algorithm to find consumer patterns in buying goods through transaction data (case study of Mizan computer retail stores). In: Journal of Physics: Conference Series. IOP Publishing, vol. 1722 no. 1, p. 012020 (2021). https://doi.org/10.1088/1742-6596/1722/1/012020
4. Tatiana, K., Mikhail, M.: Market basket analysis of heterogeneous data sources for recommendation system improvement. Procedia Comput. Sci. **136**, 246–254 (2018). https://doi.org/10.1016/j.procs.2018.08.263
5. Sun, Q., Gao, X., Wang, Z., Liu, S., Guo, S., Li, Y.: Quantifying the risk of price fluctuations based on weighted granger causality networks of consumer price indices: evidence from G7 countries. J. Econ. Interac. Coord. **15**(4), 821–844 (2019). https://doi.org/10.1007/s11403-019-00273-2
6. Sarantitis, G.A., Papadimitriou, T., Gogas, P.: A network analysis of the United Kingdom's consumer price index. Comput. Econ. **51**(2), 173–193 (2016). https://doi.org/10.1007/s10614-016-9625-9
7. Rathnayaka, S.D., Selvanathan, E.A., Selvanathan, S.: Modelling the consumption patterns in the Asian countries. Econ. Anal. Policy **74**, 277–296 (2022). https://doi.org/10.1016/j.eap.2022.02.004
8. Peixoto, V., Peixoto, H., Machado, J.: Integrating a data mining engine into recommender systems. In: Analide, C., Novais, P., Camacho, D., Yin, H. (eds.) IDEAL 2020. LNCS, vol. 12489, pp. 209–220. Springer, Cham (2020). https://doi.org/10.1007/978-3-030-62362-3_19

9. Dogan, O., Hiziroglu, A., Seymen, O.F.: Segmentation of retail consumers with soft clustering approach. In: Kahraman, C., Cevik Onar, S., Oztaysi, B., Sari, I.U., Cebi, S., Tolga, A.C. (eds.) INFUS 2020. AISC, vol. 1197, pp. 39–46. Springer, Cham (2021). https://doi.org/10.1007/978-3-030-51156-2_6

10. Chiang, L.L.L., Yang, C.S.: Does country-of-origin brand personality generate retail customer lifetime value? A big data analytics approach. Technol. Forecast. Soc. Change **130**, 177–187 (2018). https://doi.org/10.1016/j.techfore.2017.06.034

11. Munusamy, S., Murugesan, P.: Modified dynamic fuzzy c-means clustering algorithm – application in dynamic customer segmentation. Appl. Intell. **50**(6), 1922–1942 (2020). https://doi.org/10.1007/s10489-019-01626-x

12. Arunachalam, D., Kumar, N.: Benefit-based consumer segmentation and performance evaluation of clustering approaches: an evidence of data-driven decision-making. Expert Syst. Appl. **111**, 11–34 (2018). https://doi.org/10.1016/j.eswa.2018.03.007

13. Anitha, P., Patil, M.M.: RFM model for customer purchase behavior using k-means algorithm. J. King Saud Uni. – Comput. Inform. Sci. **34**(5), 1785–1792 (2022). https://doi.org/10.1016/j.jksuci.2019.12.011

14. Lipyanina, H., Sachenko, A., Lendyuk, T., Nadvynychny, S., & Grodskyi, S.: Decision tree based targeting model of customer interaction with business page. In: Proceedings of the third International Workshop on Computer Modeling and Intelligent Systems (CMIS-2020), CEUR Workshop Proceedings, (2608), pp. 1001–1012 (2020). Electronic copy at: http://ceur-ws.org/Vol-2608/paper75.pdf

15. Kanavos, A., Iakovou, S.A., Sioutas, S., Tampakas, V.: Large scale product recommendation of supermarket ware based on customer behaviour analysis. Big Data Cogn. Comput. **2**(2), 11 (2018). https://doi.org/10.3390/bdcc2020011

16. Alam, M.F., Singh, R., Katiyar, S.: Customer segmentation using k-means clustering in unsupervised machine learning. In: Proceedings of the 2021 3rd IEEE International Conference on Advances in Computing, Communication Control and Networking (ICAC3N), pp. 94–98 (2021). https://doi.org/10.1109/ICAC3N53548.2021.9725644

17. Sinaga, K.P., Yang, M.: Unsupervised k-means clustering algorithm. IEEE Access **8**, 80716–80727 (2020). https://doi.org/10.1109/ACCESS.2020.2988796

18. Customer Personality Analysis. Kaggle: Your Machine Learning and Data Science Community. https://www.kaggle.com/datasets/imakash3011/customer-personality-analysis. Accessed 10 Apr 2022

19. Fränti, P., Sieranoja, S.: K-means properties on six clustering benchmark datasets. Appl. Intell. **48**(12), 4743–4759 (2018). https://doi.org/10.1007/s10489-018-1238-7

20. Marutho, D., Hendra Handaka, S., Wijaya, E., Muljono: The determination of cluster number at k-mean using elbow method and purity evaluation on headline news. In: Proceedings of the 2018 IEEE International Seminar on Application for Technology of Information and Communication, pp. 533–538 (2018). https://doi.org/10.1109/ISEMANTIC.2018.8549751

21. Roy, S.K., Singh, G., Hope, M., Nguyen, B., Harrigan, P.: The rise of smart consumers: role of smart servicescape and smart consumer experience co-creation. J. Mark. Manag. **35**(15–16), 1480–1513 (2019). https://doi.org/10.1080/0267257X.2019.1680569

22. Bradlow, E.T., Gangwar, M., Kopalle, P., Voleti, S.: The role of big data and predictive analytics in retailing. J. Retail. **93**(1), 79–95 (2017). https://doi.org/10.1016/j.jretai.2016.12.004

23. Pantano, E.: The role of smart technologies in decision making: developing, supporting and training smart consumers. J. Mark. Manag. **35**(15–16), 1367–1369 (2019). https://doi.org/10.1080/0267257X.2019.1688927

24. Komar, M., Golovko, V., Sachenko, A., Bezobrazov, S.: Development of neural network immune detectors for computer attacks recognition and classification. In: Proceedings of the 2013 IEEE 7th International Conference on Intelligent Data Acquisition and Advanced

Computing Systems (IDAACS), pp. 665–668 (2013). https://doi.org/10.1109/IDAACS.2013.6663008

25. Hu, Z., Bodyanskiy, Y.V., Kulishova, N.Y., Tyshchenko, O.K.: A multidimensional extended neo-fuzzy neuron for facial expression recognition. Int. J. Intell. Syst. Appl. (IJISA) **9**(9), 29–36 (2017). https://doi.org/10.5815/ijisa.2017.09.04

26. Turchenko, V., Chalmers, E., Luczak, A.: A deep convolutional auto-encoder with pooling – unpooling layers in Caffe. Int. J. Comput. (18), 8--31 (2019). https://doi.org/10.47839/ijc.18.1.1270.

27. Lipyanina, H., Sachenko, S., Lendyuk, T., Brych, V., Yatskiv, V., Osolinskiy, O.: Method of detecting a fictitious company on the machine learning base. In: Hu, Z., Petoukhov, S., Dychka, I., He, M. (eds.) ICCSEEA 2021. LNDECT, vol. 83, pp. 138–146. Springer, Cham (2021). https://doi.org/10.1007/978-3-030-80472-5_12

28. Lipyanina-Goncharenko, H., Brych, V., Sachenko, S., Lendyuk, T., Bykovyy, P., Zahorodnia, D.: Method of forming a training sample for segmentation of tender organizers on machine learning basis. In: Proceedings of the 5th International Conference on Computational Linguistics and Intelligent Systems (COLINS 2021), Volume I: Main Conference, Lviv, Ukraine, 22–23 April 2021, CEUR Workshop Proceedings, 2870, pp. 1843–1852 (2021). http://ceur-ws.org/Vol-2870/paper134.pdf

Information Technology Applications - Special Session on Language Technologies

Intelligent Invoice Documents Processing Employing RPA Technologies

Vilius Kerutis and Dalia Calneryte(✉) 📍

Faculty of Informatics, Kaunas University of Technology, Studentu st. 50, Kaunas, Lithuania
{vilius.kerutis,dalia.calneryte}@ktu.lt

Abstract. The applications of Robotic Process Automation (RPA) are many and growing every year, covering banking and financial operations, insurance functions, auditing processes, logistics planning services and more, but automating invoice processing is still more challenging. However, different structure, the variety of keywords, the abundance of types of information makes the detection and retrieval of the information very complicated. Therefore, the currently solutions currently work well with predefined document structures. The aim of this study is to develop a solution based on RPA, Optical character recognition (OCR) technologies and deep learning methods for automated invoice processing without being bound to a specific document structure. The study focuses on five key fields of invoices that are most important to identify and read. The results showed that almost 83% of all invoices used in the experiments were processed correctly. In terms of the results for the detection of individual field information, the best results were found for the "date" and "total amount" fields, with 93.21% and 87.81% respectively, but the detection of the "seller" and "buyer" fields is complicated and requires extensive additional research. Experiments evaluating the document processing time of human the developed robot showed that the performance of human document processing decreases with the volume of documents processed, while the RPA time is almost constant. RPA is 1.76 times more efficient with 500 documents and 2 times faster with 1000 documents.

Keywords: Robotic Process Automation · Deep learning · Optical character recognition

1 Introduction

The automated reading of the content of financial documents using AI and software robotics technologies is a hot topic in today's business world. Robotic Process Automation (RPA) is a new technology utilizing software robots for automation of repetitive back-office processes. It can be used in a wide range of applications industries and business functions [1–3]. The main objectives of RPA are: (1) to eliminate the need for humans to work on repetitive tasks; (2) to speed up the whole process; (3) eliminate human error; and (4) maximize the robot's accuracy. The applications for RPA are numerous and growing every year, but some of the most common RPA tasks include banks and financial operations [4, 5] insurance functions [6], auditing [7], tour enquiries

© The Author(s), under exclusive license to Springer Nature Switzerland AG 2022
A. Lopata et al. (Eds.): ICIST 2022, CCIS 1665, pp. 235–247, 2022.
https://doi.org/10.1007/978-3-031-16302-9_18

[8] and logistics and planning services [9] and invoices [10]. The aim of such a service, targeted at financial documents, is to automatically scan and identify all the relevant fields of a document, regardless of the structure of the financial document. Currently, the solutions offered on the market are still dependent on the structure of the document, i.e. if a financial document is fed with a different structure than the one with which the solution has been developed, the effectiveness of the target information recognition decreases significantly [11]. If the structure of the financial document is different, the model no longer ensures correct recognition of the fields. In most cases, only a few standard fields are recognized, which are very easy to find, such as the final amount of the order, which is usually written at the bottom of the document, below the "total amount" of the order. Therefore, it makes sense to develop a solution that is able to accurately identify the information fields specified, regardless of the structure of the financial document. It is appropriate to integrate advanced artificial intelligence technologies together with RPA technologies [12, 13]. The potential customers of the system being developed are medium- to large-sized companies that sell goods or services and issue invoices. The most critical problem for such companies is the time spent on processing financial documents. The product could contribute to solving this problem by enabling the staff responsible for processing invoices to engage in other creative or intellectual activities with higher added value. This would increase the productivity and efficiency of the staff and their competence.

The most popular and commonly used solution in the business world for processing financial documents is Optical character recognition (OCR) [14]. OCR technology converts an image into text, thus extracting the necessary contextual information [15].

With the text, you can search, filter the text, or simply recognize what information is being presented, reuse that information elsewhere, etc. Identification itself can be complicated by the variety of fonts and writing styles that exist in the digital space alone, and if there are also recognizable images of handwritten text, the processing of the image and the identification of the text is even more complex.

Two methods are used to recognize as many different images as possible and convert them into text:

1. Pattern recognition. The principle is simple – the OCR logic is passed a variety of patterns for each known character. When the model receives a new image for character recognition, it applies the patterns until a match is found and the image is converted to text.

2. Feature detection. This method is much more complex than the first, but is much more widely used. It follows the rules of line drawing, for example, if there are two lines intersecting at one point, and below them there is another line crossing the previous two lines at two points, then this can be said to be the "A" symbol. This method is closely related to neural networks, and it is this principle that is used for symbol recognition.

Recognition of handwritten text in an image is performed using only feature detection [16, 17]. However, very high identification accuracies should not be expected, as handwritten text recognition is sometimes a difficult task even for humans.

Hence, the basic principle of such OCR-based solutions is very similar: a document is fed to the system, all the fields that should be identified are marked in the document, the OCR technology scans the marked areas and the marked document is fed to the recognition model for training. Real new documents are then transmitted, and the model must be able to identify the information provided.

Tesseract is an open OCR engine available under the Apache 2.0 license [18]. This engine can be used directly or (for software development purposes) by using an API to extract printed text from images [19]. For the Tesseract engine, the image is fed as an input, which is transferred onto an adaptive grid, and finally the image is converted into binary type. The contours are used to try to find the lines and words of text. Once the text lines and words are found, the character contours are combined into complete words. These words pass two levels of word recognition, and the extracted text is output as the result of the Tesseract engine.

In the context of practical solutions, the commercial products currently on the market are quite similar - all of them automate the processing of documents (mainly financial ones), all of them use OCR technology and deep learning algorithms (Conexiom [20], Klippa [21], Logikia [22], FastFour [23], and others). While these tools may appear to be the same - performing the same function - individually they all have their own advantages and disadvantages. In terms of user interface usability, price, speed of operation, Nanonets is the leader, specializing mainly in financial documents, providing a very user-friendly and understandable user interface for every user, free trials and running quite fast compared to other solutions [24]. Experiments on 20 documents with slightly different structures showed a pattern field recognition accuracy of 50%.

2 Materials and Methods

The idea of the developed project that would meet the customer's needs is presented in Fig. 1. The financial document is scanned using Adobe Acrobat Reader. The convolutional neural network then is used to find the fields required for proper document processing. Subsequently, the founds fields and their information are passed to a software robot that performs rule-based decisions, that is, decides if the found fields found meet the expected ones. Finally, after checking all the fields, the found information is saved in an MS Excel .xlsx file, which is intended to be stored in a SharePoint aggregated environment (this is not essential and can be adjusted, so it is not included in the layout of the project idea). The document is successfully flagged, and the process is repeated while there are financial documents to be processed.

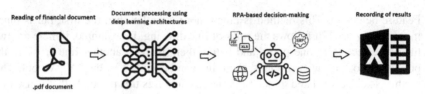

Fig. 1. Product idea layout at a high level.

The processing of visual information is based on convolutional neural networks. The target information recognition algorithm consists of two steps:

1. Target object detection and identification. Typically, OCR-based commercial decisions retrieve all the information in a financial document, but this system uses CNN
   to search for and identify only target objects that are required by the accounting
   system. FCN [25], R-CNN [26] convolutional neural network architectures were
   used to identify and segment the target objects. Their positions are then identified
   and the distances between all objects are calculated using certain metrics. Fully
   convolutional network (FCN) is responsible for finding ROI (expiration date) by
   keywords ("total sum", "order number", "booking data", etc.). It acts as a filter to
   recognize the location of the image containing the keywords, so that the recognition
   task is performed on that particular small fragment of the image rather than the entire
   region of the image to reduce computational time [27]. In addition, limiting to only
   the detected expiration date locations enables to avoid recognition errors caused by
   interference with other text in various parts of the image (see Fig. 2).

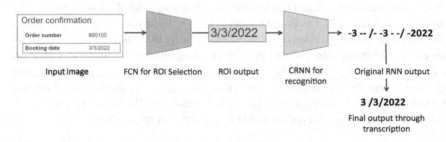

Fig. 2. Sequence for text recognition process.

2. Text recognition. CRNN (Convolutional Recurrent Neural Networks) [28], with LSTM (Long Short-Term Memory architecture) [29] and Attention-OCR [30] were used for text recognition. According to scientific research, use of these architectures enable to achieve high-precision results in identifying text and recognize textual information in different formats. The CRNN model uses a convolutional neural network (CNN) to extract visual features that are transformed and delivered to a long short-term memory network (LSTM). The LSTM output is then associated with the location of the character labels in the dense layer (see Fig. 3).

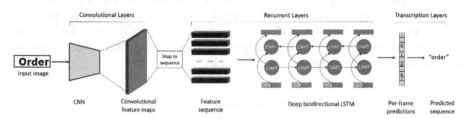

Fig. 3. Application of deep learning architectures in the system.

Decision trees are used for final processing of the information found. Decision trees are used to solve classification problems. The number of classification classes is defined in advance and corresponds to the number of fields in the accounting system.

2.1 Technologies Used for Implementation

The problem is solved in two stages. In the first stage, the image (.pdf files or photos with text) is processed. The text is derived from the image using artificial intelligence and other methods. In the second stage, for the extracted text, RPA will make a rules-based decision to decide whether what was expected has been found and selected. Artificial intelligence solutions have been implemented using the Python programming language, as it is accepted to be the most convenient and capable language when working with a wide variety of data in different formats. The Tensorflow [31] software development platform, which is specifically designed to implement such projects, has also been used.

RPA technologies are used in the second stage. There are many robotic tools and more and more new features are emerging every year (e.g. artificial intelligence), but three leaders stand out: Blue Prism [32], UiPath [33], and Automation Anywhere [34] Blue Prism technology was chosen for this study.

Fig. 4. Deployment diagram.

The deployment diagram is given in Fig. 4. The diagram shows that the process is stored on the Blue Prism server, which is accessed using RDP protocol via remote desktop. Blue Prism server directly communicates with SQL Server database via SQP Authentication connection. This diagram shows everything that is needed from a technical point of view for the process to execute.

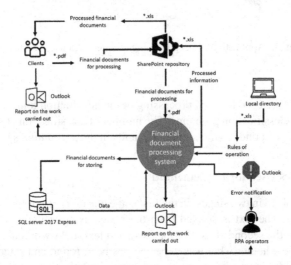

Fig. 5. Project context diagram.

The developed software is designed for operating in Windows 10 with Blue Prism v6.10 software installed. The only difference is that for the development the Blue Prism development environment is used, and after the software robot is developed, the Blue Prism production environment is used. The project context diagram is given in Fig. 5.

2.2 Developed Algorithm

The pseudo-code for the system operation algorithm that describes the entire sequence of the processes is provided below.

Pseudocode: the algorithm for the system

```
Initiliaze Blue Prism PDF_list
Initialize String textFromPDF = StringEmpty()
Loop PDF from PDF_list
   PowerShell instance = new PowerShell()
   instance.ChangeDirectory(PDF_list.getDirectory())
   instance.ConvertPDF2PNG(PDF.getFilePath())  //Usage of ImageMagick
   instance.Invoke()
   if error then                                //Any possible error
      instance.Close()
      break
   if noFileError then            //File was deleted or interrupted
      instance.TagItem("business exception")
      instance.ChangeStatus("Exception")
      instance.Close()
      break
   Environment.Sleep(10)
   Integer PNG_index = 0
   Loop PNG from PNG_list
      instance.ConvertPNG2TXT(PNG.getFilePath() + index++)
      instance.Invoke()
      if noFileError then
         instance.ConvertPNG2TXT(PNG.getFilePath())    //Tesseract-OCR
         textFromPDF = FileManagement.Read(TXT)
         break
      if error then
         instance.Close()
         break
      instance.Close()
   Loop TXT as TXT_list
      textFromPDF = textFromPDF + FileManagement.Read(TXT)
      FileManagement.Delete(TXT.getDilePath())
 GarbageCollector.DeleteAllFiles(PDF_list.getDirectory())
```

Before converting .pdf files to .png and later to .txt file formats, .pdf are already loaded from the SharePoint repository to the local environment. The developed algorithm, which is given above, specifies how .pdf files are transformed into a text format variable which can be fully interpreted by a software robot.

First, a list is received from the RPA software (Blue Prism) about queuing pending processing files. The files in .pdf format are taken from the list one after the other and processed. Power Shell is used to work with files. Thus, a Power Shell object is created and the working directory (the one in which all .pdf files are downloaded) is changed.

After changing the directory, it is possible to start the converting from .pdf to .png. A combination of Power Shell and ImageMagick is used for this. ImageMagick tool is used to convert .pdf files to .png format. Power Shell is used to activate the ImageMagick tool. ImageMagick creates as many .png files as there were .pdf pages, so later converting from .pdf to .txt requires iteration through all .png files. If an error occurs in this step, the job is completed, the Power Shell object is closed, and it is resumed from the next .pdf file.

The program then iterates through all the .png files and tries to convert them to .txt format. A Tesseract-OCR tool is used for this. It is activated by the use of Power Shell. If the .pdf file had only one page, then the .png file was created without an index at the end. During the first try the error occurs and the software tries to convert the file without an index at the end and the file is converted to .txt format and immediately stored into the final variable. After converting all .png files to .txt format, all .txt files are read one after the other into the final variable and deleted. If an error occurs in this step, the job is completed, the Power Shell object closes, and continues from the next .pdf file. Finally, all remaining files in the directory are deleted and the job is completed. The algorithm is easy to understand with an example. If we have one .pdf file that contains 5 pages, then 5 .png files will be created, which will later be converted to 5 .txt files. A total of 9 different files if the .pdf file holds 5 pages. 5 .txt files are merged into one text variable and eventually all files are deleted.

3 Experiments

250 different types of invoices were used to train the system. Testing was done with 50 new invoices from different suppliers and different structures. In the experiments, five information fields were searched for: "Seller", "Buyer", "Invoice No", "Date" and "Total amount". An example of a prepared date rule file is shown in Fig. 6. This rules file describes the individual rules for each field on different sheets. The rule syntax corresponds to the regular expression most used in search models. The software robot applies each rule one after the other to the analyzed text of the document and looks for a match. If there is more than one match, in case of date search of the document, the match is the date with the lowest start index, that is the one at the top of the document. This is because the date (regardless of the structure of the document) is usually written at the beginning of the document. The reverse case is with the final amount. The final amount search algorithm works in the same way, but if more than one match is found, the final price with the highest start index is used because it is usual (regardless of the document structure) that the final amount is usually written at the end of the document. Other fields are searched on a similar principle.

Business Acceptance Testing (BAT) showed that the developed system meets the customer's requirements and works as customers imagined at the beginning. The requirements specification specified that the program must process at least 80% of the financial documents correctly. About 83% of all financial documents used in the test were processed correctly. When evaluating the results of information detection of individual fields, the best results were detected for "date" and "total amount", 93.21% and 87.81%, respectively (see Fig. 7). The worst performers were "Seller" and "Buyer", with accuracy of just 32.69% and 33.45%, respectively. Such low accuracy results are because the data of the seller and the buyer are arranged in different places, in different formats (text, information integrated in company logos, headers, etc.), there is no keyword identifying who the buyer is and who the seller is, etc.

Rule	Example
\d{2}\.\s\d{2}\.\s\d{4}	13. 01. 2021
\d{2}\.\d{2}\.\d{4}	13.01.2021
\d{4}\.\s\d{2}\.\s\d{2}	2021. 01. 13
\d{4}\.\d{2}\.\d{2}	2021.01.13
\d{2}\-\s\d{2}\-\s\d{4}	13- 01- 2021
\d{2}\-\d{2}\-\d{4}	13-01-2021
\d{4}\-\s\d{2}\-\s\d{2}	2021- 01- 13
\d{4}\-\d{2}\-\d{2}	2021-01-13
\d{2}\s\-\s\d{2}\s\-\s\d{4}	13 - 01 - 2021
\d{4}\s\-\s\d{2}\s\-\s\d{2}	2021 - 01 - 13
\d{2}\/\d{2}\/\d{4}	13/01/2021
\d{4}\/\d{2}\/\d{2}	2021/01/13
\d{2}\s\/\s\d{2}\s\/\s\d{4}	13 / 01 / 2021
\d{4}\s\/\s\d{2}\s\/\s\d{2}	2021 / 01 / 13
\d{2}\/\d{2}\/\d{2}	13/01/21
\d{1}\/\d{2}\/\d{2}	3/01/21
\d{2}\/\d{2}\/\d{1}	21/01/3
\d{2}\-\d{2}\-\d{2}	13-01-21
\d{1}\-\d{2}\-\d{2}	3-01-21
\d{2}\-\d{2}\-\d{1}	21-01-3
\d{2}\.\d{2}\.\d{2}	13.01.21
\d{1}\.\d{2}\.\d{2}	3.01.21
\d{2}\.\d{2}\.\d{1}	21.01.3
\d{2}\s\/\s\d{2}\s\/\s\d{2}	13 / 01 / 21

Fig. 6. The example of file for date parsing rules.

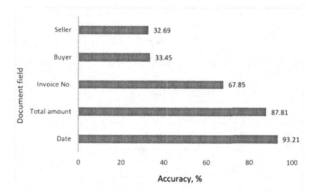

Fig. 7. Accuracy results for identification of document information fields.

The experimental results are provided in Fig. 8 to illustrate the dependence of the average processing time of a financial document on the document quality defined by the DPI value. The results show how the processing time of a document varies depending on the DPI value ranging from 75 to 1200. Experiments were also performed for different document quality $q \in \{1, 25, 50, 100\}$ for DPI values, but this did not affect the results.

To evaluate the processing time of human documents and the performance of the developed robot, an experiment was performed in one company. The results of the experiment are presented in Fig. 9. The efficiency of human document processing decreases with increasing volume of processed documents, while the RPA time is almost constant, which works with an average of 56.28 s and a standard deviation of 1.66 when experimenting with a volume of 10 to 1000 documents. As can be seen from the graph, the number of documents does not affect the RPA processing time. Although a person works a little faster with a small number of documents, processing 500 documents using

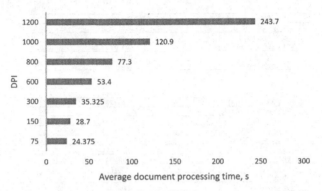

Fig. 8. Dependence of the average processing time of a financial document on the DPI value.

RPA is 1.76 times more efficient and processing 1000 documents using RPA is twice as efficient.

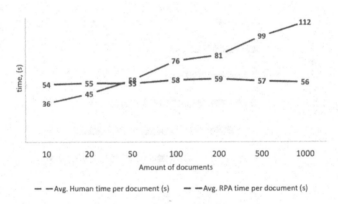

Fig. 9. Evaluating document processing efficiency: human document processing time vs. RPA robot processing time.

4 Discussion

The product under development is relatively small, but there are two risks involved that may affect the project's timing and budget:

1. Emergence of new requirements on the part of customers. Often, when developing RPA projects, there is a possibility of new requirements, which has an actual impact on the project plan over time. In the case of this project, this probability is relatively low. Knowing this risk, the project plan has already been developed with the risks involved, so the actual emergence of requirements will not affect the project plan and deadlines.

2. Excessive customer expectations for the system being developed. Often, when developing RPA products, customers think that the developed system will fully automate the physical work, but the input of customers during the life of the product is also required. During this project, it is important that, at least during the enhanced maintenance period, customers check the program results file and try to find logical errors so that they are corrected and do not recur in the future. The likelihood of this risk is also low as clients will use the results file for daily review and are likely to find any logical errors (if any). The consequence of this risk is a poorly designed system that would be abandoned in the long run, which would undermine the reputation and confidence in the RPA methodology. It is planned that if the process correctly processes at least 80% of all financial documents, the project will be considered a success and expectations will be met.

5 Conclusions

In this study, a solution for automated invoice reading was developed incorporating RPA, optical character recognition (OCR) and deep learning technologies. The aim of this study is to investigate the feasibility of advanced technologies to process invoices in completely different formats, with different types of information. The whole process has been automated and prepared for commercial applications using Blue Prism's RPA software. Different types of invoices were used to train the system, focusing on the detection and identification of five information fields: "Seller", "Buyer", "Invoice No.", "Date" and "Total". However, different structure, the variety of keywords, the abundance of types of information (words, numbers, tables, logo images) make the detection and retrieval of the information very complicated. In the experiments evaluating the results of the detection of information in the individual fields, the best results were "date" and "total", 93.21% and 87.81%, respectively. The worst performers were the "Seller" and the "Buyer", with an accuracy of only 32.69% and 33.45% respectively. Such poor results can be explained by the fact that not all invoices contain the data of the seller or buyer, they are often arranged in different places, in different formats (text, information integrated in company logos, headers, etc.), there is no keyword identifying what is the buyer and who the seller is and so on. Experiments evaluating the processing time of human documents and the performance of the developed RPA based solution have shown that the processing efficiency of human documents decreases with increasing number of processed documents, while the RPA time is almost constant (with average value of 56.28 s and standard deviation from 1.66). Robotized process is 1.76 times more efficient than human at 500 documents and 2 times more efficient at 1,000 documents.

As the experiments have shown, more detailed research and task-specific algorithms are needed to identify as much targeted invoice information as possible, including contextual information analysis, synonyms between words, and of course big and representative database.

Acknowledgments. We thank the company "Helso" UAB for providing a set of representative invoices and for contributing to the entire automation process and valuable insights and support. We also thank dr. Agne Paulauskaite-Taraseviciene for support, useful suggestions and mentoring process.

References

1. Capizzi, G., Lo Sciuto, G., Napoli, C., Shikler, R., Woźniak, M.: Optimizing the organic solar cell manufacturing process by means of AFM measurements and neural networks. Energies **11**(5), 1221 (2018)
2. Połap, D., Woźniak, M., Napoli, C., Tramontana, E.: Real-time cloud-based game management system via cuckoo search algorithm. Int. J. Electron. Telecommun. **61**, 333–338 (2015)
3. Kokina, J., Blanchette, S.: Early evidence of digital labor in accounting: innovation with robotic process automation. Int. J. Account. Inf. Syst. **35**, 100431 (2019)
4. Vedder, R., Welters, M., Mints, A., Ramkhelawan, A.: Robotic process automation in the finance function of the future (2016)
5. IBSintelligence. https://ibsintelligence.com/whitepaper/ai-rpa-in-banking-operations. Accessed 01 Apr 2022
6. Lamberton, C., Brigo, D., Hoy, D.: Impact of robotics, RPA and AI on the insurance industry: challenges and opportunities. J. Financ. Perspect. **4**(1) (2017)
7. Huang, F., Vasarhelyi, M.A.: Applying robotic process automation (RPA) in auditing: a framework. Int. J. Account. Inf. Syst. **35**, 100433 (2019)
8. RPA's Impact on the Travel Industry. https://www.uipath.com/blog/industry-solutions/rpas-impact-on-the-travel-industry. Accessed 01 Apr 2022
9. Karabegović, I., Karabegović, E., Mahmić, M., Husak, E.: The application of service robots for logistics in manufacturing processes. Adv. Prod. Eng. Manag. **10**(4) (2015)
10. Sahu, S., Salwekar, S., Pandit, A., Patil, M.: Invoice processing using robotic process automation. Int. J. Sci. Res. Comput. Sci. Eng. Inf. Technol. 216–223 (2020)
11. Polak, P., Nelischer, C., Guo, H., Robertson, D.C.: "Intelligent" finance and treasury management: what we can expect. AI & Soc. **35**(3), 715–726 (2019). https://doi.org/10.1007/s00146-019-00919-6
12. Ling, X., Gao, M., Wang, D.: Intelligent document processing based on RPA and machine learning. In: 2020 Chinese Automation Congress (CAC), pp. 1349–1353. IEEE (2020)
13. Herm, L.-V., Janiesch, C., Reijers, H.A., Seubert, F.: From symbolic RPA to intelligent RPA: challenges for developing and operating intelligent software robots. In: Polyvyanyy, A., Wynn, M.T., Van Looy, A., Reichert, M. (eds.) BPM 2021. LNCS, vol. 12875, pp. 289–305. Springer, Cham (2021). https://doi.org/10.1007/978-3-030-85469-0_19
14. Memon, J., Sami, M., Khan, R.A., Uddin, M.: Handwritten optical character recognition (OCR): a comprehensive systematic literature review (SLR). IEEE Access **8**, 142642–142668 (2020)
15. Nagy, G., Nartker, T.A., Rice, S.V.: Optical character recognition: an illustrated guide to the frontier. In: Document Recognition and Retrieval VII, vol. 3967, pp. 58–69. SPIE (1999)
16. Impedovo, S. (ed.): Fundamentals in Handwriting Recognition, vol. 124. Springer, Heidelberg (2012)
17. Plötz, T., Fink, G.A.: Markov models for offline handwriting recognition: a survey. Int. J. Doc. Anal. Recogn. (IJDAR) **12**(4), 269–298 (2009)
18. Tesseract documentation, Tesseract OCR, Github. https://tesseract-ocr.github.io/. Accessed 01 Apr 2022
19. Robby, G.A., Tandra, A., Susanto, I., Harefa, J., Chowanda, A.: Implementation of optical character recognition using tesseract with the Javanese script target in Android application. Procedia Comput. Sci. **157**, 499–505 (2019)
20. Conexiom, Ecmarket Inc., A platform for trade document automation. https://conexiom.com/. Accessed 01 Apr 2022

21. Klippa, Klippa App B.V. - KVK. Automated document processing solutions. https://www.klippa.com/. Accessed 01 Apr 2022
22. Logikia, Your solution for a smart, paperless office. www.logikia.ca/. Accessed 01 Apr 2022
23. Fast Four. https://www.fastfour.com/en/. Accessed 01 Apr 2022
24. Nanonets, NanoNet Technologies Inc. https://nanonets.com/. Accessed 01 Apr 2022
25. Shelhamer, E., Long, J., Darrell, T.: Fully convolutional networks for semantic segmentation. IEEE Trans. Pattern Anal. Mach. Intell. **39**(4), 640–651 (2016)
26. Girshick, R., Donahue, J., Darrell, T., Malik, J.: Rich feature hierarchies for accurate object detection and semantic segmentation. In: Proceedings of the IEEE Conference on Computer Vision and Pattern Recognition, pp. 580–587 (2014)
27. Gong, L., et al.: A novel unified deep neural networks methodology for use by date recognition in retail food package image. SIViP **15**(3), 449–457 (2021)
28. Fu, X., Ch'ng, E., Aickelin, U., See, S.: CRNN: a joint neural network for redundancy detection. In: 2017 IEEE International Conference on Smart Computing (SMARTCOMP), pp. 1–8. IEEE (2017)
29. Brownlee, J.: A gentle introduction to long short-term memory networks by the experts. Mach. Learn. Mastery **19** (2017)
30. Optical Character Recognition Pipeline: Text Recognition. https://theailearner.com/tag/attention-ocr/. Accessed 01 Apr 2022
31. Tensorflow. An end-to-end open source machine learning platform. https://www.tensorflow.org/. Accessed 01 Apr 2022
32. Blue Prism: Robotic Process Automation RPA, Blue Prism Limited. https://www.blueprism.com/. Accessed 01 Apr 2022
33. UiPath: Robotic Process Automation RPA, UiPath. https://www.uipath.com/. Accessed 01 Apr 2022
34. Automation Anywhere: Enterprise RPA Platform, Automation Anywhere, Inc. https://www.automationanywhere.com/. Accessed 01 Apr 2022

Topic Modeling for Tracking COVID-19 Communication on Twitter

Petar Kristijan Bogović[1,2]([📧]) [iD], Ana Meštrović[1,2] [iD],
and Sanda Martinčić-Ipšić[1,2] [iD]

[1] Faculty of Informatics and Digital Technologies, University of Rijeka,
Radmile Matejčić 2, 51000 Rijeka, Croatia
{petar.kristijanb,amestrovic,smarti}@uniri.hr
[2] Center for Artificial Intelligence and Cybersecurity, University of Rijeka,
Radmile Matejčić 2, 51000 Rijeka, Croatia

Abstract. In this study, we analyze the trends of COVID-19 related communication in Croatian language on Twitter. First, we prepare a dataset of 147,028 tweets about COVID-19 posted during the first three waves of the pandemic, and then perform an analysis in three steps. In the first step, we train the LDA model and calculate the coherence values of the topics. We identify seven topics and report the ten most frequent words for each topic. In the second step, we analyze the proportion of tweets in each topic and report how these trends change over time. In the third step, we study spreading properties for each topic. The results show that all seven topics are evenly distributed across the three pandemic waves. The topic "vaccination" stands out with the change in percentage from 14.6% tweets in the first wave to 25.7% in the third wave. The obtained results contribute to a better understanding of pandemic communication in social media in Croatia.

Keywords: Topic modeling · Latent Dirichlet Allocation · Coherence score · Croatian tweets · COVID-19 infodemic

1 Introduction

Social networks are a valuable source of information and can serve as an important communication platform during global crises such as the COVID-19 pandemic [9,12]. In the last two decades, social networks have increased the spread of information. As a result, we are now witnessing rapid propagation of information about pandemics on social media platforms, which is defined as a new phenomenon of digital society - infodemics [8,11,21,28]. The World Health Organization (WHO) defines infodemic as an overabundance of information, whether accurate or not, that makes it difficult to find trustworthy sources and reliable facts [21]. In this context, social networks may even influence the spread of the disease [26]. Therefore, analysis of content posted on social networks plays an important role in infodemic management.

© The Author(s), under exclusive license to Springer Nature Switzerland AG 2022
A. Lopata et al. (Eds.): ICIST 2022, CCIS 1665, pp. 248–258, 2022.
https://doi.org/10.1007/978-3-031-16302-9_19

This study is based on natural language processing (NLP) techniques and methods that can be used to analyse the large amount of textual content posted on social networks. With this in mind, topic modelling of text messages is one of the first steps towards a better understanding of crisis communication.

The goal of topic modelling is to identify latent semantic structure or topics from texts [5,13,20]. In general, topics can help better organise documents in the collection and enable semantically-driven clustering and classification of documents [5,18]. In the light of the pandemic management, topic modelling provides insight into the major topics of public discussion about the pandemic.

As an extremely popular and used online social network, Twitter was analysed in numerous studies during the COVID-19 pandemic. Numerous research papers reported the results of fake news detection [7,23] and sentiment analysis [1,16], topic modelling [2,27], while some of the research was devoted to the analysis of information spreading and infodemics in general [8,22].

This paper focuses on topic modelling of COVID-19 related tweets in the Croatian language published during the first three waves of the pandemic. The goal is to identify the most important COVID-19 related topics in tweets and to show how these topics change over time in terms of number and retweets.

To this end, we perform a three-step analysis. In the first step, we identify the main topics using Latent Dirichlet Allocation (LDA), i.e. the leading topics related to COVID-19 that are covered in public communication on Twitter in Croatia. We describe each topic with the top ten keywords. In the second step, we analyze the distribution of tweets on the topics and show how the trends change over time. In the third step, we quantify the spread of topics in terms of retweets.

This work is an extension of our previous study, in which we conducted topic modelling of Croatian news articles and corresponding comments related to the coronavirus outbreak [6]. In this study, we apply the same methodology, but to a different dataset sourced from social media, and extend the previous approach to include analysis of topic trends and spreading of information in the form of retweeting.

This paper is organised as follows: Sect. 2 describes the methods; Sect. 3 presents the obtained results, while Sect. 4 provides concluding remarks and directions for future research.

2 Methods

2.1 Topic Modelling

Topic modelling involves the automatic detection of latent semantic structures or topics from the co-occurrence of words in texts [5,13,20]. The topic is a probability distribution over words, while a document is a mixture of topics.

There are several branches of methods developed for topic modelling. Latent Semantic Analysis (LSA) is the basic principle of topic modelling proposed in [10]. LSA is an approach to automatic indexing and information retrieval that maps documents and terms to a representation in latent semantic space. A prominent group of methods followed LSA, Latent Semantic Indexing (LSI) and Probabilistic Latent Semantic Indexing (PLSI) [14]. PLSI is a model for automatic document indexing based on a statistical latent class model for factor analysis of count data that overcomes the limitations of the original LSI method by defining a proper generative model of the text data. The definition of a proper generative model motivated the next generation of topic modelling methods using Latent Dirichlet Allocation, which was proposed in [5] as the dominant method for topic modelling. In our research, the LDA method is used for topic modelling of tweets. Therefore, the LDA method will be explained in more detail in the continuation.

Latent Dirichlet Allocation. Latent Dirichlet Allocation (LDA) is a generative probabilistic model [20]. LDA represents documents as random mixtures over latent topics, where a topic is characterised by a distribution of words in a document. Latent Dirichlet Allocation, proposed in [5], is one of the standard methods used for topic modelling. Given a corpus D consisting of M documents and a document d containing N_d words ($d \in 1, ..., M$).

LDA assumes that a document d is generated by first sampling a topic z from the document-topic distribution ϕ, and the word w is derived according to the corresponding topic-word distribution θ. The authors in [5] suggested using the Dirichlet prior for the ϕ distribution with the corresponding parameter α and the parameter β for the θ distribution. Collapsed Gibbs Sampling is used to estimate the ϕ and θ distributions by iteratively estimating the probability of assigning each word w_i to the topic z_i [13]. The probability assignment depends on the current topic assignment of all other words in the topic-word count matrices C^{WT} and the document-topic matrix C^{DT}:

$$P(z_i = j | z_{-i}, w_i, d_i, .) \propto \frac{C_{w_i,j}^{WT} + \beta}{\sum_{w=1}^{W} C_{w,j}^{WT} + W\beta} \frac{C_{d_i,j}^{DT} + \alpha}{\sum_{t=1}^{T} C_{d_i,t}^{DT} + T\alpha} \quad (1)$$

The distribution (θ^j) for sampling a word i from topic j, and distribution (ϕ^d) for sampling topic j for document d are:

$$\theta^j = \frac{C_{ij}^{WT} + \beta}{\sum_{w=1}^{W} C_{wj}^{WT} + W\beta}, \quad (2)$$

$$\phi^d = \frac{C_{dj}^{DT} + \alpha}{\sum_{t=1}^{T} C_{dt}^{DT} + T\alpha}. \quad (3)$$

Topic Coherence. Topic coherence reflects the semantic interpretability of the extracted terms describing a topic and can be used to evaluate the topic modelling task [20]. Coherence assesses the quality of a given topic in terms of human perception of semantic understandability [19]. The selection of the number of topics is of great importance because LDA is an unsupervised method and the automatic assessment of coherence contributes to the extraction of semantically interpretable and coherent topics from the data. The highest coherence value is the indicator of the best selection of the number of topics in the data collection.

2.2   Experiment Setup

Dataset. The prepared dataset contains Twitter data, i.e. tweets collected between January 1, 2020 and May 31, 2021 during the first three epidemic waves in the Republic of Croatia. The definition of pandemic waves is explained in more detail in [3]. Data were collected using the Twitter API and filtered using a set of COVID-19 related keywords [2]. In the original version of the dataset, there were 206,196 tweets. Before proceeding with topic modelling, as is common in natural language processing, we cleaned the data by removing duplicates, stop words, emojis, and tweets that were not in Croatian. In this way, we were able to reduce the original dataset to 147,028 tweets.

Implementation. The central tool used is Gensim, a free, open-source Python library that uses unsupervised machine learning methods to automatically extract semantic topics from a document corpus by representing and processing documents as semantic vectors [25]. Word2Vec, FastText, Latent Semantic Indexing, and Latent Dirichlet Allocation are some of the methods included in Gensim. We use Gensim in three steps: first, we automatically discover collocations in a stream of sentences; second, we build a dictionary by mapping words; and third, we convert the documents into a Bag-of-Words (BoW) representation. The BoW representation is a document representation model that uses an unordered set of word or term frequencies [17]

To reduce the large number of morphological word forms in Croatian, we use the lemmatization stage of the CLASSLA pipeline [15]. Lemmatization generates lemmas (basic word forms) for each specified token. CLASSLA is a fork of the Stanford NLP Group's official Python library Stanza, which can be used to run various precise natural language processing tools [24]. CLASSLA includes numerous modifications to the Stanza library with the goal of improving the tool's performance when processing Slavic languages such as Slovenian, Croatian, Serbian, Macedonian, and Bulgarian. CLASSLA performs well on Slavic languages and provides stable lemmatization as a preprocessing step for downstream NLP tasks such as topic modelling.

Analysis of Topics. After preparing the dataset, we perform a three-step analysis. First, we identify the main topics using the LDA method and describe each topic by extracting the ten most frequent words in the dataset of tweets that belong to each topic. In the second step, we analyze the distribution of tweets among the topics. We also report the distribution of tweets across the three waves of the pandemic and the dynamics of change. In the third step, we quantify the topic spreading in terms of retweeting. For each topic, we calculate the total number of retweets and the average number of retweets. Finally, we quantify the distribution of retweets across topics and analyze how trends change over time.

3   Results

Here we report the results of topic modelling and further analysis of the distribution of tweets and retweets across different topics.

First, we train the LDA method and obtain the topics. According to the coherence score value (visualised in Fig. 1), the best coherence is obtained when we select the top seven topics. Thus, with the highest coherence score, we have identified seven main topics from the dataset of COVID-19 related tweets.

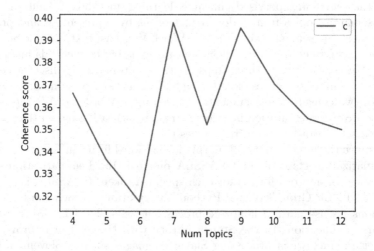

Fig. 1. Coherence scores for different number of topics obtained with LDA models trained on content of Croatian tweets.

Next, the topics are listed with their description in the form of the ten most frequent words in Table 1.

Table 1. Table showing 7 topics and top-10 keywords.

Topic name	Topic keywords
1 Epidemic prevention	maska/mask, čovjek/person, vidjeti/to see, znati/to know, doći/to come, raditi/work, htjeti/to want, nositi/to wear, doktor/doctor, nemati/to not have
2 Life during pandemic	čovjek/person, nemati/to not have, znati/to know, virus, korona/corona, zaraziti/to infect, broj/number, cijepiti/to vaccinate, doći/to come, red/queue
3 Political	pandemija/pandemic, stožer/headquarters, covid/covid, Plenković/prime minister, HDZ, izbor/choice, život/life, dijete/child, pitanje/question, medij/media
4 Vaccination	cjepivo/vaccine, cjepiti/to vaccinate, cijepljenje/vaccination, doza/dose, bolnica/hospital, covid, hrvatski/Croatian, velik/large, medicinski/medicinal, dobiti/to receive
5 Official antipandemic measures	mjera/measure, stožer/headquarters, epidemiološki/epidemiological, zaštita/protection, odluka/decision, hrvatski/Croatian, rad/work, zatvaranje /lockdown, civil/civilian, vlada/government
6 Number of new COVID-19 cases	osoba/person, nov/new, koronavirus/coronavirus, hrvatski/Croatian, sat/hour, broj/number, slučaj/case, ukupno/total, zaraza/contagion, testirati/to test
7 Epidemic prevention	županija/county, covid, samoizolacija,/self-isolation, preminuti/to die, test, hrvatski/Croatian, pozitivan/positive, zagrebača županija/Zagreb county, koronavirus/coronavirus

In the second step, we analysed the distribution of tweets among topics and the dynamics of changes during the observed period. We show the proportion of the number of tweets in each topic in Fig. 2. Looking at the entire period, most topics account for 10% to 20% of the entire dataset, respectively. The topic "Antipandemic measures", which focuses on measures taken by the Headquarters of Civil Protection, contains slightly less than 10% of the total tweets, while the topic "Coronavirus infection", which focuses on general information about specific individuals infected with COVID-19, contains less than 7% of the total dataset. During the three epidemic waves, the distribution of tweets among topics deteriorates slightly between 2.2% and 3.7%, with the exception of the topic "Vaccination", which records a gradual increase from 14.6% in the first epidemic wave to 25.7% in the third epidemic wave.

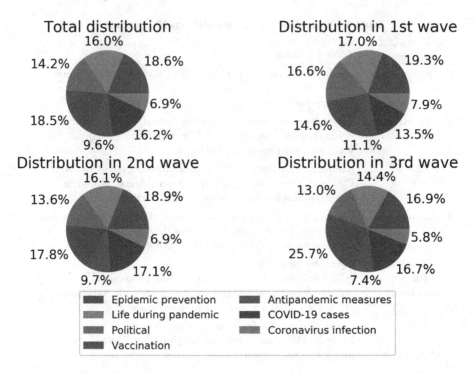

Fig. 2. Distribution of tweets in 7 topics during COVID-19 pandemic.

Figure 3 shows the evolution of the frequency of tweets, distributed over 7 topics, over time, measured on a monthly basis. The spikes observed in the graph follow the spikes in the COVID-19 bursts [3]. Most topics show an even distribution of tweets over the entire observed period, with the exception of the topic of vaccination, where the distribution of tweets increases in the fall of 2020 and in the following months.

In the third step, we study the spreading properties of topics in terms of retweets. The results are shown in Fig. 4. We can highlight the topic "Vaccination" with the highest percentage of retweets and the topic "Life during pandemic" with the lowest percentage of retweets (see Fig. 4 (A) and (B)). When we analyse the number of retweets and the ratio of retweets across months (Fig. 4 (C) and (D)), we can see that the highest number of retweets is at the beginning of the pandemic. It seems that all topics have a similar retweet distribution across months, i.e., they have peaks in the same period. The topic "Vaccination" again shows slightly different properties. Tweets on the topic of vaccination were retweeted particularly frequently in the fall of 2020, and this trend continued in 2021.

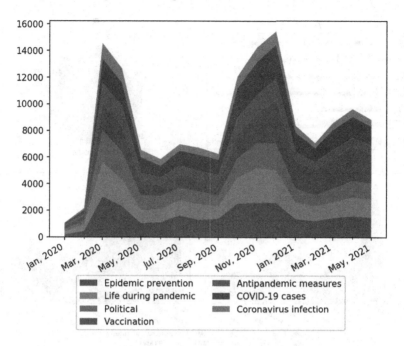

Fig. 3. Stacked area chart over tweets in whole dataset.

4   Conclusion

In this paper, we describe topic modelling of COVID-19 related tweets in the Croatian language posted during the first three waves of the pandemic. The topics are automatically derived by training the LDA model and calculating the coherence values of the reported topics.

Our results show that all seven topics are evenly distributed across the three pandemic waves and across months. Only the topic "Vaccination" stands out with the change in percentage from 14.6% tweets in the first wave to 25.7% in the third wave. The number and ratio of retweets is also similarly distributed for all topics except "Vaccination". The topic "Vaccination" has the highest number of retweets and the peak of retweets was reached in the fall of 2020. This is the beginning of a higher sharing of tweets on the topic of vaccination.

The results presented here are a first step towards a better understanding of crisis communication and information monitoring in social networks. Specifically, the themes identified can serve as a basis for longitudinal monitoring of trends, including the spreading of information in the form of retweets. The limitation of this work stems from the selection of tweets in Croatian language. Nevertheless, the proposed methodology, especially CLASSLA, can process a wide range of morphologically rich Slavic languages. In general, the transfer to other languages strongly depends on the availability of NLP resources and tools for the selected language.

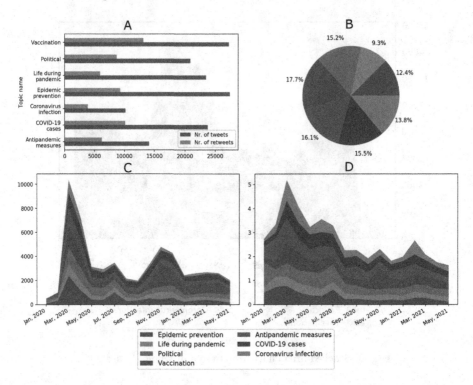

Fig. 4. Overview of retweets. (A: Comparison of number of retweets to number of tweets. B: Pie chart representing distribution of retweet ratios. C: Sum of retweets per month per topic. D: Retweets ratio per month per topic.

In the future, we plan to consider other social networks, such as Reddit and Gab. We also plan to apply a broader range of NLP methods, such as Selectivity Based Keyword Extraction Method for keyword extraction [4], Sentiment Analysis [2] and Named Entity Recognition. In this way, we would have a comprehensive overview of the content of tweets related to the COVID-19 pandemic.

Acknowledgement. This work has been supported in part by the Croatian Science Foundation under the project IP-CORONA-04-2061, "Multilayer Framework for the Information Spreading Characterization in Social Media during the COVID-19 Crisis" (InfoCoV) and by University of Rijeka projects number uniri-drustv-18-20 and uniri-drustv-18-38. PKB is fully supported by Croatian Science Foundation under the project DOK-2021-02.

References

1. Babić, K., Petrović, M., Beliga, S., Martinčić-Ipšić, S., Jarynowski, A., Meštrović, A.: COVID-19-related communication on twitter: analysis of the croatian and polish attitudes. In: Yang, X.-S., Sherratt, S., Dey, N., Joshi, A. (eds.) Proceedings of Sixth International Congress on Information and Communication Technology. LNNS, vol. 216, pp. 379–390. Springer, Singapore (2022). https://doi.org/10.1007/978-981-16-1781-2_35

2. Babić, K., Petrović, M., Beliga, S., Martinčić-Ipšić, S., Matešić, M., Meštrović, A.: Characterisation of COVID-19-related tweets in the Croatian language: framework based on the Cro-CoV-cseBERT model. Appl. Sci. **11**(21), 10442 (2021). https://doi.org/10.3390/app112110442

3. Beliga, S., Martinčić-Ipšić, S., Matešić, M., Petrijevčanin Vuksanović, I., Meštrović, A.: Infoveillance of the croatian online media during the covid-19 pandemic: one-year longitudinal study using natural language processing. JMIR Public Health Surveill. **7**(12), e31540 (2021). https://doi.org/10.2196/31540, https://publichealth.jmir.org/2021/12/e31540

4. Beliga, S., Meštrović, A., Martinčić-Ipšić, S.: Selectivity-based keyword extraction method. Int. J. Semant. Web Inf. Syst. **12**(3), 1–26 (2016). https://doi.org/10.4018/ijswis.2016070101

5. Blei, D.M., Ng, A.Y., Jordan, M.I.: Latent dirichlet allocation. J. Mach. Learn. Res. **3**(Jan), 993–1022 (2003)

6. Bogović, P.K., Meštrović, A., Beliga, S., Martinčić-Ipšić, S.: Topic modelling of Croatian news during COVID-19 pandemic. In: 2021 44th International Convention on Information, Communication and Electronic Technology (MIPRO). IEEE (2021). https://doi.org/10.23919/mipro52101.2021.9597125

7. Bunker, D.: Who do you trust? the digital destruction of shared situational awareness and the COVID-19 infodemic. Int. J. Inf. Manag. **55**, 102201 (2020). https://doi.org/10.1016/j.ijinfomgt.2020.102201

8. Cinelli, M., et al.: The COVID-19 social media infodemic. Sci. Rep. **10**(1), 1–10 (2020). https://doi.org/10.1038/s41598-020-73510-5

9. Cuello-Garcia, C., Pérez-Gaxiola, G., van Amelsvoort, L.: Social media can have an impact on how we manage and investigate the COVID-19 pandemic. J. Clin. Epidemiol. **127**, 198–201 (2020). https://doi.org/10.1016/j.jclinepi.2020.06.028

10. Deerwester, S., Dumais, S.T., Furnas, G.W., Landauer, T.K., Harshman, R.: Indexing by latent semantic analysis. J. Am. Soc. Inf. Sci. **41**(6), 391–407 (1990). https://doi.org/10.1002/(sici)1097-4571(199009)41:6⟨391::aid-asi1⟩3.0.co;2-9

11. Gallotti, R., Valle, F., Castaldo, N., Sacco, P., Domenico, M.D.: Assessing the risks of 'infodemics' in response to COVID-19 epidemics. Nat. Hum. Behav. **4**(12), 1285–1293 (2020). https://doi.org/10.1038/s41562-020-00994-6

12. Glik, D.C.: Risk communication for public health emergencies. Ann. Rev. Public Health **28**(1), 33–54 (2007). https://doi.org/10.1146/annurev.publhealth.28.021406.144123

13. Griffiths, T.L., Steyvers, M.: Finding scientific topics. Proc. Nat. Acad. Sci. **101**(suppl-1), 5228–5235 (2004). https://doi.org/10.1073/pnas.0307752101

14. Hofmann, T.: Probabilistic latent semantic indexing. In: Proceedings of the 22nd Annual International ACM SIGIR Conference on Research and Development in Information Retrieval - SIGIR 1999. ACM Press (1999). https://doi.org/10.1145/312624.312649

15. Ljubešić, N., Dobrovoljc, K.: What does neural bring? analysing improvements in morphosyntactic annotation and lemmatisation of Slovenian, Croatian and Serbian. In: Proceedings of the 7th Workshop on Balto-Slavic Natural Language Processing, pp. 29–34. Association for Computational Linguistics, Florence, Italy (2019). https://doi.org/10.18653/v1/W19-3704, https://www.aclweb.org/anthology/W19-3704

16. Lwin, M.O., et al.: Global sentiments surrounding the COVID-19 pandemic on twitter: analysis of twitter trends. JMIR Public Health Surveill. 6(2), e19447 (2020). https://doi.org/10.2196/19447

17. Manning, C.D., Raghavan, P., Schütze, H.: Introduction to Information Retrieval. Cambridge University Press (2008). https://doi.org/10.1017/CBO9780511809071

18. Martinčić-Ipšić, S., Miličić, T., Todorovski, L.: The influence of feature representation of text on the performance of document classification. Appl. Sci. 9(4), 743 (2019). https://doi.org/10.3390/app9040743

19. Newman, D., Lau, J.H., Grieser, K., Baldwin, T.: Automatic evaluation of topic coherence. In: Human Language Technologies: The 2010 Annual Conference of the North American Chapter of the Association for Computational Linguistics, pp. 100–108. HLT 2010, Association for Computational Linguistics, USA (2010)

20. O'Callaghan, D., Greene, D., Carthy, J., Cunningham, P.: An analysis of the coherence of descriptors in topic modeling. Expert Syst. Appl. 42(13), 5645–5657 (2015). https://doi.org/10.1016/j.eswa.2015.02.055

21. Organization, P.A.H.: Understanding the infodemic and misinformation in the fight against COVID-19 (2020)

22. Park, H.W., Park, S., Chong, M.: Conversations and medical news frames on twitter: infodemiological study on COVID-19 in south Korea. J. Med. Internet Res. 22(5), e18897 (2020). https://doi.org/10.2196/18897

23. Pulido, C.M., Villarejo-Carballido, B., Redondo-Sama, G., Gómez, A.: COVID-19 infodemic: more retweets for science-based information on coronavirus than for false information. Int. Sociol. 35(4), 377–392 (2020). https://doi.org/10.1177/0268580920914755

24. Qi, P., Zhang, Y., Zhang, Y., Bolton, J., Manning, C.D.: Stanza: a python natural language processing toolkit for many human languages. In: Proceedings of the 58th Annual Meeting of the Association for Computational Linguistics: System Demonstrations (2020)

25. Rehurek, R., Sojka, P.: Software framework for topic modelling with large corpora. In: Proceedings of the LREC 2010 Workshop on New Challenges for NLP Frameworks, pp. 45–50. CiteSeerX (2010)

26. Xia, C., et al.: A new coupled disease-awareness spreading model with mass media on multiplex networks. Inf. Sci. 471, 185–200 (2019). https://doi.org/10.1016/j.ins.2018.08.050

27. Xue, J., Chen, J., Chen, C., Zheng, C., Li, S., Zhu, T.: Public discourse and sentiment during the COVID 19 pandemic: using latent dirichlet allocation for topic modeling on twitter. PLoS One 15(9), e0239441 (2020). https://doi.org/10.1371/journal.pone.0239441

28. Zarocostas, J.: How to fight an infodemic. Lancet 395(10225), 676 (2020). https://doi.org/10.1016/s0140-6736(20)30461-x

Efficiency of End-to-End Speech Recognition for Languages with Scarce Resources

Vytautas Rudzionis[1]([envelope]), Ugnius Malukas[2], and Audrius Lopata[2]

[1] Vilnius University Kaunas Faculty, Muitines 8, Kaunas, Lithuania
vytautas.rudzionis@knf.vu.lt
[2] Kaunas University of Technology, Studentu 50, Kaunas, Lithuania

Abstract. Modern deep learning based speech recognition methods allow for achieving phenomenal speech recognition accuracy. But it requires enormous amounts of data to train such systems to achieve high recognition accuracy. Many less widely spoken languages simply do not possess the necessary amounts of speech corpora. The paper presents attempts to evaluate DeepSpeech-based speech recognition efficiency with the limited amounts of training data available and the ways to improve the accuracy. The experiments showed that the accuracy of Deep-Speech2 recognizer with about 100 h of speech corpora used for training is quite modest but the application of simple grammatical constraints allowed to reduce the word error rate to 23–25%.

Keywords: Speech recognition · Hybrid methods · Machine learning · End-to-end speech recognition

1 Introduction

Automatic speech recognition has been a hot topic of research for a long time. But only in recent years have such systems matured to the level that is good enough for the vast majority of practical applications. This is well illustrated by the fact that according to Deepgram survey from 2021 about 99% of the respondents in North America indicated they are currently using ASR in some form. Most, about 78%, are using ASR systems to transcribe and analyze voice data from consumer-facing devices – largely voice assistants within mobile apps. This clearly indicates that the technology is mature enough.

The advent and development of various methods using so-called deep learning was the key element of the progress with speech recognition in the recent decade. The research included the neural network composed of restricted Boltzmann machine stacking and conducted layer-by-layer training for the network. Improve the over-fitting problem of neural networks by using dropout. DNN-HMM became the main acoustic model, showing strong recognition capability in the recognition of large vocabulary. With the further development of technology, more neural networks began to invest in the field of speech recognition, such as CNN and RNN. Particular success has been caused by the LSTM model.

A. Lopata et al. (Eds.): ICIST 2022, CCIS 1665, pp. 259–264, 2022.
https://doi.org/10.1007/978-3-031-16302-9_20

Further progress has been achieved using so-called end-to-end models. The model is simpler because it does not require calculating acoustic features but makes attempt to map directly audio signals to text. There were several generations of this type of model usually called DeepSpeech and version number. It has been shown that such systems are able to achieve extremely high recognition accuracy when huge amounts of training data are presented [1]. Unfortunately, there are not so many speech corpora available for many less widely spoken languages. The aim of this study was to investigate the accuracy of end-to-end speech recognition systems when applying limited training sets available as well as the ways to achieve higher recognition accuracy.

2 Deep Neural Networks for Speech Recognition

Artificial neural networks have been around for over half a century and their applications to speech processing have been almost as long. Prager with colleagues [2] suggested the use of Boltzmann machines for speech recognition. This is one of the earliest attempts to use this type of models for speech recognition. The idea was interesting but the Boltzmann machine was inadequate due to its high need of computation time also in the recognition stage and limited computational resources available at that time. In the period immediately after the proposal of backpropagation training algorithm a series of proposals how neural networks could be used for speech recognition were made. Multilayer perceptrons were suggested by by Bourlard and Wellekens ASR [3] and by Watrous and Shastri for feature analysis [4] in 1987. In 1989, Waibel et al. published a report describing the TDNN and its use for isolated phoneme recognition [5]. Later the use of radial basis functions (RBF) has been proposed too. Their role was similar to GMM models and essentially they made an alternative to mixtures of Gaussian distributions used in HMM. Looking back it is not difficult to see that despite high expectations neural networks failed to achieve the results anticipated. For more than ten years, neural networks have been used in ASR with scores comparable with those reached by traditional recognizers as CD-HMM. But CD-HMM used simpler architecture, required less parameters and consequently lower computational resources and less (then this meant feasible) time to train the recognition system. It was not until around 2010 with the resurgence of neural networks (with the "deep" form) and with the start of deep learning that all the difficulties encountered in 1990s and 2000s have been overcome, especially for large vocabulary ASR applications.

Situation changed significantly with the development of probabilistic speech models characterized by the distribution parameters in the graphical modeling framework and a different type of deep generative models characterized by neural network parameters. They were called Deep Belief Networks [6]. In the deep learning era, neural networks has shown significant improvement in the speech recognition task. Various methods have been applied such as convolutional neural networks (CNNs), recurrent neural networks (RNNs), while recently Transformer networks have achieved great performance too [7].

Recurrent neural network (RNN), captures useful temporal patterns in sequential data such as speech to augment recognition performance [8]. An RNN architecture includes hidden layers that retain the memory of past elements of an input sequence. RNN has succeeded in improving speech recognition performance because of its ability to learn sequential patterns as seen in speech, language, or time-series data. Convolutional neural networks (CNN) learn hierarchical patterns at multiple layers using a series of 2D convolutional operations.

All these advances led to a significant increase in large vocabulary and continuous speech recognition accuracy [9]. Most modern systems have an accuracy of 75% to 85% off-the-shelf, but training can improve that level further. Some of the teams from several leading companies (Google, IBM, Baidu, Microsoft) announced the recognition accuracy of 95–97% using clean speech in laboratory environments. But all these results were achieved for widely spoken languages and using extremely large speech corpora to train the system (often reaching over 3000 h of speech). Corpora of such size aren't available for the vast majority of not-so-widely spoken languages. Our task was to evaluate end-to-end speech recognition system's accuracy using corpora whose size is available for many not-so-widely spoken languages. Section 3 presents the results of this investigation.

3 Efficiency of Lithuanian End-to-End Recognition

So-called end-to-end speech recognition appeared in recent years as one of the most efficient methods to recognize speech. End-to-end is a system that directly maps a sequence of input acoustic features into a sequence of grapheme or words. A system that was trained to optimize criteria that are related to the final evaluation metric that we are interested in (typically, word error rate). Conventional ASR systems involve separately trained acoustic, pronunciation and language model components which are trained separately. Curating pronunciation lexicon, and defining phoneme sets for a particular language requires expert knowledge, and is time-consuming. It can be seen that end-to-end speech recognition greatly simplifies the complexity of traditional speech recognition. There is no need to manually label information, the neural network can automatically learn language or pronunciation information. What is even more important end-to-end systems achieved remarkable results and have been shown to be very efficient.

It is possible to see that high-accuracy end-to-end systems were trained using enormous amounts of training data. E.g. original version of DeepSpeech2 recognizer was trained using 11,940 h of labeled speech containing 8 million utterances, and the Mandarin system uses 9,400 h of labeled speech containing 11 million utterances. This requires huge computational resources available to only very few institutions in the world and huge linguistic resources that are available for only several widely spoken languages. Lithuanian like many other not-so-widely spoken languages does not possess linguistic resources of such size.

Efficiency of end-to-end approach when there is only limited amount of training data remains open question: there are no known studies investigating about the end-to-end systems efficiency using no more than 100 h recordings to train the system. Since limited resources are common situation for many not so widely used languages this inspired us to investigate end-to-end efficiency for less popular languages.

As the basis of the study it has been selected slightly simplified end-to-end architecture called DeepSpeech2. It was used 5 hidden layers among them 3 recurrent layers, number of neurons in hidden layers 494 while training has been performed using batch size 32. The number of layers has been limited to 5 since some studies showed that using higher number of layers does not lead to further reduction in error rate or even can cause lower recognition accuracy.

The first group of experiments was carried out on small vocabulary task - 10 Lithuanian digits. The corpora contained utterances of 100 speakers (80 speakers used for training while 20 speakers for testing). Each speaker pronounced every digit name 10 times. For the comparison CD-HMM recognition has been applied on the same task. The experiments were performed using three different SNR levels 0 15, 10 and 5 dB. Table 1 shows the results of the experiment.

Table 1. Recognition accuracy of 10 Lithuanian digits using CD-HMM and ETE neural network recognizers, WER in %

SNR,dB	CD-HMM, monophones	CD-HMM, triphones	ETE, 51 iterations	ETE, 62 iterations
15	0.47	0.35	0.26	0.23
10	1.9	0.9	0.7	0.68
5	9.93	5.55	0.98	0.96

The results of the experiment showed slight superiority of ETE approach for high quality speech and obvious advantage over CD-HMM for relatively noisy speech in the case of limited vocabulary.

The same ETE configuration was applied for the large vocabulary speaker-independent Lithuanian continuous recognition with limited resources for training. 50 h of reading continuous Lithuanian speech with the addition of other Lithuanian spoken language examples were used for training and testing (about 70 h of speech corpora). Cross-validation has been used: 10% of continuous speech corpora were used for testing and not used for training. When applied without language model and error post-processing it was achieved rather poor recognition accuracy: depending on the initial parameters set for training and the dataset used in the experiments the WER varied between 38% and 62% (average accuracy of 12 runs is 45.4%). Such results can't be treated as satisfactory.

A detailed analysis of errors has been performed. The original text had 96198 words while the output of the recognizer produced 94489 words. Comparing the original text with the generated by the recognizer it was found 44318 differences between the lexical units in original and generated texts. It was observed that many errors were caused by improper splitting or joining of recognized words (e.g. visatameditacija instead of visa ta meditacija). The errors of such type were corrected bycomparing the 2–3 words in the original text with 2–3 words in the generated text and looking if the generated text could be made identical to the original by splitting or joining together 2–3 words in the context. After such post-processing 40784 (42.4%) differences between the original text and the generated text remained. It should be noted that not all errors of this type have been corrected after processing because the check was limited to 2–3 neighboring words. Then the obvious errors with hand letters have been corrected in the situations when such errors could be corrected without ambiguities (e.g. only orthographic inscription ma\u{z}i is possible while ma\u{z}\c{i} is an obvious mistake). After that 37521 (39%) differences between the original and generated text were left. At the next step it was checked how many remaining differences are the words that aren't present in standard vocabulary. There were 32245 out of vocabulary words. Such words have been changed to the closest word in the vocabulary using Levenstein distance. After this processing 18322 errors were left plus 5276 words present in the vocabulary (24.53%). Error analysis allowed to make assumptions about the potential of the ETP approach with limited linguistic resources for training if a statistical language model would be applied.

At the final stage, we tried to implement a statistical language model into the ETE recognizer. In the traditional approach, DeepSpeech type recognizers implement language model not on the word but on letter level exploiting statistical dependencies on letters frequencies in predefined language. Such a model wasn't available for Lithuanian. Instead, n-gram language model has been applied for continuous speech recognition. For this purpose, two or three most similar words from the vocabulary have been generated as the alternatives and then Lithuanian n-gram model has been applied. The recognition accuracies obtained are presented in Table 2. In these experiments, only clean speech recordings were used.

Table 2. Recognition accuracy using ETE recognizer with and without grammar, WER in %

	Without grammar	2 alternatives	3 alternatives
Accuracy, WER in %	45.4	24.8	23.3

These results suggests that the use of language model allows to reduce recognition error rate significantly but the recognition accuracy is lower comparing with the accuracy achieved using LSTM networks. At the first view this observation contradicts with the results achieved in other studies using ETE and LSTM type neural networks. It is necessary to emphasize that we used significantly smaller in size linguistic resources to train our models. It could be speculated that with limited training resources LSTM model allows to receive higher recognition accuracy than ETE approaches. The bigger amounts of training resources needs to be used to obtain low WER using end-to-end speech recognizers even when using grammar models.

4 Conclusions

Modern large vocabulary continuous speech systems require huge corpora to train the system for very high accuracy. At the same time, the recognition size of speech corpora will be a problem for many less widely spoken languages. The training of end-to-end LVCSR system for Lithuanian using big size as for Lithuanian speech corpora (about 100 h) resulted in relatively modest performance even with clean speech (word error rate above 40%). These leaves open the question of how to improve the recognition accuracy in such a situation. Implementation of grammar restrictions allowed to reduce the WER to 23–25%.

References

1. Battenberg, E., et al.: Exploring neural transducers for end-to-end speech recognition. In: Proceedings of 2017 IEEE Automatic Speech Recognition and Understanding Workshop (ASRU), pp. 206–213, Okinawa, Japan (2017)
2. Prager, R.W, Harrison, T.D., Fallside, F.: Boltzmann Machines for Speech Recognition, Computer, Speech and Language, vol. 1, pp 3–27, Academic Press. Cambridge (1986)
3. Bourlard, H., Wellekens, C.J.: Multilayer perceptrons and automatic speech recognition. In: Proceedings of IEEE First International Conference on Neural Networks. San Diego, Calif, pp. 407–416 (1987)
4. Watrous, R.L., Shastri, L.: Learning phonetic features using connectionist networks. In: Proceedings of IEEE First International Conference on Neural Networks, San Diego, pp. 381–388 (1987)
5. Waibel, A., et al.: Phoneme recognition using time-delay neural networks. IEEE Trans. Acoust. Speech Signal Process. **37**(3), 328–339 (1989)
6. Hinton, G., Osindero, S., Yee-Wee, T.: A fast learning algorithm for deep belief nets. Neural Comput. **18**(7), 1527–1554 (2006)
7. Chang, F.J., et al.: Context-aware transformer transducer for speech recognition. In: Proceedings of 2021 IEEE Automatic Speech Recognition and Understanding Workshop (ASRU), pp. 503–510 (2021)
8. Graves, A., Mohamed, A.R., Hinton, G.: Speech recognition with deep recurrent neural networks. In: Proceedings of 2013 IEEE International Conference on Acoustics, Speech and Signal Processing, pp. 6645–6649 (2013)
9. Amodei, D., et al.: Deep speech 2 end-to-end speech recognition in English and mandarin. In: Proceedings of the 33rd International Conference on International Conference on Machine Learning, pp. 173–182, New York (2016)

Improvement of Speech Recognition Accuracy Using Post-processing of Recognized Text

Vytautas Rudzionis[1]([⊠]), Ugnius Malukas[2], and Renata Danieliene[1]

[1] Vilnius University Kaunas Faculty, Muitines 8, Kaunas, Lithuania
vytautas.rudzionis@knf.vu.lt
[2] Kaunas University of Technology, Studentu 50, Kaunas, Lithuania

Abstract. Modern deep learning-based speech recognition methods allow for achieving phenomenal speech recognition accuracy. But this requires enormous amounts of data to train. Unfortunately, developers of recognizers for less widely spoken languages are often facing the problem of scarce resources to train recognizers. The paper presents a novel method to increase recognition accuracy by post-processing of the text outputs of two different speech recognizers. The method is using machine learning to find a more likely symbol or group of symbols from two different deep learning-based recognizers. The experiments showed that the method allows increasing recognition accuracy by 3%.

Keywords: Speech recognition · Hybrid methods · Machine learning · Text processing

1 Introduction

Automatic speech recognition has been a hot topic of research for a long time. In the 1980s, after IBM applied HMM to speech recognition, HMM has been playing an important role in speech recognition, and HMM/GMM has become the mainstream acoustic model. In 2006, after Li Deng and Hinton proposed the use of deep learning in speech recognition, the neural network became a research upsurge of speech technology, which turned from the ANN to the DNN. The research included the neural network composed of restricted Boltzmann machine stacking and conducted layer-by-layer training for the network. Improve the over-fitting problem of neural networks by using drop-out. DNN-HMM became the main acoustic model, showing strong recognition capability in the recognition of large vocabulary. With the further development of technology, more neural networks began to invest in the field of speech recognition, such as CNN and RNN.

However, establishing a speech recognition system is a complicated process, which requires a lot of professional knowledge. Various attempts have been made in recent years to reduce the complexity of ASR. Among such attempts is the idea of directly mapping speech to tags. End-to-end speech recognition has been proposed as a method to directly map speech to text.

All these efforts resulted in significant improvement in speech recognition accuracy and consequently the widespread use of spoken language as an interface for human-computer communication in many practical applications. Current best large vocabulary

© The Author(s), under exclusive license to Springer Nature Switzerland AG 2022
A. Lopata et al. (Eds.): ICIST 2022, CCIS 1665, pp. 265–270, 2022.
https://doi.org/10.1007/978-3-031-16302-9_21

continuous speech recognition systems achieve recognition accuracy of 4–6% WER in laboratory conditions (some evaluations of these systems in real-world conditions achieves a lower accuracy level). Such results are close to the human ability to recognize continuous speech correctly. It should be noted that this level of accuracy has been achieved only for several widely spoken languages (e.g. English or Mandarin Chinese) that have huge linguistic resources that could be used for training. Lithuanian language (as many other not so widely spoken languages) does not have so well trained recognizers. Adaptation of the most promising recognition methods for such languages requires not only linguistic resources but often also expert knowledge of how lexical, morphological, and syntactic features of a particular language could be exploited in the best way.

2   Review of Methods

Artificial neural networks have been around for over half a century and their applications to speech processing have been almost as long. Representative early work in using shallow (and small) neural networks for speech includes the studies reported in [1, 2]. However, these neural nets did not show superior performance over the GMM-HMM technology based on generative models of speech trained discriminatingly for many years. Several key reasons caused this vanishing gradients and weak temporal structure modelling to name a few. These difficulties were investigated in addition to the lack of big training data and big computing power. It was not until around 2010 with the resurgence of neural networks (with the "deep" form) and with the start of deep learning that all the difficulties encountered in 1990s and 2000s have been overcome, especially for large vocabulary ASR applications.

Deep Belief Networks or DBNs [3, 4] was the first deep neural networks-based model which showed a significant advantage over common for the period CD-HMM based models. This was possible due to three essential elements introduced into the topology of neural networks. To remove the complexity of rigorously modeling speech dynamics, one can for the time being remove such dynamics but one can compensate for this modeling inaccuracy by using a long time window to approximate the effects of true dynamics which led to the introduction of recurrence into the network. And the dynamics of speech at the symbolic level can then be approximately captured by the standard HMM. The second essential idea was to reverse the direction of information flow in the deep models – from top-down as in the deep generative model to bottom-up as in the DNN, in order to make inference fast and accurate (given the models). However, with many hidden layers, neural networks were very difficult to train. In order to solve this problem, the third idea was implemented: using a DBN to initialize or pre-train the DNN based on the original proposal of [3]. It was found that with bigger amounts of training data available and with careful pre-training the vanishing gradients problem was no longer the problem. These first attempts to use the deep learning approach for speech recognition showed similar accuracy as CD-HMM and GMM models common for the period but they showed the potential of neural networks for solving this task and opened the window of opportunities for other approaches.

However, soon recurrent neural networks (RNNs) [5] architectures including long-short term memory (LSTM) [6] outperformed DBNs and became state-of-the-art models.

The superior performance of RNN architectures was mainly because of their ability to capture temporal contexts from speech. Later, a cascade of convolutional neural networks (CNNs), LSTM with fully connected (DNNs) layers were further shown to outperform LSTM-only models by capturing more discriminative attributes from speech. The similar to LSTM models architecture had gated recurrent units (GRU) networks which showed similar performance as purely LSTM networks.

All previously mentioned models are using feature-based speech representation largely similar to the representation used in pre-NN era speech recognition systems. A completely different approach was implemented in so-called end-to-end (ETE) systems pioneered by [7] and originally called DeepSpeech 1. DeepSpeech 1 doesn't require a phoneme dictionary, but it uses a well-optimized RNN training system. The major building block of Deep Speech is a recurrent neural network that has been trained to ingest speech spectrograms and generate English text transcriptions. The purpose of the RNN is to convert an input sequence into a sequence of character probabilities for the transcription. The RNN has five layers of hidden units, with the first three layers not being recurrent. At each time step, the non-recurrent layers work on independent data. The fourth layer is a bi-directional recurrent layer with two sets of hidden units. One set has forward recurrence while the other has a backward recurrence. After prediction, Connectionist Temporal Classification (CTC) loss is computed to measure the prediction error. Training is done using Nesterov's Accelerated gradient method.

The further development of ETE was DeepSpeech 2 model [8]. The architecture used in this model has up to 11 layers made up of bidirectional recurrent layers and convolutional layers and is using batch normalization for optimization. For the activation function, they use the clipped rectified linear (ReLU) function. At its core, this architecture is similar to Deep Speech 1. The architecture is a recurrent neural network trained to ingest speech spectrograms and output text transcriptions. The model is trained using the CTC loss function.

It should be noted that all successful studies used very large amounts of training data which often aren't available for languages with scarce linguistic resources. The question which model allows to achieve acceptable recognition accuracy and in some sense is more "economical" in similar situations remains open.

3 Hybrid Approach

The main problems when implementing two different classifiers lies in the fact that different classification algorithms has very different topologies and their parameters falls into very different ranges of values. To apply those parameters directly seems to be complicated task. Additional problems arises from the fact bigger practical value has not the outputs of neural network itself but the outputs of language model. Language model inevitably suppress some variations in neural network parameters differences. Having in mind these considerations we selected outputs at the end of each speech recognizer: sequences of letters, syllables and words or other lexical units.

So in the presented group of experiments, the inputs of a hybrid classifier have been used as outputs generated by the two different neural network-based classifiers using LSTM and EndToEnd approaches (abbreviated as LST and ETE here). The text of the original text file, text generated by the LST recognizer, and text generated by the ETE recognizer were used during training. Both texts generated by the LST and ETE recognizers were normalized before training trying to equalize the lengths of words. Equalization was performed using several manually derived rules. Several examples of the rules: if one recognizer generated the word with symbols at the end while another one without in this case empty symbols were added to make both words of equal length or if one recognizer generated two words at the output while another one these words were joined together (e.g. Lithuanian words ne mažiau and nemažiau). For normalization was used Levenstein distance in the neighborhood of 2–3 symbols trying to find lost or inserted symbols and split or joined together words (orthographic realizations).After normalization texts generated by each recognizer were sued to derive the rules or to train classification and regression trees and other types of classifiers. As the reference, the word and all its symbols from the original text were used. Training and testing were done using the symbol-by-symbol principle: taking the symbols from the output of two recognizers and as the target using the letter in the original text. All experiments were performed in a speaker-independent model. Trying to evaluate the possibilities to use a hybrid approach we checked the efficiency of the proposed approach on different speakers. There were selected 7 different speakers that have been hard to recognize speech in previous experiments. Table 1 shows the recognition accuracy for each selected speaker and both for LST and ETE recognizers.

Table 1. Recognition accuracy for different speakers using LTM and ETE, (WER in %)

Speaker	LST	ETE
ADAM	10,84	18,9
ARM6	27,7	29,9
BADY	23,4	28,14
LRVR	20,96	21,65
PRIV	66,37	69,98
SPEK	21,89	18,88
TVR	25,81	33,12

The results showed that the hybrid method allowed to reduce the number of errors in the majority of cases and the majority of speakers. CARTs rule-based methods worked slightly better than naive Bayes or single perceptron. We treat it as important if the accuracy of speech recognizers produced a higher relative improvement was achieved applying the hybrid approach. Applying a hybrid classifier when both recognizers are producing the same symbol at the output the overall number of errors slightly increases: a hybrid classifier needs to be applied only when different outputs are generated by LST and ETE (Table 2).

Error analysis showed that roughly half of the remaining errors were in the situation when LST or ETE made the deletion or insertion error (one of the recognizers made than insertion or deletion error while another did not). We hypothesize that this was

Table 2. Recognition accuracy for different speakers combining outputs of LTM and ETE recognizers using various decision making methods, WER in \%, (NB - Naive Bayes, PC - perceptron, RF - random forest, DT - decision table)

Speaker	NB	PC	RF	J48	DT	JRIP
ADAM	9.85	9.3	8.98	7.99	8.0	8.53
ARM6	24.1	28.1	23.18	23.83	24.11	24.07
BADY	22.9	22.45	22.0	22.12	22.78	22.78
LRVR	20.34	20.75	19.14	19.89	19.45	19.66
PRIV	66.5	75.14	64.32	68.41	69.4	72.14
SPEK	21.12	22.0	19.2	19.74	20.11	20.54
TVR	24.04	26.14	23.67	23.88	23.88	24.07

caused by the fact that always in such a situation the same symbol was used to mark the absence of the symbol at the output of one recognizer (in this case w because a symbol isn't used in the Lithuanian alphabet) and the algorithm has a bias towards deletion over other recognized symbol. If the correct recognition result would be accepted recognized symbol instead of considering the insertion error led to inconclusive observations: for the speaker ADAM the WER would drop down to 6.4% while for speaker LVRV it will grow up to 28.4%.

Trying to improve recognition accuracy further we reduced the number of symbols available. This has been done treating all diphtongs and compounds such as ch, dž as single elements (sounds). The results are shown in Table 3.

Table 3. Recognition accuracy for different speakers combining outputs of LTM and ETE recognizers using various decision making methods, WER in \%, (NB - Naive Bayes, PC - perceptron, RF - random forest, DT - decision table)

Speaker	NB	PC	RF	J48	DT	JRIP
ADAM	9.6	9.25	8.85	7.99	8.12	8.36
ARM6	24.42	27.56	22.89	23.34	24.75	24.78
BADY	22.44	22.56	21.56	22.12	22.34	22.34
LRVR	19.15	20.34	18.77	19.11	18.88	19.15
PRIV	64.36	72.33	63.45	67.35	69.05	71.11
SPEK	20.32	21.56	18.45	19.08	19.66	20.12
TVR	24.15	26.78	23.19	23.88	23.19	23.88

The results proved that proposed model enables to improve overall recognition accuracy. This is especially true in the case of the speakers that are hard to recognize properly.

This model is difficult to implement in real time but could be used for post-processing of long texts to reduce the amount of humans text editing after recognition.

4 Conclusions

The speech recognition accuracy still remains a problem for the languages with limited speech corpora available. Since the collection of speech recordings is long and expensive task researchers there are need to find other ways to increase recognition accuracy.

A novel method to increase recognition accuracy using the text outputs of two different deep learning recognizers was proposed. The method relies on using machine learning to find the more likely symbol or symbol group at the output of the recognizer. The experimental evaluation showed that the method allows an increase in the overall accuracy by 2–3%. The improvement depends on the speaker and training material. Since the method is relatively easily implemented it could be used to achieve higher recognition accuracy with small efforts.

References

1. Bourlard, H., Morgan, N.: Connectionist Speech Recognition: A Hybrid Approach. Kluwer Press, Amsterdam (1994)
2. Tebelskis, J.: Speech recognition using neural networks. Ph.D. thesis, CMU (1995)
3. Hinton, G., Osindero, S., Yee-Wee, T.: A fast learning algorithm for deep belief nets. Neural Comput. **18**(7), 1527–1554 (2006)
4. Hinton, G., et al.: Deep neural networks for acoustic modeling in speech recognition: the shared views of four research groups. IEEE Signal Process. Mag. **29**(6), 82–97 (2012)
5. Saon, G., Chien, J.: Large-vocabulary continuous speech recognition systems: a look at some recent advances. Signal Process. Mag. **29**(6), 18–33 (2012)
6. Graves, A., Jaitly, N., Mohamed, A.-R.: Hybrid speech recognition with deep bidirectional LSTM. In: Poroceedings of 2013 IEEE Workshop on Automatic Speech Recognition and Understanding, Olomouc, Czech Republic, pp. 273–278 (2013)
7. Hannun, A., et al.: Deep speech: scaling up end-to-end speech recognition (2014). https://arxiv.org/abs/1412.5567
8. Amodei, D., et al.: Deep speech 2: end-to-end speech recognition in English and mandarin. In: Proceedings of the 33rd International Conference on International Conference on Machine Learning, New York, pp. 173–182 (2016)

Information Technology Applications - Special Session on Smart e-Learning Technologies and Applications

Technology-Enriched Challenge-Based Learning for Responsible Education

Jurgita Barynienė[1], Asta Daunorienė[2], and Daina Gudonienė[3($\boxtimes$)]

[1] Faculty of Social Sciences, Arts and Humanities, Kaunas University of Technology, Mickeviciaus str. 37, 44244 Kaunas, Lithuania

[2] School of Economics and Business, Kaunas University of Technology, Gedimino str. 50, 44239 Kaunas, Lithuania

[3] Faculty of Informatics, Kaunas University of Technology, Studentu str. 50, 51367 Kaunas, Lithuania

daina.gudoniene@ktu.lt

Abstract. The paper presents a study on the relevance of the challenge-based learning (CBL) approach in today's learning process, introduces the stages of CBL and their key elements, reviews the possible ways of learning incorporating technologies and provides key recommendations for a successful and effective learning process for responsible education. The main objective of this paper is to analyze how technology-enriched learning can ensure the successful implementation of CBL in the study process. The paper also presents good practice and the existing experience of the authors and provides a wide range of technological solutions for the application of CBL.

Keywords: Challenge-Based Learning (CBL) · Educational technologies · Responsible education · E-learning · Higher education policy

1 Introduction

Contemporary complex, chaotic and fast-changing society faces the challenges of how to act together in individual and collective ways. The main task of higher education policymakers and other education actors is to answer the question of how to prepare students for life as active and responsible citizens [3, 5]. For this reason, higher education institutions are constantly looking for new and innovative study methods that are student-centred and actively engage students in the learning process. However, technology transforms learning and teaching and opens new possibilities for achieving learning outcomes.

It is agreed that recently the context of higher education has been significantly influenced by the global sustainability agenda and responsible management education imperatives (United Nations (UN) Principles of Responsible Management Education (PRME), UN Sustainable Development Goals (SDGs), UN Global Compact, UN Decade of Education for Sustainable Development (ESD), *etc.*) [3]. Discussions on trends in higher education are increasingly focusing not only on graduates' knowledge and skills, but also

© The Author(s), under exclusive license to Springer Nature Switzerland AG 2022
A. Lopata et al. (Eds.): ICIST 2022, CCIS 1665, pp. 273–283, 2022.
https://doi.org/10.1007/978-3-031-16302-9_22

on their values and attitudes, which form the basis for contributing to global economic, environmental, and social challenges, and encourage them to take responsibility for their own decisions in global, as well as local contexts [3]. According to this, responsible education is considered the most powerful instrument to enable students to contribute to and benefit from an inclusive and sustainable future [3, 14].

Typically, a sustainable future is associated with sustainable development, in which local and global debates in the public sphere, including education, law, policy-making and political-socio-economic negotiations are going in a variety of ways and represent the interests of many groups and communities [3].

An important aspect of responsible education emerges which emphasizes the combination of subject-specific competences with generic competences that enable graduates to navigate through unfamiliar contexts and find sustainable solutions for society by collaborating with society, business, and other stakeholders in a meaningful and responsible way. According to this, challenge-based learning (CBL) can be seen as the most appropriate method. Furthermore, higher education institutions as knowledge providers are closely interconnected with social challenges and the transformation to a sustainable society. One learning approach in the Higher Education Institutions (HEI) – often described as "challenge-based" - is to manage how to tune theory with practice in addressing real-world problems in collaboration with stakeholders in society [9].

There are various definitions of CBL in the scientific literature [9]. Analysis of scientific literature shows that CBL draws from different educational theories and pedagogical methods, for example, problem-based learning and inquiry-based learning (IBL). Problem-based learning has been widely adopted in medicine and engineering education, due to the expected benefits in improving student critical thinking, self-directed learning, generic skills, and long-term retention [10, 17]. The CBL method can be described as a special form of problem-based learning (PBL), in which the problems are of realistic, open-ended nature. Additionally, the CBL contains features of experiential and project-based learning approaches.

The authors [8] declare that CBL is a multidisciplinary approach that encourages students to actively work with peers, teachers and stakeholders in society to identify complex challenges, formulate relevant questions, and act for sustainable development. This method is a student-oriented learning approach that empowers them to solve complex challenges which appear in the real world. In addition, this method encourages students to collaborate in interdisciplinary and intercultural teams, work with peers, teachers, and experts in their communities, and promotes self-directed learning both inside and outside the classroom [7, 9]. CBL focuses on the real world and surfaces the essential relevance of the core subjects at the same time [7]. In this paper, it is argued that CBL can be viewed as an evolution of the Concept of Conception, Design, Implementation, and Operation (CDIO), expanding, as well as deepening, the learning experience.

CBL from different perspectives was analyzed and discussed by many authors [2, 4, 12, 16, 21], however, our focus is on the technologies for the implementation of CBL in practice. The global pandemic COVID-19, with all its implications, highlighted the importance of technology in teaching and learning processes. It should be noted that today's rapid development of technologies and their implementation in the study process significantly influence the principles of traditional and distance learning and raises new theoretical and practical issues for higher education institutions. CBL as an engaging multidisciplinary approach to teaching and learning encourages students to take advantage of the technology they use in their daily lives to solve real-world problems. In this context, the main objective of this paper is to analyze how technology-enriched learning can ensure the successful implementation of CBL in the study process.

The technological implementation solutions of CBL ensure a successful and effective educational process. CBL is supported by the provision of Digital Experimentation Toolkits (DExTs) which comprise materials, initial instructions, references to web resources, and specific software tools. Technological challenges lie in the ease of use in accessing these data and communicating the learners' requests and specifications of the learners to remote sites [1].

2 Characteristics of CBL

The changing context, new trends in the labour market, and the transformation of the higher education paradigm place new demands and expectations on competence and its structure. Competence is commonly described as a combination of knowledge, skills, and attitudes (which are closely interdependent) that enable an individual to perform a task or an activity successfully within a given context [11, 15]. OECD (2019) presented the "Learning Compass 2030" to reopen the discussion of educational transformation at all levels in order to equip learners with crucial skills for future life, well-being and responsible citizenship [13]. The responsible education approach stimulates discussions about the wider goals of education and puts emphasis on orientation towards the responsible future (individual and collective well-being). This approach emphasizes the need for students to learn how to navigate through unfamiliar contexts and find direction in a meaningful and the most responsible way (Fig. 1).

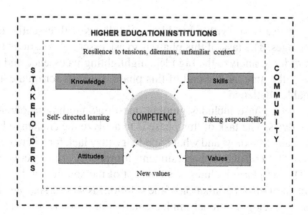

Fig. 1. Key aspects of responsible education

The main elements of CBL can be identified which create added value for the learners and the larger society and contribute to responsible education: (1) involvement of stakeholders (e.g. companies, start-ups, municipalities, public institutions, etc.); (2) the real challenges are posed by stakeholders; (3) iterative application of innovation approaches; (4) teamwork in interdisciplinary and interdisciplinary student groups; (5) effective oral communication; (6) deliberate competition between teams and independent evaluation of the results achieved; (7) practical activities, study visits and other experiences that complement theoretical knowledge acquired in lectures; (9) a focus on the value creation process and the development of entrepreneurial skills. CBL enhances learners' collaboration, creativity, problem-solving, critical thinking, communication, and other skills that are crucial for future decision making. According to the model, CBL has three main phases: (1) engage, (2) investigate, and (3) act (Fig. 2).

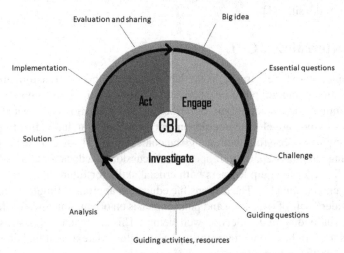

Fig. 2. CBL phases

The Engage phase starts with a big idea and follows with essential questions and actionable challenges. The task of this phase is to ask essential questions from different perspectives in order to analyze the big idea, highlighting its essence and relevance for each learner and all teams. At the end of this phase, students formulate and propose a concrete actionable challenge.

The investigation phase includes guiding questions, guiding resources, as well as activities and analysis. The task of this phase is to analyze the challenge by identifying what the students already know and what knowledge they lack for a better understanding of the challenge. At the end of this phase, students formulate a primary concept for solving the challenge. The act phase includes the concept of the solution and its development, solution implementation and evaluation of the solution, as well as sharing. The main task of this phase is to develop a rational implementation of it in a real-world environment. At the end of this phase, students evaluate the solution, improve it, and share the results. Each phase includes activities that prepare the students to move on to the next phase. The whole learning process is supported by a continuous process of documentation, reflection, and information sharing. The role of the educator is to work with students to assimilate the multidisciplinary standards-based content, relate it to what is happening today, and turn it into an experience where students make the solutions that transform their communities.

According to the analyzed CBL process, the unique aspects of this method related to responsible education are expressed by several key aspects: (1) the teams define their own challenge to work on, take responsibility and ownership of the learning process; (2) students enter the real world, involving all stakeholders and community members necessary in the process; (3) final result is not predictable and the process itself determines the direction; (4) process allows to recognize challenges and find opportunities that are environmentally, socially, and economically sustainable.

3 Technology-Enriched CBL

For CBL to be successful technological enriched, certain prerequisites are necessary (Fig. 3).

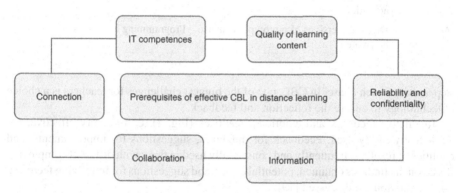

Fig.3. Prerequisites of Effective CBL in distance learning

A critical prerequisite for the success of CBL is a communication infrastructure that includes access to hardware and software and the ability to receive technical support in real time. An equally important component is competence, i.e., sufficient ICT literacy for both students and lecturers, communication basics, and the basics of online collaboration.

Successful studies are not possible without high-quality learning content, which includes digital resources of sufficiently high quality according to the field of study and the object of study. Trust in the consistency of the technology and the reliability of the information is also important. Also, information capture: protocols for storing, tagging, and retrieving digital material. Collaboration: existing or emerging networked communities, collaborative knowledge/output creation (blogs, wikis, etc.).

CBL can be applied on campus and online; however, in this way, the biggest focus should be on the technologies for the learning processes implementation. The authors are suggesting several solutions on how technologies can be involved and what technologies could be used for the CBL implementation (Table 1).

It is also important to emphasize that both individual and group reflection of students is crucial to the CBL. Reflection on the learning experience should be done after each

Table 1. CBL application using technologies

CBL phase	How can technologies be involved?	Technologies
Engage	Technology for communication with stakeholders and the community Open data basis, open educational resources Communication student-to-student For teamwork in order to be sustainable oriented (collaboration platforms instead of flipchart paper, etc.)	Collaborative Writing Tools Digital recordings Digital text Virtual learning environments
Investigate	Delving into online learning resources to answer research questions The following digital technologies can be used in addition to tagging and prioritizing issues, resources and activities	Computer-assisted language learning Student response systems Automated feedback on MCQs Evaluation tools Intelligent tutors
Act	Digitized versions of prototypes can also be created	Programming languages

step and after each phase. In CBL, one of the biggest challenges for teachers is a choice of technology to ensure the reflection and feedback.

Regulative feedback and emotional feedback (Fig. 4). Can be very effective, but are actually rarely used. Feedback for diagnosis, suggestions for improvements, and qualities of results is frequently and consistently used in tasks with different complexity. Based on the findings obtained, potential causes and suggestions for improving feedback implementation are discussed [19].

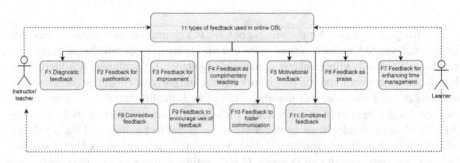

Fig. 4. Types of feedback.

Feedback is crucial to competence development and is used extensively in online CBL, but the lack of consistent positive effects on learning is a concern. Additionally, feedback in the context of CBL is not well understood. Therefore, it is crucial to investigate how feedback is actually used and how feedback practice can be improved [18].

Moreover, access to peer feedback and the feedback information peers have received from the teacher, together with peer and teacher discussions through virtual learning environments (VLE) (such as Moodle, Blackboard, or Google Classroom) provide additional input that if engaged with through a critical and evaluative filter can also aid in the understanding of academic standards in a way similar to on-display assignments. Using the open feedback environment as a resource for formative assessment allows emergent examples of the high-quality application of course content from learners to be highlighted for the group [20].

Furthermore, CBL supportive technologies can ensure a successful learning process and will give added value by ensuring qualitative and effective feedback in the CBL process: (1) Educator to student feedback, (2) Computer-to-student feedback, (3) Peer to students' feedback, (4) Self-feedback [6] (Fig. 5).

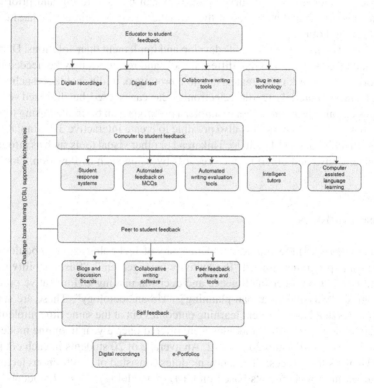

Fig. 5. Supporting technologies for CBL.

In the engagement phase of applying traditional learning, depending on the available infrastructure, human resources, time, etc., students can meet face to face and get to know the challenge provider, the potential target group, or the context in which the challenge solution will be deployed. However, technology can be used to speed up these processes.

The use of databases and resources from universities, libraries, museums, archives, NGOs, and other organizations is recommended, which can be accessed both live and virtually. Student collaboration in all phases could be via email, social networks, etc.

In an attempt to narrow down an initially broad, abstract challenge, if the necessary tools are available, students can use large-format paper, sticky notes, markers, (smart) whiteboards, etc. to mark ideas, draw mind maps, etc. However, in order to optimize traditional classroom learning and contribute to sustainability by saving resources, it is still recommended to use technological solutions for such processes. For this purpose, the Internet is full of commercial but also partially or completely free, often open-source, solutions that can be accessed on a wide range of devices with different operating systems (e.g. Coggle, Stormboard, LucidChart, Mindnode, and others).

During the research phase, students could further explore the sources of information mentioned above, or access them online. At this phase, students make a list of guiding questions, prioritize them, and conduct the research. In all activities of this phase, traditional and technological solutions can be used. Additional technological tools such as Google or other interactive survey platforms can be used to tag and prioritize the questions, resources, and activities of the presenters (e.g. Mentimeter, AhaSlides, Poll Everywhere, and others).

In the third action phase, students develop and implement their solutions. Depending on the challenge being addressed, different tools and resources may be needed to build the prototype. If the task is to create a tangible prototype, traditional tools such as paper, paint, containers, materials, textiles, electronics, etc. can be used, but digitized versions of prototypes can also be created. For example, a prototype can be created using tools such as Scratch, CAD, and others. It is also possible to create interactive 3D simulations and models with tools such as SketchUp, Tinkercad or other visual tools such as infographics (e.g. Visme, Canva and others), video records by using such as Powtoon, Doodly and others.

4   Case Findings

A CBL has been used in several Kaunas University of Technology study modules in postgraduate study programs entitled "Productivity management", "Sustainability management and law", "Computer intelligence and decision making", "Innovative production technologies", "Sustainable urban planning", "Urban sociology". These are six credit study modules that have different learning outcomes but at the same time implement the CBL methodology. The study modules were offered once a year in online mode during the period of 2019/2020 and 2021/2022. An average of 20 students in each course participated in the study process. The study modules consisted of synchronous lectures and authentic learning assignments based on CBL methodology. 40% of students' grades were based on the knowledge of the course, the other 60% were from CBL. During the study process, the students used different technologies to work together. The data on technology usage were collected during the study process in the study modules. The second table summarizes the technologies that are the most frequently used during the CBL process (Table 2).

The collected data shows that for communication between students, the teachers and stakeholders, Zoom and Teams platforms. Before the implementation of the CBL process, students used Trello to create a work plan and allocate task responsibilities among team members. For the Big idea analysis students actively used Jamboard and

Table 2. Frequently used technologies applying CBL activities

Activities \ Technology	Zoom	Teams	Goole Classroom	E.mails	Trello	Stormboard	Jamboard	Coggle	Mindnote	Mindmup	Google Docs	Miro	Moocs	Padlet	CAD	Mentimeter	Miro	Youtube	Google Forms	Flinga	Scratch	Tinkercad	SketchUp	Visme	Canva	Powtoon
Communication between students	X	X																								
Communication with teacher	X	X		X																						
Communication with stakeholders	X	X		X																						
Work Organization					X																					
Big idea analysis (essential questions)							X			X		X														
Identification of guided questions							X				X	X														
Research											X	X	X						X							
Prototyping															X						X	X				
Sharing																		X						X	X	X
Documentation							X				X															
Feedback	X															X	X		X							
Reflections							X									X	X		X							

Mindnote platforms. In order to collect guided questions, students used Google Docs, Miro, and Jamboard. To complete the research students worked with Google forms and Moocs. For the prototyping sessions Scratch, Tinkercad and CAD platforms were used. For the sharing sessions, students integrated YouTube channels, Visme, Canva, and Powtoon platforms. For the feedback and reflection sessions, teachers mostly used Miro, Mentimeter and Google Forms.

5   Conclusions

The research results reveal that technologies can be effectively used to promote CBL methodology in an online mode. Research results indicate that students actively use different technologies in order to solve challenges, communicate, and work together. Active student involvement in the technologies has a positive impact on the changing study process with the implementation of active study methods such as CBL. It proves the idea that teachers do not necessarily have to be technological experts in the CBL course. The students take on most of the responsibilities by choosing the right platform for their activities and responsibilities.

The most significant aspect should be considered. There is an extensive recommendation to use the technologies in the study process. However, these recommendations are general and should not be necessary and should be valuable for the concrete study process embedding different methodologies. The research results helped allocate the recommended technologies for each stage of the CBL process. The recommended list is valuable for teachers and students working with the CBL methodology. This list could help to choose the technology much easier. Moreover, teachers can prepare a short presentation video with advice for the students on how the technologies can help them to succeed in the CBL study process. In other words, the CBL process could be more immersive by using different technologies and rewarding students to use the technologies. In terms of responsible education, the active and meaningful usage of technologies can help students to know and trust themselves, understand others, and to explore different technologies of improving social skills.

References

1. Baloian, N., Hoeksema, K., Hoppe, U., Milrad, M.: Technologies and educational activities for supporting and implementing challenge-based learning. In: Kumar, D., Turner, J. (eds.) Education for the 21st Century — Impact of ICT and Digital Resources. IIFIP, vol. 210, pp. 7–16. Springer, Boston, MA (2006). https://doi.org/10.1007/978-0-387-34731-8_2
2. Campos, J.M., Lozano, E.A., Urzúa, J., Calderón, J.G.: Challenge-based learning: a fast track to introduce engineering students to data science. In: 2021 Machine Learning-Driven Digital Technologies for Educational Innovation Workshop, pp. 1–6. IEEE (2021)
3. Cicmil, S., Gough, G., Hills, S.: Insights into responsible education for sustainable development: the case of UWE, Bristol. Int. J. Manag. Educ. 15(2), 293–305 (2017)
4. Conde, M.Á., Rodríguez-Sedano, F.J., Fernández-Llamas, C., Gonçalves, J., Lima, J., García-Peñalvo, F.J.: Fostering STEAM through challenge-based learning, robotics, and physical devices: a systematic mapping literature review. Comput. Appl. Eng. Educ. 29(1), 46–65 (2021)

5. Council of Europe (2018). Reference framework of competences for democratic culture. https://rm.coe.int/prems-008318-gbr-2508-reference-framework-of-competences-vol-1-8573-co/16807bc66c

6. Dawson, P., et al.: Technology and feedback design. In: Spector, M., Lockee, B., Childress, M. (eds.) Learning, Design, and Technology, pp. 1–45. Springer, Cham (2018). https://doi.org/10.1007/978-3-319-17727-4_124-1

7. Johnson, L.F., Smith, R.S., Smythe, J.T., Varon, R.K.: Challenge-based learning: An approach for our time, pp. 1–38. The new Media consortium (2009)

8. Kohn Rådberg, K., Lundqvist, U., Malmqvist, J., Hagvall Svensson, O.: From CDIO to challenge-based learning experiences–expanding student learning as well as societal impact? Eur. J. Eng. Educ. **45**(1), 22–37 (2020)

9. Leijon, M., Gudmundsson, P., Staaf, P., Christersson, C.: Challenge based learning in higher education–a systematic literature review. Innovations Educ. Teach. Int. 1–10 (2021)

10. Lund, B., Jensen, A.A.: PBL teachers in higher education: Challenges and possibilities. In: Peters, M.A. (ed.) Encyclopedia of teacher education, pp. 1–6. Springer Singapore, Singapore (2020). https://doi.org/10.1007/978-981-13-1179-6_385-1

11. Mulder, M., Gulikers, J., Biemans, H., Wesselink, R.: The new competence concept in higher education: error or enrichment? J. Eur. Ind. Train. **33**(8/9), 755–770 (2009)

12. Gerardou, F.S., Meriton, R., Brown, A., Moran, B.V.G., Bhandal, R.: Advancing a design thinking approach to challenge-based learning. In: The Emerald Handbook of Challenge Based Learning, pp. 93–129 (2022)

13. OECD Learning Compass 2030. Prieiga internete. https://www.oecd.org/education/2030-project/teaching-and-learning/learning/

14. OECD (2018) The future of education and skills: Education 2030. OECD Education Working Papers

15. Rychen, D.S., Salganik, L.H.: Key Competencies for a Successful Life and a Wellfunctioning Society. Hogrefe & Huber, Göttingen Germany (2003)

16. Salinas-Navarro, D.E.: Design a challenge-based learning model for higher education, an application case in a beverage company. In: VI IEEE World Engineering Education Conference. IEEE (2021)

17. Strobel, J., Van Barneveld, A.: When is PBL more effective? A meta-synthesis of meta-analyses comparing PBL to conventional classrooms. Interdis. J. Prob.-Based Learn. **3**(1), 44–58 (2009)

18. Tekian, A., Watling, C.J., Roberts, T.E., Steinert, Y., Norcini, J.: Qualitative and quantitative feedback in the context of competency-based education. Med. Teach. **39**(12), 1245–1249 (2017)

19. Wang, H., Tlili, A., Lehman, J.D., Lu, H., Huang, R.: Investigating feedback implemented by instructors to support online competency-based learning (CBL): a multiple case study. Int. J. Educ. Technol. High. Educ. **18**(1), 1–21 (2021). https://doi.org/10.1186/s41239-021-00241-6

20. Wood, J.: A dialogic technology-mediated model of feedback uptake and literacy. Assess. Eval. High. Educ. **46**(8), 1173–1190 (2021)

21. Woschank, M., Pacher, C., Miklautsch, P., Kaiblinger, A., Murphy, M.: The usage of challenge-based learning in industrial engineering education. In: Auer, M.E., Hortsch, H., Michler, O., Köhler, T. (eds.) Mobility for Smart Cities and Regional Development - Challenges for Higher Education: Proceedings of the 24th International Conference on Interactive Collaborative Learning (ICL2021), Volume 2, pp. 869–878. Springer International Publishing, Cham (2022). https://doi.org/10.1007/978-3-030-93907-6_93

Open Course Integration into Formal Education: Case on Databases Course

Rita Butkienė, Linas Ablonskis, and Algirdas Šukys[✉]

Department of Information Systems, Kaunas University of Technology, Studentų St. 50-307a, 51368 Kaunas, Lithuania
algirdas.sukys@ktu.lt

Abstract. Open online courses are often used in formal education to provide added value for the students by helping gain new skills and competences or as extra material tasks in addition to the formal education course. The course described in this paper is developed and piloted fully open online. It is also integrated into formal education. This paper presents a case on integration of open databases course into formal education together with student feedback on the course quality and effectiveness of course delivery process.

Keywords: MOOC · Databases · Formal education · Open resources

1 Introduction

Possibilities and learning outcomes of open education are highly dependent on the strategy of the course. Instructors are constantly looking for improved ways to provide course materials and ensure achievement of learning outcomes. They experiment with different technologies and learning approaches while investigating the effect achieved. Research shows that there is no one-size-fits-all approach in education. Sharing experiences on application of various methods in education helps others when planning changes in their own courses.

The open online course "Entity-Relationship Modelling" has been developed and integrated into the formal course "Databases". The "Databases" course is of 6 ECTS credits and is delivered for the second-year students who are studying Computer Science. The course is delivered by instructors having more than 10 years of experience in teaching. The main challenges encountered during lectures of this course were maintaining attention of students, ensuring attendance and active involvement of students and accounting for different student aptitudes.

Mastering the technique of entity-relationship modelling requires a lot of practice. Therefore, inspired by applications of educational learning technologies, we decided to redesign the "Databases" course and implement a flipped [3, 4, 8] or inverted [18] classroom approach for delivering the topic of entity-relationship modelling. This allows students to learn at home from video records and discuss the issues on campus. The redesigned topic materials were implemented in the open online course "Entity-Relationship Modelling". This course was developed as a self-directed learning course

© The Author(s), under exclusive license to Springer Nature Switzerland AG 2022
A. Lopata et al. (Eds.): ICIST 2022, CCIS 1665, pp. 284–295, 2022.
https://doi.org/10.1007/978-3-031-16302-9_23

based on instructional videos to provide background knowledge of entity-relationship modelling. The face-to-face lectures were used for modelling practice.

The biggest challenge for instructional designers lies in the decomposition of the topic and adoption of self-directed learning. According to [24], these challenges can be divided into four categories: human and non-human resources [13, 15], lack of skills, preparation of teachers, resistance with instructional change [7, 20], design [12, 19], and evaluation [17, 19].

To ensure that the redesigned course met our expectations and to plan for further improvements, we have conducted a student survey after running the pilot of the course. The survey was designed to gather student feedback. We have also investigated student learning activities by analyzing data gathered by the Learning Management System of Moodle environment. The student feedback was positive and has provided some insights for further improvements. Analysis of student learning activities has allowed to assess student attitude towards learning and design further improvements of teaching strategy.

The rest of this paper is organized as follows. We begin with related work section where we provide a review of the literature on the application and benefits of MOOC courses. Further, in Sect. 3, we present the development methodology used for our MOOC course for university students. We introduce the basics of how we created the MOOC course for the subsection of formal course "Databases" covering topics related to entity-relationship modeling. In Sect. 4, we present and analyze usage data of the course and results of the student survey. Additionally, we provide our insights and observations related to this course. Finally, in Sect. 5, we present conclusions.

2   Related Works

Massive Open Online Courses (MOOC) have entered the higher education environment in many forms as a way of acquiring knowledge. Teachers have been incorporating MOOCs [10, 11, 26] with more or less success in a traditional classroom setting to support various learning preferences, introduce a new way of learning to students, and to make learning available to those who might not be able to follow traditional instructions [5, 21, 23].

There are several important aspects to consider when we use open educational resources or open courses in formal education: (1) increased possibility to use open resources, (2) changes to assessment approach, and (3) increased adoption of the self-directed learning approach [22].

A blended education - mixing online and traditional education - has positive effects on student outcomes in terms of achievement and engagement. MOOCs have been blended with traditional education into various formats with mixed results [1]. Literature review presented in [2] shows, that student achievements in MOOC mostly depends on the following factors: (1) quality of the course instructions, (2) design of the course, (3) pedagogy and (4) social media tools.

Some authors have examined the use of MOOCs in campus-based courses and found no statistical difference in pass rate or final score, but the feedback concerning rating, interest, difficulty, and amount learned was better for traditionally taught classes. In [5] a MOOC has been offered as an alternative activity to project work, credited towards the final grade in the course. Both activities have been aligned to achieve the same learning outcomes. There was a two-folded goal for the introduction of a MOOC in the course: to give students more online learning experience and to help part-time students, who are not able to fully participate in campus teaching, meet the learning outcomes of the course.

The study [25] investigated that the learning outcomes, related instruments, and assessment characteristics of these instruments in MOOCs. The study results indicate that quizzes and exams can be used to test the knowledge that participants have acquired in the course. While complex tasks and practical assignments allow to assess cognitive skills.

Paper [6] discusses the results of a longitudinal study on the integration of MOOCs in university classrooms and their influence on academic performance. The relationship between academic performance, course design and the type of student participation are discussed. Academic performance has been assessed through evidence of learning, while the design and influence of the type of participation have been checked using TAM (Technology Acceptance Model) and IMMS (Instructional Materials Motivation Survey). Evidence obtained shows that participation in a MOOC improved learning results and that both types of course design (defined by intensive use of social networks and e-activities) and active participation have an influence on the level of academic success.

The video becomes increasingly prevalent in educational settings. Research presented in [16] presents an empirical study of how video production decisions affect student engagement and makes recommendations on what to look for when creating online educational videos. One of the recommendations is about the duration of videos. Authors state that shorter informal instructional videos are more engaging than long pre-recorded lectures from classrooms. Research presented in paper [14] investigated what feedback instructors need regarding their students' engagement and learning even if video technologies are equipped to provide viewing analytics and collect student feedback. Authors of [9] state that data on user behavior collected in the course environment can be used to improve the quality of MOOC courses, reduce the rate of dropouts, and increase support for participants. This could be done with the help of software agents that analyze user behavior.

3   Structure of Entity-Relationships Modeling MOOC

The "Entity-Relationships Modeling" course was created primarily for students of formal education. The grade obtained for the completion of the "Entity-Relationships Modeling" course tasks was included in the calculation of the overall grade of the "Database" course with a relatively small impact. The MOOC was introduced to enable students study on their own and learn the course material better. After completing the course, students were invited to participate in a survey and tell if this way of presenting learning material was attractive.

The MOOC was designed to provide the most relevant information in a concise manner. As the material in the "Databases" course is comprehensive, presenting the most important topics concisely proved to be a challenge. It was hard to decide which parts from the learning material are most relevant and must be included and which parts can be omitted. Eventually, 11 subtopics were identified, focusing on the ER modeling process:

1. Introduction to ER modelling;
2. ER modeling notation;
3. ER modelling process, modelling of attributes;
4. Unique identifier of entities;
5. Relationships: modelling structural business rules;
6. Example of ER modeling;
7. Types of relationships;
8. Modelling of changes in time;
9. Modelling of categories;
10. Modelling of structure;
11. Modelling of hierarchy.

At the beginning of the MOOC, students are introduced to the elements of ER model (entities, attributes, unique identifiers, etc.). Then they are taught how to create models – to identify entities, their attributes, relations, cardinalities, etc. The last topics of the course are used to explain specific modeling situations, such as categories, hierarchical relations and modelling of changes in time.

For each topic, there is a video, 3 to 6 min long. In the videos, the instructor presents the topic by showing slides and commenting. Watching videos is recommended, but not mandatory. For each topic students are able to take a test and check if they have learned the topic well. A number of test attempts is unlimited. The number of questions in the test range from 1 to 5. There are questions of different types: multiple choice, drag-and-drop and matching. To complete the test, the student should receive the maximum grade. Navigation between questions is not restricted.

At the end of the course, students can take the final task and final test to assess the knowledge learned. The final task is accessible if all the course videos have been watched. The final task is preparatory and mandatory for the completion of the final test. Questions of the final test are directly associated with the final task and cover all the stages of ER modeling. Therefore, only those students who have learned the material of the whole course can answer correctly. The correct answers are not displayed immediately but shown only after the final test is completed.

4 Analysis of MOOC Delivery

4.1 Analysis of Course Usage

In this section, we analyze data about student learning activities gathered from Moodle system of the course. The data was analyzed to answer the following questions related to the impact of the new topic delivery strategy on student learning:

- Did the students watch the video and how many times?
- Did the students view the test and how many times?

- Did the student complete the test and how many attempts were required?
- How many students completed the activities?
- How many videos have students watched?
- How many tests have students completed?
- How many students did complete the final activities?
- How many attempts were required to complete the final activities?

This analysis provides insights into student learning behavior, motivation and how much attention were paid to the learning material and activities. The data collected allows drawing preliminary conclusions only and lends itself to raising some hypotheses. To test the hypotheses, more detailed studies are required. For example, if the number of video views is high, it can be assumed that this is either because the topic is very interesting or the topic is very complex and needs to be simplified. Also, some data points are not completely reliable. For example, the number of views of the video material does not mean that students have watched the entire video from the beginning to the end. The students could have only clicked on the video and skipped the watching altogether.

We start the analysis with the chart showing the percentage of students who watched videos a certain number of times on a particular topic (see Fig. 1). Most students watched all the videos a single time.

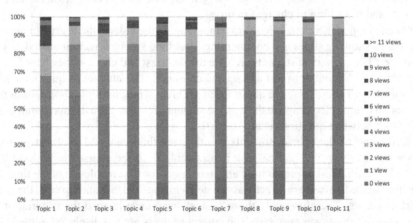

Fig. 1. Percentage of students who completed a certain number of video views.

Videos of Topics 5 and 6 were viewed 6 and more times by the highest percentage of students. This can be explained by the fact that Topic 5 explains one of the most challenging parts of entity-relationship modelling – establishing relations. And Topic 6 provides an example of ER model which summarizes all previous topics and helps to understand ER modelling principles better.

The chart presented in Fig. 2 shows the percentage of students who viewed tests a certain number of times on a particular topic and reveals which test required the most effort. The numbers correspond to views of each question (page loads) in the test. Students were allowed to navigate freely between test questions. This could have generated a significant number of views. For example, Test 5 was viewed from 26 to

50 times by the highest percentage of students. The diagram in Fig. 2 repeats the trends visible in the previous chart. Test 5 deals with one of the most difficult topics and it is natural that it requires the most effort to solve. It requires not only knowledge but also logical thinking and imagination because this test asks to mark elements in graphical ER models. Test 8 has only one multiple choice question; therefore, it is not surprising that it requires the least amount of effort.

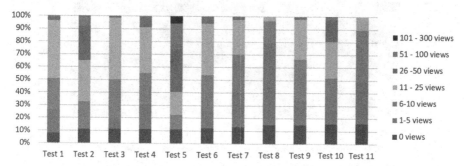

Fig. 2. Percentage of students who performed a certain number of test views.

The following chart (see Fig. 3) shows how many attempts were required to complete each test. For more complex topics, students needed more attempts. Test 5 stands out the most. The completion of Tests 4 and 9 also required many attempts for many students. These tests contain not only multiple-choice questions but also questions where ER diagram needs to be completed by dragging and dropping elements to correct positions or the correctness of the presented diagram should be assessed.

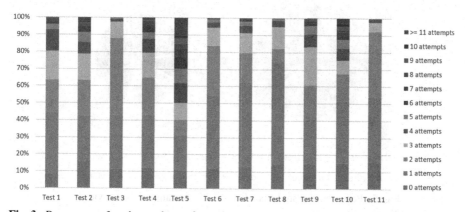

Fig. 3. Percentage of students who performed a certain number of attempts to complete the test.

The chart in Fig. 4 shows the percentage of students who viewed videos and the percentage of students who completed tests on each topic. There appears to be no correlation between these two activities. Each of the videos was watched at least once by a number of students ranging from 80% to 90%. The percentage of students who completed tests varies more significantly. Understandably, this percentage is lower for more complex tests, i.e., ones that required more attempts to complete.

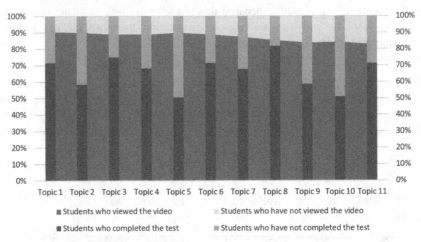

Fig. 4. Percentage of students who completed the activities.

The chart in Fig. 5 shows the percentage of students who viewed a certain number of videos. 81% of students viewed all 11 videos. 4% of students were inactive and did not view any video. The remaining 15% viewed a different number of videos: 2% viewed 10 videos, 6% maybe just wanted to try and watched 1 or 2 videos only.

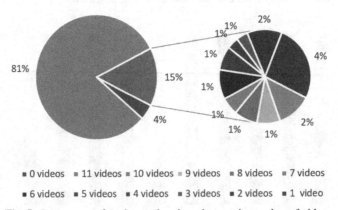

Fig. 5. Percentage of students who viewed a certain number of videos.

The chart in Fig. 6 shows the percentage of students who completed a certain number of tests. About half of the students completed from 1 to 10 tests in approximately equal proportions. 14% of students had good motivation at the beginning, showed effort and completed 5 to 7 tests, but failed to complete all the tasks. More detailed research should be done to find out why students lost motivation during the course. 10% of students were inactive and did not complete any test: whether they failed to answer all the questions or did not try at all.

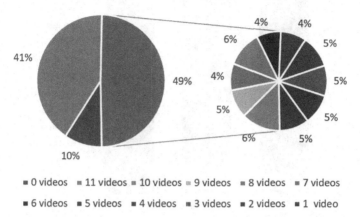

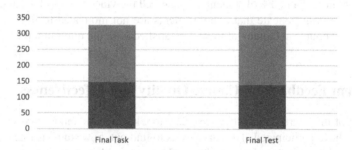

Fig. 6. Percentage of students who completed a certain number of tests.

The chart in Fig. 7 shows how many students managed to complete the final task and final test. Only those who viewed all the videos could try the final task. However, it was not mandatory to complete all the tests. The chart shows that 45% of students completed the final task. A very similar number of students passed the final test. It is very likely that most of these students are those who have passed either all 11 tests (41% of total) or 10 tests (6% of total).

Fig. 7. Number of students who completed final activities.

The diagram in Fig. 8 shows how many attempts students needed to complete the final task and final test. To complete the final task and final test, all questions must be answered correctly. Only after completing the final task, students were allowed to take the final test. It took two attempts to complete the final task for the largest group of students, however a significant number of students required 6 or more attempts. Only one or two attempts were required for most students to complete the final test. It can be assumed that completing the final task helped students to repeat and learn the essential knowledge in this course and prepare for the final test.

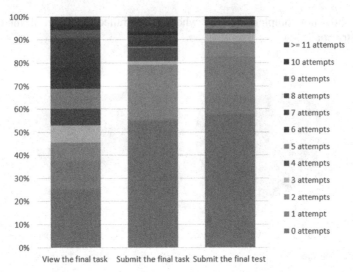

Fig. 8. Percentage of students who performed a certain number of attempts to complete the activity.

The analysis of MOOC usage data has resulted in the following insights:

- Short (~5 min. length) videos are appropriate for learning the topic of the course presented. For most students, 1 view was enough to grasp the knowledge.
- There are topics (e.g., Topic 5) that require more attention and efforts from students.
- Although more than 80% of students watched all the videos, only 41% passed all the tests. This might indicate that many students are not motivated to fully master the topic of the course and many of them are satisfied with the minimum passable grade only.

5   Student Feedback on Course Quality and Effectiveness

At the end of the course, students were asked to take an anonymous survey. A total of 39 students have participated. The survey was to find out, how students rate the course, which aspects they liked, and which did not. They were able to submit grades on a scale of 1 to 7. The following diagrams (see Fig. 9, Fig. 10) show that most students (77%) rated their satisfaction as good or very good and gave a score of 6 or 7. 18% of students rated their satisfaction as average and gave a score of 5. The willingness to recommend the course to friends or colleagues was rated similarly.

Students were also asked to answer whether they were attending a MOOC for the first time. Most students (80%) took MOOCs for the first time, while 18% have already attended such courses. The answers indicate that this type of the course is not widely available to students at our university and based on student satisfaction ratings, it appears promising.

When answering a question about the length of the course, most students (64%) rated it positively. However, they had some remarks about the length of the course - 30% of

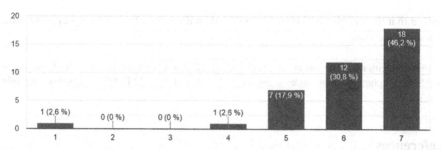

Fig. 9. Evaluation scores for the question "Overall, to what extent are you satisfied with the course, or the part of the course implemented differently?".

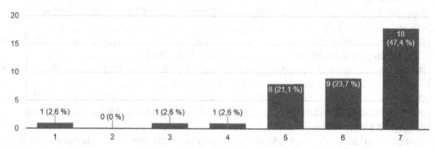

Fig. 10. Evaluation scores for the question "Would you recommend this course to your friends, acquaintances, or colleagues?".

students rated the course as long or very long. This suggests that the course may need to be shortened or some of the additional topics should be omitted.

Students also had the opportunity to write what they liked and disliked about the course. They liked the idea of breaking down the course material into short videos that provide basic information quickly. Students also appreciated the consistency of topics and the smoothness of transition between the topics. The possibility to view the tests an unlimited number of times was also mentioned as a positive thing.

As a negative thing, students mentioned the final task, which turned out to be too difficult and demanding for some. Additionally, some tests were seen as having too many questions and some multiple-choice questions were seen as being too complex.

6   Conclusions

We have presented our experience in providing a part of the learning material of the "Databases" module to students as a MOOC. We have analyzed the statistics provided by the course Moodle system – how many times videos or tests were viewed, how many times students attempted to complete the test, etc. The analysis resulted in some insights on the learning habits of students and student motivation. We have also found out, if the topics of the course are presented clearly, and if the complexity of the tasks is of the appropriate level. We also have presented the results of the survey where students have provided their feedback about the MOOC and presentation of learning materials. We believe that the insights and observations gathered can be of use when preparing other courses in the future.

Acknowledgements. The paper is developed in the framework of the MODEIT project in ERASMUS+ grant program under grant no. 2019-1-DE01-KA203-005051 (https://www.mode-it.eu/).

References

1. Agasisti, T., Azzone, G., Soncin, M.: Assessing the effect of Massive Open Online Courses as remedial courses in higher education. Innovations Educ. Teach. Int. 1–10 (2021)
2. Baig, M.A.: Impact of Massive Online Open Courses (MOOCs) on students' achievement-a research review (2019)
3. Bergmann, J., Sams, A.: Flip Your Classroom: Reach Every Student in Every Class Every Day. International society for technology in education (2012)
4. Bergmann, J., Sams, A.: Flipped Learning: Gateway to student Engagement. International Society for Technology in Education (2014)
5. Bralić, A., Divjak, B.: Integrating MOOCs in traditionally taught courses: achieving learning outcomes with blended learning. Int. J. Educ. Technol. High. Educ. 15(1), 1–16 (2018). https://doi.org/10.1186/s41239-017-0085-7
6. Castano-Garrido, C., Garay, U., Maiz, I.: Factores de éxito académico en la integración de los MOOC en el aula universitaria/Factors for academic success in the integration of MOOCs in the university classroom. Revista española de pedagogía, 65–82 (2017)
7. Clark, R.M., et al.: Flipping engineering courses: A school wide initiative. Adv. Eng. Educ. 5(3), 1–39 (2016)
8. Clark, R.M., Kaw, A., Besterfield-Sacre, M.: Comparing the effectiveness of blended, semi-flipped, and flipped formats in an engineering numerical methods course. Adv. Eng. Educ. 5(3), n3 (2016)
9. Daradoumis, T., Bassi, R., Xhafa, F., Caballé, S.: A review on massive e-learning (MOOC) design, delivery and assessment. In: 2013 Eighth International Conference on P2P, Parallel, Grid, Cloud and Internet Computing, pp. 208–213. IEEE (2013)
10. de Lima Guedes, K.K.: Integrating MOOCs into traditional UK higher education: lessons learnt from MOOC-blend practitioners. Education 4, 29–36 (2020)
11. de Moura, V.F., de Souza, C.A., Viana, A.B.N.: The use of Massive Open Online Courses (MOOCs) in blended learning courses and the functional value perceived by students. Comput. Educ. 161, 104077 (2021)
12. Enfield, J.: Looking at the impact of the flipped classroom model of instruction on undergraduate multimedia students at CSUN. TechTrends 57(6), 14–27 (2013)
13. Ferreri, S.P., O'Connor, S.K.: Redesign of a large lecture course into a small-group learning course. Am. J. Pharm. Educ. 77(1) (2013)
14. Fong, M., et al.: Instructors desire student activity, literacy, and video quality analytics to improve video-based blended courses. In: Proceedings of the Sixth (2019) ACM Conference on Learning@ Scale, pp. 1–10 (2019)
15. Giannakos, M.N., Krogstie, J., Chrisochoides, N.: Reviewing the flipped classroom research: reflections for computer science education. In: Proceedings of the Computer Science Education Research Conference, pp. 23–29 (2014)
16. Guo, P.J., Kim, J., Rubin, R.: How video production affects student engagement: an empirical study of MOOC videos. In: Proceedings of the First ACM Conference on Learning@ Scale Conference, pp. 41–50 (2014)

17. Ivala, E., Thiart, A., Gachago, D.: A lecturer's perception of the adoption of the inverted classroom or flipped method of curriculum delivery in a hydrology course, in a resource poor university of technology. In: Proceedings of the International Conference on e-Learning, pp. 207–214 (2013)
18. Lage, M.J., Platt, G.J., Treglia, M.: Inverting the classroom: a gateway to creating an inclusive learning environment. J. Econ. Educ. 31(1), 30–43 (2000)
19. Lee, J., Lim, C., Kim, H.: Development of an instructional design model for flipped learning in higher education. Educ. Tech. Res. Dev. 65(2), 427–453 (2016). https://doi.org/10.1007/s11423-016-9502-1
20. Loo, J.L., et al.: Flipped instruction for information literacy: five instructional cases of academic librarians. J. Acad. Librariansh. 42(3), 273–280 (2016)
21. Pearson, M., Swartz, E., Vazquez, E.A., Striker, R., Singelmann, L.: Driving change using MOOCS in a blended and online learning environment. In: 2019 IEEE Learning With MOOCS (LWMOOCS), pp. 96–100. IEEE (2019)
22. Ponti, M.: Self-directed learning and guidance in non-formal open courses. Learn. Media Technol. 39(2), 154–168 (2014)
23. Sanz Martínez, M.L., Er, E., Dimitriadis Damoulis, I., Martínez Monés, A., Bote Lorenzo, M.L.: Supporting teachers in the design and implementation of group formation policies in MOOCs: a case study (2018)
24. Shnai, I.: Systematic review of challenges and gaps in flipped classroom implementation: toward future model enhancement. In: European Conference on e-Learning, pp. 484–490. Academic Conferences International Limited (2017)
25. Wei, X., Saab, N., Admiraal, W.: Assessment of cognitive, behavioral, and affective learning outcomes in massive open online courses: a systematic literature review. Comput. Educ. 163, 104097 (2021)
26. Wong, K.T., Abdullah, N.B., Goh, P.S.C.: A cross examination of the intention to integrate MOOCs in teaching and learning: an application of multi- group invariance analysis. Int. J. Emerg. Technol. Learn. (iJET) 14(19), 106 (2019). https://doi.org/10.3991/ijet.v14i19.10642

The Ways of Recognition of Open Online Courses

Tim Brueggemann[1], Rita Butkiene[2], Edgaras Dambrauskas[2]([⊠]), Elif Toprak[3],
Cengiz Hakan Aydin[3], Carlos Vaz de Carvalh[4], Diana Andone[5], and Vlad Mihaescu[5]

[1] Fachhochschule Des Mittelstands, Bielefeld, Germany
[2] Kaunas University of Technology, Kaunas, Lithuania
edgaras.dambrauskas@ktu.lt
[3] Anadolu University, Eskişehir, Turkey
[4] Instituto Politecnico Do Porto, Porto, Portugal
[5] University Polytechnic Timisoara, Timişoara, Romania

Abstract. This paper presents the national cases on the open online courses recognition. This result is directly related to the non-formal education, i.e. which means as a collective term for all forms of learning and education which happens in all fields outside of formal educational systems. The lack of accreditation is an issue to be addresses to policymakers. The lack of formal recognition for MOOCs could be a reason why they are taken by participants who already have university degrees, because they are taking courses to update their skills. The paper shows some national cases of the open courses recognition.

Keywords: Digital transformation framework · Competence model · Curriculum development · Self-directed learning · Higher education

1 Introduction

The **recognition**, accreditation and certification of **MOOCs** could be defined in many different ways, but generally, it refers to establishing a set of arrangements to make visible and value all learning outcomes which has been gaining political momentum in Europe since early 2000s [1]. According to the MOONLITE project results (https://moonliteproject.eu/about/mooc-recognition/) we are following the scenarios conception and provide different conceptions in the countries. The aim of the document is to provide a series of recommendations on MOOCs recognition for non-formal learners are expected in Germany, Lithuania, Romania, Turkey and Portugal.

Massive Online Open Courses (hereinafter – MOOCs) falls under the category of distance learning as is primarily aimed at learners being able to acquire new skills or knowledge remotely, without the inherent need for face-to-face interaction. Due to their accessibility and convenience, MOOCs as such, has gained significant popularity during the recent years, especially due to the pandemic situation when technological solutions were necessary as institutions of Higher Education utilised MOOCs to steer the shift to online form of education [2]. The usefulness of MOOCs is further strengthened by

A. Lopata et al. (Eds.): ICIST 2022, CCIS 1665, pp. 296–304, 2022.
https://doi.org/10.1007/978-3-031-16302-9_24

the notion of additional benefits, such as provision of self-paced environment, allowing learners to learn at their own pace [3] and encouragement of lifelong learning [4] which is more complicated to achieve via traditional educational approach.

In general, MOOC popularity as well as mobile learning solutions for MOOCs [5] have been increasing for some time already with the popularity peaking during the COVID 19 period as "numerous universities have adopted online courses and a large number of university students are studying at home" [6] even though some studies [7] indicate that learners may prefer unstructured informal learning courses provided by non-university entities. It has led to services, provided by the private companies to gain additional interest and active users. The report by Class Central[1] indicates that the growth is stable and the top MOOCs providers such as Coursera, edX, FutureLearn or Swayam show numbers, indicating strong positions in the market with the leader, Coursera, having 97 million learners, 6000 courses, 910 microcredentials and 34 degrees by 2021. Due to the volume and popularity of MOOCs as well as new emerging providers, a question of recognitions arises.

Frequently, MOOCs are offered by private entities and therefore there are differences in the process of certification or recognition, in some cases a fee, depending on the type of the course, has to be paid as well. Policy-wise the issue of recognition has been raised by international organizations some time ago[2], even before the spike in their popularity during the pandemic period. The Education 2030 Framework for Action was adopted by 184 UNESCO Member States on 4 November 2015 in Paris, acknowledging that "the provision of flexible learning pathways, as well as the recognition, validation and accreditation of the knowledge, skills and competencies acquired through non-formal and informal education, is important"[3].

Among the established practices of recognition, a number of methods may be distinguished mainly on the basis of transferability and the division of formal and informal education. Farrow et al. [8] distinguish the following categories of recognition methods, all of which are currently in use (Table 1).

Academic credits may act both as a quantitative as well as a qualitative measure [9] and therefore they may be considered to be preferable among higher education institutions as measurement in ETCS becomes comparable between institutions even though slight difference of workload in terms of hours per credit point. While being highly effective for recognition purposes among higher education institutions, a significant share of MOOC providers are business entities, that ten to use their own methods. This is further complicated in the case of informal education as it their acceptance in different institutions may vary greatly. It has to be mentioned, though, that different stakeholders may differ in needs, and due to the lack of unified approach the issue of recognition remains. So far, there is no effective national or worldwide system for collecting, connecting, searching, and comparing current information regarding learning outcomes and credentials in a standard language or format that is globally understood and accessible. This

---

[1] https://www.classcentral.com/report/mooc-stats-2021/.

[2] https://moocbook.pressbooks.com/chapter/recognition-accreditation/.

[3] https://apa.sdg4education2030.org/education-2030-framework-action.

Table 1. Summary of recognition methods (Farrow et al.)

Main category	Sub-category	Brief description
Academic credit	Non-transferable	Academic credit can only be applied to a program offered by the same university
	Transferable	Academic credits can be transferred, either because ECTS are awarded or because specified universities have agreed to accept the credits
Professional credit	Formal	Awards credit hours or credits from formal professional accreditation bodies
	Informal	Informal awards such as a certificate from the MOOC platform or badge from content provider
	Endorsements	Professional certificate backed by business leader, enhancing credibility and increasing work relevance
Combined	Combined	Academic and professional credits awarded. Increases utility for learners

lack of information and systems adds to a sense of confusion, distrust, and rash decision-making when it comes to the recognition of talents and certifications both locally and on the international level [10].

Cha et al. [11] claim that recognition is more than credentialisation but rather combines it with the assessment as well processes that lead to the acknowledgement of learning accomplishments. Assessment is a step of assessment that occurs at various points within the learning process, whereas credentials are issued after formal learning units are completed and "in both cases, these evaluative processes entail a formal endorsement of learning and lead to recognition of achievement of the learner by third parties". The need for recognition of skills gained through informal learning is no less important and continuous skill upgrading and enhancing will help to overcome skilled worker shortages [12]. Today there are solutions that are aimed at learners who constantly have to update skills and knowledge through certification in such fields as healthcare. In such cases, microcredits or badges become the method of choice, although as noticed by Littlejohn et al. [13] it is not an ideal choice for other fields, such as programming where actual skills and being able to demonstrate your skills may be valued more than certifications or qualifications.

While fulfilling their immediate function, microcredentials are still lacking. Inconsistent terminology coupled with low standardization and limited stackability and transferability are key obstacles that have to be overcome in order to adapt to fast-changing market requirements [14]. Unlike formal degrees obtained at higher education institutions, MOOC micro-credentials and degrees provide individuals with an opportunity to adapt to the changing demands of the industry as MOOCs are compatible with work life, up-to date and comparatively low-cost [15]. Consequently, recognition and acceptance of MOOC courses results in continuing professional development, upskilling, reskilling [16].

Moreover, there is important integrating MOOCS into traditional higher education [17, 18]. For some of these professional-development students, the ones who completed and excelled in the courses, the question quickly became: How might my achievement be recognized and validated?

At the same time, universities were beginning to offer MOOCs that were the same as or equivalent to courses offered in their own degree programs. Students who completed these courses also indicated an interest in receiving academic credit for them [18].

Moreover, there is benefit if the courses integrated into the formal education [18, 19, 21] programs. Authors [19, 20] presented developed in the past different methods of integration: as a full course recognition, partial course recognition, or project/activity based recognition of a MOOCs course completion, into a traditional higher education face-to-face course.

2 Cases on Recommendations for MOOC's Recognition in the Countries

As far as the common practices go, there is a significant variety of approaches and points of focus across European countries. This chapter will delve deeper into the exemplary practices of different countries inside and outside EU. In the case of **Germany**, an implementation of the PICK & STUDY concept by the FHM Online University responds to the needs of learners towards receiving flexible and personalized education. The PICK & STUDY program is considered an individual modular study program for all those who want to be prepared for the dynamically changing professional requirements, who need individual credit points (ECTS) for the recognition of their knowledge at a university, or who just want to further educate themselves in a subject area concerned. Instead of completing the entire study course, learners can choose a module of their specific interest to acquire targeted knowledge, skills and competences. Each module is offered fully online and is composed of a series of scientific texts, audio and video files, and tests. The studies are completely self-paced allowing for completing the module while working. The start is possible at any time.

After completing the Pick & Study program, two types of the learning recognition are possible, either issuing a **certificate of attendance** or a **university certificate.** The Certificate of Attendance can be issued to learners who are interested in attending a specific module without receiving credit points. For this type of the recognition, learners do not need to fulfill any admission requirements. To prove the attendance of the module, learners need to complete tests at the end of each subject unit. Learners are free in selecting the date and time of the assessment (assuming it will be completed during the period agreed in the study contract). The number of attempts is unlimited. Once learners have passed all tests of the module, they will receive a certificate of attendance to be attached to their personal resume. The certificate will display all study contents included in the module concerned. In such case, no examination is required.

Meanwhile, the University Certificate option can be chosen by learners who are interested in receiving credit points of the module they attended. In order to get registered for the option University Certificate under the FHM Pick & Study Program, learners have to fulfil specific admission requirements, such as having a general university entrance qualification, a technical college entrance qualification or vocational training with work experience. The University Certificate displays the module grade, the course contents as well as the credit points according to ECTS (European Credit and Accumulation Transfer System). This allows for recognizing the university certificate for any regular course of study at the FHM or at other accredited universities in the European Higher Education Area. in this manner, the University Certificate can be considered as a micro-credential.

In order to obtain the University Certificate, learners have to pass an official university examination after having studied all the module contents. The exam can be conveniently taken as an e-exam without leaving home. Each failed exam can be repeated a maximum of two times during the agreed contract period of six months. The MOOC Competitor Analysis elaborated under the MODE IT project will be added to the Pick & Study program of the FHM Online University by offering two recognition options as described above. The attendance of the module will be free of charge. Only the issuing of the Certificates as well as an examination fee will be charged.

In **Lithuania (Kaunas University of Technology)**, MOOCs are used online for general access (institutional MOOCs platform https://open.ktu.edu/) and those materials are sufficient in scope and quality of content and required associated activities to enable a learner to acquire the competences defined in the expected learning outcomes, and if the university is able to assess the competences, then credits or certificates can be easily awarded. Among the advantages offered by MOOCs, Erasmus exchange students studying MOOCs can be seen as participating in virtual exchanges. Thus, the university must be assured of the quality of the MOOC that a student will study – a process which would be codified in agreements similar to Erasmus agreements. Furthermore, the Summer School scenario can go with Erasmus exchange possibilities, because in this case although the learner is a current student the hosting organization, student can gain ECTS credits from a university with no relationship with her/his current university.

Credits or Certification may be utilized as proof of assessment the learner using the methods it has decided are appropriate for its own MOOC and offers credits to be taken. The parallel in traditional university education would be organized Continuing Professional Development courses (CPD) where individual modules are studied without enrolment into a degree programme. Flexible approach to recognition is an advantage for further skill development or continuing learning after a time gap. For this reason, Recognition of Prior Learning (RPL) may be organized to varying extents to enable entry to degree programmes of students whose background does contain suitable academic study for automatic entry. Allowing learners who have studied using open learning materials to enter a university, some form of recognition of prior learning will normally be required. If the learner is able to explicitly prove that a specific set of learning outcomes has been assessed in the MOOC, the burden of RPL will be much reduced.

Currently, there are currently five traditional scenarios in Anadolu, **Turkey**. Although it is not an institutional policy, the professors/teachers in Anadolu University are able to ask their students complete some MOOCs as a requirement of their formal courses. This type of a MOOC integration is gaining popularity among professors/instructors due to the fact that there is a growing interest in MOOCs among students. They are not only completing a requirement of their courses and getting a credit but also often receiving certificates to be included into their curricula vitae. In addition, we are collaborating with several worldwide known MOOC providers to establish MOOC based online graduate programs, such as master's program on "technology-based learning", "educational communications" and certificate programs like "online teaching", "corporate teaching", etc. So that, we will be able to integrate MOOCs into formal curricula in different fields.

Anadolu University has MOOCs platform, titled as AKADEMA, where it offers more than 130 MOOCs in Turkish. A great deal of these courses are created from scratch to be able to (1) show the HE community and especially decision makers in Turkey that with the right design any subject and competencies including science, music, psychomotor skills, etc., can be taught online as effectively as face-to-face, and (2) to help academic staff to gain online teaching skills and knowhow in their fields. There are two types of MOOCs: self-paced (always open) and guided (facilitated by real instructors, with certain start and end dates, interaction with the facilitator is a must, offered three times in a year). The course subjects vary from soft skills to employability skills, from sports to science, from personal development to corporate affairs. The primary target group of these MOOCs is students in Anadolu's distance and face-to-face (25K) programs. The courses are free of any charge. Students who complete a MOOC receive a "completion document" but those who would like to get a "achievement certificate" should pay a nominal fee and take proctored online exams in local branches of Anadolu University located throughout the country. Courses especially focusing on employability skills, such "how to prepare a CV", "Effective Job Interviews", etc. are among the most preferred courses among the students.

Anadolu uses MOOCs especially in the AKADEMA platform as a testbed environment for piloting some of the innovative instructional strategies and tools before integrating into formal courses and programs. For instance, an advance notification system that provides feedback and recommendations based on the students' time-spend-on-tasks was developed and tested in a MOOC. And then, after revisions it was integrated into formal courses. It is also seen as the MOOCs in the AKADEMA platform as supplementary materials, or remedial instructional opportunities for those students who fall behind in formal courses. For instance, in the theology program it was noticed that some students were not able to progress and dropped-out the program due to shortage of Arabic language skills. Anadolu has created several MOOCs on Arabic Language in different levels and then offered to not only those theology students but everyone who would like to learn. Some of the theology students took benefit of these courses and started to perform better in their formal courses.

Regarding the international students, in AKADEMA platform, Anadolu univesity also offers MOOCs on Turkish language for those who would like to learn Turkish. These courses are recommended to those Erasmus students or any other students coming from outside Turkey or refugees who would like to study or pursue their education in Anadolu. Although the international students can also enroll the face-to-face Turkish language prep courses when they come to Anadolu, those who complete the MOOCs before coming the Anadolu spend less or no time in those language prep courses.

In **Portugal**, the traditional learning scenarios is still very much oriented towards face-to-face and blended learning using a customized Moodle platform (http://moodle.isep.ip.pt). MOOCs are used to complement some curses either by recommendation of the teachers or by initiative of the learners themselves but they are not credited in the formal programme. With MODE-IT several courses have integrated MOOC-based learning as formal pedagogical approaches and are formally credited as such. Erasmus possibilities for recognition based on several virtual or blended mobility courses and activities running at PPORTO but they don't use MOOCs as the basis for the contents. These students and the traditional mobility Erasmus + students normally enroll in the Learning Management System provided by PPORTO. Summer Schools run only in face-to-face mode. They are recognized as an independent training programme, not included in the formal academic programmes. Teachers might recommend MOOCs as part of the training course.

As for the credits and certification, during the implementation of MODE-IT several courses have integrated MOOC-based learning as formal pedagogical approaches and are formally credited as such. Before that the MOOC components were not formally recognized or credited. Recognition of Prior Learning (RPL), however, is subject to formal state regulations and is normally subject of an evaluation by professors either to enable entry to degree programmes or to give equivalence to some courses. The recognition of MOOC-based credits is not usual and must be received through a recognized academic entity.

In **Romania** there are several scenarios which exist. All UPT students are enrolled in the Virtual Campus of University Polytechnic Timisoara (UPT), a Moodle based virtual learning environment (VLE), https://cv.upt.ro/. Even if some courses are created in a MOOC-alike format, the courses are not "open" and also many of them are not "massive". Another scenario involves integration of external MOOCs into the Bachelor of Master programs courses. Some teachers are giving as a project based activity or as an exam activity the completion of external MOOC courses, related to the university's course topic.

Finally, several MOOCs are implemented on the open VLE/MOOC platform of UPT, UniCampus, https://unicampus.ro/. These are open for everyone to register and are offered by teachers from UPT and also from some project partners. All courses on UniCampus are self-paced and have some sort of examination. Depending on the completed MOOC, participants might receive a digital open badge or a digital certificate. Meanwhile, Erasmus students are encouraged to enroll in MOOC courses from the UniCampus platform. However, they cannot choose a MOOC course to be recognized through the ECTS system.

Regarding credits and certification, UPT respects the ECTS standards. The list of credits obtained by the student is reported in the Transcript of Records issued by UPT. There is an internal university process, respecting the national legislation, for offering credits on the supplement diploma or for offering a post-university studies certificate for those completing certain MOOC courses. UPT, through the Centre for eLearning, has started promoting the use of microcredentials and digital open badges also. However, the national legislation is very strict regarding the official recognition of these. Some MOOC courses offer a pre-course self-assessment, based on which recommendations are made to learners into which modules of the MOOC to focus upon.

3 Conclusions

As it was discussed, recognition practices differ region-to-region, however, the variety of recognition types even within the same institution indicates that higher education institutions are constantly looking for solutions, suitable to improve current practices. It is also important that countries focus not only on the formal education but on informal one as well in an attempt to include learners who continue improving their knowledge and skills later in life or choose to supplement their skills with new ones and require a proof of their newly-acquired knowledge. Lastly, it is vitally important that similar practices are implement not only on a national level, as transnational cooperation and recognition will allow learners to receive more advantageous mobility options both physically and remotely by finding institutions or organizations providing study programmes or courses abroad without facing acceptance issues in their home country.

References

1. Villalba-García, E.: Validation of non-formal and informal learning: the hero with a thousand faces? Eur. J. Educ. **56**(3), 351–364 (2021)
2. Baudo, V., Mezzera, D.: Insights from a MOOC Platform during COVID-19 Pandemic in Italy. In: EDEN Conference Proceedings, No. 1, pp. 401–409 (2021)
3. Rafiq, K.R.M., Hashim, H., Yunus, M.M.: MOOC for training: how far it benefits employees? In: Journal of Physics: Conference Series, vol. 1424, no. 1, p. 012033. IOP Publishing (2019)
4. Aljaraideh, Y.: Massive Open Online Learning (MOOC) benefits and challenges: a case study in Jordanian context. Int. J. Instr. **12**(4), 65–78 (2019)
5. Antonova, A., Bontchev, B.: Investigating MOOC platforms as a prospective tool for mobile learning. In: 16th International Conference Mobile Learning, pp. 2–4 (2020)
6. Nasulea, C., Nasulea, D.F.: Teaching economics In: The Cloud: Assessing the Efficiency of Online Economics Teaching Methods. In Proceedings of EDULEARN21 Conference, vol. 5, p. 6th (2021)
7. Kang, K., Wang, T., Chen, S., Su, Y.S.: Push-pull-mooring analysis of Massive Open Online Courses and college students during the COVID-19 Pandemic. Front. Psychol. **12**, 755137 (2021)
8. Farrow, R., Ferguson, R., Weller, M., Pitt, R., Sanzgiri, J., Habib, M.: Assessment and recognition of MOOCs: the state of the art. J. Innovation Polytech. Educ. **3**(1), 15–26 (2021)
9. O'Sullivan, T.: Lessons from 'MOOCs for credit'-turning non-formal learning into formal credit
10. Chakroun, B., Keevy, J.: Digital credentialing: implications for the recognition of learning across borders (2018)
11. Cha, H., So, H.J.: Integration of formal, non-formal and informal learning through MOOCs. In: Burgos, D. (ed.) Radical solutions and open science. LNET, pp. 135–158. Springer, Singapore (2020). https://doi.org/10.1007/978-981-15-4276-3_9
12. Kiers, J., Van Der Werff, J.H.: The future of work requires a future of professional learning: from stand-alone, academic MOOCs to programmes that are relevant for professionals. In: EMOOCs-WIP, pp. 247–253 (2019)
13. Littlejohn, A., Pammer-Schindler, V.: Technologies for professional learning. In: Harteis, C., Gijbels, D., Kyndt, E. (eds.) Research Approaches on Workplace Learning. PPL, vol. 31, pp. 321–346. Springer, Cham (2022). https://doi.org/10.1007/978-3-030-89582-2_15

14. Resei, C., Friedl, C., Staubitz, T., Rohloff, T.: Micro-credentials in EU and Global. Corship, July (2019)
15. Lewis, M.J., Lodge, J.M.: Keep calm and credential on: linking learning, life and work practices in a complex world. In: Ifenthaler, D., Bellin-Mularski, N., Mah, D.-K. (eds.) Foundation of digital badges and micro-credentials, pp. 41–54. Springer International Publishing, Cham (2016). https://doi.org/10.1007/978-3-319-15425-1_3
16. Özbek, E.A.: Digital transformation, MOOCS, micro-credentials and MOOC-based degrees: implications for higher education. In: International Open and Distance Learning Conference Proceedings Book, p. 37
17. Geng, L., Xu, M., Wei, Z., Zhou, X.: Learning deep spatiotemporal feature for engagement recognition of online courses. In: 2019 IEEE Symposium Series on Computational Intelligence (SSCI), pp. 442–447. IEEE (2019)
18. Sandeen, C.: Integrating MOOCs into traditional higher education: the emerging "MOOC 3.0" era. Change Mag. High. Learn. **45**(6), 34–39 (2013)
19. Harris, J., Wihak, C.: The recognition of non-formal education in higher education: where are we now, and are we learning from experience? Int. J. E-Learn. Distance Educ. **33**(1), 1–19 (2018)
20. Andone, D., Mihaescu, V., Ternauciuc, A., Vasiu, R.: Integrating MOOCs in traditional higher education. In: Proceedings of the Third European MOOCs Stakeholder Summit, pp. 71–75 (2015)
21. Dubbaka, A., Gopalan, A.: Detecting learner engagement in MOOCs using automatic facial expression recognition. In: 2020 IEEE Global Engineering Education Conference (EDUCON), pp. 447–456). IEEE (2020)

A Case Study on Gaming Implementation for Social Inclusion and Civic Participation

Afxentis Afxentiou[1], Peter Frühmann[2], Maria Kyriakidou[3], Maria Patsarika[3],
Daina Gudoniene[4(✉)], Andrius Paulauskas[4], Alicia García-Holgado[5],
and Francisco José García-Peñalvo[5]

[1] Center for Social Innovation, 62 Rigenis Street, Nicosia, Cyprus
`afxentis.afxentiou@csicy.com`
[2] ZB&V - Narrative Research, Esdoornplantsoen 11, 1326 BW Almere, The Netherlands
`peter@storybag.nl`
[3] Educational Association Anatolia, 17 Sevenidi St., 55535 Thessaloniki, Greece
`{markyria,mpatsarika}@act.edu`
[4] Kaunas University of Technology, Studentu 50, 51367 Kaunas, Lithuania
`{daina.gudoniene,andrius.paulauskas}@ktu.lt`
[5] GRIAL Research Group, Computer Science Department, University of Salamanca,
Salamanca, Spain
`{aliciagh,fgarcia}@usal.es`

Abstract. The aim of the paper is to present the processes of the game implementation and design. Nowadays technologies could play an active role in promoting social inclusion and equal participation by providing people with interactive experiences on these subjects. Paper authors are developing a game that will engage learners and motivate them to learn from simulated experience-enhancing critical reflection on social and political circumstances, build skills and stimulate interest for collective action. The paper presents a case study on gaming implementation in practice.

Keywords: Game · Social · Civic inclusion

1 Introduction

Nowadays, students are significantly influenced by the digital era and are constantly handling digital information. As a result, they form their personalities in the light of flexible communities, pursue to be directly connected, require prompt responses and social interaction and prefer learning based on experiences [1]. Moreover, the authors highlight the importance of playing and games themselves in human development; to briefly present learning theories that support the use of games in learning; to define the main characteristics of game-based learning; to define board games in relation to adult education - learning outcomes of board games and competences that may be built and developed through board games. This paper is part of the research within an international cooperation project that aims to develop and implement game-based learning in adult education through board games and role-plays [2].

A. Lopata et al. (Eds.): ICIST 2022, CCIS 1665, pp. 305–314, 2022.
https://doi.org/10.1007/978-3-031-16302-9_25

However, there is also an important focus on minorities of students. Gaming has not only been for entertainment purposes, but has also been used to improve and engage minority students. The exploration of meaningful experience for both classroom and gaming technology has been a challenge in developing new problem-solving strategies for minorities globally. Minorities continue to experience disparities in different domains based on various factors such as ethnicity, culture, socio-economic background and gender. The disparity is also vastly influenced by the local cultural trends [3].

Social orders that create disparities based on gender, religion, or ethnicity do not happen without reason and are not predetermined. According to [3], effective educational practices can make a positive difference in understanding and building awareness of those practices and also help us challenge and transform those social practices. Education is much more than getting ready for the job market; education provides us tools for our social conduct, the strength of character, and self-respect [3]. Educational elements can be integrated into the gameplay, which will be subconsciously acquired by the players during the gaming process [4].

Authors discuss about the technology and social inclusion and different participation through different perspectives. The paper presents a general framework for the game levels implementation.

2 Literature Review

In the field of game studies, there are multiple perspectives on what is a game, although it is possible to identify some common aspects, such as the existence of rules that orient and limit players; conflict or contest; a clear goal-orientation or outcome-orientation; activities, processes, or events that involve decision-making [5].

The technology could play a role in promoting social inclusion and equal participation through different perspectives:

1. in terms of information distribution;
2. technology involves the younger generation, but live communication is more conducive to a sense of community and involvement and empathy; through the media and social networks;
3. it makes communication easier and more participants can be involved;
4. technology could help with getting involved in activities and share the practical information;
5. it helps to understand the problems and possible solutions;
6. technologies are growing and getting better and better very quickly, so it could play a role in promoting social inclusion and equal participation soon;
7. technologies are just a tool to present;
8. it makes people aware of social injustices and engages them to participate;
9. a visualization tool to engage or to help to understand the problem;
10. it expands the target group by involving more people in civic engagement using social networks, web-based technologies, electronic billboards and more;
11. technology gives opportunities to reach broader audiences, everybody who is using Internet is equal (clothing, surroundings, devices cannot be seen, judged);

12. technology also is used to maintain the motivation;
13. it is an important facilitator of social inclusion for people with disabilities in society as it helps to deliver real-time services that can enable individuals to learn (even fully participate in education), work, socialize, shop, and interact with the community without being subject to physical barriers;

Furthermore, technology could play an active role in promoting social inclusion and equal participation by providing people with interactive experiences on these subjects. In particular, we are developing a game that will engage learners and motivate them to learn from simulated experience-enhancing critical reflection on social and political circumstances, build skills and stimulate interest for collective action, i.e. (1) a lot of these types of games (serious, educational) have an imbalanced development focus. They tend to sideline the gameplay and game design part of development. It's necessary to strike for the perfect balance; (2) a game needs to have the properties that a usual addictive online game has; (3) project goals should not overwhelm the game itself; (4) the game should be oriented towards quality (professional design, models, sounds, etc...), better less scope than less quality; (5) a game should include some form of gamification and could use social networks; (6) one of the most important aspects of any kind of learning is relevance and authenticity; (7) when it comes to virtual learning, we can consider interactivity, connectivism, engaging tasks, gamification aspects, and high-quality graphics.

This work describes a case study on gaming for social inclusion and civic participation developed in the frame of the INGAME project, an Erasmus + project funded by the European Union that involves institutions from Spain, Romania, Greece, Lithuania, The Netherlands, Cyprus, Italy and Poland. The presented case study is based on the results of the Transnational INGAME Ecosystem Mapping Report which was developed by compiling the INGAME National Reports and the EU Report developed by the project partners. According to the Dutch national report, the game should inform players, stimulate encourage players to engage, and stimulate reflection and conversations on the topics. One has to be sure that the stated final learning objectives are achieved within a defined timeframe. Greek stakeholders suggested that INGAME should necessarily have good and engaging storytelling and that it should definitely be user friendly, with nice graphics and gender-sensitive avatars, including decision making options that would promote cultural diversity. Lithuanian results indicate that it is necessary to find a perfect balance between the development part related to gameplay and game design. The project goals should not overwhelm the game itself; a game should include some form of gamification and could use social networks. The game will not be too complicated so that anyone with no experience can go through several levels. It has to be interactive, with a friendly environment, attractive and possibly based on levels. According to the Polish stakeholders, gamification solutions must be supported by clear instructions for users to understand how to proceed and what is their aim. The game should be easily accessible, have good graphics and interesting content. One of the suggestions is that the game should have feature realistic scenarios and should be available on different devices, not only on PC, but mobile devices and should include good practices – some practical examples, also it would be great if there will be a possibility to connect with other users.

Regarding the Cyprus national report, video games could be based on realistic social and political issues e.g., a game combating racism, social inequality, empowering critical thinking, learning through experience, socializing and meeting other people, making decisions with teammates. A video game should be also competitive. Also, in terms of their structure, it is important that this game is interactive and multiplayer in order to promote collaboration between players and their interactivity. Italian stakeholders indicate that. the game, while dealing with serious topics, should maintain its playful aspect; it should simulate situations and circumstances very similar to reality, stimulate further reflections and propose in-depth analysis, depending on the game choices. Through a scoring system, the game should challenge the user to act not only in the virtual world but also in reality. Moreover, the Spanish stakeholders highlighted some technical characteristics. In particular, the game should be open access and take into account user accessibility. From the perspective of the narration, of the characters, the game should adhere to real-life without giving up the playful element. Furthermore, the gamification could be used to enhance critical reflection on the social and political circumstances of young adults, i.e. (1) it could provide a better framework of reference, introduce more external motivators, thus somewhat increasing motivation; (2) through engaging activities and discovery of relevant topics; (3) It helps to involve young people; (4) Virtual reality-based games can improve many skills; (5) gamification can help in the political actions as well; (6) gamification should take race, gender, religion and free will of people into account. Giving freedom to reflect the ideology of the player and not be punished because of this. There should be no discrimination due to his/her gender or race or religion. More interactive and task solving should be involved; (7) gamification can be used as a tool to maintain the motivation to participate more and acquire deeper knowledge about social and political circumstances.

E-participation in the games, as any means of engagement with the common good, is, however, a difficult area of human motivation as it can be seen to exist outside the common hurdles of everyday life and where the effects of participation are often invisible or take a long time to materialize. Recent trends of digitalization, such as gamification; a popular approach for stimulating motivation, have been proposed as remedies to foster e-participation [6].

Another paper aims to demonstrate the role played by gamification in encouraging citizens to create well-founded and concrete proposals, and to obtain, as a consequence, answers by politicians (qualified responses in the following) [7].

In the context of *smart communities*, an active and continuous collaboration between citizens, organizations and institutions is essential. There are several cases where citizens may be asked to participate such as in the public decision-making process by informing, voting or proposing projects or in crisis management by sharing precise and timely information with other citizens and emergency organizations [8].

However, gaming has revealed several distinct differences between players of varying gameplay motivations. Social motivations, including an interest in socializing, forming relationships, and engaging in team play, have been found to positively affect users' feelings of happiness and well-being [9]. Another author [10] examined relations among civic engagement, political efficacy, and social responsibility by young people. His finding pointed out that political efficacy is related to four domains of civic engagement:

helping, community action, formal political action, and activism. The unresolved young people issues result in unemployment and disengagement with the social transformation. In the EU, the most important social challenges are given by the EU.

One of the emerging trends in the field of public participation is gamification. Participatory processes increasingly apply strategies and dynamics borrowed from games to promote a more diverse demographic of engagement and to incentivize desirable behaviour by the participants. While many scholars and practitioners highlight the practical benefits of gamification, others warn us of the potential risks of the ludification of public participation, especially if applied in a learning context [11].

Gamification is an umbrella term used when referring to game elements in non-game systems being used to improve user experience and engagement [12]. Furthermore, recent studies indicate that gamification show positive results in acquiring new skills and optimizing the learning process [13]. Current studies indicate that gamification can be used as a tool for increasing learner engagement and motivation if a teacher is able to use it correctly in a timely manner [14]. Therefore, it should be noted that gamification has been frequently addressed and used in the field of education, where maintaining and increasing interest is a continual issue [15]. Rapp et al. claim that today progress has been made in determining the processes through which gamification can achieve better results in comparison with a non-gamified approach. Individual game mechanics can have an influence on individual behavioural results, according to the study. As a result of these developments, some critics believe that gamification research has matured [16].

The concept of gamification, its uses and effectiveness are related to the popularity and success of such well-known applications as Duolingo for language learning or Codeacademy for learning how to code [17]. While skill development apps are a common space for the application of gamification, the motivation it provides can be further applied to achieve lasting real-life effects as well as positive behaviour changes. Gamified mHealth applications are a potential way to get people to modify their health habits. MHealth applications, in particular, have the potential to help with illness management and prevention, as well as supporting healthier lifestyle by encouraging physical activity and a balanced diet [18].

While standpoints on gamification for education varies as well as its reception, studies tend to show positive results. A study by Chapman and Rich show that almost two thirds of participants in an organizational behavior course reported that the educational gamification environment used increased their perceived motivation further amplified by components that include tracking one's own and others' progress, as well as those that provide feedback on performance [19].

Games not only help in the learning process but also increase users' knowledge of the virtual world or virtual space in which the game takes place [20].

3 Levels Based Games Implementation

The game we are developing is a 'coming of age journey' of a (humanoid) youngster from a remote civilisation from outer space who lands on earth and has to learn about our planet, its inhabitants and their ways. The avatar (the player) is supported and nudged by a 'mentor' (NPC), challenged and questioned by 'others' (NPC), and facilitated through information (NPC). In six levels it grows up to become a young adult. It becomes more and more aware of human (inter)actions, what works in society and whatnot, and what the consequences of all that are for the planet. In total, 6 levels are used in the game (see Fig. 1).

Level 1 – gender (equality). The avatar (player) has to find out/learn about (the difference between) sex (and sexual orientation) and gender (gender identity, gender equality, gender norms, gender roles, gender discrimination, etc.). It will encounter its first humans and their stories of experience. There are three (overlapping) issues within this level: 1. Gender and sex, 2. gender identity and gender roles; gender (in) equality), and 3. gender norms and exclusion (discrimination).

Level 2 – education (equality and equity). Education (at home and in school) plays an important role in knowledge (of the world) and development of the 'self' (i.e. identity, self-esteem), but also an individual's background (i.e. socio-economic, cultural) we also have to understand that 'equal chances' are not as equal as we think. It goes for society in general, but specifically for education. The player has to find out/learn about (the difference between) 'equality' and 'equity', how cultural and socio-economic backgrounds, political and social trends and discourses (and prejudices) shape the whole education process and the self-perception up to finding a place in society and the job market. The player should develop empathy (with other (young) learners) and an increased understanding of the right to a good education for everyone.

Level 3 – social inclusion. We want the player to become aware that social exclusion (including stigmatisation, stereotyping, discrimination, racism) can happen in different spaces: the labour market, in the participation in communities, in public policy and (service) institutions, in legal norms and rights, in informal (community) norms and practices, and in (basic) human capabilities in dealing with 'others'. The player will experience a moment of exclusion and will have to find out and learn how to turn that around towards (social) inclusion by either choosing solutions that promote that and/or finding out 'the hard way' how we sometimes fail in offering support. In the end, an increased sense of 'equity' and justice, but also empathy and compassion for others, will lead to successful inclusion.

Level 4 – city life. We want the player to become aware of policies and visions (or no vision) of governments and municipalities when it comes to city development now and in the (far) future.

Create awareness of (possible) neighbourhood (citizens') initiatives that promote cohesion and sustainability, and the potential resourcefulness of mixed, diverse neighbourhoods. But also awareness of discrimination (e.g. migrant neighbourhoods) and the people who live there. Awareness of 'renovation' of old neighbourhoods (often low income) that favours 'gentrification' and disadvantages lower incomes. Finally, a glimpse of the cities of the future: greener, more social, self-sufficient and sustainable.

Level 5 – environment/climate change. We want the player to become aware of a number of issues around the environment, the urban and the global, and that – in a way – they go hand in hand. Water pollution (urban, agriculture, industry), and its consequences for hygiene and health (humans, plants, animals) and ocean life. Air pollution (urban, agriculture, industry, transport, etc.) and its consequences on the atmosphere (carbon dioxide and other 'greenhouse' gas emissions) and thus global warming. The

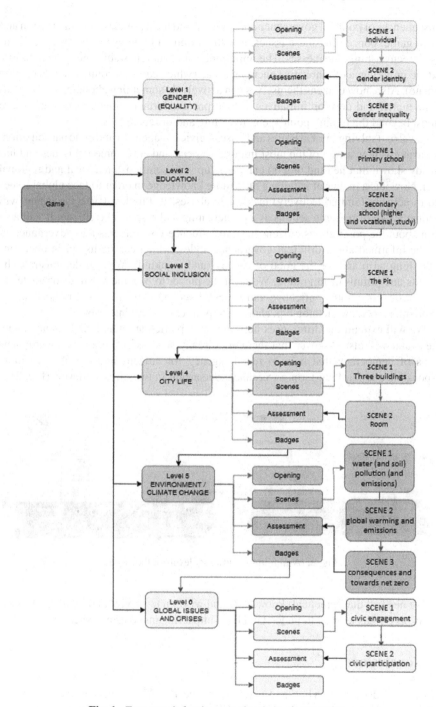

Fig. 1. Framework for the game levels implementation.

consequences of political governance and national and local policies (procrastination and blame game) concerning these issues, and the turning a blind eye to (or even facilitating) 'greenwashing' businesses. The importance of clean renewable energy generation, and the importance of innovative energy storage (which can also contribute to a cleaner climate). Also, how citizens themselves can actively do something about the seriousness of the matter and develop initiatives to help prevent further climate warming ('we're almost beyond the tipping point'), e.g. recycling and/or reusing.

Level 6 – (solving) global issues and crises – civic engagement and civic participation. The avatar is now aware of the most important social and environmental issues and has already shown that he (and others) can come up with solutions on a local and regional level. Now it is a matter of gaining a little more knowledge in order to face global issues and to actively (and collectively) tackle any abuses. In this last level, the avatar will become aware of possible actions as a participating and responsible citizen. It will also learn about the possibilities citizens have to influence governments and governance. It will be informed about different governance styles, which can be useful in decisions in the long term and for the good of society (and mankind). We will demonstrate the benefits and pitfalls of migration. We want the player to become aware of obstacles to democratic, cooperative, effective and peaceful societies (polarization, radicalization, terrorism, autocracy, dictatorship, short-term political (party) interests…).

We will explain the differences between civic participation and civic engagement. The avatar will also discover that there are already successful initiatives towards new forms of democracy that help to regain agency for citizens and can lead to more responsible and fair long-term governance. See avatar in two different levels (Fig. 2).

Fig. 2. Avatar in two different levels of the game.

We need all that (practical) knowledge and wisdom to survive and by its actions our avatar/player has learned to understand that (https://ingame.erasmus.site/).

4 Conclusions

Educational design, storyline and narrative of the INGAME solution and the overall content can further be used for fostering EU citizens' positive attitudes towards social inclusion, gender equality, civic participation as well as the development of competences and intercultural skills.

INGAME encourages players to explore, engage and participate: this theme corresponded to the challenge of empowering and building resilience in young people to participate in society on many levels, and develop capacities to socially and culturally engage and enter the labour market. This is achieved by presenting multiple game levels, each of them corresponding to a specific society-wide issue, presented in an easily understandable format.

The digital transformation of society offers new challenges but also tremendous opportunities in achieving social and civic inclusion via technological and creative solutions, allowing easier visualisation of issues as well as increased engagement with the topic.

Acknowledgement. This project was undertaken with the support of the Erasmus+ Programme of the European Union in its Key Action 3: "Social inclusion and common values: the contribution in the field of education and training. Project INGAME - Gaming for Social Inclusion and Civic Participation – A holistic approach for a cultural shift in education and policy (Reference number 612166-ES-EPPKA3-IPI-SOC-IN) (https://ingame.erasmus.site/lt/results-2/#). The European Commission's support for the production of this publication does not constitute an endorsement of the contents, which reflect the views only of the authors, and the Commission cannot be held responsible for any use which may be made of the information contained therein.

References

1. Anastasiadis, T., Lampropoulos, G., Siakas, K.: Digital game-based learning and serious games in education. Int. J. Adv. Sci. Res. Eng. **4**(12), 139–144 (2018)
2. Boghian, I., Cojocariu, V.M., Popescu, C.V., Mâță, L.: Game-based learning. Using board games in adult education. J. Educ. Sci. Psychol. **9**(1) (2019)
3. Misra, R., Eyombo, L., Phillips, F.T.: Minority experiences and use of games in education around the world. In Research Anthology on Developments in Gamification and Game-Based Learning, pp. 1549–1559. IGI Global (2022)
4. Zhonggen, Y.: A meta-analysis of use of serious games in education over a decade. Int. J. Comput. Games Technol. (2019)
5. Costa, C., Marcelino, L., Neves, J., Sousa, C.: Games for education of deaf students–a systematic literature review. In: ECGBL19-Proceedings of the 13th European Conference on Game Based Learning, pp. 170–181, October 2019
6. Hassan, L., Hamari, J.: Gameful civic engagement: a review of the literature on gamification of e-participation. Gov. Inf. Q. **37**(3), 101461 (2020)
7. Bianchini, D., Fogli, D., Ragazzi, D.: Promoting citizen participation through gamification. In: Proceedings of the 9th Nordic Conference on Human-Computer Interaction, pp. 1–4, October 2016
8. Romano, M., Díaz, P., Aedo, I.: Gamification-less: may gamification really foster civic participation? A controlled field experiment. J. Ambient Intell. Humaniz. Comput. 1–15 (2021)
9. Castillo, R.P.: Exploring the differential effects of social and individualistic gameplay motivations on bridging social capital for users of a massively multiplayer online game. Comput. Hum. Behav. **91**, 263–270 (2019)
10. Perko, I., Mendiwelso-Bendek, Z.: Gaming for introducing social challenges and responsibility to Young people. J. Contemp. Issues Econ. Bus. **64**(4), 34–47 (2018)

11. Meloni, M., Antunes, S.: Games for citizen participation. In: International Conference Democracy and Participation in the 21st Century. ISA (2017)
12. Deterding, S., Sicart, M., Nacke, L., O'Hara, K., Dixon, D.: Gamification. using game-design elements in non-gaming contexts. In: CHI 2011 Extended Abstracts on Human Factors in Computing Systems, pp. 2425–2428 (2011)
13. Alhammad, M.M., Moreno, A.M.: Gamification in software engineering education: a systematic mapping. J. Syst. Softw. **141**, 131–150 (2018)
14. Zainuddin, Z., Chu, S.K.W., Shujahat, M., Perera, C.J.: The impact of gamification on learning and instruction: a systematic review of empirical evidence. Educ. Res. Rev. **30**, 100326 (2020)
15. Majuri, J., Koivisto, J., Hamari, J.: Gamification of education and learning: a review of empirical literature. In: Proceedings of the 2nd International GamiFIN Conference, GamiFIN 2018. CEUR-WS (2018)
16. Rapp, A., Hopfgartner, F., Hamari, J., Linehan, C., Cena, F.: Strengthening gamification studies: current trends and future opportunities of gamification research. Int. J. Hum. Comput. Stud. **127**, 1–6 (2019)
17. Van Roy, R., Zaman, B.: Need-supporting gamification in education: an assessment of motivational effects over time. Comput. Educ. **127**, 283–297 (2018)
18. Schmidt-Kraepelin, M., Thiebes, S., Sunyaev, A.: Investigating the relationship between user ratings and gamification–a review of mHealth apps in the apple app store and google play store (2019)
19. Chapman, J.R., Rich, P.J.: Does educational gamification improve students' motivation? If so, which game elements work best? J. Educ. Bus. **93**(7), 315–322 (2018)
20. Noemí, P.M., Máximo, S.H.: Educational games for learning. Univ. J. Educ. Res. **2**(3), 230–238 (2014)

Designing MOOC Based on the Framework for Teacher Professional Development in STEAM

Renata Burbaitė[1] ⓘ, Ligita Zailskaitė-Jakštė[1(✉)] ⓘ, Lina Narbutaitė[1],
Armantas Ostreika[1] ⓘ, Aušra Urbaitytė[1], Piet Kommers[2] ⓘ, Sümeyye Hatice Eral[3] ⓘ,
Ceyda Aydos[3], and Şükran Koç[3]

[1] Kaunas University of Technology, Donelaičio str. 73, 44249 Kaunas, Lithuania
`ligita.zailskaite@ktu.lt`
[2] BothSocial, Keulenstraat 12, 7418 ET Deventer, The Netherlands
[3] Directorate of General Innovation and Educational Technologies, Ministry of National
Education, Emniyet Mahallesi Milas Sokak No:8, 06500 Yenimahalle/Ankara, Turkey

Abstract. Massive Open Online Courses (MOOCs) can be especially useful in the Science, Technology, Engineering, Arts and Mathematics (STEAM) field to provide a large number of teachers with appropriate content for their professional development. On the other hand, we still have to think, how to use STEAM in virtual platforms for robotical learning (r-learning) and ensure appropriate skills attainment of teachers.

Best practices, how to design better MOOCs for teacher's professional development, are still in search. In this paper, we offer MOOCs with a theoretical background describing STEAM models for teachers continues professional development (TCPD).

The aim of the paper is to present the relationship between proposed framework for teachers' professional development in STEAM and MOOC platform.

The objectives of the study are: 1) to presents the analysis of the existing STEAM models for teachers' professional development; 2) to presents framework for teachers' professional development in STEAM Teacher Training & Training Curriculum model with robotical education; 3) to presents methodology for MOOC design on Framework for Teacher Professional Development in STEAM usage for r-learning implementation.

Keywords: MOOCs · STEAM · Teacher continues professional development · 21st-century skills

1 Introduction

The teacher's professional development in the STEAM is of big importance but at the same time it raises a lot of challenges. One of them is appropriate content preparation and integration into the MOOCs in order to provide a large number of the teachers with

A. Lopata et al. (Eds.): ICIST 2022, CCIS 1665, pp. 315–330, 2022.
https://doi.org/10.1007/978-3-031-16302-9_26

training, to ensure the teachers satisfaction and appropriate knowledge obtainment. The MOOCs usage should be intuitive and don't distract from the learning activities.

Another important issue in the STEAM field is the material about robotics integration in MOOCs. Different robotics kits are tangible and more understandable, when learners can touch and to constrain them. When we want to transfer content from offline to online environments trying to incorporate r-learning in MOOCs we have to think about educational, methodological characteristics (hardware and software parts) and how to ensure teachers professional development with all the requirements for the 21st century skills.

The paper consists of three parts: first part discloses the literature review of existing models and for teachers' professional development necessary in STEAM; second part presents the framework for teacher professional development in STEAM field; third part presents the MOOC design based on the proposed framework.

2   The Search of Teachers Professional Development Framework

Teachers face a special urgency to stay 'life-long learners' themselves. Not only in order to keep complimenting the fast evolution of content domains like in STEAM. MOOCs can provide teachers with easy accession of appropriate resources for their professional development.

Even more urgent as the notion of 'learning' in the 21st century is evolving so quickly and essential. Subsequently, the 'framework' for teachers' professional development should be an agile and a dynamic one. Traditionally it has been teacher inservice training courses that were the best occasions to update teachers' skills and expertise. Nowadays it is "teachers' 'communities of practice' that have the best reputation. And even more recently they are 'Web-based Communities' for sharing best practice specimens. So, in the search for a proper 'framework', the overall metaphor for developing teacher competences is 'sharing' and 'collaborative design' so that an optimal momentum from many corners from the educational fields will penetrate.

The STEAM field requires a holistic approach for teachers' role in the educational process. The analytical existential models have been traced and typified as below.

2.1   The Analysis of Existing Models

There are a lot of models, which try to emphasize main aspects necessary for teachers' professional development in the 21st century in the STEAM field. These aspects should be based on the holistic theory application for teachers' role in the educational process. Using the holistic theory in STEM field we have to base teachers' professional development on the set of approaches, techniques, and tools enabling a smooth transition from schoolchildren's unplugged activities to high school children's and students' model-based and computer-based simulations and to integrate it with computation thinking [1]. Learners can examine the confluence of r-learning by combining arts disciplines with STEM (Science, Technology, Engineering, and Mathematics). The arts have the ability to open up new views, ways of thinking, and learning opportunities. The Arts ("A") component of STEAM education that adds to its effectiveness is r-learning. The use of robots in education can help students develop cross-disciplinary knowledge in social and humanistic sciences [2, 3].

The variety of STEAM models for teachers' professional development are presented in Table 1.

Table 1. The variety of STEAM professional development models for teachers.

Name	Main aspects		Authors
Digital Competence Framework for Educators (DigCompEdu)	Main domain	Professional engagement, digital resources, Teaching and learning, assessment, Empowering learners, facilitating learners' digital competence	[4]
	Sub-domains	Digital competences, Subject-specific competencies, Transversal competencies as educators' and learners' competences	
A Highly Structured Collaborative STEAM Program: Enacting a Professional Development Framework	Design and development	Common vision and design, targets (teachers' orientation, knowledge and practices, which are closely related to the learner outcomes), context (individual contexts, environment and high-reliability organizations);	[5]
	Implementation Phase	Whole group engagement, classroom implementation and four phases of active implementation (plan, make, study, act)	
	Evaluation	Design, contexts, cycles, connections, measures and assessment, outcomes	
	Research	The main aspects are teacher's knowledge and teachers' orientation and measure of these components	

(continued)

Table 1. (*continued*)

Name	Main aspects		Authors
Kolb's Experiential Learning Cycle as a Base of Teacher Training Framework	Phases	Concrete Experience, Reflexive Observation, Abstract Conceptualizing; Active Experimenting	[6, 7]
STEM-driven conceptual model	Components	Pedagogy driven activities, technology-driven processes, knowledge transfer channels; educational environment (tools, STEM library and etc.); learning outcomes	[8, 9]

DigiCompEdu. The concept emphasizes the teachers' ability to raise professional competencies as educators, pedagogical competencies, or learners' competencies, and how these abilities are crucial in the STEAM area. This brings us to the conclusion that we need to improve various teacher competencies while also ensuring that they are digitally savvy. According to [10], in r-learning field training, the teacher should have the competences listed above, as well as experience teaching technology, programming knowledge, and the ability to motivate students to participate in project creation.

A highly structured collaborative STEAM program. Although all of these phases of this model are critical in the STEAM sector, the model appears to overlook teachers' abilities to employ specific technological tools, digital tools, and learner preferences in the context of r-learning. The utilization of computational tools and activities in mathematics and science courses, according to [11], gives students a more realistic grasp of these areas, better preparing them for jobs in these fields.

Kolb's Experiential Learning Cycle. We may detect some correlations with computational thinking skills in this paradigm, such as the ability to think abstractly and divide large perspectives into little chunks [12]. These elements are also crucial in r-learning for teachers. First, teachers have to understand the process by themselves in order to teach others.

STEM-driven conceptual model of the computational thinking (CS) curriculum. We used model for STEM-driven computational thinking curriculum from the perspective of teachers [8, 9]. Computational thinking is particularly valued in the field of computer science, and it complements critical thinking as a method of reasoning for solving issues, making decisions, and interacting with our environment. This model was suggested as a framework for the instructors' framework creation to the partners. This assertion was made for a variety of reasons. It's hampered by the teachers' approach. This paradigm can be used in a variety of fields, not just computer science.

Mentioned models disclose particular aspects of the teachers' pedagogical development framework elements such as digital, collaborative, computational thinking competences which are necessary in the 21st century.

2.2 Theories and Models Adaptable in the STEAM Context

Teachers must comprehend the shift from a teacher-centered to a learner-centered approach, as well as the role of learners in a learning context and their own function in this context.

We will discuss the ideas and models that can be used to augment the educational STEAM field in this subchapter (Table 2).

Meaningful learning model. This paradigm is applicable to both STEAM and r-learning, as it stresses the learners' own responsibility for participating in various activities, collaborative learning, and so on. We emphasize the learner-centric approach in the STEAM area, where the instructor serves as a mentor to the learner group and both the teacher and the student share responsibility for the learning goals.

Activity Theory. Engineering, human-computer interaction, and other STEM fields employ activity theory. This theory aids in the comprehension of human behavior, social interactions, and dynamics involving various social actors. One of the most widely used and researched theories is activity theory.

Table 2. Main components of theories and models applicable for STEAM education.

Name model/theory	Main aspects		Authors
Meaningful learning model	Active	Manipulative, observant	[13]
	Constructive	Articulate, reflective	
	Cooperative	Cooperative, conversational	
	Authentic	Contextualized, complex	
	Intentional	Reflective, regulatory	
Activity theory	Subject	Who implementing activity	[14, 15]
	Object	Task, which leads to an outcome	
	Community	Participants of activity	
	Rules	Defines how problem-solving and decision making will be organized	
	Specific tools (instruments)	Collaborative tools	
	Division of labor	Divides labor between parties	

3 Proposed Framework for Teachers Professional Development in STEAM

The primary components of STEAM-driven Learning Content (curriculum) (see Fig. 1) are covered in the first cycle: Five components make up the model: pedagogy-driven

activities, technology-driven processes, knowledge transfer channels; educational environment (tools, STEM library, etc.); and learning outcomes. Two-sided arrows connect
the first cycle's components.

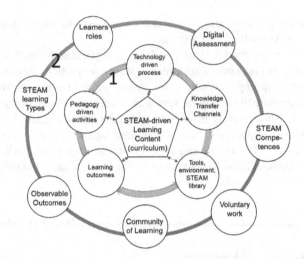

Fig. 1. Two-cycle STEM-driven conceptual model (2CSTEAM) (final model).

Digital Assessment, STEAM Competences, Voluntary Work, Community of Learning, Observable Outcomes, STEAM Learning Types, Learners Identity and Needs are
all part of the second cycle.

It was used layered learning design provided by Boyle to develop the framework
(2009) [16]. The pedagogical aspects are located in the top layer (No. 2). The deeper
layer includes STEAM learning components (No. 1). The arrows do not link the two
layers together. The surface layer's components can be linked to the surface layer's
components.

Despite the fact that we developed a model for teachers' professional development
in the STEAM sector, we included as an important component - learners' roles, which
are linked to learners' preferences; needs that influence learning motivation and identity:

- Learners' preferences for the course are based on their prior experience, what they've
learned, what they'd like to learn, and the best learning style for them.
- Motivation and needs. Learners have varying needs for teacher assistance, and teacher
assistance can influence learners' motivation.
- When it comes to thinking about one's interactions with others and oneself in the
learning process, identity is complex.

In the next part, it will be presented, how the MOOC is designed according to the
framework key elements.

4   Methodology

The aim of the current research is to explore the MOOC design based on the Framework for Teacher Professional Development in STEAM. This study's target group was trainees (teachers) who participated in piloting study. The perspective 'students-as co-creators' was used in order to get constructive trainees ratings and reviews about the MOOCs as well to evaluate their experience [17].

The quantitate methods was used to collect information about MOOC usage regarding the development of Framework of Teacher Professional Development in STEAM to get effectively robotically literacy knowledge.

5   Results and Discussion

This section presents a solution for the MOOC design which was based on Framework for Teacher Professional Development in STEAM, course learning units' correlation and the survey results.

5.1   Key Topics of Platform

The MOOC was designed seeking teachers to provide access to the learning material and ensure the assessment capabilities of their knowledge learners. As we mentioned in the previous part, the learners' preferences, motivation, needs and identity are important but this aspect requires human interaction. Therefore, we paid attention just to particular aspects of learners' roles.

The trainees at the first get basic information about the MOOC: how to browse and track the progress, which learning material was already reviewed, which tasks are finished and where are places to discuss the problematic issues of the course. Learning content resources and activities are subject to the automatic completion of activities under specified conditions, e.g. view, answer the question, submit the results, complete activity and non-automatic mark as done for practical tasks. The progress bar is visible to the right of the course.

The e-course learning material was divided into four parts (see Fig. 2):

- Unit 1. Introduction to integrated STE (A) M teaching & relevant teaching methods.
- Unit 2. STEAM subjects and how STEM careers are contextualized at school
- Unit 3. Subject-specific details for teachers
- Unit 4. Robotics

Learning material in Unit 3 and Unit 4 was presented in two levels for beginners and intermediates.

Each section provides lessons on the topic using the interactive content tool H5P course presentation. Each lesson presents self-monitoring questions and tasks for mastering the learning material, testing comprehension, and sharing experiences with colleagues. To this end, each lesson includes one or more questions for self-monitoring and an individual practical task. Additional resources are used at the end of the unit.

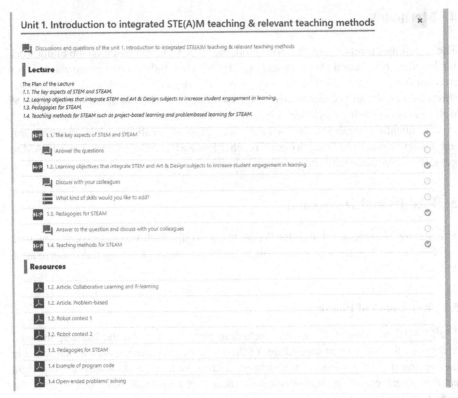

Fig. 2. Example of the Unit 1 structure.

The learning content of the Unit 1, 2 and 3 was provided in interactive form using H5P. The assessment was integrated into the content (see Fig. 3). This tool provided the assessment tools. Usually when the assessment is integrated in the teaching content, the assessment process can become simple and easy.

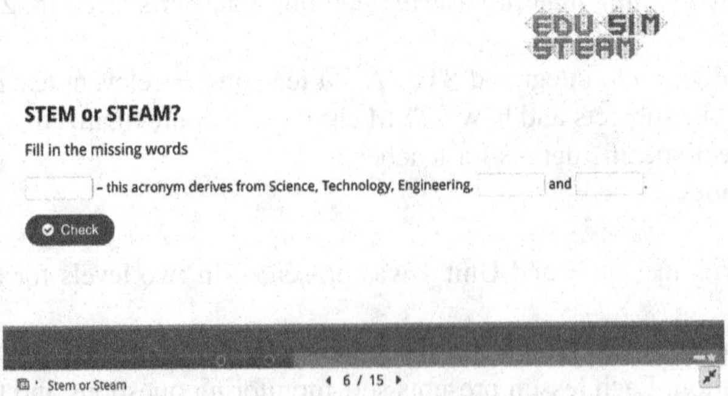

Fig. 3. Assessment integration into the interactive content.

5.2 MOOC's Relationship with the Proposed Teachers Professional Development Framework in STEAM

The first cycle components of the Framework for Teachers Professional Development in STEAM are presented in Table 3.

Table 3. First cycle components.

No.	Course section	Level	Activities and resources	Detailed explanation about implemented components
1	General	General	Discussion forum Page Book	To help and to discuss any question and share experience References for more read To introduce about course and how to study
2	Unit 1	General	Discussion forum Page 4 H5P interactive presentations File and URL	To discuss and answer the question about Unit To introduce about the unit plan The interactive content with self-questions and task for share and discuss with your colleagues Additionally resources for download or more to read
3	Unit 2	General	Discussion forum Page 4 H5P interactive presentations File and URL Assignment	To discuss and answer the question about Unit To introduce about the unit plan The interactive content with self-questions and task for share and discuss with your colleagues Additionally, resources for download or more to read To introduce individual work and to submit results for mentor To share experience with colleagues
4	Unit 3	Beginners Intermediates	Discussion forum 2 File	To discuss and answer the question about Unit Task to read and complete Example Task

(continued)

Table 3. (*continued*)

No.	Course section	Level	Activities and resources	Detailed explanation about implemented components
5	Unit 4	Beginners Intermediates	Discussion forum File and URL H5P interactive presentations Assignments	To discuss and answer the question about Unit The resources for read more or complete the task To introduce with project by level To share results of the solved tasks
6	To finish	General	Questionnaire Certificate	To get feedback To download certificate for successful completion

Second cycle components are presented in Table 4. These components are more important for trainees when they start to teach their students.

6 Evaluation of the STEAM Course Oriented Toward r-learning in MOOC

In the evaluation process, mentors analyze the first draft of the MOOC, give their feedback for improvement of the platform and content. After improvement of the MOOC, participants join the MOOC, follow all steps of the tasks and develop STEAM scenarios. Participants conduct a survey and give an interview to give their feedback on the MOOC at the end. In this survey, we search participants' ideas about content of the MOOC, platform features, participants' experience and attitude to the MOOC. 227 of trainees from 252 completed the questionnaire.

The respondents had to answer closed questions as well we used Likert scale: from 1 - Strongly disagree to 7 - Strongly agree and binary questions.

Figure 4 presents the aspects in which course provided knowledge to respondents. The biggest number of respondents 143 (62%) got knowledge of "STEAM teaching scenarios creation", 141 (61%) trainees got STEAM knowledge of teaching, 129 (56%) respondents got STEAM knowledge, 122 (53%) participants got knowledge of robotics integration into the subject, and 15 (7%) participants got some other knowledge.

The biggest number of respondents 140 (61%) mentioned, that creating of STEAM learning scenarios helped to obtain teaching practice (see Fig. 5). 112 (49) of respondents got knowledge of robotics integration into the subject.

The statement "I have gained practical ideas on how I can improve my professional practice in STEAM learning scenarios and robotics" evaluation average was 5,0 points (Table 5).

For the platform simplicity evaluation was used binary questions, to which respondents answer "Yes" or "No". 165 (73%) of the respondents answered 'Yes', the platform

Table 4. 2nd Cycle components of 2CSTEAM.

No.	Sub-component	Component	Detailed explanation about implemented components
1	STEAM learning types (educational approaches)	Problem-based, Project-based, Inquiry-based, Design-based, Storytelling, Others	Content presents main STEAM learning types such as Problem-based learning, inquiry-based science education
2	Learners' role	Preferences, Identity, Needs and Motivation	Teachers on this platform were as a learners (trainees)
3	Digital assessment	Flexible, Functional, Useful, Free, Interactive, Personalized, Formative	H5P assessment can be integrated into the slides
4	Teachers Competences in STEAM Field	Innovativeness, creativity, Creation of a learning environment, usage of varied teaching strategies, Ability to identify learners, needs, good communication abilities, ability to collaborate, capability to interact with all learners	The trainees had opportunity to discuss in discuss forums; To evaluate the results each other's solved tasks, To communicate with mentors
5	Voluntary work	Intentional; regulatory; reflective work	Mentors engagement was based on the voluntary activities
6	Community of learning	Platforms for collaboration and communication, Relationship with peers/groups nurturing	The discussion forums were possible to use during the training period
7	Observable outcomes	Developed critical thinking, Collaboration skills in groups, Project development, Technical knowledge, New educational methods, New content creation skills	The trainees has possibility to upload the results of their tasks, for example, prepared scenarios; they peers has opportunity to evaluate each other's

was easy to use, but 62 (27%) of the respondents answered "No". This direct us to the MOOC improvement.

The framework can be adopted in the MOOCs, but some concepts can be integrated offline or blended learning. For r-learning its necessary to combine tangible and intangible aspects of learning process in order to provide appropriate knowledge for the respondents.

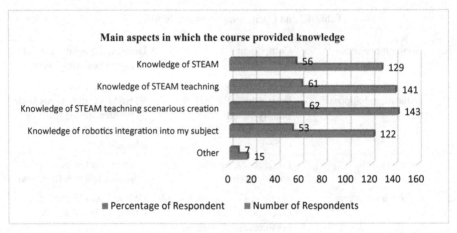

Fig. 4. Main aspects in which course provided knowledge.

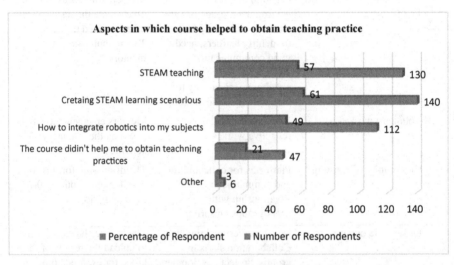

Fig. 5. The aspects in which course helped to obtain teaching practice.

Table 5. Practical ideas on how I can improve my professional practice in STEAM learning scenarios and robotics.

I have gained practical ideas on how I can improve my professional practice in STEAM learning scenarios and robotic	1	2	3	4	5	6	7
Number of respondents	14	8	23	34	47	37	**64**
Percentage of respondents	6	4	10	15	21	16	**28**

The platform was adopted for teachers, therefore the identification of the learners (students' role) will be important in the future, when the teacher will start to work with his/her students.

The understanding of different learners' roles is important for every teacher.

In order to adopt the framework fully it is essential to ensure the continuity of the project and the ideas to transfer to the students into other platforms.

The capability to give teachers to transfer fonts into their schools' MOOCs will be a big advantage as well. In such a way the teachers could transfer the training content into an offline environment and provide the students with tangible robotics kits.

7   Findings

In this section, we will present objectives and content of the MOOC, features of the platform, monitoring and evaluation of the MOOC.

7.1   Objectives of the MOOC

MOOC offers high-quality free courses for all teachers as well as for other educational professionals interested in STEAM [18]. In the scope of EDUSIMSTEAM project, it is crucial to design a TCPD MOOC on STEAM, which offers teachers opportunities to make synchronous and asynchronous activities, create STEAM scenarios, share them with their MOOC mates and get peer feedback in the process. We can list the objectives of the MOOC as follows:

- To support creativity, innovation and entrepreneurship at all levels of education,
- To develop teachers' skills and competences in STEAM education and robotics practices,
- To increase teachers' digital competencies, entrepreneurship and 21st century skills,
- To make teachers productive and creative individuals who have scientific thinking.

7.2   Content of the MOOC

EDUSIMSTEAM project offers a needs analysis report [19] on STEAM education, and project members design the MOOC based on this needs analysis report. In the MOOC, any teacher can find synchronous and asynchronous training, attention-grabbing visuals, engaging videos, different inspiring examples and ideas about STEAM education and robotics practices, STEAM scenarios, summary parts and module tasks. Participants can use discussion forums and join a community on Facebook to share their MOOC experience. At the end, they can earn certificates if they complete the training successfully. The content of the MOOC was listed above in the subchapter 4.1. "Overview of the Platform".

7.3 Features of the Platform

The open source learning platform, Moodle, is used to present the MOOCs of the EDUSIMSTEAM Project. The Moodle allows different types of activity or resources for creating the course contents like lesson, peer assessment, quiz, forum, workshop etc. Also there are other applications available for creating the course content. The H5P application is an interactive content which could be integrated with Moodle. In the EDUSIMSTEAM Project, the H5P application is used to create MOOC content. The content presentations come with the H5P without much interactivity, so it's possible to add some interactivity: to add a self-monitoring question or task, or other more visual and interactivity elements (image juxtaposition - to show changes; short interactive video - to illustrate the practical assignments; find one or multiple hotspots - to show functionality; Cornell notes - to attach by teachers notes and ideas to a text, a video, a practical task etc.; and others). Visual presentation of content in Moodle platform is a MOOC format which displays topics as "Tiles" in a grid. This format can be changed to more visual design or to modify as adaptive learning. It is used in a lot of MOODLE activities such as "Assignment", for example, Results of the solved tasks, when teachers have to upload completed tasks, but nobody checks them and the feedback is not ensured. Also is used in a few MOODLE activities such as "Database", "Forum", when teachers can evaluate each other's work or to comment on them. The activity Moodle "Assignment" can be replace other activities.

7.4 Monitoring of the MOOC

The MOOC takes 4-week time to complete all units and tasks. Volunteer teachers from Europe can sign up for the MOOC, and mentors engage the MOOC to guide these teachers to carry out all STEAM and robotics tasks. In addition, mentors organize live events based on relevant units for the participants each week. In the process of the MOOC, first, participants follow all steps in each unit, and they carry out all tasks in the units. Then, they create a STEAM scenario and get involved in peer assessment. Finally, they conduct a survey to give their feedback for the MOOC.

8 Limitations

In order to validate this TCPD framework, we have already implemented a pilot teacher training in Turkey and Spain based on the framework and got feedback from teachers. The teachers' involvement into the evaluation helped to improve MOOCs and develop the final TCPD framework in STEAM.

The platform piloting in other countries can provide with valuable insights about MOOC design for teachers professional continual development in STEAM Education. However, the other countries can have distinctive needs in STEAM education.

9 Conclusions

We presented the design of the MOOCs that seeks to involve the main components related to the teachers continues professional development in the STEAM field for r-learning.

In this study, we presented the training framework for teachers continues professional development in the STEAM field adaptation in MOOCs and we hope that the framework for teaching methodologies will serve as guidelines STEAM field adoption for teachers' professional development.

The architecture given here may be utilized for both synchronous and asynchronous sessions, and that it can be customized to the educational systems in different European countries.

Acknowledgment. This study is a part of the Erasmus+ project "Fostering steam education in schools (EDUSIMSTEAM)" dissemination activities. The project EDUSIMSTEAM (612855-EPP-1-2019-1-TR-EPPKA3-PI-FORWARD) is co-funded by European Commission.

References

1. Dolgopolovas, V., Dagienė, V.: Computational thinking: enhancing STEAM and engineering education, from theory to practice. Comput. Appl. Eng. Educ. **29**(1), 5–11 (2021)
2. Damaševičius, R., Maskeliūnas, R., Blažauskas, T.: Faster pedagogical framework for steam education based on educational robotics. Int. J. Eng. Technol. **7**(2.28), 138–142 (2018)
3. Burbaite, R., Zailskaite-Jakste, L., Blazauskas, T., Narbutaite, L., Ostreika, A.: Conversational robots for steam education
4. Punie, Y. (ed.), Redecker, C.: European Framework for the Digital Competence of Educators: DigCompEdu, EUR 28775 EN. Publications Office of the European Union, Luxembourg (2017). ISBN 978-92-79-73718-3 (print), 978-92-79-73494-6 (pdf). https://doi.org/10.2760/178382 (print), https://doi.org/10.2760/159770 (online), JRC107466
5. Bush, S.B., Cook, K.L., Ronau, R.N., Rakes, C.R., Mohr-Schroeder, M.J., Saderholm, J.: A highly structured collaborative STEAM program: enacting a professional development framework. J. Res. STEM Educ. **2**(2), 106–125 (2016)
6. Kolb, A.Y., Kolb, D.A.: The learning way: Meta-cognitive aspects of experiential learning. Simul. Gaming **40**(3), 297–327 (2009)
7. Kolb, D.: Experiential Learning: Experience as the Source of Learning and Development. Prentice-Hall (1984)
8. Burbaitė, R., Drąsutė, V., Štuikys, V.: Integration of computational thinking skills in STEM-driven computer science education. In: 2018 IEEE Global Engineering Education Conference (EDUCON), pp. 1824–1832. IEEE, April 2018
9. Štuikys, V., Burbaite, R., Blažauskas, T., Barisas, D., Binkis, M.: Model for introducing STEM into high school computer science education. Int. J. Eng. Educ. **33**(5), 1684–1698 (2017)
10. Jung, S.E., Han, J.: A comprehensive review on r-learning: authentic r-learning beyond the fad of new educational technology. Int. J. Adv. Smart Converg. **9**(2), 28–37 (2020)
11. Weintrop, D., et al.: Defining computational thinking for mathematics and science classrooms. J. Sci. Educ. Technol. **25**(1), 127–147 (2015). https://doi.org/10.1007/s10956-015-9581-5
12. Selby, C., Woollard, J.: Computational thinking: the developing definition (2013)
13. Jonassen, P., Peck, K.L, Wilson, B.G.: Learning with technology: a constructivist perspective (1999)
14. Engestrdm, Y.: Learning by expanding: An activity-theoretical approach to developmental research. Orienta-Konsultit, Helsinki (1987)
15. Engeström, Y.: Making expansive decisions: An activity-theoretical study of practitioners building collaborative medical care for children. In: Allwood, C.M., Selart, M. (eds.) Decision making: Social and creative dimensions, pp. 281–301. Springer, Dordrecht (2001). https://doi.org/10.1007/978-94-015-9827-9_14

16. Boyle, T.: Generative learning objects (GLOs): design as the basis for reuse and repurposing. In: First International Conference of e-Learning and Distance Education, March 2009
17. Deng, R., Benckendorff, P.: What are the key themes associated with the positive learning experience in MOOCs? An empirical investigation of learners' ratings and reviews. Int. J. Educ. Technol. High. Educ. **18**(1), 1–28 (2021). https://doi.org/10.1186/s41239-021-00244-3
18. Ministry of National Education [MoNE]. Fostering STEAM Education in Schools (2022). https://edusimsteam.eba.gov.tr/?page_id=104&lang=en. Accessed 6 Apr 2022
19. Ministry of National Education [MoNE], Fostering STEAM Education in Schools Needs Analysis Report (2022). https://edusimsteam.eba.gov.tr/?p=766&lang=en. 7 Apr 2022

Author Index

Printed in the United States
by Baker & Taylor Publisher Services